The Politics of New
Immigrant Destinations

Edited by STEFANIE CHAMBERS, DIANA EVANS,
ANTHONY M. MESSINA, AND ABIGAIL FISHER WILLIAMSON

The Politics of New
Immigrant Destinations

Transatlantic Perspectives

TEMPLE UNIVERSITY PRESS
Philadelphia • *Rome* • *Tokyo*

TEMPLE UNIVERSITY PRESS
Philadelphia, Pennsylvania 19122
www.temple.edu/tempress

Library of Congress Cataloging-in-Publication Data

Names: Chambers, Stefanie.
Title: The politics of new immigrant destinations : transatlantic
  perspectives / edited by Stefanie Chambers, Diana Evans, Anthony M.
  Messina, and Abigail Fisher Williamson.
Description: Philadelphia : Temple University Press, [2017] | Includes
  bibliographical references and index.
Identifiers: LCCN 2017018898 (print) | LCCN 2016057424 (ebook) | ISBN
  9781439914625 (cloth : alk. paper) | ISBN 9781439914632 (pbk. : alk.
  paper) | ISBN 9781439914649 (E-Book)
Subjects: LCSH: Emigration and immigration—Government policy—Cross-cultural
  studies. | Immigrants—Government policy—Cross-cultural studies. |
  Emigration and immigration—Political aspects. | Emigration and
  immigration—Social aspects. | Immigrants—Political activity.
Classification: LCC JV6271 .P68 2017 (ebook) | LCC JV6271 (print) | DDC
  325/.1—dc23
LC record available at https://lccn.loc.gov/2017018898

Printed in the United States of America

9 8 7 6 5 4 3 2 1

For Joe, who supports my scholarly endeavors and holds down the fort when my research takes me away from home.
—STEFANIE CHAMBERS

For my father, Zane Evans, whose lifelong love of books and learning became my own.
—DIANA EVANS

For Katrina, with affection and gratitude.
—ANTHONY M. MESSINA

To Chris and Peggy Williamson, for parenting with unsurpassable grace and love.
—ABIGAIL FISHER WILLIAMSON

Contents

Preface and
Acknowledgments

The collaboration that culminated in this volume was spawned during a meeting of the editors in late February 2012 during which we discussed our respective research agendas on the politics of immigration. Despite having different individual research backgrounds and scholarly expertises, we soon discovered that we shared an interest in the topic of new immigrant destinations. From this starting point we decided to convene a conference on the subject at Trinity College, our home institution, in October 2013. With the exceptions of the essay by Rhys Andrews, which first appeared in the journal *Rural Sociology* 76 (2011), Erica Dobbs's chapter on Ireland, and Claudio Holzner's and Melissa Goldsmith's contribution on the politics of place, all of the chapters in this volume were presented at the 2013 conference.

As cited in the Introduction, this volume addresses the major challenges posed for governments, majority populations, and immigrants as a consequence of the proliferation of cultural, ethnic, and/or religious diversity in new immigrant destinations in Europe and the United States. More specifically, its collective chapters explore the dilemmas precipitated by immigration-related diversity in "intermediate" destination countries; regions or subnational administrative units with especially distinctive cultural and/or political identities; new destination locales within traditional destination countries; and "early migration cycle" countries.

The book's publication arrives at an especially trying moment for many immigration-receiving countries in Europe. Fleeing war-torn countries such as Iraq, Libya, and Syria, hundreds of thousands of asylum seekers and refugees have migrated to the European Union (EU) since 2015 and, in so doing, have precipitated a humanitarian management crisis on a scale not witnessed since the early post–WWII period. Although most migrants will eventually settle permanently in Germany, a traditional immigration country, new destination states such as Hungary, Greece, and Italy too are likely to be significantly impacted over the long term as thousands of asylum seekers and refugees from the Middle East gain permanent residence in their respective societies.

We are deeply indebted to the numerous individuals, groups, and organizations at Trinity College who supported the 2013 conference that ultimately culminated in this book. We especially wish to thank our colleagues in the Department of Political Science for permitting us to utilize the resources of the Albert L. E. Gestmann Fund in International Organizations and Programs that financially got the conference off the ground. We believe our former colleague Bert Gastmann would be pleased with the volume's contents and scope. We also owe considerable thanks to Xiangming Chen, the founding dean and current director of the Center for Urban and Global Studies, and Dario Del Puppo, the chairperson of the Cesare Barbieri Endowment for Italian Culture, for supporting our funding proposals to their respective institutions.

We also are grateful to the numerous European and American scholars who traveled to Hartford, Connecticut, to participate in the conference. Although several did not ultimately contribute chapters to this book, their participation in the conference nevertheless profoundly influenced our thinking about the topic of new immigrant destinations. First and foremost, we wish to thank Joaquín Arango and Rodney Hero for delivering outstanding keynote addresses. We continue to be inspired by their respective intellectual insights and ability to engage a diverse audience of assembled comparativists and Americanists. The conference also was enriched by the participation of Roxana Barbulescu, Hamutal Bernstein, Janet Bauer, Els de Graauw, Xavier Escandell, Bryan Fanning, Chris Gilligan, Daniel J. Hopkins, Michael Jones Correa, J. Celeste Lay, Elitsa Molles, Marc Swyngedouw, Kim Williams, and Jamie Winders.

Many others at Trinity also facilitated the success of the conference and the completion of the book. Mary Beth White, our department's administrative assistant, assisted us in planning and executing the conference. David Tatem helped us construct the maps presented in the book's introductory chapter. Ali Caless, Rachel DiPietro, Natalia Kolakowska, Rose Lichtenfels, Pornpat Pootinath, and Wes Simon, Trinity College undergraduates all, ably served as conference panel discussants and/or chairs. Moreover, Jane Bisson, Kaitlyn Sprague, and Brooke Williams cheerfully assisted us in putting the book together.

Finally, we wish to thank the team at Temple University Press for its assistance at each step of the production process. Aaron Javsicas, the press's editor-in-chief, expressed his enthusiasm for our project early on and waited patiently for us to deliver the final manuscript. He also offered us valuable advice throughout the trying moments of revising the manuscript. Finally, and not least of all, we wish to acknowledge the valuable and insightful criticisms offered by the manuscript's two anonymous reviewers.

The Politics of New
Immigrant Destinations

Introduction

Dimensions of Variation in Newly Diverse Transatlantic Destinations

ANTHONY M. MESSINA

ABIGAIL FISHER WILLIAMSON

> And so everything changed just like that! A society with a long aptitude for squeezing out surplus family members . . . threw open its doors unequivocally to four hundred million fellow Europeans and conditionally to cherry-picked migrants from elsewhere. No statue of Liberty or Ellis Island was needed. No grand proclamations of an Irish Dream were issued. . . . In less than a decade Irish society experienced its greatest transformation since the 1846 Famine.
>
> —BRIAN FANNING, *New Guests of the Irish Nation*

> Spain is a laboratory of diversities because practically all the main forms of diversity are in interplay with each other.
>
> —RICARD ZAPATA-BARRERO, "Managing Diversity in Spanish Society"

> Key aspects of [U.S.] Southern locales, especially their racial histories and lack of recallable immigrant histories, do create differences in the context of reception.
>
> —JAMIE WINDERS, *Nashville in the New Millennium*

As has been extensively documented (Loyal 2011; Ó'Riain 2014), Ireland's unprecedented economic growth during the 1990s rapidly transformed it into a major country of immigration. Historically an emigration country, Ireland rather unexpectedly became a country in which relatively few immigrants resided to one in which they currently comprise nearly 17 percent of its total population, thus ranking it third among contemporary Western European societies in terms of its foreign-born population (OECD 2013). Over a similar period and in somewhat equivalent economic circumstances, the size of the foreign-born population also dramatically increased in the southern American state of Georgia. At the height of the immigration wave during the early twentieth century, when immigrants made up 15 percent of the American population (Gibson and Jung 2006), less than 3 percent of the population in Georgia was foreign born (Bankston 2007). By 2014, in contrast, 10 percent of Georgia's total population consisted of immigrants (Brown and Patten 2014), thus making the absolute size of its foreign-born population the ninth highest among American states.

Georgia's relatively recent experience with accelerating immigration flows is certainly not unique. Indeed, in 1990, fully 73 percent of immigrants resided in only a handful of traditional destination states: California, New York, Texas, Florida, New Jersey, and Illinois (Singer 2004); by 2012, in contrast, the proportion of immigrants who resided in the aforementioned states had declined to less than 65 percent (American Community Surveys 2008–2012). As Figure I.1 illustrates, while immigrants remain spatially concentrated in the traditional destination states, foreign-born populations since 1990 have expanded most rapidly in states like Georgia and, more generally, across other nontraditional immigrant destinations in the Southeast and Midwest. Moreover, in addition to their residential dispersion within and across regions, migrants to the United States are now altogether avoiding or increasingly migrating from metropolitan areas and choosing to settle in suburban and rural destinations (Marrow 2005; Singer 2008).

As the previously cited examples suggest, migration to new destinations in Europe and the United States has expanded exponentially over the past few decades, and, within these destinations, immigrant populations have become increasing dispersed geographically. As a consequence, numerous local and regional destinations on both continents are experiencing new varieties of ethnic, cultural, and/or religious diversity. Informed and inspired by this transatlantic phenomenon, this volume is centrally concerned with the challenges posed by the proliferation of diversity for governments, majority populations, and immigrants. More specifically, its collective essays assess the effectiveness of the policy and political responses that have been spawned by increasing diversity in four types of new immigrant destinations: "intermediate" destination countries (Ireland and Italy); regions or subnational administrative units with especially distinctive cultural and/or political identities (Catalonia, the American South); new destination locales within traditional destination countries (cities in the American state of Utah and in rural England); and "early migration cycle" countries (Latvia and Poland).

What *specifically* defines a new immigrant destination? New immigrant destinations are European countries and cities and regions in Europe, the United States, and elsewhere that, until relatively recently, had not been sites of immigrant settlement for at least a century, if ever (Goździak and Bump 2008). Originally conceived by American social scientists to describe the geographic dispersion of immigrants revealed in data generated by the 2000

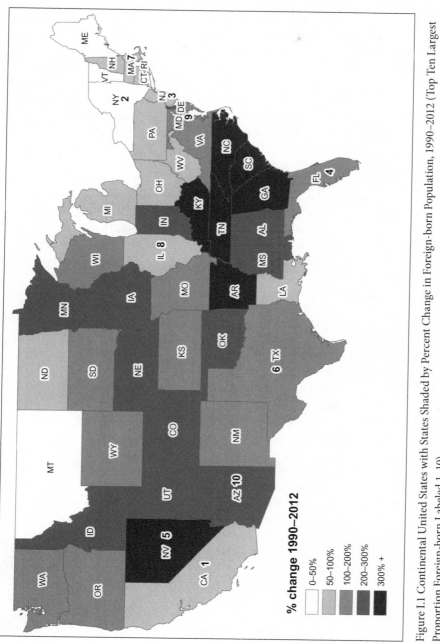

Figure I.1 Continental United States with States Shaded by Percent Change in Foreign-born Population, 1990–2012 (Top Ten Largest Proportion Foreign-born Labeled 1–10)

U.S. Census (Marrow 2005; Zúñiga and Hernández-León 2005a), the concept of new immigrant destinations has now been embraced by numerous scholars in Europe (Morales 2014; Schnell and Azzolini 2015; Urso and Carammia 2014) who are investigating a similar phenomenon across the Atlantic (Messina 2009).

In the American context, "new" immigration implies a reference point of "old" immigration during the late nineteenth and early twentieth centuries. In Europe, on the other hand, old, or traditional, migration tends to refer to the immediate post–World War II period.[1] While these reference points and time frames obviously differ, the recent experiences of new immigrant destinations on both sides of the Atlantic are nevertheless similar along several dimensions.

The phenomenon of mass migration to both Ireland and the American state of Georgia, for example, can largely be attributed to a similar set of facilitating economic conditions and a confluence of national and/or supranational changes in public policy. In the case of Georgia, the enactment of the 1986 Immigration Reform and Control Act (IRCA), which regularized the status of undocumented immigrants nationally, facilitated immigrants' freedom of movement across the country while also increasing security at traditional crossing points along the U.S. southern border (Massey, Durand, and Malone 2002). At the same time, many midwestern and southern American states experiencing economic growth rates exceeding those elsewhere in the country served as a powerful magnet for foreign workers (Donato, Stainback, and Bankston 2006; Duchón and Murphy 2001; Johnson, Johnson-Webb, and Farrell 1999). Similarly, in Ireland, a booming economy, dubbed the "Celtic Tiger," attracted tens of thousands of labor migrants from Africa, Asia, and elsewhere in Europe during the 1990s (Ruhs 2003). Moreover, Ireland was among the first European Union (EU) member states to open its labor market to the ascension states in 2004, thus precipitating a significant inflow of migrants from Eastern Europe and particularly Poland (Honohan 2010). Although migration to Ireland has significantly slowed since the onset of the recent global recession, the demand for foreign workers in the advanced sectors of its economy and a steady inflow of asylum seekers from Nigeria, Pakistan, and China have persisted and have only solidified Ireland's status as a country of immigration (OECD 2013).

Significant migration to and immigrant dispersion within new destinations are thus clear trends on both sides of the Atlantic. Indeed, even as the intermediate countries of immigration in Europe (e.g., Greece, Ireland, Italy, Portugal, and Spain) grapple with the challenges posed by the proliferation of diversity from previous decades, newer immigrant destinations continue to emerge, both subnationally and in new countries. For example, like many of its contemporary Southern, Central, and Eastern European neighbors, Poland, though still predominantly a country of emigration, now depends on a significant annual influx of migrants to buoy its economy and compensate for its shrinking population and increasingly suboptimal demographic profile (Drbohlav 2012; King and Mai 2008; Klementjeviene 2010; Matysiak and Nowok 2007; Peixoto et al. 2012). Owing to demographic pressures and in an effort to avoid future labor shortages and depopulation, analysts argue that Poland must admit approximately 5.2 million foreigners for permanent settlement by 2050 (Funacja Energia dla Europy 2013). In light of these forecasts, will Poland follow in the footsteps of Ireland and the Western European nations that preceded it and thus embark on the path of becoming a major country of immigration? While some observers are skeptical (Iglicka and Gmaj 2010), if and when it does so, Poland will join the ranks of numerous new immigrant destinations in Europe and the United States experiencing the proliferation of cultural, ethnic, and/or religious diversity resulting from mass immigrant settlement (Włoch 2013).

To aid in differentiating among the various immigration and immigrant settlement patterns across both new and older destinations, we begin this introductory chapter by touching base with Freeman's well-known typology of immigrant-receiving states. According to Freeman (1995: 881), a first set of traditional immigration countries (Australia, Canada, New Zealand, and the United States) are united by their "histories of periodically open immigration, machineries of immigration planning and regulation, and densely organized webs of interest groups contesting policies." In these societies the phenomenon of mass immigrant settlement features prominently in both their founding narratives and subsequent political and social development. In contrast, a second set of traditional destination countries (Belgium, Britain, France, Germany, the Netherlands, Sweden, and Switzerland) initially experienced mass immigration only after World War II, with significant immigrant settlement beginning in the immediate postwar period up until the mid-1960s. Migrants from geographically proximate Southern European labor-surplus countries or colonial or former colonial territories eventually settled permanently in these Western European countries and, in so doing, were assigned identities as new ethnic or racial minorities (Messina et al. 1992). Yet a third set, the intermediate destination countries, which are located primarily in Southern Europe (Greece, Portugal, Spain, and Italy, but also Ireland), did not begin to experience mass immigrant settlement until the late 1980s and early 1990s. All of the aforementioned countries have been challenged by the experience of mass immigration against the backdrop of accelerating intergovernmental and supranational initiatives to forge common immigration and immigrant policies within the framework of the EU. We also consider a fourth set of immigration-receiving states in this volume: the contemporary early migration cycle countries of Central and Eastern Europe (e.g., Hungary, Latvia, Lithuania, and Poland) that have experienced significant immigration only within the past decade. Figure I.2

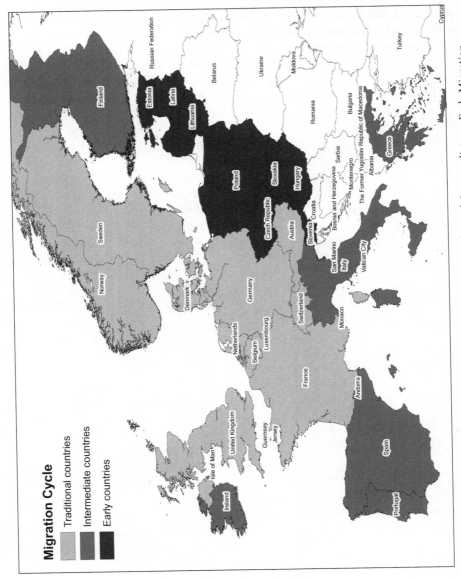

Figure I.2 European Countries Shaded to Indicate Their Status as Traditional, Intermediate, or Early Migration

Cycle Countries

illustrates the geographical distribution of traditional, intermediate, and early migration cycle countries across contemporary Europe.

In Europe, scholarship on new immigrant destinations has hitherto largely focused on cross-national comparisons. In the United States, on the other hand, similar scholarship has focused on subnational comparisons. In folding the United States into the aforementioned cross-national comparisons and by drawing attention to subnational variation not only in the United States but also in Europe, a key objective of this volume is to generate yet additional comparisons (Winders 2014). While we aspire to identify similarities in the transatlantic processes of new immigrant dispersion, we particularly aim to highlight two dimensions of variation among these destinations. First, new destinations vary with regard to their historical experience of cultural, ethnic, and/or religious diversity in ways that likely affect their policy and political responses to new immigrant populations. Second, as suggested by the EU-U.S. comparisons we offer below, new destinations differ in their scale and relationships to traditional destinations, whether as constituent units within traditional destinations—cities or regions—or as geographically proximate neighbors. Because their responses to diversity and formulation of immigrant integration policies are visible from their earliest stages, the observed variation in responses across new destinations presents immigration scholars with an opportunity to better understand the contextual factors that facilitate effective immigrant integration practices.

New Destinations: Key Dimensions of Similarity

What differentiates the new from the traditional immigrant destinations? Especially rapid immigrant flows, a lack of immigrant integration infrastructure, and an unusual pattern of immigrant settlement are among the key characteristics that virtually all new immigrant destinations share. On the first score, it is the unusual velocity by which immigrant populations have penetrated the new destinations that typically distinguishes these destinations (Winders 2013: 17). Indeed, several intermediate destination countries in Europe have accepted more persons for permanent settlement within their first decade of mass immigration than the traditional countries did during their first three decades as major destinations (Barbulescu forthcoming). Much like the aforementioned Irish experience, the foreign-born population in Spain, for example, increased more than fivefold from 1998 to 2010, or from 3 percent to 16 percent of the total Spanish population (Morales and Echazarra 2013: 347). During the same decade, the size of the foreign-born population increased by over 300 percent in Italy (OECD 2013: 386). Similarly, the foreign-born population in Greece expanded by 227 percent between 2001 and 2010, before modestly declining in 2011 (384). New immigrant destinations within the United States have also experienced high immigration velocities over a relatively short period. As Figure I.1 illustrates, though the American states of Indiana, Minnesota, and Utah had foreign-born populations of 3 percent or less in 1990, from 1990 to 2010 their foreign-born populations grew by more than 200 percent. Over the same period, immigrant populations in Georgia, North Carolina, and Tennessee—states with less than a 3 percent foreign-born population in 1990—expanded by between 389 percent and 525 percent (American Community Survey 2008–2012). Overall, almost 40 percent of all migrants to the new destination states in the United States have arrived since 1999 (Terrazas 2011).

Partly as a result of their relatively recent and accelerated experience with mass immigrant settlement, new destinations also often lack an adequate legal and/or political infrastructure to respond adequately to the needs of immigrants (Drbohlav 2009: 53; Zapata-Barrero 2013: 4). Indeed, they have been particularly slow to develop a coherent or comprehensive immigrant integration regime (Boucher 2008; Davis 2009: 137; Waters and Jiménez 2005: 118). Moreover, even in those new destinations where a national integration regime is eventually established, albeit often hastily (Triandafyllidou 2009: 49), the primary administrative unit responsible for executing its objectives has frequently fallen to resource-strapped regional and/or local governments (Caponio 2010; Milly 2014: 163; Singer 2004: 16), a pattern especially prevalent in Italy, Spain, and the United States, where regional or state governments exercise considerable policy-making autonomy on matters of immigrant integration (Rodriguez 2008; Triandafyllidou 2009: 49). Perhaps not so coincidently, and as we discuss below, immigrant integration outcomes and the majority population's reception of immigrants within these countries vary considerably from one region to the next (Escandell and Ceobanu 2010; Koff 2006: 188; Zamora-Kapoor 2013).

In addition to their especially rapid immigration flows and lack of an adequate immigrant integration infrastructure, new destinations are distinguished by their unusual subnational dispersion of immigrants. As compared with the highly concentrated residential settlement pattern that was prevalent within the traditional destinations early in their immigrant history, new immigrants have settled far beyond a small number of subnational destinations (Massey and Capoferro 2008: 26; Suro and Tafoya 2004). For example, as Table I.1 demonstrates, only two of Spain's seventeen autonomous communities had an immigrant population of greater than 3 percent in 1998; in contrast, by 2013 all but three had an immigrant population of 6 percent or greater, with an average increase in foreign-born population of more than 10 percentage points. The contemporary residential dispersal pattern in Italy is similar, with immigrants making up more than 6 percent of the total population in thirteen of of the country's twenty regions (Table I.2). Moreover, each of Ireland's twenty-six counties has a foreigner population greater than 7 percent (Central Statistics Office 2012: 10). Across con-

TABLE I.1 FOREIGNER POPULATION AND "IMMIGRATION A MAJOR
PROBLEM" WITHIN SPAIN'S AUTONOMOUS COMMUNITIES IN PERCENTAGES

Community	Foreign-born Proportion (1998)	Foreign-born Proportion (2013)	Increase (1998–2013)	Perception of Immigration as One of Three Major Problems (2012)
Islas Baleares	4.8	20.1	15.3	10.2
Islas Canarias	3.4	14.2	10.8	4.1
Comunidad Valenciana	2.5	16.8	14.3	3.6
Madrid	2.3	14.7	12.4	3.8
Cataluña	2.0	15.3	13.3	8.2
Andalucía	1.4	8.6	7.2	3.4
Murcia	1.1	15.7	14.6	15.4
La Rioja	1.0	13.7	12.7	9.6
Navarra	0.8	10.5	9.7	10.6
País Vasco	0.7	6.8	6.1	4.8
Galicia	0.7	4.0	3.3	1.0
Aragón	0.7	12.9	12.2	5.8
Castilla–La Mancha	0.6	10.5	9.9	2.5
Cantabria	0.6	6.5	5.9	3.5
Castilla y León	0.6	6.5	5.9	3.3
Asturias	0.6	4.5	3.9	1.5
Extremadura	0.4	3.7	3.3	5.5
Spain	1.4	10.9	9.5	4.9

Sources: Centro de Investigaciones Sociológicas 2012; González and Lázaro y Torres 2005: 40; Instituto Nacional Estadística 2013.

temporary Ireland there are no fewer than sixty towns in which foreigners equal or exceed 20 percent of the population (11); even relatively small towns (i.e., between 7,000 and 9,500 residents) now have a sizeable immigrant population. Given this geographic dispersal pattern, there are now few corners of Ireland, Italy, and Spain that have not been culturally, politically, and socially impacted by immigrant settlement (Fanning 2007). Similarly, the dispersion of immigrants to new destinations in the United States has been marked by migration not only to new cities but also increasingly to suburban and rural destinations (Marrow 2005; Singer 2008). Along these lines, 30 percent of U.S. towns and cities had foreign-born populations of at least 5 percent in 2012 (American Community Survey 2008–2012), as compared to 16 percent in 1990 (U.S. Census 1990).

TABLE I.2   GEOGRAPHICAL DISTRIBUTION OF IMMIGRANTS IN TOP
THIRTEEN ITALIAN REGIONS, 2010

	% Regional Population	% Distribution in Italy	Incidence*
Emilia-Romagna	11.3	8.5	1.5
Umbria	11.0	2.2	1.5
Lombardia	10.7	11.0	1.4
Veneto	10.2	11.0	1.4
Toscana	9.7	8.0	1.3
Lazio	9.5	11.8	1.3
Marche	9.4	3.2	1.3
Piemonte	8.9	8.7	1.2
Trentino–Alto Adige	8.7	2.0	1.2
Fruili–Venezia Giulia	8.5	2.3	1.1
Liguria	7.8	2.7	1.0
Valle d'Aosta	6.8	0.2	0.9
Abruzzo	6.0	1.7	0.8
Italy	7.5	100	1.0

Source: ISTAT 2012: 42.

* Represents the ratio between the number of foreigners/immigrants living in the region (percentage of total regional population) and the total number of foreigners in the country (percentage of the total national population).

The aforementioned similarities of new destinations in Europe and the United States have generated settings that create an opportunity to better understand how governmental responses to diversity and immigration eventually emerge and shape the process of immigrant integration (Waters and Jiménez 2005). Moreover, rapid immigrant settlement, often in places without any previous experience of ethnic, cultural, and/or religious diversity, provides a laboratory within which we can investigate how social and political relations evolve in the context of growing diversity (Winders 2014: 151). Similarly, migration to destinations without preexisting policies that address the integration needs of immigrants enables us to observe the early formulation of such policies. The resulting subnational and cross-national variation in integration policies can also illuminate how varying policy regimes affect immigrant integration outcomes.

Defining Key Terms: Diversity and Integration

Before discussing two key mediating factors—a prior history of diversity and the scale and relationships to traditional destinations—that likely influence the policy and political responses of new immigrant destinations, it is necessary to briefly define *diversity* and *integration*, concepts that admittedly have contested meanings within the contemporary scholarly literature.

Diversity

In the most general terms, Thomas Faist (2009: 174) observes that *immigration-related diversity* typically refers to "a plurality of languages, religions, and ethnic groups." Anna Triandafyllidou (2012: 24), on the other hand, more specifically defines the phenomenon of *cultural diversity* as the presence of a critical number of individuals or groups that have a different ethnic descent (ethnic diversity); physical characteristics (racial diversity); cultural traditions, customs, and language (cultural diversity); and/or religion (religious diversity) from the majority group within a particular country, region, or locale. Contrary to the simple notion of *difference*, which, according to Thomas Eriksen (2006: 14), "refers to morally objectionable or at least questionable notions and practices in a minority group or category," diversity implies "largely aesthetic, politically and morally neutral expressions of cultural difference."

Ruud Koopmans and Merlin Schaeffer (2013: 6) further argue that diversity is characterized by three dimensions: the relative size of the in-group, the unequal balance of populations over out-groups, and the variety of out-groups. Following from this definition, they observe that the "situation in most European immigration countries is generally a quasi-monoethnic one: a clear national majority is accompanied by a number of comparatively small minority immigrant groups." As we emphasized earlier, a condition of quasi-monoethnicism need not be applicable exclusively to countries. Traditional regions and localities within countries too may be accurately characterized as quasi-monoethnic (Waters and Jiménez 2005: 111–113). As a result, each level may be appropriately classified as more or less diverse (Voyer 2013). As Schaeffer (2014: 51) persuasively argues, a key variable here is that "it makes a difference whether the population is equally distributed over three or twenty ethnic groups." Indeed, as we discuss below, a growing literature, primarily generated by scholars in Europe, has been investigating the phenomenon of *superdiversity*, or what David Hollinger (1995) has characterized as the "diversification of diversity." According to Steven Vertovec (2007: 1024), *superdiversity* is a "condition distinguished by a dynamic interplay of variables among an increased number of new, small and scattered, multiple-origin, transnationally connected, socio-economically differentiated and legally stratified immigrants." It is defined by the unprecedented proliferation since the 1990s of ethnic, cultural, and/or religious identities within and across established territorial boundaries (Sniderman and Hagendoorn 2007: 124; Vertovec 2007: 1048).

Integration

As cited above, national and subnational governments across Europe and the
United States have adopted a variety of policies in response to the proliferation of diversity and the numerous policy and political challenges it poses.
Although the essays in this volume do not speak to all of the key dimensions
of these challenges, it is nevertheless helpful to have a baseline understanding of the concept of *integration* before moving forward. While no definition
is universally embraced (Ireland 2004: 15; Miera 2012: 193), integration as
scholars and policy makers employ it in most contexts has a positive connota-
tion. If only for this reason, integration can be usefully distinguished from
adaptation, acculturation, assimilation, multiculturalism, and other related
terms that tend to evoke less-than-positive responses from immigrants themselves and/or their detractors (Castles et al. 2002: 115–119; Green 2007).

Rinus Penninx and Marco Martiniello (2004: 141) broadly characterize
integration as "the process of becoming an accepted part of society." Irene
Ponzo et al. (2013: 2) argue that it is "the dynamic, multi-actor process of
mutual engagement that facilitates effective participation by all members of
a diverse society in the economic, political, social and cultural life, and fosters a shared and inclusive sense of belonging." More specifically, Mitja
Žagar (2008: 315–316) describes social integration "as a continuous process
of voluntary, equal and full inclusion of all individuals, especially those who
are marginalized, such as immigrants, persons belonging to ethnic and/or
other minorities or deprived (social) groups, as well diverse distinct communities (as collective entities) into societies where they live." In identifying
its key dimensions, Spencer Boyer (2009: 3) further defines the process of
"successful" integration as one "that includes, but is not limited to, the
spread of educational and economic mobility, social inclusion, and equal
opportunity for newcomers and minorities into the mainstream of a society." On the opposite side of the coin, he argues, "poor integration results in
the formation of an ethnically segregated bottom class composed of immigrant groups and/or communities of color."

In addition to Penninx and Martiniello's (2004: 141) characterization
of integration as "the process of becoming an accepted part of society,"
immigrant integration, as we define it here, can be empirically measured
as the progress immigrants are making along four major axes within a
given society: employment, education, social inclusion, and active citizenship (Table I.3). As articulated by the Council of the European Union
(2004a: 13):

> Employment is a vital part of the integration process, and efforts in
> education are essential in helping immigrants to become successful
> and more active participants in society. Not only access to the labor

TABLE I.3 IMMIGRANT INTEGRATION MEASURES IN THE EU	
Policy Area	**Core Indicators**
Employment	Employment rate Unemployment rate Activity rate
Education	Highest educational attainment (share of population with tertiary, secondary, and primary or less than primary education) Share of low-achieving fifteen-year-olds in reading, mathematics, and science Share of thirty- to thirty-four-year-olds with tertiary educational attainment Share of those who leave education and training early
Social inclusion	Median net income—the median net income of the immigrant population as a proportion of the median net income of the total population At risk of poverty rate—share of population with net disposable income of less than 60 percent of national median Share of population perceiving their health status as good or poor Ratio of property owners to nonproperty owners among immigrants and the total population
Active citizenship	Share of immigrants who have acquired citizenship Share of immigrants holding permanent or long-term residence permits Share of immigrants among elected representatives

Source: European Ministerial Conference on Integration 2010.

market is important but also entry into society more generally, which makes social inclusion an important area. The participation of immigrants in the democratic process as active citizens supports their integration and enhances their sense of belonging.

While other axes could be profitably added to this list, the aforementioned capture the commonly accepted priority areas of immigrant integration. Taken together, they permit scholars to assess the degree to which immigrants are included within the immigration-receiving society (Penninx and Martiniello 2004).

Integration, of course, is not simply the accommodation of a host society to the objective needs and interests of its newcomers; rather, it is necessarily a two-way process requiring the continual adaptation of both immigrants and the receiving society (Castles et al. 2002: 113). Thus, the degree to which majority populations perceive immigration and the immigrants themselves with concern and the extent to which immigrants feel the discriminatory effects of this concern are potentially problematic for the integration process. Moreover, as numerous scholars have observed, immigrants and their receiving society are far from equal partners in the immigrant integration process. As Penninx (2003: 1) emphasizes, "The receiving society, in terms of its institutional structure and the way it reacts to newcomers, has much more say in the outcome of the process." Along these lines, national integration models, or what Dan Rodríguez-García et al. (2007: 15–16) label *incorporation models*, can be subsumed under three categories:

> [A]ssimilationist or republican (based on the idea that equality can be achieved through the full adoption of the rules and values of the dominant society and through the avoidance of any considerations of diversity, as in the case of France); multiculturalist or pluralist (based on the respect for and protection of cultural diversity within a framework of shared belonging, as in the cases of Sweden, the Netherlands, the UK, and Canada); and a segregationist or exclusion model . . . characterized by separation between, or fragmentation of, ethnic-cultural communities, and distinguished particularly by its restrictive legal framework regarding access to citizenship, based on the ethno-racial criterion of *jus sanguinis*, as in the cases of Austria, Germany, and Switzerland.

Although other scholars have adopted and employed somewhat different typologies (Soysal 1994), Rodríguez-García et al.'s categories represent fairly well the range of immigrant integration models currently prevailing among the traditional immigrant destinations (Boyer 2009: 3).

This said, Gary Freeman (2004: 960) appropriately cautions that "rather than anticipating a small number of distinct 'modes of immigrant incorporation' that might characterize the policies of particular countries, we should expect different modes in particular domains—state, market, welfare, culture—within individual states; the overall outcome being a mixed bag not fully assimilationist, pluralist, or multicultural." As we discuss below, we are especially mindful of Freeman's caution when he suggests that modes of immigrant integration can also vary at the subnational level. Such variation results in part because, irrespective of the destination—that is, local, regional, or national (Ireland 2004: 234)—the immigrant integration process is nearly always inherently conflict ridden. While destinations necessarily vary in the degree of conflict they experience, the immigrant integration process, as Frauke Miera (2012: 196) astutely observes, is one "in which the status quo is maintained and defended and that therefore entails dissent and conflict in order to produce something new."

Dimensions of Variation and Resulting Questions

As the preceding sections make clear, new immigrant destinations share an experience of rapid in-flows, a nascent and/or suboptimal integration infrastructure, and an atypical pattern of immigrant dispersion that make them theoretically interesting sites in which to observe the formulation of policy and political responses to increasing diversity. New immigrant destinations nevertheless differ from one another in important ways, including their respective historical experiences of cultural, ethnic, and/or religious diversity and, relatedly, their relationship to traditional destinations. As a result, each of these dimensions of variation generates competing hypotheses about the overall prospects for success in pursuing a local, regional, or national project of immigrant integration.

Variation in Historical Experiences with Diversity

Many new immigrant destinations had little if any experience of ethnic and/ or racial diversity prior to the 1980s (e.g., Ireland, Greece, and the U.S. states of Maine and Minnesota). Conversely, other new destinations (e.g., Spain and the American southern states) had been afflicted by long-standing ethnic or racial tensions that were exacerbated and/or made more complex by the relatively recent arrival and settlement of immigrants (Barker 2015: 157; Lee and Bean 2010; Messina 1992; Winders 2008; Zapata-Barrero 2013). As useful shorthand, we characterize the latter category of destinations, with their intersecting forms of diversity, as superdiverse. In this context it is hardly surprising that whenever people from significantly dissimilar backgrounds inhabit and interact within the same economic, social, and political space, interpersonal and intergroup frictions can ensue. Thus, to the extent that diversity precipitates especially thorny political and policy-related challenges, we can usefully ask whether such challenges are most acute in new destinations where diversity is unprecedented or in superdiverse destinations where new diversity overlies historically embedded cultural, ethnic, and/or racial tensions. Different theories of intergroup relations in the context of diversity offer conflicting answers.

Conflict, or group-threat, theory generally assumes that the increased presence of out-groups in a given society fuels ever-greater competition with in-groups, thus ultimately resulting in out-group prejudice and in-group solidarity (Blalock 1967; Key 1949). Alternatively, and more recently, Robert Putnam (2007: 149) has introduced "constrict theory," arguing that the proliferation of diversity erodes both in- and out-group solidarity, a phenomenon he summarizes as "hunker[ing] down." Both theories contend that greater diversity spawns greater societal tension and, in so doing, implicitly suggest that superdiverse new immigrant destinations will be especially conflictual.

Contrary to conflict and constrict theories, contact theory does not predict that greater diversity will necessarily precipitate greater discord. Rather, it posits the more optimistic view that intergroup contact will yield relative social harmony if the interacting groups enjoy a similar status, work cooperatively toward a shared goal, and have the blessing of the relevant authorities (Allport 1954; Pettigrew and Tropp 2006). Although a positive outcome is hardly predestined, contact theory offers the prospect that places with experience in navigating the challenges of diversity, such as superdiverse destinations, may be better prepared to integrate immigrant newcomers.

The existing scholarship on immigrant integration in new destinations, in fact, supports both hypotheses. In advancing the thesis that superdiverse destinations produce greater conflict, several social scientists have suggested that these more diverse settings produce not one but two tiers of immigrant integration conflict (Messina 1992; Zapata-Barrero 2010: 388). On the first tier, the aspirations, claims, interests, and very often the cultural, ethnic, and/or religious identities of immigrant populations conflict with those of a significant fraction of the national majority population. On a second tier, the aspirations, claims, interests, and identities of immigrant populations directly or indirectly collide with those of regional minority communities (Chiba 2010; Kymlicka 2001: 65) that identify themselves as "distinct in . . . their culture, language, history, religion, tradition or political past" (Thompson and Rudolph 1989: 2). In this view, many, if not most, indigenous minority communities are ambivalent about immigrants and immigration. On the one hand, regional governments and employers across Europe and numerous new immigrant destination states in the United States have recruited foreign workers and/or facilitated their entry into the economy in order to alleviate labor shortages, ameliorate declining birthrates, and spur greater economic growth and productivity (Fernández-Huertas Moraga and Ferrer-i -Carbonell 2007; Krissman 2000; Migration Observatory 2013). On the other hand, in those regions with an especially distinctive cultural, ethnic, and/or religious identity, the dominant regional population oftentimes perceives immigrants as potentially threatening of the status they have assiduously worked to achieve (Núñez 2002: 229; Tarchi 2007: 189).

In these superdiverse new destinations, public policies that were formulated by national governments to ameliorate historical ethnic conflicts, such as sovereignty-sharing arrangements within multinational states, have often proved inadequate to meeting the challenges posed by the establishment of new cultural, ethnic, and/or religious minorities (Bousetta 2009; Gilligan, Hainsworth, and McGarry 2014; Hainsworth 1998; Messina et al. 1992; Zapata-Barrero 2013: 4). In Spain (as discussed in Chapter 3 herein, by Amado Alarcón), new social cleavages spawned by mass immigration in recent decades have been awkwardly superimposed over older cleavages that were associated with the country's transition to democracy and the dominant presence of "minority nations" in the historical regions of Catalonia and the Basque Country (Zapata-Barrero 2009, 2013). Similarly, in the United States, civil rights policies formulated to rectify the historical injustices of slavery and Jim Crow illuminate that responses to diversity are designed to serve marginalized ethnic minorities rather than foreign nationals (Bloemraad 2006a; Kasinitz et al. 2008).

On the other hand, however, superdiverse new destinations more often than not have some experience implementing policies that aim to navigate successfully at least some form of historical diversity. The policies and the institutions that have developed in response may, in some cases, be reshaped to successfully address new immigrant diversity (Waters and Kasinitz 2013), as Helen B. Marrow's description of the contemporary American South in Chapter 4 of this volume suggests. In this respect, and at least in the short-term, unprecedented diversity may pose greater challenges for politics and policy makers than new diversity that has been superimposed on long-standing social cleavages. Indeed, in previously homogeneous new destinations, governments are often challenged to combat popular outbreaks of discrimination and prejudice that accompany the transition from relatively homogeneous to heterogeneous social settings (Juhasz 2010; Marrow 2011: 247–251; Walker and Leitner 2011: 159). Along these lines, Daniel Hopkins (2010) has discovered that, in the American context, majority populations in the host communities are especially likely to respond negatively when they experience a sudden influx of immigrants at a time when national rhetoric politicizes immigration. Clearly, then, the literature and experience of new destinations present conflicting accounts as to how prior experience with diversity shapes the reception of new immigrant populations, a key dimension of variation that the collected essays in this volume explore.

Variation in Relationship to Traditional Destinations

In addition to new destinations with distinctive histories of diversity, contemporary immigrants are entering political and social settings that have been informed, if not directly influenced by, the experiences of the traditional immigrant destinations (Arango 2012: 50–51; Drbohlav 2012: 195). In the case of the subnational dispersion of immigrants, as in the American state of Georgia, the new destination is nested within a traditional receiving country whose policies and historical experiences more or less inevitably shape subnational responses to immigrants (Marrow 2011). In the case of dispersion to the new immigration-receiving countries within Europe, new destination responses may be influenced by the experiences of traditional immigrant-receiving countries and the supranational policies of the EU, as the EU has incrementally pressured its member state countries to harmonize their immigrant and immigration policies in recent decades (Bijl and Verweij

2012: 12–14; Palidda 2009: 360). As a consequence, the policies of the EU member states are reputed to be converging, particularly in the area of anti-discrimination policies (Givens 2014). This said, the degree to which the experiences of the traditional receiving countries are pertinent for new destinations remains a subject of spirited debate (Faßmann and Reeger 2012: 67). Inspiring this discussion is the key question of whether the politics of immigrant settlement in the new destinations are following a similar trajectory to that in the traditional destinations (Messina 2009).

It is, of course, premature to arrive at a definitive answer to this question. Both the early immigration countries and the intermediate countries are but in the preliminary stages of receiving, accommodating, and integrating their respective immigrant populations. Even Italy, one of the "oldest" of the intermediate destination countries, continues to be severely tested in transforming its immigrant population into ethnic minority citizens (Bonifazi, Strozza, and Vitiello 2012; Colombo and Sciortino 2004). Nevertheless, Joaquín Arango (2012: 56–57) hypothesizes that "historical precedence has significantly conditioned the immigration policies of Southern and Eastern European countries, and therefore their experiences and realities. This is because they have grown, or are starting to grow, as countries of immigration at a time in which other, more developed immigration countries existed nearby."

If proximity to countries, regions, or municipalities with a long-standing experience of immigration *does* significantly shape the experience of new destinations in coping with immigrant integration, it is not unreasonable to assume there is something resembling a common dynamic that is driving the immigration/immigrant integration process, a dynamic that perhaps compels a nascent country of immigration to travel along a familiar political-policy pathway (Messina 2007). On the other hand, it may be equally likely that the new destinations that are emerging during this period will remain distinct from their earlier counterparts as a result of a cohort effect. Moreover, greater variation in destinations both nationally and subnationally may ultimately result in greater variation in integration policies, immigrant outcomes, and the resulting political dynamics. Indeed, despite the efforts of federal and supranational systems, immigrant integration policies are not necessarily harmonized across all levels of government (Jeram 2013; Marrow 2011: 234). Moreover, even the best-designed and best-intentioned immigrant integration initiatives formulated and implemented at one governmental level can be effectively undermined at other levels (Alexander 2004: 59; Caponio 2010; Jones-Correa 2011), especially but not exclusively in federal systems of governance (Joppke and Seidle 2012; Kinney and Cohen 2013; Varsanyi 2010a). Thus, it is conceivable that the rise of new immigrant destinations could result in a divergence rather than a convergence of immigrant integration outcomes.

While divergence remains possible, several comparative scholars have presented evidence of convergence in integration policies and public responses in the new destinations that is driven less by the phenomenon of policy diffusion or emulation (Bennett 1991; Cornelius and Tsuda 2004: 17) than by a kind of parallel path development, a process during which the new immigrant destinations, as the traditional destinations before them did, initially embrace mass immigration primarily for economic reasons (Ambrosini 2013) and subsequently experience similar political and social repercussions (Messina 2009). If so, such a common pathway is likely punctuated by discrete steps or stages in which permanent immigrant settlement occurs and the general process of immigrant integration more or less predictably unfolds within a new immigrant destination (Faßmann and Reeger 2012).

While evidence from the traditional and intermediate immigrant destinations suggests the existence of such a common pathway, it is unclear whether intermediate destinations will necessarily continue along this trajectory. Moreover, it is still too soon to know whether the early migration cycle countries or the new subnational destinations will follow the political-policy pathway forged by older destinations. Thus, we conclude this introductory chapter by investigating whether traditional, intermediate, and early immigrant destinations currently diverge with regard to the general political and social environment within which immigrants are being received. Although space constraints prevent us from addressing this question comprehensively, we nevertheless wish to establish an empirical foundation upon which it can be fruitfully investigated in the future.

Traditional and New Destinations: Distinct "Newness" or Convergent Pathway?

The existing data that are available to investigate the extent to which the recency of the experience of immigration shapes responses and outcomes are largely cross-national and predominantly drawn from the member states of the EU. We begin our investigation by considering whether the policy responses and immigrant integration outcomes across the traditional, intermediate, and early migration cycle countries of the EU differ significantly. Following this, we present the available data on how subnational responses and outcomes vary with the recency of immigration, including within the United States. In doing so, we raise and address four questions. First, do the policies hitherto adopted by the traditional, intermediate, and early immigration countries to facilitate immigrant integration diverge significantly? Second, do the general publics in the traditional, intermediate, and early immigration countries differ significantly in their perceptions of the salience of immigration and the social fallout of immigrant settlement? Third, to what extent do immigrants in the traditional, intermediate, and early immigration countries perceive themselves as victims of ethnic, linguistic, national, racial, and/or religious discrimination? Finally, are there considerable differences in the way that the experiences of mass immigration and immigrant settlement are perceived by subnational or regional populations?

Integration Policies and Public Perceptions of Ethnic Discrimination across Destinations

In considering how the recency of immigrant settlement shapes integration policies, the Migrant Integration Policy Index (MIPEX) offers a useful tool by which to compare the immigrant integration policies of countries across the EU. Employing 148 total indicators, the MIPEX collapses seven policy areas—antidiscrimination, education, family reunion, labor market access, long-term residence, access to nationality, and political participation—in measuring the progress of settled immigrants toward full citizenship. As the data in Table I.4 reveal, on the basis of their composite MIPEX scores, the intermediate countries, on average, are no less formally committed to integrating their immigrant populations than the traditional destination countries. Indeed, Sweden and Portugal, the leaders by a wide margin within their respective immigrant destination categories, have almost identical MIPEX scores. Somewhat predictably, on the other side of the ledger are the early migration cycle countries that have relatively underdeveloped immigrant integration regimes. Latvia and Slovakia occupy the lowest rungs on the MIPEX index within this set. Thus, the MIPEX data offer preliminary evidence for policy convergence among the European traditional and intermediate destinations. At the same time, these data offer evidence that the newest destinations remain distinct, suggesting that if a common political policy pathway exists, the aforementioned are at an earlier stage of development. Finally, the MIPEX data offer evidence of interdestination variation, suggesting that the long-term presence of immigrants does not necessarily correlate with more comprehensive integration policies. To illustrate, Austria, a traditional destination country, scores lowest among the thirteen Western European countries.

While MIPEX offers an objective measure of the robustness of each country's integration policy regime, it is also worth asking how residents perceive a nation's progress toward immigrant integration. For example, do the native-born publics of the immigrant destination countries perceive ethnic minorities as a target of discrimination? The data presented in Table I.4 shed light on this question, though they must be interpreted cautiously, since in some countries the label "ethnics" includes so-called traditional or invisible minorities (e.g., Russian language speakers in Latvia). Nevertheless, as the data make clear, the publics of the traditional immigrant destination countries, on average, are much more inclined than those in the intermediate and especially

TABLE I.4 IMMIGRATION STARTING POINT AND IMMIGRANT INTEGRATION SCORE IN TRADITIONAL, INTERMEDIATE, AND EARLY MIGRATION CYCLE DESTINATION COUNTRIES

| Immigration Countries | Approximate Immigration "Starting Point" | Immigrant Integration Measures | |
		Total MIPEX Score (2010)	% Who Perceive Ethnic Discrimination as Widespread (2012)
Traditional destinations	*1956*	*60*	*64*
Austria	1962	42	48
Belgium	1945	67	68
Denmark	1968	53	70
France	1956	51	76
Germany	1955	57	51
Netherlands	1964	68	70
Sweden	1954	83	75
United Kingdom	1946	57	57
Intermediate destinations	*1988*	*60*	*55*
Greece	1975	49	70
Ireland	1992	49	35
Italy	1988	60	61
Portugal	1993	79	53
Spain	1991	63	58
Early migration cycle destinations	*2002*	*42*	*38*
Czech Republic	*2002*	*46*	*52*
Estonia	—	46	37
Hungary	1999	45	70
Latvia	1997	31	26
Lithuania	2001	40	17
Poland	2002	42	26
Slovakia	2006	36	44
Slovenia	2007	49	35

Sources: European Commission 2012: 29; Kovalenco et al. 2010: 38, 45; Messina 2007: 24; OECD 2015: 268; OECD SOPEMI 1995: 95, 2007: 301; Venturini 2004: 10; http://www.mipex.eu/usa.

the early migration cycle countries to perceive ethnic discrimination as pervasive within their societies. The French, Danes, and Dutch are especially cognizant of ethnic discrimination within their respective countries. On the other side of the ledger, in only two of the eight early migration cycle countries (Hungary and the Czech Republic) does a majority of the public perceive ethnic discrimination as pervasive. Lithuanians, Latvians, and Poles are the least inclined publics to see evidence of discrimination.

At least two reasons might explain the divergence of popular perceptions across destinations. First, because of their repeated exposure to numerous empirical studies on ethnic discrimination in the popular media (European Commission 2012), the general publics in the traditional immigrant destination countries may be especially well aware of the existing objective evidence of discrimination. Second, because the new ethnic minorities in these countries tend to exercise greater voice and rights than immigrants in the intermediate and early migration countries, including the right to formal political expression and representation (Heath et al. 2013), the publics of the traditional destination countries are probably more cognizant of minority claims of discrimination (Koopmans et al. 2005: 146–179).

In sum, whereas objective measures of integration policy suggest a convergence of comprehensive integration policies, with few differences evident between the intermediate and traditional destinations, public perceptions of the treatment of immigrants paint a different story. Where immigrants have been present longer, the public is more likely to see them as the target of discrimination. This finding offers suggestive evidence with respect to whether "new" or "super" diversity presents greater challenges for politics and policy. On this score, the recency of diversity alone is not responsible for the prevalence of discrimination against immigrants, or at least not for public perceptions of such discrimination.

Public Attitudes across Immigrant Destinations

What can we determine about public attitudes on the salience and value of immigration? As discussed above, several scholars have predicted that unprecedented diversity may present special political and policy challenges that, in turn, precipitate an illiberal backlash (Walker and Leitner 2011). On the other hand, it is possible, if only because of "immigration fatigue" ("Immigrants Have Worlds to Offer" 1992), that the majority populations in the traditional immigration countries would express greater frustration with new or continuing immigration. The common political-policy pathway alluded to above suggests that the general public's unease with immigration may indeed increase over time.

The survey data presented in Table I.5 do not fully confirm either hypothesis, however. On the one hand, when asked in 2013 whether immi-

TABLE I.5   FOREIGN POPULATION, "IMMIGRATION IMPORTANT," "CULTURAL LIFE ENRICHED," AND DEREX INDEX SCORE OF TRADITIONAL, INTERMEDIATE, AND EARLY MIGRATION CYCLE DESTINATION COUNTRIES

	% Foreign-born Population (2011)	% Who Perceive Immigration as One of Two Most Important Issues (2013)		% Who Perceive Cultural Life as Enriched by Diversity (2007)	DEREX score* (2010)
		Country	EU		
Traditional destinations	**12.8**	**17**	**18**	**72**	**2.73**
Austria	16.0	13	8	62	4.44
Belgium	14.9	16	21	72	2.90
Denmark	7.9	17	19	74	0.93
France	11.6	12	23	72	4.53
Germany	13.1	16	22	77	2.74
Netherlands	11.4	4	12	76	1.19
Sweden	15.1	13	16	72	0.66
United Kingdom	12.0	33	23	73	5.11
Intermediate destinations	**11.0**	**5**	**10**	**69**	**7.61**
Greece	6.6	5	15	60	16.96
Ireland	16.8	9	8	84	3.56
Italy	9.0	8	16	70	8.26
Portugal	8.3	1	3	61	6.87
Spain	14.6	2	8	71	2.40
Early migration cycle destinations	**8.2**	**4**	**13**	**72**	**10.50**
Czech Republic	6.4	2	13	66	7.40
Estonia	15.7	2	15	69	5.84
Hungary	4.7	2	10	77	20.73
Latvia	14.4	11	22	75	20.79
Lithuania	6.4	8	14	76	—
Poland	1.8	3	9	70	6.52
Slovakia	4.6	1	8	67	6.60
Slovenia	11.2	0	10	73	5.29

Sources: European Commission 2007: 16, 2013: 12, 16; Kasileva 2011: 2; OECD 2013: 271, 273, 360; Political Capital 2010: 4.

*The Demand for Right-Wing Extremism (DEREX) Index tracks changes in popular attitudes and values in thirty-two countries. DEREX's data are culled in response to twenty-nine questions in the European Social Survey's database, which are divided into four categories: "Prejudice and Welfare Chauvinism"; "Anti-Establishment Attitudes"; "Right-Wing Value Orientation"; and "Fear, Distrust and Pessimism," with the index increasing with the incidence of these factors.

gration was one of the two most important issues for their respective countries and the EU, the aggregate publics in the traditional immigrant destination countries predictably viewed the issue as more salient than the respective publics in the intermediate and early migration cycle countries. Immigration was an especially salient concern for Britons and Danes. On the other hand, contrary to expectations, and despite their longer experience with mass immigration, the aggregate publics in the intermediate immigrant destinations were slightly *less* inclined than the publics in the early migration cycle countries to perceive immigration as an important issue. Within the former set of countries, immigration was perceived as most salient by the publics in Ireland and Italy and least so in Portugal and Spain. These mixed results suggest that length of immigrant presence is not in and of itself determinative of the public's estimation of the salience of immigration.

Greater agreement prevailed, however, among the aggregate publics in the traditional, intermediate, and early migration cycle countries with regard to the question of whether cultural life in their respective countries is "enriched by diversity." As the data in Table I.5 reveal, on this score there was virtually no difference across the three sets of immigrant destinations in 2007; almost two-thirds of the aggregate publics in each set concurred that the cultural life of their respective countries was enriched by diversity. However, public attitudes *within* each destination category did diverge, especially within the intermediate and early migration cycle countries. Among the populations in the former group, for example, far fewer Greeks were willing to embrace diversity than were the Irish. Similarly, among the early migration countries, Czechs and Slovaks were decidedly less likely to value diversity than Lithuanians and Hungarians. Despite their experience as citizens of a major country of immigration since the early 1960s, Austrians were the least inclined European public to embrace diversity. Here, the recency of immigration appears to be largely unrelated to whether the public values the resultant diversity.

In contrast to these findings, the traditional, intermediate, and early migration cycle countries divided along fairly predictable lines in 2010 with regard to their average DEREX scores, a composite measure of the public's disposition toward prejudice and welfare chauvinism, anti-establishment attitudes, right-wing value orientation, and fear, distrust, and pessimism (Political Capital 2010). Put simply, the longer a country's experience with liberal democracy (irrespective of its particular history with immigration) the less likely its population was to espouse values that were compatible with discriminatory, anti-establishment, and authoritarian ideologies—that is ideologies that are obviously antithetical to tolerating the presence of immigrants. To some extent, however, the substantially higher DEREX scores in the intermediate and early countries are driven by the exceptionally high scores of outliers such as Greece, Hungary, and Latvia. In sum, public opinion data on immigration do not suggest that the new destination countries are uniquely prone to xenophobia. At the same time, however, the data also do not provide strong evidence of an increase in "immigration fatigue" over time.

Immigrant Perceptions across Destinations

Clearly, the recency of migration alone is not determinative of the broader public's views on immigration. What can we determine about the perceptions of immigrants? Do immigrants in the traditional, intermediate, and early immigration countries significantly differ with regard to their perception of the security of their social status and, more specifically, whether they are the target of ethnic, linguistic, national, racial, and/or religious discrimination? Utilizing survey data from the second (2004–2005) and third (2006–2007) waves of the European Social Survey, Stéfanie André, Jaap Dronkers, and Fenella Fleischmann (2010) analyzed responses to this question by adult immigrants who had at least one parent born outside of their country of residence (Table I.6). Included in their analysis were eight traditional countries of immigration, two intermediate countries, and three early migration cycle countries. Interpreting and drawing firm conclusions from their data is obviously fraught with risk. In addition to the fact that too few countries are represented in the categories of intermediate and early migration cycle destinations is the problem that more than a quarter of the permanent Estonian population is Russian, an artifact of the large number of ethnic Russians who were offered incentives to settle in Estonia during the Soviet era. As a consequence, the Estonian case is not on a par with the immigration countries of Western Europe.

Nevertheless, two tentative conclusions can be drawn from the data. First, there was a gap, indeed frequently a chasm (e.g., in Austria, France, the Netherlands, Denmark, Spain, and the Czech Republic), in the data between natives and immigrants with regard to whether they perceive themselves as victims of discrimination. On the whole, immigrants were more than three times as likely as natives to see themselves as having been discriminated against. Second, and more importantly, the data suggest that the propensity of immigrants to perceive themselves as targets of discrimination appears to be unrelated to whether they reside in a traditional, intermediate, or early migration cycle country. More specifically, immigrants in Sweden (a traditional destination), Ireland (an intermediate destination), and the Czech Republic (an early migration cycle country) perceive themselves as targets of discrimination in approximately the same percentages.

Country	% Immigrants Perceiving Discrimination	% Natives Perceiving Discrimination	Difference
TABLE I.6 NATIVES AND IMMIGRANTS WHO PERCEIVE IN-GROUP DISCRIMINATION ON ONE OF FIVE GROUNDS (ETHNICITY, LANGUAGE, NATIONALITY, RACE, OR RELIGION) IN EU (IN PERCENTAGES)*			
Traditional destinations			
Austria	15.1	0	15.1
Belgium	8.6	2.3	6.3
Denmark	8.4	0	8.4
France	12.3	3.1	9.2
Germany	10.2	7.1	3.1
Netherlands	11.7	0	11.7
Sweden	7.8	6.7	1.1
United Kingdom	15.9	8.0	7.9
Intermediate destinations			
Ireland	6.6	4.8	1.8
Spain	18.3	2.9	15.4
Early migration cycle destinations			
Czech Republic	7.4	0	7.4
Estonia	22.4	5.0	17.4
Slovenia	3.0	1.8	1.2
Average	**11.4**	**3.2**	**8.2**
Source: André, Dronkers, and Fleischmann 2010: 34.			
* Unweighted data are from the second and third wave of the European Social Survey.			

Public Perceptions at the Subnational Level

What can we determine about the perceptions of regional publics (Koff 2008: 86)? Survey evidence from Spain, an intermediate immigrant destination, and the United States, a traditional immigrant destination, reveals that inter-regional differences can and often do vary as much as intercountry differences with regard to public opinion on immigration and immigrant settlement. Moreover, in both cases there appears to be no strong correlation linking the recency of immigration and the general public's attitudes toward immigration and immigrants.

As the data in Table I.1 indicate, the Spanish public's perception that immigration poses a major policy problem generally tends to be correlated with a high immigrant presence within a region. Indeed, it is undoubtedly no coincidence that three of the autonomous communities (Murcia, Navarra, and Islas Baleares) in which more than 10 percent of the public perceives immigration as being especially problematic are home to a foreigner population exceeding 10 percent. On the other side of the coin, no greater than 3.3 percent of the public identifies immigration as a major problem in three of four of the least immigrant-penetrated autonomous communities (Galicia, Asturias, and Castilla y León). This noted, there are several obvious outliers in the data. For example, although the residents of Madrid and Islas Canarias live and work alongside a relatively high number of immigrants (i.e., more than 14 percent of the regional population), a supermajority of them seem to be comparatively relaxed about immigration. Conversely, a critical minority of the residents of Extremadura, an autonomous community populated by relatively few immigrants (3.7 percent), are disproportionately disturbed by their presence.

Some evidence of correlation, however weak, is equally evident with respect to the recency of significant migration to a region and the regional public's perception that immigration poses a major policy problem in 2012. As Table I.1 indicates, Spain had eight autonomous communities (Islas Baleares, Islas Canarias, Comunidad Valenciana, Madrid, Cataluña, Andalucía, Murcia, and La Rioja) with a foreigner population of approximately 1 percent or greater in 1998. These are the communities that were among the earliest and most popular immigrant destinations. By comparison, the communities of the next nine immigrant-penetrated destinations during Spain's early years as a country of immigration had a foreigner population of between 0.38 and 0.81 percent. Somewhat predictably, in the first set of communities, an average of 7.3 percent of the public agreed that immigration was one of three major problems in 2012, as compared with an average of only 4.3 percent of the public in the least immigrant-penetrated communities in 1998. This said, the aforementioned trend was not without its conspicuous outliers, as the publics of several of the slower evolving immigrant destination communities (Navarra, Aragón, and Extremadura) were more inclined to identify immigration as a problem in 2012 than four of the most immigrant-penetrated communities (Islas Canarias, Comunidad Valenciana, Madrid, and Andalucía) in 1998.

Evidence from a 2012 survey of Americans with substantial state-level samples also reveals intracountry variation in popular attitudes, but in this instance public opinion in the new immigrant destination states, on average, showed decidedly less tolerance of immigrants than in the old immigrant destination states (CCES 2012). The survey posed six questions that, in the aggregate, gauged popular concern with immigration and immigrants: whether illegal immigrants should be granted legal status, whether border patrols should be increased, whether to allow police questioning of illegal immigrants, whether businesses that hire the unauthorized should be fined, whether illegal immigrants should be prohibited from accessing emergency health care and public school, and whether the American-born children of illegal immigrants should be denied U.S. citizenship. Table I.7 compares the

TABLE I.7 POPULAR ATTITUDES TOWARD IMMIGRANTS IN SELECT TRADITIONAL AND NEW IMMIGRATION U.S. STATES, 2013 (IN PERCENTAGES)

State	% Immigrants 1990	% Immigrants 2012	% Romney Vote 2012	% Grant Legal Status to Illegal Immigrants	% Increase Border Patrol	% Allow Police Questioning of Illegal Immigrants	% Fine Businesses That Hire Illegal Immigrants	% Prohibit Illegal Immigrants from Public School	% Deny Citizenship to Children of Illegal Immigrants
California	22	27	37	51	49	32	57	28	35
Florida	13	20	49	48	57	42	62	31	35
Illinois	8	14	41	50	52	36	61	31	35
New Jersey	13	21	41	50	54	36	57	29	34
New York	16	23	35	54	50	31	51	25	29
Texas	9	16	57	47	61	42	62	34	40
Traditional average	*13*	*20*	*43*	*50*	*54*	*36*	*58*	*30*	*34*
Delaware	3	9	40	50	53	43	62	33	34

Georgia	3	10	53	48	59	41	62	31	36
Indiana	2	5	54	42	62	43	66	34	39
Kansas	3	7	60	42	57	43	69	33	40
Minnesota	3	8	45	50	50	38	65	30	35
Nebraska	2	7	60	40	59	50	72	39	47
North Carolina	2	8	50	45	58	43	63	30	35
Oklahoma	2	6	67	41	61	48	70	36	43
South Carolina	1	5	55	39	64	49	67	37	42
Utah	3	8	73	46	55	39	66	27	38
New destination average	*2*	*7*	*56*	*44*	*58*	*44*	*66*	*33*	*39*
Difference (% points)	*11*	*13*	*-12*	*6****	*-4****	*-7****	*-8****	*-3****	*-5****

Source: CCES 2012

Note: New destination states are defined here as those that had 3 percent or less foreign-born persons resident in 1990, had 5 percent or more foreign born in 2012, and over this period exhibited foreign-born growth of greater than 200 percent. *** p <.001.

responses to these questions from the six most concentrated foreign-born states, as compared with ten new destination states, defined here as those that were 3 percent or less foreign born in 1990, 5 percent or more foreign born in 2012 and exhibited foreign-born growth over this period of greater than 200 percent. In response to every question posed in the survey, the residents of new destinations indicated greater concern about immigrants. Although these questions specifically gauged sentiment toward unauthorized immigrants, an analysis of a 2013 survey that asked questions about general immigration threat generated similar results (Table I.8). Again, in response to every question posed—whether newcomers threaten American values, immigrants are changing American life for the worse, the American way of life needs to be protected against foreign influence, the idea of a majority nonwhite America is bothersome, and all illegal immigrants ought to be arrested and deported—the respective publics in the new immigration states were, on average, more inclined to feel threatened.

Of course, the aforementioned differences between the new and traditional destination states are not uniformly large. Moreover, the popular views on immigration expressed in this and other public opinion surveys tend to correlate with political partisanship, as the new destinations were, on average, more Republican. Indeed, in 2012, the average proportion voting for Republican presidential candidate Mitt Romney among the new destination states exceeded the proportion in the traditional destination states by 12 percentage points. Thus, using the CCES data, we can analyze whether residence in a new destination state predicts restrictive attitudes toward immigrants among whites, holding constant the respondents' ideology, gender, and education. What we find is that whites in new destinations, regardless of ideology, are less likely to advocate granting legal status to undocumented immigrants and more likely to support allowing the police to question undocumented immigrants and fining businesses that hire undocumented immigrants. Once ideology is held constant, however, whites in new destinations are not especially predisposed to advocate greater border security, disallow unauthorized immigrants to access public services, or deny citizenship to the children of unauthorized immigrants (results available upon request). While the results on the whole are mixed, this analysis indicates that non-Hispanic white Americans residing in new immigrant destinations are somewhat more concerned about the presence of immigrants than those in traditional destinations. Although we cannot draw firm conclusions from the data, it appears that the effect of subnational recency of immigrant settlement on public opinion varies with context. Specifically, in the United States, it appears that new immigrant destinations are sites of greater friction over immigration, while in Spain the recency of immigration appears to have impacted public attitudes less.

TABLE I.8   POPULAR ATTITUDES TOWARD IMMIGRANTS IN SELECT TRADITIONAL AND NEW IMMIGRATION U.S. STATES, 2013 (IN PERCENTAGES)

State	% Newcomers Threaten Customs and Values	% Immigrants Change American Life for the Worse	% American Way of Life Needs Protection from Foreign Influence	% All Illegal Immigrants Should Be Deported	% Idea of Majority Non-white America Is Bothersome
Traditional destinations					
California	33	25	48	21	13
Florida	42	25	51	24	13
New York	33	24	48	31	12
Texas	36	25	58	28	13
Average	**36**	**25**	**51**	**26**	**13**
New destinations					
Indiana	44	28	61	26	16
Minnesota	33	21	49	25	16
Pennsylvania	37	29	56	32	15
Average	**38**	**26**	**55**	**28**	**16**
Difference	**2**	**1**	**4**	**2**	**3**

Source: Public Religion Research Institute 2013 (sufficient samples of only three nontraditional states available in data).

While a more sophisticated analysis is required to answer fully the question posed here, this analysis indicates that recency of migration alone is clearly not determinative. Although the data on integration policies point toward some degree of convergence in the EU beyond the early migration cycle countries, this policy convergence is not paralleled by a consensus among these countries in terms of native or immigrant public opinion. On the whole, the data suggest the importance of identifying mediating factors that shape the relationship between recency of immigration and integration policies and outcomes. Under which circumstances does "newness" pose particular challenges?

The data presented here echo Rogers Brubaker's (1992) thesis that distinct modes of national "self-understanding" primarily determine whether immigrants gain greater or lesser access to citizenship and acceptance into the political community. The findings suggest that from the perspective of the state it is not inexperience with mass immigrant settlement that poses the greatest challenge for managing diversity successfully in new immigrant destinations—although this *is* self-evidently important (Blommaert and Verschueren 1998: 11–21; Waters and Jiménez 2005; Wessendorf 2014)—but, rather, several other mediating factors. Although this volume is by no means exhaustive, its chapters explore how four factors mediate the relationship between recency and immigrant integration: (1) the velocity of the flow of immigrants into a destination over time (Mollenkopf and Pastor 2013; Zapata-Barrero 2009: 1114); (2) the extent to which immigrants are geographically dispersed and, hence, whether the economic, political, and social costs of immigrant settlement are either concentrated or diffuse (Freeman 1995; Morales and Echazarra 2013; Papademetriou 2006: xxxi); (3) the accessibility, adaptability, and permeability of the destination's formal economic, political, and social institutions (Niessen 2000: 31), including its social welfare regime (Buckley 2013; Penninx 2003: 1; Weldon 2006); and (4) how a particular destination defines itself as a cultural, political, and social community (Cinalli and Giugni 2011; Escandell and Ceobanu 2010; Triandafyllidou 2010: 210–212; Walker and Leitner 2011: 165; Winders 2013: 24).

In sum, the chances of successfully managing diversity or superdiversity are most likely a function of both subjective and structural factors. On the one hand, we find evidence of policy convergence across the traditional and intermediate destinations. On the other, this is not matched by a parallel convergence in public attitudes or immigrant integration experiences. Thus, policy convergence does not, in and of itself, ensure convergent integration outcomes. Moreover, new immigrant destinations are not inherently troubled; nor are traditional destinations inherently evincing "immigration fatigue." As such, the passage of time may not, in and of itself, facilitate successful immigrant integration. Rather, some settings appear more conducive to immigrant integration even if the process of immigrant settlement began relatively recently. The rise of new immigrant destinations in both Europe and the United States offers an opportunity to identify the factors that condition successful immigrant integration, a task that the collected essays in this volume undertake.

Plan of the Book

With the aforementioned dimensions of variation in mind, this volume is organized in five parts. Part I introduces several of the major issues raised by the proliferation of diversity in two intermediate destination countries (Ireland and Italy). Part II considers the policy and political implications of new migration to regions with a distinctive cultural or ethnic identity (the American South and Catalonia). The essays in Part III identify several of the unique challenges that migration poses to new destination locales within traditional destination countries (subnational immigrant dispersion in the United States and the United Kingdom). The chapters in Part IV introduce two examples of "early migration cycle" destinations (Poland and Latvia)— that is, pre-new destination countries in Europe (Okólski 2009: 6). Part V helps bring the book to a close with three chapters that collectively address the degree to which new immigrant destinations differ from the traditional destinations and/or from one another with regard to the success of their efforts to integrate immigrants.

The essays in Part I of the volume introduce two intermediate new destination countries in Europe—Ireland and Italy—that have attracted a significant number of foreign workers and their dependents since the 1980s. Like the traditional immigration countries in Europe during the 1950s and 1960s (Hammar 1985; Messina 2007: 20–30), both Ireland and Italy emerged as new countries of immigration as a direct result of acute labor shortages that were precipitated by rapid economic growth. However, unlike the other countries subsumed under Freeman's (1995) three modes of immigration politics, neither Ireland nor Italy was a traditional destination for refugees, had "mother-country" ties to former colonies, or (at least prior to the 1980s) had experienced a significant influx of foreign workers. Therefore, their respective national governments did little to forge comprehensive immigration or immigrant integration policies until relatively late in the immigration cycle.

Against the backdrop of Ireland's sluggishness in addressing the challenges of immigrant integration, Erica Dobbs asks in Chapter 1 whether, in the context of their self-appointed mission to foster and facilitate immigrant social and civil engagement, state actors can perform the function of accelerating immigrant electoral incorporation. Analyzing the Dublin City Council's efforts to engage the city's immigrant community in the 2009 local elections, she discovers that the ability of state bureaucrats to act as agents for immigrant electoral incorporation is, in practice, significantly circumscribed. Specifically, in the face of the unwillingness and/or failure of Ireland's political parties to politically socialize and mobilize Ireland's new immigrants, local bureaucrats are largely unable to fulfill these roles.

Adopting a somewhat broader view of the role of politics in the immigrant integration process, Tiziana Caponio and Francesca Campomori underscore in Chapter 2 the need to look to beneath the national level—that is, regionally and/or locally—in order to better assess the opportunities and obstacles associated with immigrant integration. They find that the immigrant integration programs of two Italian regions (Emilia-Romagna and Veneto) more closely reflect the policy frames and ideological orientation of their respective governing political parties than the prevailing policy frame at the national level. As a consequence, different and often conflicting frames are in play in the context of decision making within each region and, thus, presumably, across Italian regions generally. In this context Caponio and Campomori persuasively argue that "national" models of immigrant integration have not been especially useful in understanding the dynamics of the immigrant integration process in Italy (Ireland 2004).

The essays in Part II, by Amado Alarcón (Chapter 3) and Helen B. Marrow (Chapter 4), also address the regional level but expand upon Caponio and Campomori's study of Emilia-Romagna and Veneto by showing that the challenges posed by immigrant integration at the subnational level—in Catalonia for Alarcón and in the American South for Marrow—are further complicated by the interaction of new immigrants with indigenous minority populations. At specific issue for Alarcón is whether immigrants and their dependents assimilate in Catalan, Spanish, their mother tongue, or some combination of the three languages. He finds that a lack of correspondence between linguistic integration and socioeconomic immigrant integration leads to an illusion of fully integrated youth. Particularly among poorly educated Latin Americans, the use of Catalan is conspicuously low because of its lack of utility in the workplace.

In building upon her earlier scholarship (Marrow 2011), Marrow's chapter offers an updated and nuanced analysis of elite versus nonelite black-Hispanic relations across various institutional domains within the American South. Her survey of recent trends within the region reveals a bifurcation by level and domain that suggests that several color lines may still be emerging and, in the process, transforming the region. Although the rigid and long-standing hierarchy between whites and blacks continues to predominate, the relational and material place of Hispanic newcomers may be inching closer to that of African Americans in several ways, while staying relationally closer to that of whites in other respects.

The contributions by Claudio A. Holzner and Melissa M. Goldsmith (Chapter 5) and Rhys Andrews (Chapter 6) in Part III broadly assess the phenomenon of immigrant dispersion in new destination locales—cities in the U.S. state of Utah and in rural England, respectively—within two traditional countries of immigration. Holzner and Goldsmith ask whether the local communities in which immigrants settle increase or decrease the likelihood that they will be incorporated successfully into politics. Utilizing a dataset that combines individual-level demographic information on all Utah residents with official voter records and city-level contextual variables for 243 cities and towns, the authors investigate the effects of city size, municipal forms of government, and immigrants' local political experiences on the likelihood that immigrants voted in the 2008 presidential election. What they ultimately discover is that direct experiences with local political activity increase the probability that immigrants will vote in presidential elections. In contrast, residing in a large city depresses immigrant voter turnout. In sum, their findings generally confirm the importance of local politics for immigrant political incorporation in new destinations.

In Chapter 6, in contrast, Andrews identifies an unusual but significant *subjective* variable relevant for the social integration of new immigrant groups: the bridging social capital that is associated within mainline religious communities. In modeling the separate and combined effects of religious communities and economic in-migration on social cohesion in rural areas across England, Andrews finds that religious communities and recent immigration have an especially large statistically significant independent effect on overall citizen perceptions of social cohesion. More specifically, Andrews's data analysis suggests that mainline Protestant communities enhance intergroup social cohesion in rural England, while evangelical communities do not. As a consequence, the social integration of immigrants appears to be broader and deeper where mainline Protestant and Catholic communities are strongest.

To gain insight into why new immigrant destinations emerge and how they subsequently respond to their new status, the descriptive chapters in Part IV of the volume offer two examples of "early migration cycle" destinations that seem to be transitioning from net emigration to net immigration countries: Poland and Latvia (Okólski 2009: 6). With regard to why these two countries have attracted an increasing number of migrants since the early 1990s, and especially since their accession to the EU, Chapter 7 (Poland), by Aleksandra Kazłowska and Magdalena Lesińska, and Chapter 8 (Latvia), by Dace Akule, arrive at much the same conclusion: As a consequence of rapid economic growth, periodic labor shortages, and persistent problems of low fertility and/or demographic aging, each early migration cycle economy now requires a significant number of foreign workers. Moreover, as a subset of these workers have incrementally settled into their host society, foreign workers have been propelled by inertia, family-related considerations, and/or the immediate or anticipated threat of government-imposed immigration restrictions to establish permanent roots.

In both countries, the process of integrating immigrants, however modest their current numbers, has raised pressing challenges for the government, the host society, and the immigrants themselves. For the Polish and Latvian governments, the most significant of the aforementioned challenges has been whether and how to craft new immigrant integration policies and reform the main tenets of their national citizenship law in ways that conform to the requirements of the EU without creating an incentive for otherwise temporary or circular migrants to settle permanently. For the majority population of each host society, the central dilemma is how to embrace diversity without compromising the national identity and core cultural values upon which this identity is founded. As Kazłowska and Lesińska point out in Chapter 7, for immigrants to Poland, the major quandary is whether to risk rupturing their in-group relations and the social mores, linguistic heritage, and cultural practices of their home country in order to better conform to the expectations of their adopted country and host society. As Akule highlights in Chapter 8, all of the aforementioned challenges have been made more difficult in Latvia as a result of the 1993 entrance onto the national political stage of an illiberal political party that is explicitly opposed to naturalizing nonethnic Latvians. Although Kazłowska and Lesińska perceive Poland's political climate as more tolerant and accommodating than Latvia's, here too immigrants are not so easily integrated.

Chapter 9, by Monica Varsanyi et al.; Chapter 10, by Melissa Marschall; and Chapter 11, by Katia Pilati and Laura Morales, in Part V, help conclude the volume by offering different perspectives on the degree to which new immigrant destinations differ from traditional destinations and/or from one another in their attempts and successes in integrating immigrants. Considered together, they present a fairly encouraging picture of the structural and political conditions in which immigrants are currently integrating within new destinations and the summary judgment that there is greater convergence than divergence of such conditions across destinations.

Chapter 9 introduces the section by addressing the issue of policing in new immigrant destinations across the United States and, specifically, the important role of law enforcement in the process of immigrant integration. Utilizing quantitative data from two national surveys of police chiefs and qualitative data from an in-depth case study conducted in Allentown, Pennsylvania, Varsanyi and her co-authors find that new destinations do not differ significantly from more traditional immigrant destinations in terms of policing *practices*, but new destinations are somewhat behind the curve in developing official immigrant-related *policies*. Although new destination localities may be quickly gaining ground—and perhaps even developing innovative, forward-thinking practices with bureaucracies such as the police leading the way—it remains to be seen to what extent new public policies will ultimately lead to new practices by law enforcement.

Complementing the previous contribution by Varsanyi et al., Chapter 10 investigates how schools situated in different "contexts of reception" address the needs of both immigrant parents and students. Holding constant a number of variables, Marschall examines the differences between new and old destinations in school policies for limited-English-proficiency (LEP) students, staffing to support these students, and outreach to LEP parents, all on the basis of data culled from the National Center for Educational Statistics Schools and Staffing Surveys (1987–2007). Marschall's findings are broadly positive in the sense that they suggest that new immigrant destinations are performing very well compared to more established destinations, in terms of the incorporation of LEP students and their families. Marschall concludes that the lack of experience with immigrant and LEP populations in new destinations (compared to established immigrant destinations and border counties) has not hampered the ability of schools to implement programs that serve the needs of these populations.

On the European side, Chapter 11 explores patterns of civic and political engagement in nine European cities, including both new and old destinations. In pursuing this line of inquiry, Pilati and Morales analyze the factors affecting immigrant engagement in ethnic, native, and pan-immigrant organizations, as well as their political engagement in mainstream and immigrant-related activities in Budapest, Barcelona, Geneva, Lyon, London, Madrid, Milan, Stockholm, and Zurich. They find that the contextual effect of new and old destinations depends on the type of civic and political engagement examined. Specifically, immigrant destination type significantly affects immigrant engagement only in native and pan-immigrant organizations and engagement in mainstream politics. Neither ethnic organizing nor immigrant-related activities is especially affected by whether the country is a new or an old destination.

NOTE

1. The editors are grateful to Michael Jones-Correa for sharing this insight.

I

New Destination
Countries

1

Bureaucrats and the Ballot Box

State-Led Political Incorporation in Ireland

ERICA DOBBS

In this chapter, Dobbs analyzes both the impetus toward and resistance to the political incorporation of immigrants in Ireland. She demonstrates that while some local government bureaucrats in Dublin see the merits of engaging immigrants in electoral politics as voters and/or candidates, the political party activists who could play a role in that process are more resistant.

The latest wave of migration to Western democratic societies has reopened old debates about the political incorporation of new immigrants. Of particular interest to both scholars and policymakers is electoral incorporation, namely the process by which immigrants not only register for and actively participate in elections, but are also treated as a constituent voting group by politicians seeking office. While electoral incorporation has long been viewed as a key stage in the citizenship process (Marshall 1964), it has taken on particular urgency in recent years, as the reaction of political parties to contemporary immigration has ranged from benign neglect (Andersen 2010) to active mobilization of anti-immigrant sentiment for electoral gain (Ford and Goodwin 2014; Spanje 2010).

At the same time that parties are seemingly giving up on immigrants as a constituent group, new immigrant communities may not have the capacity or know-how to mobilize themselves within the context of mainstream electoral politics in their newly adopted countries. This is particularly true in new destination societies where immigration is a novel phenomenon: lacking both an understanding of the receiving country's political institutions and processes and well-established civic and social organizations that are dedicated to representing the interests of migrant communities, immigrants in new destinations may have few political guides and allies (Waters and Jiménez 2005). With little interest in mobilization coming to them from above, and a limited capacity for mobilizing themselves from below, immigrants seem condemned to be acted upon by the political system, rather than engaged actors within it.

However, recent studies of social and political incorporation suggest a third way: incorporation via the state. State funding for immigrant community organizations and civic education programs has been shown to increase the likelihood of both naturalization and civic participation (Bloemraad 2005; 2006a). Beyond distributing state funding, however, bureaucrats may not just act as agents of the state, but may also see themselves as advocates for immigrant communities (Chen 2012; Marrow 2009b). The increasingly obvious role that state actors play in fostering and facilitating different forms of social and civic engagement begs the question: Can bureaucrats play a similar role when it comes to elections?

In this chapter I explore the role of bureaucrats in facilitating electoral incorporation using Ireland as a case. Ireland is relatively unique in that it allows all noncitizen adults to participate in local elections, regardless of their immigration status. The only requirements are that a voter be over the age of eighteen and demonstrate residency in the state for at least six months before Election Day.[1] Given that access to citizenship is usually prior to access to electoral politics, and different immigrant groups may have different pathways to citizenship, using Ireland as a case allows us to focus on when and why migrant voter-mobilization efforts occur without having to take into account differences in eligibility among immigrant groups.[2] Ireland is also interesting because, despite how open its electoral institutions are to immigrants, the documented lack of party engagement with immigrant communities is somewhat puzzling.[3]

Beyond its electoral institutions, Ireland's status as a new destination country for immigrants makes it an important case for exploring contemporary processes of immigrant electoral incorporation. Until the 1990s, Ireland was largely a country of emigration, but from 1981 to 2006, the foreign-born population rose from 6.7 percent to 15.8 percent (see Table 1.1). The relative newness of migration means that unlike, for example, the Democratic Party's relationship to the Irish in the United States, political parties (and civic associations) in Ireland do not have long historic ties with immigrant populations.[4] As a new destination country, Ireland also lacks a dominant historical narrative defining itself as a "nation of immigrants" like that used in American political debates. Shared narratives play an important role in offering guidance in a time of uncertainty (Ganz 2011; Zald 1996),

TABLE 1.1 FOREIGN-BORN PERSONS AS A PERCENTAGE OF IRISH POPULATION, 1981–2006		
	Foreign born	Foreign Born—U.K. Citizens
1981	6.7	1.3
1986	6.3	1.3
1991	6.5	1.6
1996	7.5	2.1
2001	11.4	4.7
2006	15.8	9.0
Source: CSO 2016.		

and these kinds of historical narratives play a role in facilitating incorporation by normalizing the idea that immigrants should be a part of civic life (Griffith 2008). Finally, Ireland represents a new and interesting case for exploring the dynamics of incorporation: much of what we know about immigrant political incorporation comes from studies of countries where the process was driven by mass industrialization and/or imperial relationships—yet many of today's new destination states at the periphery of Europe are not too far removed from poverty and emigration themselves. The lessons drawn from Ireland—a small, late-developing country with a history of domination by its more powerful neighbor—may be far more relevant for the new destination states of Southern and Eastern Europe than the lessons drawn from the industrial powers of Northern Europe and North America.

In order to explore the role of bureaucrats in fostering electoral incorporation, I offer a close case study of efforts by the Dublin City Council (DCC) to engage the city's immigrant population in the 2009 local elections. I find that the ability of bureaucrats to act as agents for electoral incorporation is relatively limited. While the direct impact of bureaucrat-led voter-registration initiatives on overall immigrant voter-registration rates cannot be determined ex post, efforts to engage political parties with immigrant communities clearly failed. However, bureaucrats were successful in building stronger working relationships between themselves and immigrant-serving community organizations. In addition, the diversity of the groups selected to participate in the voter campaign led to a great deal of inadvertent bridge building across disparate immigrant organizations. Together, findings from the Dublin case suggest that bureaucrats may not be particularly well positioned to affect the relationship between immigrants and political parties or to foster partisan interest in politics. However, they are capable of facilitating both learning about the political system and bridge building between not only city officials and immigrant organizations but among immigrant organizations

TABLE 1.2 INTERVIEW SCHEDULE	
Party and elected officials	7
Government officials	3
NGOs	18
TOTAL	28

that deal with very different issues and communities. While this bridging role was not necessarily what organizers intended, it does directly address a growing critique that state support for explicitly ethnic organizations is counterproductive because these groups are too disconnected from the host society (Strömblad and Adman 2010; Vasta 2007). By acting as a matchmaker among diverse immigrant ethnic organizations and a conduit between ethnic organizations and the state, bureaucrats can help foster the kinds of bridging social and political networks that the critics of ethnic organizations claim is lacking.[5]

These findings were developed through a review of public documents, including press statements, newspaper articles, and reports from both government agencies and NGOs. In addition, twenty-eight interviews with immigrant community leaders, bureaucrats, and party officials were conducted in the wake of the 2009 local election cycle (see Table 1.2). Interviewees were selected due to their involvement with immigrant electoral incorporation efforts (both with and outside of the DCC campaign) or with party politics. Interviews were held in Dublin just after the local elections in June and July 2009 and during a follow-up visit from March to June 2010. Given that many immigrant organizations rely on government funding, and that the issue of immigration is politically sensitive, participants were guaranteed anonymity, except in cases where, given the outsized role they played in the campaign, this would be impossible.

The chapter is structured as follows: section two outlines the challenges specifically facing immigrant communities when it comes to incorporation and the potential role of both parties and bureaucrats in fostering immigrant participation in elections. Section three explains both the changing dynamics of immigration in Ireland and the institutional context of political incorporation. Section four introduces the case of the DCC immigrant voter-registration campaign and presents the key findings, and section five presents a brief discussion of the findings and some concluding remarks.

Challenge of Incorporation

What are some of the key variables that affect immigrant political incorporation? Hochschild et al. (2013) identify six: (1) immigration status, (2) linguistic capacity, (3) contextual knowledge of receiving country politics, (4) political socialization in the home country, (5) transnational relationships, and (6) perceptions of inclusion.

Immigration status is a key barrier to political incorporation, for although a growing number of countries allow limited voting rights for non-citizens (Earnest 2006), in most countries, access to citizenship is a prerequisite for voting rights. Linguistic capacity, contextual knowledge, and political socialization are significant because they are immigrant-specific variables that upend much of the traditional literature on political behavior. In studies that focus on native political behavior, individuals who engage in electoral politics tend to be more educated, better off, and more involved in community organizations than those who do not (Brady, Verba, and Schlozman 1995; Rosenstone and Hansen 2002). New immigrant populations may be quite well off economically, highly educated, and fluent in the language, but if they are not familiar with local political dynamics or are reluctant to engage in political activity because of differences in past political socialization, their levels of electoral engagement will remain low (Tam Cho 1999). In addition, recent work on immigrant civic organizations suggests that while association membership generally boosts political engagement among immigrants, this is not the case for ethnic associations (Strömblad and Adman 2010). Therefore, the experience of being an immigrant works against electoral incorporation in a way that is distinctive from natives and counters much of the literature on native political behavior.

Transnational relationships and perceptions of inclusion can also affect political engagement, and sometimes these two variables can interact. Past work on immigration and minority group politics shows that being the target of hostile legislation and/or perceptions of exclusion can have a positive impact on electoral participation, as minority groups make their displeasure known at the ballot box (Pantoja, Ramirez, and Segura 2001). However, research focusing specifically on immigrants finds that some may actually seek refuge in transnational civil society rather than host country politics when faced with exclusion in the receiving community (Itzigsohn and Giorguli-Saucedo 2005), although this experience may differ by gender (Jones-Correa 1998b).

Beyond the specifics of immigrant communities, there are external factors that may affect political incorporation as well. Party politics and power relations can have a serious impact on immigrant political incorporation, particularly when it comes to electoral participation. First, a given party's position within the political system may have an effect on its eagerness to mobilize new immigrants: groups looking to increase their vote share may see the organization of new immigrant voters as a way of expanding their base—and their power (Dahl [1961] 2005). Conversely, in a situation where one party utterly dominates a given district or political system, there may be little incentive to seek support from new arrivals (Erie 1988; Jones-Correa 1998a). Second, the candidates that a party selects can affect immigrant turnout or interest in voting: research on minority politics in the United States suggests that having a coethnic on the ballot increases voter turnout among members of that group (Barreto 2007; Barretto, Villareal, and Woods 2005; Whitby 2007). Finally, being approached matters: individuals who are directly contacted and asked to vote are more likely to do so (Wong 2005), and this effect is even greater for those contacted by coethnics (Michelson 2003).

Yet despite the potential for electoral benefit from registering and mobilizing immigrants, many political parties, particularly in Europe, have sought and found electoral success not by recruiting new immigrant voters, but by mobilizing against immigration. The National Front in France, Golden Dawn in Greece, the Swedish Democrats, the Freedom Party in the Netherlands, the Danish People's Party, the Finns Party of Finland, and the Swiss People's Party have all found some electoral success in recent years, in no small part due to their anti-immigration platforms. With parties using politics as a weapon against immigrant communities that may not have the linguistic ability, legal right, or political knowledge to push back against these policies, it is increasingly unclear where or how—or if—immigrant electoral incorporation will happen in the future.

Bureaucrats and Incorporation

With parties either alienated from or actively opposed to immigrant communities, might bureaucrats have an impact on electoral incorporation? As the key agents tasked with implementing policy, bureaucrats—particularly at the local level—may be the first point of contact with the state for new immigrants, and can thereby play a critical role in shaping how immigrants understand their role within that given society. Bloemraad (2006a: 4) notes that interaction with the state can affect "understandings of citizenship, especially of immigrants' legitimate political standing." In addition, given that home-country effects are not necessarily fixed over time and may diminish through resocialization in the receiving country (White et al. 2008), bureaucrats are uniquely positioned to contribute to this process due to their frontline interaction with immigrants. This said, the remit of bureaucrats may be limited depending on the nature of their position: local school officials may be more interested and invested in the civic engagement of immigrant communities than, say, law enforcement officials (Marrow 2009b). Bureaucrats may also face some limits due to the dynamics of the principal-agent relationship they have with elected officials: bureaucrats who stray too far from the policy intent of legislators or who actively challenge or criticize policy may find their budgets slashed or their departments cut altogether. Yet despite these challenges, given their close contact with immigrant communities, the role of bureaucrats in potentially facilitating electoral incorporation warrants further investigation.

Old Challenges, New Destinations: Immigrants in Ireland

Historically, Ireland has been a country of emigration, not immigration. Due to a combination of political and economic reforms in the 1980s and the booming "Celtic Tiger" economy of the 1990s, Ireland not only attracted attention from overseas investors, but overseas workers as well. Between 1991 and 2006, the foreign-born population grew at an unprecedented rate, rising from 6.3 percent in 1986 to 15.8 percent in 2006. This growth rate is even more dramatic when U.K.-born residents—many of whom are ethnically Irish—are removed from the equation: between 1996 and 2002, the non-U.K. foreign-born population more than doubled, from 2.1 percent to 4.7 percent, and by 2006 it increased again to 9 percent.[6]

Not only did Ireland's immigrant population grow exponentially during the period, but it also became more diverse. Prior to the Celtic Tiger boom of the 1990s, most foreign-born residents of Ireland were citizens of the United Kingdom, United States, or Australia—in other words, the countries that were long a haven for Irish emigrants seeking work. As the economy improved in the 1990s and the reserve labor pool began to dry up, a growing number of African and Asian professionals began to fill gaps in the labor market within IT and health services (CSO 2008). Beginning in the late 1990s, Ireland also saw a significant increase in asylum seekers, rising from only thirty-nine in 1992 to just under twelve thousand in 2002 (ORAC 2001: 62; 2004: 67). However, 2004 represented a major turning point for Irish immigration flows, as Ireland was one of only three members of the European Union (EU) that allowed new EU accession members access to the labor market.[7] This decision led to an unexpected and dramatic increase in the Eastern European population, most notably Poles, in Ireland: a 2008 report by the CSO (2008) noted that the Polish population increased by 90 percent between 2004 and 2006, to 63,276.[8] The same report also highlighted the diversity of the non-Irish national population: while over a quarter identified as British, and 15 percent as Polish, no other national group made up more than 6 percent of the total.[9]

The rapidly increasing size and diversity of the foreign-born population presented several key challenges to the process of political incorporation. First, the shift away from Anglophone countries as a source of migration introduced significant linguistic barriers to incorporation. Second, the diversity in the population, and, in particular, the increase in migration from other EU member states, created a tiered system of access to electoral politics: non-EU

TABLE 1.3 VOTING RIGHTS BY CITIZENSHIP STATUS IN IRELAND				
Eligibility Criteria	Local Elections	European Parliamentary Elections	General Elections (Dáil)	Referenda in Republic of Ireland
Eighteen years old	x	x	x	x
On register of elections	x	x	x	x
Citizen of Ireland	x	x	x	x
Citizen of United Kingdom	x	x	x	
Citizen of the European Union (not United Kingdom)	x	x		
Citizen of country outside of Ireland, the United Kingdom, or the European Union	x			
Source: DECLG 2013.				

citizens are only allowed to participate in local elections; their European counterparts, on the other hand, have more expansive voting rights (see Table 1.3). Finally, the diversity of sending countries meant that the immigrant population had an extremely broad range of previous experience with political and civic engagement before arriving in Ireland. Whatever happened with immigrant electoral incorporation in Ireland, it was unlikely to be a one-size-fits-all solution.

Irish Electoral Institutions

Despite the challenges of incorporating a diverse population into politics, Ireland's formal electoral institutions are remarkably open to foreigners. According to the Department of Environment, Heritage and Local Government, every adult individual in Ireland can run for office or vote in local elections as long as they are at least eighteen years old and have been resident in the state for at least six months. The focus is on presence in the state: there are no citizenship requirements, and noncitizens are not required to have legal permanent residency. The only other restrictions are related to timing, as voter registration forms must be submitted at least six months before an election. After six months, voters must have their form stamped by the Garda (the Irish police) in order to verify that the six-month residency requirement was met. Compared to most other democratic societies, Ireland has one of the most accessible electoral regimes in the world for noncitizens.

Interestingly, Ireland's universal local voting rules were not created in response to, or in anticipation of, immigration. Instead, they are an administrative carryover from efforts in the 1960s to simplify voting rules in order to include rural landowners who were also British citizens. The transcripts from the parliamentary debates over the proposed electoral reform at that time are instructive:

> In the case of local elections, it is proposed to allow every person aged 21 years or more who normally resides or occupies property in the area of a local authority to be registered there as a local government elector, irrespective of whether or not he is an Irish citizen. At present a person who is not an Irish citizen can be registered as a local government elector only if he has occupied the property in the area of a local authority for six months, or is the wife of such an occupier, and is a British subject. The number of non-citizens who will receive the local government franchise as a result of the proposal will be small, but considerable simplifications in registration procedures will result from the change.[10]

Although it is certainly open to outsiders, the Irish voting system can be very confusing, as the country uses the relatively rare system of proportional representation (PR) with the single transferrable vote (PR-STV).[11] For the 2009 local elections, each voting district in Ireland had between three and seven seats, and there are no formal limits on the number of candidates who can contest seats within a given district.[12] Within each district, candidates are listed on the ballot in alphabetical order, and voters rank their preferences from number one through any number of candidates. Votes are tallied in rounds, and as candidates fall short of the necessary votes in each round, they are eliminated, and their preference votes are transferred to other candidates. The "count" continues until all seats are filled within a given constituency.

While Ireland's electoral institutions do not create legal barriers to immigrant participation (such as a citizenship requirement), the relatively unique process does present a significant hurdle in terms of immigrant knowledge of the system. Since noncitizens are not allowed to vote in most countries, most immigrants do not know that they have this right in Ireland. In addition, the PR-STV system is relatively unique; even immigrants who speak the language and are interested in voting may not know how to actually do so. Therefore, the legal rules governing Irish elections are not what present hurdles to immigrant electoral participation, but rather the knowledge gap that is part and parcel of being a new arrival in an unfamiliar system.

In addition to formal voting rules, informal institutions play a key role in Irish politics. Helmke and Levitsky (2004: 727) draw a clear distinction between formal and informal institutions:

> We define informal institutions as *socially shared rules, usually unwritten, that are created, communicated, and enforced outside of*

officially sanctioned channels. By contrast, *formal* institutions are rules and procedures that are created, communicated, and enforced through channels widely accepted as official. This includes state institutions (Courts, legislatures, bureaucracies) and state-enforced rules (constitutions, laws, regulations). (emphasis added)

Research on Irish parties and local elections suggests that social networks and the ability to mobilize voters play a significant role in determining if and how individuals interact with parties and candidates. Weeks and Quinlivan (2009) note that door-to-door canvassing is an integral part of local elections, in part because most local candidates do not have access to the national media market, but also because Irish voters expect politicians to knock on the door and ask them for their votes. Therefore, party outreach to voters is not—with the notable exception of election posters hanging off of every tree and lamppost in the country—a mass campaign, but rather an intimate, one-on-one affair. This in and of itself is not necessarily a problem, and as previously noted, direct personal appeals have a positive effect on both likelihood of registration and voting behavior. However, the Irish door-knocking list is driven by the voter registration list, and some political parties, most notably Sinn Féin and Fianna Fáil, use the list to engage in massive election day voter-turnout campaigns, including providing transit vans to help people get to the polls. Subsequently, not appearing on the voter registry creates a "chicken or the egg" problem for new immigrant communities: without registering, they are less likely to be asked to vote, less likely to have information about different parties and candidates, and less likely to be targeted by turnout efforts on election day, but new arrivals need information about the process in order to register in the first place and, in general, voters are far more likely to register and vote in elections if they are actively recruited to do so.

Migration and the Changing Context of Irish Elections

Despite the dramatic increase in the immigrant population and the relative lack of institutional barriers to immigrant political incorporation, Irish political parties were not particularly engaged with new immigrant communities in the early 2000s. A 2003 report noted that none of the major parties saw immigrants as potential members, and none had developed policies or practices to encourage them to join (Fanning, Mutwarasibo, and Chadamoyo 2003). One party, the Progressive Democrats, went so far as to bar non-Irish citizens from membership. A similar study found that no party addressed immigration or attempted to reach out to migrant communities in their party platforms during the 2007 national election cycle either (Fanning et al. 2007). Not surprisingly, few immigrants participated in the 2004 or 2007 elections, either as candidates or as voters.

However, the years between the 2004 and 2009 local elections would prove to be a turning point for immigrant communities and political engagement in Ireland. In April 2004, the government introduced a proposal in the Dáil (the Irish Parliament) to limit immigrant access to birthright citizenship through holding a constitutional referendum. The referendum initiative would strip birthright citizenship from the constitution, and place citizenship policy in the hands of the legislature. The government maintained that the asylum process was being used as a backdoor to immigration, and echoing the debates over "anchor babies" in the United States, argued that non-EU (i.e., Asian and African) women were claiming asylum in Ireland in order to give birth in Ireland and then claim residency through their citizen child.[13] Despite howls of protest from opposition parties in the Dáil, immigrant rights groups, and even the Referendum Commission (the government agency tasked with overseeing referendums), the referendum proposal was extremely popular with the general public, and passed with close to 80 percent support (DECLG 2013). While immigrant-serving organizations were uniformly unhappy with the results, the referendum was a particularly troubling experience for the African immigrant community, which felt targeted by the increasingly racialized public debate over asylum and citizenship (Fanning and Mutwarasibo 2007; Lentin 2007).

The May 2004 election cycle did offer one bright spot for immigrant communities: Rotimi Adebari, a Nigerian immigrant, was elected to the town council of Portlaoise, a community outside of Dublin that has one of the highest percentages of black residents in Ireland. Having borne the brunt of much of the anti-asylum invective surrounding the referendum debate, the Nigerian community took particular pride in Adebari's election. The bruising experience of being targeted by negative campaigning combined with the uplifting experience of seeing an African candidate successfully standing for office convinced many African community activists that engagement in electoral politics was critical to securing both their legal and social position in Irish society.

Events outside of Ireland also began to change how local bureaucrats viewed immigrant political engagement. In 2005, urban riots involving young people, primarily of West and North African descent, swept across Paris and other large French cities, causing millions of euros in property damage and alarming public officials across the continent.[14] Local officials with the DCC took notice, and council bureaucrats began brainstorming about new ways to ensure that the city's immigrant population would and could air concerns and grievances through the political process, rather than contentious street politics. Subsequently, in the mid-2000s, city officials established an Office of Integration within the DCC and began both developing integration plans and launching a series of outreach efforts targeting immigrant communities.

Finally, the enormous influx of Central and Eastern Europeans—in particular, Poles—also changed the dynamics of immigrant civic engagement between 2004 and 2009. The Polish community in Ireland was disproportionately made up of young, male migrant workers—the very group that is least likely to vote (Goerres 2007). Nevertheless, the Polish community in both the United Kingdom and Ireland took great interest in the 2007 Polish national elections, which pitted the increasingly nationalistic Law and Justice Party, led by the Kaczynsky twins, against the pro-European Civic Platform party, led by Donald Tusk. Tusk traveled to Dublin to campaign, and local Polish activists focused on mobilizing voters to participate in the election. After contributing to the turnout of 22,000 Polish voters in Dublin, Cork, and Galway—over one-third of the Polish population in Ireland— these community leaders turned their attention to Irish politics.

Ready for 2009?

The net effect of the political and demographic changes that took place in Ireland in the 2000s, and in particular between local election cycles in 2004 and 2009, was that both immigrant community leaders and bureaucrats within the DCC increasingly saw immigrant electoral participation as critical to both the long-term political integration of the immigrant community and the maintenance of social stability. While motives varied, both across immigrant groups and between immigrant activists and the DCC, they shared a common goal: insuring that immigrants were seen as not just a group to be acted upon but rather constituents to be consulted with and listened to. For local bureaucrats, the need to maintain social cohesion meant that they had to take direct civic engagement with immigrant communities seriously. Immigrant community leaders, on the other hand, increasingly felt that the only way to avoid being a target of the political system was to demonstrate their ability to mobilize and make a difference in local elections. Thus, despite their different motives, both bureaucrats and activists were primed to take action in order to facilitate immigrant electoral integration for the 2009 local election cycle.

DCC Campaign

In early 2008, Cormac O'Donnell, an official in the Dublin City Council Office of Integration, began recruiting immigrant community leaders to join a steering committee that would engage in a migrant voter-outreach campaign. O'Donnell enjoyed strong working and personal relationships with an assortment of immigrant community activists, particularly within the Polish community. In order to round out the group and expand participation beyond his existing network, O'Donnell also relied on references from

TABLE 1.4 STEERING COMMITTEE MEMBERS
AkiDwa
Arab Communities
Base Youth Project
Chinese Business Association
Czech Association
Immigrant Council Ireland
Integrating Ireland
Ireland-India Council
Islamic Foundation Ireland
Lithuania Organization
Migrants Rights Centre Ireland
National Consultative Committee on Racism in Ireland (NCCRI)
New Communities Partnership
North West Inner City Network
Parish Integration Project
Polish Federation of Organizations
Russian Enterprise Centre

other immigrant activists and umbrella organizations. Ultimately, the steering committee included seventeen organizations that served immigrant communities in different capacities and contexts (see Table 1.4).

In April 2008, the DCC officially launched the voter registration drive during a press event at Mansion House, the official residence of the Lord Mayor of Dublin. According to a city press release: "Facilitating participation in the political life of the city is a key element in promoting and supporting the integration of ethnic minorities in the life of the city" (Dublin City Council 2008). Increasing migrant voter electoral participation was central to this goal: by getting more immigrants on the voter list, the committee would increase the likelihood of contact with Irish party officials, and by encouraging immigrant voter participation, the committee hoped to foster a stronger sense of community belonging. While immigrant community activists were committed to political integration efforts and objectives as defined by the DCC, many participants had another goal: with a good showing at the polls by noncitizen voters, Irish parties might have to take the concerns of immigrant communities more seriously.

With these goals in mind, the DCC campaign attempted to engage in three key activities designed to increase migrant voter registration and electoral participation: (1) addressing the information gap, (2) direct registration campaigns, and (3) network building with Irish political parties. Not all of these efforts, however, got off of the ground.

Addressing the Information Gap

The first step was a public education campaign. The committee produced a basic template for a voter education poster that advised migrant communities of their voting rights, and they relied on committee volunteers to translate the template into over a dozen languages. The committee then worked with the city to install the posters at bus stops in areas with significant immigrant populations. Digital versions of the poster were also distributed through steering committee LISTSERVs, and paper copies were distributed to immigrant-serving community organizations and DCC offices to be hung on bulletin boards and in waiting areas. Finally, a multilingual Web site (now defunct) was established in order to provide information on registration and voting procedures to potential immigrant voters.

Direct Outreach Campaigns

The next step was to focus on direct migrant voter outreach through training volunteers not only about the Irish political system, but how to register new voters. Steering committee members partnered with the Vincentians, a religious order, to launch "train the trainer" programs whereby committee members would teach people in their networks about immigrant voting rights and procedures, and they in turn would not only register new voters, but would train others. Once a pool of voter-registration volunteers was trained, steering committee members worked with these new partners on direct voter-registration drives within their own communities. In this way, Dublin's diverse immigrant groups would all have the same basic information about how voter registration and elections worked, but could distribute it in a way that was culturally and linguistically appropriate.

One aspect of the voter-registration process that proved to be challenging for some committee members was the requirement that new voters who registered less than six months before the elections had to have their application stamped by An Garda Síochána (commonly referred to as the "Garda"), the Irish police force that was also tasked with immigration enforcement. As one immigrant community activist noted: "Even if you have not done anything wrong, it is a very awkward thing to walk into a police station!" (NGO4, personal interview, Dublin, July 2009).[15] This was especially true for immigrants from countries where the police were to be feared, avoided, or bribed. Some groups decided to get creative in order to demystify the Garda: one even decided to invite Garda officials to an Easter celebration, which allowed officers to discuss and even stamp voter registration forms in an environment that felt more comfortable and less forbidding than a police station (NGO1, personal interview, Dublin, June 2009). Another committee member joked that the Garda were so good about attending community banquets when asked that "they are all getting quite fat!" (NGO12, personal interview, Dublin, April 2010).

Despite the positive experiences of some, there did seem to be some variation when it came to dealing with the Garda and voter registration. Several committee members reported that some immigrants who had tried to register for the 2009 elections were erroneously told that they were in the wrong place, or that they could not register at all. Although they were careful to point out that this was not seen as a systemic issue but as a problem of random individuals with bad information, given that many immigrants in Dublin (particularly asylum seekers) had extremely negative interactions with the police in their home countries, and working up the nerve to approach the police was already difficult, the miscommunication about voting rights at some Garda stations was disheartening.

Party Outreach

Far more problematic were attempts by the steering committee to build bridges between immigrant communities and Irish political parties. The committee originally planned to host a community forum featuring representatives from every Irish party. The forum would be held at the DCC office, and hosted by the national broadcaster, RTÉ. However, for reasons that were unclear to committee members, the forum fell apart when some parties decided not to participate (it is not known which parties declined). Several committee members speculated that the political parties were not interested in immigrant outreach because, given the economic downturn, they expected migrant workers to go home. This do-nothing approach was seen as par for the course; one committee member noted that when the economy was good and people were arriving en masse, the government's response was "this is new, so we don't know what to do and we can't do anything," and when the economy soured, the government's response was "well they're all going to leave anyway, so we shouldn't do anything" (NGO2, personal interview, Dublin, June 2009).

Party officials had a different take on the situation. One political operative who did not participate on the committee noted that the parties had little incentive to engage in mass immigrant voter-registration drives because they did not know how new immigrants would actually vote (Party1, personal interview, Dublin, July 2009). This concern was exacerbated by the fact that under Ireland's PR-STV system, voters could give transfer votes to candidates from multiple parties. From the perspective of the official, it was a risky strategy to spend precious resources mobilizing an unknown group who might then turn around and give transfer votes to rivals. Interestingly, an official from a different party that actively supported full economic, political, and social citizenship for immigrants opined that many new arrivals, Poles in particular, tended to be relatively religious, and there were concerns that mobilizing them would bolster conservative Catholic politicians (Party3, personal interview, Dublin, April 2010).

This is not to say that the political parties had no contact with members of the committee. On the contrary, there seemed to be a fair amount of back-channel communication between some committee participants and party officials. At least one participant was approached to run for office, and another was a party member with close ties to coethnic political candidates. One committee affiliate, the New Communities Partnership (NCP 2010), even cohosted events with other African organizations that brought in candidates to talk to immigrant voters. However, back-channel outreach was not always appreciated. One committee member indignantly noted: "[We were not going to be] handing the people to political parties . . . they would have to sweat to get to the people. We weren't there to work for their election campaigns" (NGO7, personal interview, Dublin, July 2009).

This is also not to say that the parties had no contact with immigrant communities whatsoever. In a sharp contrast to 2004, the two largest parties, Fianna Fáil and Fine Gael, hired migrant outreach coordinators for the 2009 election cycle. Both were Eastern European, and both parties made Polish-language materials available on their Web sites. Interestingly, Ireland's left-wing parties that were more sympathetic to immigrants' issues (and that opposed the citizenship referendum) had less explicit outreach to immigrant communities: while immigration was mentioned in party platforms, they did not have staff specifically dedicated to migrant outreach. Two parties, Labour and the Green Party, did have immigrant candidates, and those individuals became a focal point for connecting the parties to immigrant communities.

Assessing the Campaign

Because this study was conducted after the elections, there is no way to measure how the campaign affected the political socialization process (in this case, the effect of the information campaign on individual knowledge about Irish politics). It is also unclear if the campaign had a significant impact on immigrant voter-registration rates. Although immigrant voter registration increased in the run-up to the 2009 local elections, according to data from the City Manager's Office in Dublin, it increased during the previous election cycle as well: the number of non-European adults on the Dublin City electoral register rose from 6,773 in 2007/2008 to 8,306 in 2008/2009, a 22 percent increase, but registration increased 21percent for the 2006/2007 to 2007/2008 cycle (e-mail correspondence, May 2010). While at least one steering committee partner claimed some credit for boosting noncitizen turnout (NCP 2010), the timing of noncitizen voter-registration interests suggests that it may just be part and parcel of election year interest, rather than the outcome of immigrant voter campaigns. This said, this is an area that is ripe for future research.

The campaign also highlighted that for many of Ireland's new immigrants, home country ties and prior political socialization still profoundly shape political behavior, particularly among Ireland's newest labor migrants. A report from University College Dublin notes that although over 18 percent of the population of Dublin was foreign born, only 4 percent of the registered electorate was (Fanning et al. 2007). However, reports from both the Polish government and the Irish media note that just over 20,000 Poles living in Ireland registered to vote remotely in Polish national elections in 2007, representing almost 37 percent of the eligible electorate.[16] The Polish example highlights that some immigrants may still feel more politically connected to their countries of origin than their country of residence, despite efforts to encourage participation in host country politics.

Interestingly, there is one area where the campaign may have had an effect on political socialization, and that is with Garda relations. The dynamic between the police and immigrant communities—in particular, second- and third-generation communities—is one of the most contentious and urgent areas of migration-related state-society relations in Europe: the 2005 riots in Paris and the 2011 riots in London were triggered by confrontations with the police. Given how volatile immigrant-police relations are across much of Europe, the willingness of Garda officials to attend immigrant community events is notable. It is not clear how this positive relationship between the Garda and immigrant communities holds across groups and jurisdictions, but given the urgency of the issue across much of Europe, this is also an area where future research would be useful.

Although efforts to build stronger networks between immigrants and parties through a DCC-sponsored forum failed, network-building efforts had greater success within the committee itself. Prior to their inclusion on the steering committee, many participants did not know each other or had not worked with each other directly. After the elections, however, participants were positive about their interaction with other committee members, with one noting that it was a "fantastic opportunity to come together with other organizations, and with people from such a diverse background" (NGO6, personal interview, Dublin, July 2009). Several participants also commented that they had a newly developed, positive relationship with local government: because many immigrant organizations focus on national immigration policies (such as asylum law or citizenship), they had little interaction with the Dublin City Council prior to the campaign.

One other notable aspect of the DCC campaign was the fact that although it was bureaucrat led, it was immigrant driven. While the DCC provided modest funding and office space, and used its ties to other public agencies such as Dublin Bus in order to spread the word about elections to new immigrant communities, the steering committee participants were the ones with principal responsibility for crafting the campaign message, recruiting volunteers, and launching community-specific registration drives. The leeway that groups had to organize voter-registration events how they saw fit was also consistent with emerging best practices in the field: in other contexts, researchers have noted that election campaign attendance figures are highest when voter-registration efforts are linked to some other kind of community religious or cultural event (Takle 2013).

The primary visible effects of the city-led immigrant voter initiative were strengthened ties both between Dublin City Council bureaucrats and immigrant community elites and across Ireland's diverse immigrant groups. In other words, while it is unclear whether this kind of bureaucrat-led campaign can link individual voters to the political process, and it seems ill-suited to link immigrant communities to political parties, this initiative was quite effective in creating new bridging and bonding networks among disparate groups that are at the front lines of the political, social, and economic incorporation process. This said, future work is needed in order to determine the extent to which potential immigrant voters are even aware of these campaigns, or if they affect electoral participation. Additional research as to whether or not there is a positive signaling effect of these kinds of campaigns might also be useful in shaping incorporation policy: even if these kinds of campaigns do not actually affect immigrant electoral participation, they may have a positive impact on interpretive citizenship.

Conclusion

The focus of this case study was to identify the role that bureaucrats can play in the process of immigrant electoral incorporation. Despite the relatively limited scope, these findings make a strong case for taking seriously the role that informal institutions play in inhibiting political incorporation, as well as the shifting role of the state in fostering civic engagement. The fact that the voter-registration campaign largely drew on volunteer and symbolic resources—the use of train-the-trainer schemes, the public launch with support from city elected officials, and so on—is also notable, for although austerity policies across Europe have hit funding for migrant organizations and state-led incorporation initiatives extremely hard, many of the DCC initiatives were low cost. As one local bureaucrat put it, "Leadership is free" (BUR1, personal interview, Dublin, July 2009).

This said, when it comes to partisan electoral engagement, it is unclear that bureaucrats can successfully bring together new immigrants and parties. The specific partisan interests of parties make state-sponsored nonpartisan mobilization efforts seem a distraction at best and, at worst, a threat to the status quo. Given both the individualized nature of the PR-STV voting system and the emphasis on the personal networks of candidates when canvassing, the best bet for building strong ties between immigrant ethnic communities and parties may be for parties to run strong immigrant candidates, a tactic that has worked to build immigrant and ethnic minority turnout in both European and North American elections. Even setting aside Ireland's relatively unique political institutions, it is difficult to imagine a process of electoral incorporation that does not involve the very actors and organizations that contest elections. Electoral incorporation requires some level of engagement between voters and the partisan groups contesting elections, and fostering this interaction may simply be beyond the remit of non-partisan bureaucrats.

NOTES

1. The Irish Citizens Information Board outlines voting procedures here: http://www.citizensinformation.ie/en/moving_country/moving_to_ireland/introduction_to_the_irish_system/right_to_vote.html.

2. For example, access to citizenship can be affected by an individual's refugee status or whether or not an immigrant's country of origin is a former colony of the receiving country. For example, in Spain, immigrants from Latin American countries have a much shorter pathway to citizenship than immigrants from Morocco or Senegal.

3. Although it is not altogether puzzling: party apathy toward new immigrant communities is well documented. See Jones-Correa (1998a) and Andersen (2010).

4. For analysis of the historical relationship between the Democratic Party and the Irish community in the United States, see Rakove (1976) and Erie (1988).

5. Bridging networks refer to those that link groups that are fundamentally different, while bonding networks refer to relations within a group (Putnam 2000). The primary critique of ethnic organizations is that they focus exclusively on bonding networks, whereas host country governments would prefer to see migrant organizations engage with native and other "out"-group organizations as well (i.e., bridging networks).

6. Removing U.K. citizens from the analysis is significant because many individuals living in Ireland who were born in the U.K. self-identify as Irish nationals on the census. The Irish census asks both: Question #5, "What is your place of birth?" and Question #6, "What is your nationality?" While the U.K.-born population in Ireland was listed as 271,768 in 2006 (CSO 2016), the number of people who self-reported having U.K. nationality was only 112,548 (CSO 2008).

7. The other two countries were the United Kingdom and Sweden.

8. The dramatic increase in the Polish population was completely unexpected in Ireland. When EU expansion was being debated in the Dáil (the Irish Parliament), the then-chair of the European Affairs committee asserted, "The suggestion that huge numbers of unwanted and unneeded people will come in does not stand up. When Ireland

joined the European Union in 1973 . . . large numbers of emigrants did not leave our shores for Germany, France, Italy and other countries. We had emigration, but it was to traditional markets . . . the same will prevail in Central and Eastern Europe" (Dáil Éireann, line 19 at: http://oireachtasdebates.oireachtas.ie/debates%20authoring/debateswebpack .nsf/takes/dail2002090400005?opendocument).

9. This refers to Question #6 of the census, "What is your nationality?"

10. The exact statute is available on the Oireachtas website at: http://debates .oireachtas.ie/dail/1963/02/27/00058.asp.

11. PR-STV is primarily used in Ireland, parts of the United Kingdom, and countries of the British Commonwealth (albeit at the regional, not primarily the local and national, level, as in Ireland).

12. Districts were consolidated and reshuffled for the 2014 local elections.

13. Irish Naturalization and Immigration Service, CITIZENSHIP REFERENDUM: The Government's Proposals (April 2004), available online at: http://www.inis.gov.ie/en /INIS/Govtproposals.pdf/Files/Govtproposals.pdf.

14. For an analysis of the root causes of the 2005 riots in France, see Schneider (2008).

15. All interviews were coded by type of organization (NGO, BUR for bureaucrats, EF for elected officials) and numbered in chronological order. The location and date of each interview is included in the citation.

16. "20,000 Poles Cast Votes in Ireland for Polish Election," The Irish Independent, October 21, 2007.

2

Immigrant Integration Policy Frames in Italy

A Multilevel Governance Perspective

TIZIANA CAPONIO

FRANCESCA CAMPOMORI

As the previous chapter by Dobbs demonstrated, immigrant political incorporation that is embraced and advanced by local party organizations is arguably a precondition for the creation of optimal public policies for immigrant groups, in part because such policies can be expected to reflect the policy frame of the governing political party. In this chapter Caponio and Campomori demonstrate the importance of differences in regional policy frames as embodied in the positions of the dominant political parties for immigrant incorporation in Italy, another new immigrant destination country.

Immigrant integration in Italy has been explicitly addressed in public debates only since the first half of the 2000s, following a number of dramatic focus events such as September 11, 2001, the bombings in Madrid (March 2004) and London (July 2005), the murder of filmmaker Theo Van Gogh in Amsterdam (November 2004), and the Danish cartoon crisis (September 2005). Italy is a recent immigration country in the European context, and migration there started slowly in the 1970s, only to gain momentum in the second half of the following decade. Border controls and the mass arrivals of undocumented migrants have always monopolized both the media and the political debate. For a long time, immigrant integration was not a salient issue: immigrants were welcomed insofar as they were able to access the labor market, even if informally, as consistent with a conception of immigration based on considerations of utility for the Italian economy.

In this chapter we address changes in the framing of immigrant integration in Italy through a multilevel governance perspective. Our goal is to understand which kind of policy frames of integration have been emerging at a regional level in Italy and if developments in national legislation and public debates in the mid-2000s triggered a change in the policies pursued by these levels of government, considering that, after the federalist reform of 2001, the regions have enjoyed complete autonomy in the field of social policy, including immigrant integration. To this end, we investigate policy frames in two politically opposite regions, namely Veneto, governed since 2000 by a center-right majority, including the openly anti-immigrant Northern League Party (Lega Nord), and Emilia-Romagna, governed over the same period by a center-left majority, encompassing the ex-Communist Party and leftwing Catholics.

By adopting a multilevel governance perspective and considering frames at different levels of government, that is, national and regional, we aim to contribute to the scholarly debate on immigrant integration models (see Bertossi and Duyvendak 2009; Boswell, Geddes, and Scholten 2011). This type of research has rarely considered southern Europe and, even less, subnational levels of government; nevertheless, focusing on the regional meso-level appears crucial not only to provide a more accurate assessment of the policies actually pursued in a specific national context, but also to flesh out the factors accounting for the emergence of different approaches and policy discourses within one country. As Patrick Ireland (2004: 8) states, "At the local level, theory meets practice. National models for immigrant settlement run headlong into organizational and practical realities." Moreover, the process of decentralization taking place all over in Europe since the mid-1990s has transferred significant decision-making powers to the regional, provincial, and municipal levels, together with implementation tasks, for which they have not always had the experience and the administrative capacity (Ireland 2004). Therefore, the subnational level is undoubtedly the fundamental setting to investigate and understand the actual frames and dynamics of immigrant integration policies.

The chapter is structured as follows. In the next section we discuss the scholarly literature on immigrant integration policy frames in order to identify the gaps. Section three introduces the Italian context by illustrating the main developments in the national policy framing of immigrant integration from the early 1980s through 2010. Section four provides the methodological details of our research on Emilia-Romagna and Veneto, while section five presents the empirical evidence and research findings. In section six the similarities and differences in the two regions' policy frames are identified, and we discuss the factors that account for the processes of convergence, with particular attention paid to the impact of the national culturalist turn. In the conclusion, the relevance of this study for research on immigrant integration policy making is assessed.

Argumentative Turn in the Analysis of Immigrant Integration Policy: Promises and Gaps

The study of policymaking and processes of policy framing is quite new to the immigration policy scholarly literature. Since the early 1990s the historical neo-institutionalist approach (Hall and Taylor 1996) has dominated the field, dictating a research agenda that is almost exclusively concerned with the analysis of nationally and historically rooted policy models or integration regimes (e.g., Brubaker 1992). The dynamics of these models have for a long time remained unexplored, even though, as early as the late 1990s, comparative studies on local policies pointed out the internal complexity and inconsistencies of national integration models.

Notwithstanding increasing criticism of the "model" metaphor for its excessive emphasis on macroinstitutional variables and oversimplification of social integration processes (Favell 2001), national models resurfaced in public and scholarly debate at the beginning of the 2000s following a series of studies aimed at evaluating their effectiveness (Böcker, Michalowski, and Thränhardt 2004; Koopmans 2003). The results in general have indicated a poor performance of Dutch multicultural policy, presented in terms of a failure of this model to keep up to its promises (Sniderman and Hagendoorn 2007). At the same time, a greater convergence of old models towards some kind of (pan-) European, neo-assimilationist paradigm has been observed (Joppke 2007), due to the introduction of so-called civic integration programs, which link admission and/or permanent residence of third-country nationals to the obligation of acquiring a basic knowledge of host country language and culture.

However, a critical approach to the notion of integration models has also emerged that challenges and deconstructs its scientific soundness (Bertossi and Duyvendak 2009; Scholten 2011). Usually presented as useful heuristic devices for the sake of cross-country comparative analysis, models have actually assumed a semblance of internally coherent and consistent historical reconstructions of integration policies (Scholten 2011: 31). This has led not only to a neglect of the discrepancies produced in the context of implementation processes, but also to an inadequate consideration of the different discourses on immigrant integration that can in a certain period underpin policymaking on immigration. To address these gaps, a new argumentative turn to the study of integration policy has been advanced, looking at models in terms of competing policy frames, or policy discourses, and trying to elucidate the actors and dynamics that account for their rise and fall in the context of policy-making processes.

This emerging literature adopts a conception of policy frames focused on processes of "framing" and "naming" (Schön and Rein 1994) emerging from political debates around immigration and immigrant integration. Christina

Boswell, Andrew Geddes, and Peter Scholten (2011), for instance, define policy narratives as composed of three components: (1) a set of claims about the policy problem to be addressed, and in particular about its nature and scale; (2) a set of claims about what causes the problem and to what extent the problem can be controlled; (3) a set of claims about how policy interventions have affected or are likely to affect the considered policy problems. In a similar vein, Erik Bleich (2003: 29), in his analysis of race politics in Britain and France, defines a policy frame as a set of "cognitive and moral maps that orient an actor within a policy sphere. Frames help actors to identify problems and prioritize their interests and goals. . . . Frames give direction to policymaking and help account for policy outcomes." Put more explicitly, frames contribute to defining the terrain of action and then influence action within that terrain, which means that they constrain actions.

Similar to the national models literature, though, this emerging argumentative approach seems almost exclusively concerned with national-level policy and with a limited number of "old" European immigration countries such as the Netherlands, France, Germany, and the United Kingdom (see Scholten 2011 on the Netherlands; Bleich 2003 on France and the United Kingdom; Boswell 2009 on Germany and the United Kingdom). As a matter of fact, thus far only a few studies have tried to look into policy frames in the context of local processes of agenda setting (Mahnig 2004), and even fewer have gone so in-depth as to consider those emerging from implementation processes (Caponio and Borkert 2010).

This narrow perspective is especially problematic, since in contemporary multilevel contexts, where different levels of government (vertical governance) as well as various public and private actors (horizontal governance) are likely to intervene on such a complex issue as immigration, national policy frames can only account for a small part of the story. Moreover, national integration models, even in the old immigration countries with a historically clearly defined approach to integration (assimilationist or multiculturalist), have often displayed inconsistencies when compared with the actual decision making and policy implementation at the local level (Penninx and Martiniello 2004). Put differently, whereas the national level accounts for the rhetoric and national political discourse, the regional and local levels represent privileged contexts for analyzing practices of integration.

In this chapter we offer a systematic analysis of the policy frames emerging from regional policies by considering a Southern European case, Italy, a country lacking a strong and consistent national integration model and where the role of subnational governments in the framing of immigrant integration has always been crucial. However, we look at regional policy frames from a multilevel governance perspective, that is, in relation with framing processes at other level of government, and in particular at the national level, since immigration laws cannot but represent an unavoidable point of reference in the definition of what has to be understood as immigrant integration in a certain social and political context.

Context: Frames of Immigrant Integration in a Fragmented and Regionalized Political System

Throughout the 1980s and early 1990s, immigrants' integration only barely surfaced in the public debate on immigration in Italy, since the focus was on border control, illegal immigration, and criminality (Colombo and Sciortino 2004). Yet the first immigration law approved in 1986 did not completely neglect the issue: the regions and local authorities were assigned the task of promoting cultural programs and social inclusion measures, yet no specific funding was provided to this end.

Immigrant integration policies received some political attention during the second half of the 1990s, during the first center-left Prodi government. The 1998 Immigration Law had the ambition of establishing a distinctive Italian model of integration, the so-called reasonable integration model, implying the support of both nationals' and immigrants' physical and psychological well-being on the one hand, and positive interaction between different groups on the other (Zincone 2011). On the basis of these two principles, policies aimed at fostering individual equality and at promoting intercultural relations were devised in all the crucial spheres of immigrant incorporation: employment, health, education and professional training, housing, and civic participation. Regions were held responsible for policy implementation, and to this end they had to draft, in collaboration with local tiers of government, specific immigrant integration programs to be financed by the National Fund for Immigrant Policy.

Yet this division of tasks was to be challenged by the approval in May 2001 of the federalist reform, which gave the regions complete autonomy on matters of social policy, including immigrant integration. The National Fund for Immigrant Policy merged into a broader Social Policy Fund, and since 2003, when the reform was in force, the regions have been receiving its resources and are completely responsible for establishing priorities on matters of social policy and allocating resources. As a consequence, they are not obliged anymore to undertake specific programs for the integration of immigrants.

Parallel to this decentralization of immigrant integration policy, at the national level, the early 2000s were marked by the beginning of a debate about preserving Italian identity against multiculturalism and Islam, following reactions to September 11. At its start such a debate had no impact on immigrant integration policy: the 2002 second Berlusconi government reform of the immigration law introduced a link between job contract and residence permit, implying that immigrants willing to enter Italy legally had to obtain a job offer before leaving their country, somehow reinventing the old Northern European—and German in particular—guestworker model (Caponio and Graziano 2011). Employment clearly represented the crucial precondition in order to stay and integrate in Italy.

However, the culturalist discourse took more and more ground in the middle of the decade, triggered by the terrorist attacks in London and Madrid. Center-right MPs and ministries of the then third Berlusconi government expressed radical positions. The Northern League minister for devolution, Roberto Calderoli, for instance, during a TV program in February 2006, showed a T-shirt reproducing one of the contested Danish cartoons on Islam as a demonstration of liberty of expression in Europe.[1] Against these risks of radicalization, the second center-left Prodi government, elected in May 2006, did not attempt to restore the "reasonable integration model" anymore, but actually adhered to the new cultural definition of Italian identity, trying at the same time to downplay anti-Islam positions. This is clearly demonstrated by the initiative of the then minister of the interior, Giuliano Amato, to promote the drafting of a Charter of the Values of Citizenship and Integration.[2] Initially intended as a set of principles to be signed by new religious organizations in Italy, Minister Amato gradually enlarged its scope. The document was to be accepted by all foreign citizens aspiring for Italian nationality, and it established an integration path that—similar to the French *Contract d'Accueil*—would have required "the learning of the Italian language, of the basic notions of the Italian history and culture, as well as the sharing of the principles regulating our society."[3]

Such an approach to immigrant integration was reinforced by the fourth Berlusconi government, elected in April 2008, which was able to combine the new culturalist discourse with recurrent slogans about immigrants as would-be criminals and a threat for public security (Caponio 2012). As early as June 2008, the Northern League minister of the interior, Roberto Maroni, presented to the Senate a bill called the Security Law that was essentially concerned with introducing new restrictions against undocumented immigrants. At the same time, this law also formally sanctioned the new Italian culturalist approach toward integration, defined as the "process aimed at promoting cohabitation [*convivenza*] between Italian and foreign citizens on the basis of the respect of the Italian Constitution." To this end, the so-called Integration Agreement (IA) was introduced: this is to be signed by the immigrant at the moment of issuing the first residence permit, and the IA commits him/her to achieve specific integration goals in a time span of two years. These goals include a sufficient level of knowledge of the spoken Italian language (level A2), of the principles of the Italian Constitution, as well as of Italian civic life and institutions (labor market functioning, fiscal obligations, and so on).

However, the IA entered into force only in March 2012, after the implementation rules were finally approved by the Monti government. Meanwhile, funding for the undertaking of language and civic integration courses for immigrants had already been provided to the regions on the basis of a series of special agreements signed with the Ministry of Labour and Social Policy since 2005 (Stuppini 2012). Since 2007 this kind of intervention has become more and more institutionalized, thanks to the financial resources provided to this end by the European Integration Fund (EIF), which the Ministry of the Interior decided to assign to the regions.

As is clear, the culturalist frame of immigrant integration that gradually emerged in the mid-2000s had both a rhetorical and institutional meaning. The debate about Italian identity, multiculturalism, and immigrant integration ran parallel to an increasing effort on the part of national executives, regardless of their political colors, to invest more and more in civic integration courses consistent with the 2004 European Union Common Basic Principles on Integration and even more with the 2007 EIF priorities.[4] At the same time, the National Social Policy Fund has experienced considerable cuts, leaving the regions fewer resources for implementing specific programs on immigrant integration.

In the following section, through an analysis of immigrant integration policy frames in Emilia-Romagna and Veneto, we intend to assess if and to what extent the new culturalist orientation of national policy has been incorporated at the regional level. We could expect an increasing convergence of regional policy frames on civic integration as a result of both the rhetorical and institutional changes taking place at the national level in the mid-2000s. Yet an alternative hypothesis might be that there is a certain independence of regional policy frames, due to the high level of autonomy to define immigrant integration policies enjoyed by the regions, as well as the necessity of answering to specific local pressures around this highly politicized issue.

Methodological Note

According to Donald A. Schön and Martin Rein (1994), the formulation of a policy is a process characterized by the intertwining of two different kind of frames: rhetorical frames, which consist of the persuasive use of story and argument in policy discourse; and action policy frames, which inform policy practice in the sense that they are used by an institutional actor to construct the problem in a specific situation. In this chapter, we reconstruct both elements as emerging from the official documents on immigrant integration approved in Emilia-Romagna and Veneto. We focus on "annual integration programs," which are executive programs in the sense that they set the guidelines for local-level implementation processes and provide the related financial resources. Hence, these documents can be regarded as informing policy practice, that is, as yielding the policy frames underlining regional actors' policy actions.

The two selected regions are similar in numerous relevant respects: (1) their economic development is centered on small- and medium-sized firms

TABLE 2.1 IMMIGRANTS IN TOTAL POPULATION OF EMILIA-ROMAGNA AND VENETO, 2002–2010 (IN PERCENTAGES)									
	2002	2003	2004	2005	2006	2007	2008	2009	2010
Emilia-Romagna	4.1	5.2	6.2	6.9	7.5	8.5	9.7	10.5	11.3
Veneto	4.2	5.2	6.1	6.8	7.3	8.4	9.3	9.8	10.2
Source: ISTAT n.d.									

(Bagnasco 1977); (2) they have high levels of social capital (Putnam, Leonardi, and Nanetti 1993); and (3) they have high and continuously increasing rates of immigration relative to the total population (see Table 2.1).

However, Veneto and Emilia-Romagna also present opposite political traditions and have traditionally been ruled by different political parties, the Christian Democrat Party in the former case and the Communist Party in the latter. During the post–WWII period, two different policy and administrative styles emerged, whose legacy is still evident today. Whereas in Veneto, according to the principle of subsidiarity, regional authorities have always been particularly disposed to devolve the responsibility for service delivery to private actors and voluntary associations, in Emilia-Romagna, a policy-making model characterized by a strong coordinating role of the region emerged, albeit in a context with a tradition of municipal autonomy. Furthermore, from the beginning of the 1990s, the two regions began to diverge also in terms of politicization of the immigration issue.

In Veneto the Northern League (Lega Nord) gained a high of popular support that peaked in the 2008 national elections, with more than 25 percent of the vote. The Northern League was founded in 1982 the northern regions (mainly Lombardy and Veneto) and mobilized the discontent of this area of the country against the national government, which was accused of imposing taxes to maintain the "parasitic" Roman bureaucracy and the underdeveloped southern regions. A call for a separation of the Padania (basically the rich and industrialized North) from the rest of Italy (and in particular the South), has always dominated the League's political discourse, even though in 1994, with the participation of the Northern League in the first Berlusconi government, its separatist claim took the shape of a petition for devolution. At the same time, the party mobilized its rhetoric against immigration, which quickly became a central theme in its political discourse, emphasizing the risks of competition in the job market and increased public insecurity. Anti-immigration rhetoric has especially surfaced at the local level, where a number of mayors engaged throughout the 1990s and 2000s in (mainly symbolic) policies aimed at limiting immigrants' rights and opposing the manifestation of cultural and religious difference. In contrast, the left-wing coalitions, which have been governing in Emilia-Romagna in the same period, have attempted to counter politicization by adopting a positive view of immigration, usually described as an opportunity for social and cultural enrichment.[5]

Therefore, comparing Emilia-Romagna and Veneto provides an opportunity to test the impact of the national culturalist turn in the framing of immigrant integration in regions characterized by different political orientations. As mentioned above, we could expect convergence, given the fact that ad hoc funding is provided by the national government in order to implement civic integration policies. Yet, given the traditional autonomy enjoyed by regions in this policy field, it might be also the case that different approaches to immigrant integration will persist, influenced by other relevant local factors such as welfare systems, labor markets, and so on. In order to reconstruct regional policy frames, and to shed light on the factors accounting for these frames, the *espoused theory* of regional decision makers (what they declare about immigrant integration) has to be compared with the *theory in use* (the goals actually pursued and the interventions undertaken).[6] The espoused theory has been operationalized in terms of *direct labels*, which are definitions, analogies, metaphors and symbols that aid actors in conceptualizing a political or social situation (Bleich 2003): in our case, we refer to those definitions explicitly associated with the notions of "immigration" and "integration," whereas the theory in use has been operationalized through an analysis of *indirect labels*, which can be inferred by looking at official documents' policy priorities and implementation structures: indirect labels are therefore the actual priorities and projects listed in the annual integration programs.[7]

In particular, as indicated in Table 2.2, as far as policy priorities are concerned, the regional governments' actual commitments can be inferred by looking at the budget attached to each policy and at the degree of specification of the envisaged interventions. Clearly defined policy priorities, with the identification of a precise action to be pursued and the specification of a budget and of the institution/organization responsible for implementation, indicate a strong commitment of the regional government to achieving a

TABLE 2.2 OPERATIONALIZATION OF THE ESPOUSED THEORY AND THEORY IN USE	
Espoused theory	**Direct labels**: *Analogies, metaphors, symbols, adjectives, and statements associated with the words "immigration/immigrants" and "integration"*
Theory in use	**Indirect labels**: *Policy priorities in terms of:* • *Budget* • *Specification of the actions to be undertaken and the actors charged with implementation*

specific policy goal. On the other hand, nonbinding policy priorities, whose implementation is totally delegated to the local authorities, signal a less strong interest in pursuing a certain course of policy action.

Immigrant Integration Policy Frames in Italian Regions

Emilia-Romagna and the Culture-Friendly Approach

The labeling of immigrants in Emilia-Romagna's immigrant integration programs seems to underscore an acknowledgment on the part of regional authorities of their increasing settlement. The heading of the 1999 program talks about the "activities of welcome and assistance in favor of immigrants." In 2004 this heading was replaced with the expression "Actions for Immigrants' Social Integration," while immigrants started to be explicitly defined as "citizens." Beginning in 2006 this definition even becomes part of the heading "Program for the Social Integration of Foreign Citizens." This framing of immigrants as would-be citizens is reinforced by the strong critical stance toward the center-right 2002 immigration law, accused of keeping immigrants in a permanent precarious legal status.

With regard to the direct labels linked to the definition of the immigration phenomenon, the 2001 program emphasized "the opportunities and the enrichment brought by immigration" in terms of cultural diversity and hoped for the establishment of "a multicultural society . . . based upon immigrants' full and acknowledged status of citizens." In subsequent years, appreciation of immigration as a cultural asset was complemented by a greater emphasis on economic aspects. In the 2006–2008 program we find an appraisal of the EU's The Hague Program (Council of the European Union 2004b: 11), arguing that "if immigration flows are regulated and well managed, each single state can get gains: stronger economies, better social cohesion and better sense of security." The program particularly emphasized the necessity of putting pressure on national policy makers for more favorable legislation, allowing for a greater match between new inflows and the region's economic needs. Furthermore, the introduction to the 2009–2011 triennual program[8] stated that "the perception according to which integration costs are higher than the economic advantages is wrong, given that the growing access of foreign people to welfare services, due to their disadvantaged socio-economic conditions at the beginning, is later compensated by the taxes that foreign workers pay to the Italian State."

Hence, vis-à-vis national legislation and political discourse, Emilia-Romagna's official integration programs disclose a critical stance, especially toward the restrictiveness of admission policies, which do not take into account the regional labor market needs. The debate about Italian culture and immigrants' civic integration does not seem to be echoed in these documents. Also the indirect labels, which can be uncovered by looking at the specific content of the recurrent policy priorities, do not seem to emphasize issues of Italian language and culture. These are four: (1) immigrant participation and involvement in social, cultural, and political life at the local level; (2) intercultural initiatives; (3) actions for preventing and combatting discrimination; and (4) provisions in favor of asylum seekers and trafficked persons.

As for the first priority, since the 2000 program, Emilia-Romagna has encouraged immigrants' participation in local politics and promoted activities in favor of their associations. The 2002 program deemed it important to establish consultative councils at the provincial level, and, according to the 2004 program, foreign citizens' representative bodies should be directly elected from legally resident immigrants.

Intercultural initiatives (second priority) cover a wide array of social interventions, Italian language and civic education courses included. These are put on the same plane with worker training, communication activities in schools, and professional training in journalism for young immigrants. The third priority is aimed at supporting the setting up of structures devoted to monitoring, informing, and providing legal assistance to immigrants who have experienced discrimination. As for the fourth priority, a specific project was launched in the mid-2000s to promote the integration of refugees and asylum seekers, while for trafficked women, since 1996 the Emilia-Romagna region has funded a project called Oltre la Strada (Beyond the street), which is implemented by municipalities in cooperation with nonprofit organizations.

However, it is almost impossible to rank these four policy priorities according to the budget assigned to each one, because of the specific implementation structure adopted by the region, which is based on a high level of devolution to local authorities. Between 1999 and 2004, resources were assigned to the nine provinces, which were held responsible for deciding how much to invest in each policy issue. Since 2004, 70 percent of the total regional budget started to be assigned to the so-called social districts (thirty-eight in total), which are small- and medium-sized municipalities' joint ventures responsible for the delivery of social services on a specific territory. Social districts have been charged with the implementation of the above-mentioned four priorities, while provincial plans have assumed a secondary role, benefiting from the remaining 30 percent of the resources, to be devoted primarily to tasks of monitoring of the phenomenon (provincial immigration observatories) and coordination of local interventions in the areas of interculture, antidiscrimination, political representation and asylum seeker and refugee services.

Table 2.3 summarizes the main findings of the analysis of the Emilia-Romagna regional programs. A high degree of consistency between direct and

TABLE 2.3 DIRECT LABELS, INDIRECT LABELS, AND POLICY PRIORITIES IN EMILIA ROMAGNA'S IMMIGRANT INTEGRATION POLICIES	
Direct labels	**Immigration:** • Opportunity for enrichment • Economic advantages higher than costs (since 2006) **Immigrants:** • Citizens **Integration:** • Multicultural society
Indirect labels	• Immigrants' political participation • Intercultural services
Policy priorities	• Language and civic education • Cultural mediators • Intercultural centers • Journalists of immigrant origin • Antidiscrimination • Asylum seekers and trafficked women

Source: Emilia-Romagna Regional Integration Programs (1999–2011).

indirect labels can be seen: on one hand, immigrants are defined as "new citizens," and the building of a multicultural society is positively regarded; on the other, the theory in use assigns considerable relevance to policy priorities such as immigrants' political representation, intercultural services, and antidiscrimination, that is, actions directed at promoting cultural difference in a context of equal opportunities. National policy priorities such as Italian language and civic culture courses are also considered, but these do not seem to have a central relevance. Overall, a culture-friendly framing of integration can be highlighted, which rests on a soft or liberal understanding of multiculturalism (Castles and Miller 2003) in the sense that it does not go so far as to endorse a policy of recognition, but simply acknowledges the positive value of cultural difference for the host society. This goes hand in hand with a flexible implementation structure, since local governments are autonomous in choosing which priorities to favor among those proposed in the regional programs.

Veneto and the Assimilationist Approach

In Veneto's immigrant integration programs, immigration is framed mostly as a phenomenon that must be regulated in order to be socially sustainable and consistent with regional economic development. An emphasis on "legality and regularity" surfaces in all the analyzed policy programs, since they explicitly sanctioned that social interventions should target legal immigrants exclusively. Contrary to Emilia-Romagna, Veneto's documents declare their appreciation of the center-right 2002 immigration law[9] for its emphasis on legality. The word "integration" only started to appear in 2004, in the heading of one of the identified policy priorities, "Education and Social Integration," and, from 2007, a new heading, "Pact of Welcome and Integration," was introduced to indicate the intention to support immigrants' civic integration courses, implying not only Italian language training but also the socialization to Venetian culture and labor and safety rules. As a matter of fact, Veneto foreshadows the national IA that, as pointed out above, was introduced only in 2009.

The analysis of the direct labels associated with immigrants provides some further insights into the framing of the integration issue and on its overall consistency with the cultural turn occurring at a national level in this decade. Until 2003, immigrants were usually referred to as *extracomunitari*. This word literally means "people from a non–EU country," but it has a negative and pejorative meaning, and has always characterized the political rhetoric on migration of center-right parties, and in particular of the Northern League. In contrast to what we have seen in Emilia-Romagna, the term "citizen" is never used. At the same time, immigrants are constantly compared to Venetian past emigrants and their descendants.[10] Both the 2001–2003 and 2004–2006 triennial programs gave the latter preference in access to social provisions, as opposed to the subordinate position associated with the *extracomunitari*. This emphasis on co-ethnics clearly echoes the national center-right governments' policies, since the 2002 immigration law introduced for the first time a privileged entry quota for immigrants who could demonstrate to have Italian origins, in particular from South America (Argentina, Venezuela, and Brazil).

Indirect labels reveal a framing of the issue of immigrant integration predominantly based on: (1) housing, (2) employment, and (3) vocational training. Housing can be regarded as primarily a local issue, since in the 2000s this issue was scarcely considered by national policies. Throughout the period studied, this was the main item in the Venetian programs' total budget (35–40 percent). The 2002 program argued that housing was an essential requirement for integration and allocated significant economic resources for the building of around one hundred accommodations devoted to immigrants and return emigrants of Venetian origin. The 2004–2006 programs declared their appreciation for those employers engaged in supporting their foreign employees in finding suitable accommodation, while at the same time emphasizing the need to avoid competition with the native population. Since 2007 the region has been committed to the launching of an Ethnic Housing Fund for low-income immigrants and native people.

Employment, on the other hand, the second precondition for effective integration, reflects the 2002 national immigration law emphasis on the link between legal status and participation in the labor market, which Venetian programs explicitly appreciate. In order to aid immigrant employment,

Venetian programs provide for programs such as professional training either in Veneto or in the country of origin before arrival. The programs also stress the necessity for greater involvement of Italian regions in the decisions about annual entry quotas.

As for the measures included under the heading "Vocational Training," these seem to converge toward the national cultural turn, since a particular emphasis is put on Italian language and civic education courses, as well as on courses on labor safety regulations. In the plans for 2004–2006 and later, a fourth priority was introduced, school and social integration of immigrant children. Similar to Emilia-Romagna, resources were designated for refresher courses for schoolteachers, support in the learning of the Italian language, intercultural education programs, and cultural mediation.

Also in Veneto, policy implementation is delegated to local authorities, yet when compared to Emilia-Romagna, these authorities have much less room to maneuver. The budget is allocated to the policy priorities mentioned above, and local governments cannot choose which one to favor but rather are required to develop specific projects for each area.

Table 2.4 summarizes the main findings of the analysis of the Veneto region's integration programs. Compared to Emilia-Romagna, a quite different

TABLE 2.4 DIRECT LABELS, INDIRECT LABELS, AND POLICY PRIORITIES IN VENETO'S IMMIGRANT INTEGRATION POLICIES	
Direct labels	*Immigration:* • *Must be socially sustainable* • *Must be consistent with regional development* *Immigrants:* • *Extracomunitari* • *Noncommunitarian/foreign immigrants* • *Return emigrants first* *Integration:* • *Legality and regularity* • *Ordered and civic coexistence*
Indirect labels	• *Housing* • *Employment*
Policy priorities	• *Vocational training for newcomers and potential immigrants* • *Vocational training* • *Language and civic education* • *Social workers and cultural mediators* • *Safety regulation in job places* • *Re-insertion into the countries of origin* • *Education and social integration*
Source: Veneto Regional Integration Programs (2002–2008).	

framing of immigrants' integration emerges. Direct labels underscore a clear concern for social cohesion, economic development, and the cultural identity of the region. Comparing *extracomunitari* and return emigrants of Venetian origin stresses the cultural otherness of the former, while constructing the idea of a regional community bound together by a common ethnic origin. Consistently, indirect labels pursue socioeconomic integration, providing for individuals' basic needs, such as access to housing and employment as well as, starting in 2007, requiring cultural assimilation, as indicated in the Pact for Welcome and Integration.

An assimilationist frame of integration emerges, which appears consistent with the mid-2000s culturalist turn in national policy, yet it would be incorrect to consider Venetian immigrant integration programs as simply reflecting this. Actually, this region foreshadowed changes in national policy, as clearly indicated by the constant emphasis on the necessity to preserve local community values and traditions, to give a right of way to return emigrants, and to engage *extracomunitari* in a "Pact for Welcome and Integration."

Similarities and Differences in the Framing of Immigrant Integration: What Convergence?

The analysis carried out above highlights both the differences and similarities in the framing of integration in Emilia-Romagna and Veneto, and as a consequence different degrees of convergence not only with respect to the national culturalist policy turn, but also between the two regions themselves.

As for vertical convergence, that is, between national and regional policy frames, if the national culturalist turn was forestalled by the Veneto region rhetoric on immigrant integration, it was almost not considered at all by Emilia-Romagna. The official programs of these regions consistently regard immigrants as would-be citizens whose cultural difference should be appreciated. However, if we move from the plan of the direct labels—definitions, metaphors, and analogies about immigration and immigrants—to that of the indirect labels, of the policy priorities actually pursued, it emerges how Emilia-Romagna, under the heading "intercultural services," has always recommended to local authorities the undertaking of Italian language and civic integration, similarly to Veneto, which considered these measures as part of the "vocational training" priority. It is interesting to note that the two regions justified these interventions on the basis of similar arguments, to favor immigrants' access to the labor market and to strengthen their capacity of interacting with social services, in particular with schools. This de facto convergence seems to have been reinforced after 2005 because of the introduction of ad hoc national (and since 2007, also European) funding for language and civic integration courses.

Regarding horizontal convergence, that is, between the two regions, if we consider the direct labels, opposite ideas of integration prevail: whereas Emilia-Romagna shows a greater openness to cultural diversity and social participation, Veneto conceives integration as a process of assimilation, both socioeconomic and cultural. Direct labels reflect the different ideological stances toward immigration of the center-left and center-right majorities governing the two regions and, more generally, their different political cultures, that is, a center-left commitment to support civil rights and diversity more generally, and a center-right, more conservative, orientation focused on the national/local community and the family.

It could be also hypothesized that these different discourses on integration are indirectly influenced by the respective electoral constituencies: whereas the center-left is likely to be motivated by its desire to turn immigrants into center-left voting citizens, the center-right's rhetoric and policies (in particular regarding the Northern League) could be driven by the expectation that immigrants will never vote for them. Yet, this hypothesis has to be rejected on three grounds. First, in order to vote in Italy, even at a local level, immigrants have to become citizens, and this is a long and complicated process, requiring ten years for naturalization and two additional years minimum for the processing of the application. Secondly, preliminary studies on the electoral participation of Romanian citizens, who since 2007 can vote at a local level, as can all EU citizens, show extremely low turnouts.[11] Last, but not least, the assumption that immigrants lean politically left is challenged in the case of Eastern European immigrants: coming from exsocialist regimes, they tend to vote for moderate center-right parties.

If from the direct labels we move to an in-depth analysis of the indirect labels, various elements of similarity emerge between the two regions, which challenge the primacy of political ideology. In fact, in the considered decade, the two regions seem somehow to converge toward each other. In particular, in the case of Veneto, from the mid-2000s on the programs show an increasing appreciation of intercultural education and cultural mediation, following the approach that has characterized the Emilia-Romagna programs since the very beginning. The main factor accounting for such an intercultural frame shift is the pressure from local administrations (municipalities) and grassroots practitioners, especially in the schools, as explained in the 2004–2006 Veneto immigrant integration program:

> In this new social context, the fact that immigration in Veneto is a phenomenon diffused on the territory and not just concentrated in the main cities, and that there is a multiplicity of public and private organizations working in the sector of integration, represent *main causes* for the continuous arising of new funding requests. . . . In particular, an important share of these new requests concerns initiatives

aimed at supporting access to education and school integration, which are presented by school units or networks of schools, municipalities, provinces, associations working in the field. (Deliberazione del Consiglio regionale n. 53/2004, *Programma regionale triennale 2004–06 in materia di immigrazione*, 5, emphasis added)

On the other hand, in the second half of the decade, Emilia-Romagna seems to have moved somewhat toward Veneto in considering immigration more and more as an economic asset for the regional labor market. This is particularly evident in the 2006–2008 integration program, where, as pointed out above, immigration began to be defined both as a cultural and economic asset. This new framing is reflected in the ambition of the region to assume a more relevant role in national policy making on entries and admissions, as already advocated for quite a while by Veneto. To justify this frame shift, local labor market needs are particularly emphasized. These are analytically illustrated in section 7 of the 2006–2008 Emilia-Romagna's immigrant integration program, depicting a scenario that is very similar to that sketched in the 2004–2006 integration program of the Veneto region. Declining fertility rates, an aging population, and higher levels of education among the younger generations are mentioned as factors leading to increasing gaps in the need for low- and medium-skilled workers. The two regions appear to reach similar conclusions:

The Veneto region will work, together with the responsible Ministry and the local Venetian actors involved in economic production and professional training for the establishing of a permanent system of immigrant training and recruitment abroad. . . . The region will encourage inflows consistent with labor demands expressed by the Venetian industrial and services sectors, as well as by families in relation to their care and domestic needs, taking into account the unemployment rate of Italian and foreign workers living in Veneto. (Deliberazione del Consiglio della regione Veneto n. 53/2004, *Programma regionale triennale 2004–06 in materia di immigrazione*, 5)
The region reasserts its involvement in estimating the annual foreign workforce needs . . . and reasserts also its choice for a preliminary confrontation with the social partners and local authorities in order to pursue the strategic goal of active management of immigrant inflows, according to the regions' quantitative and qualitative labor force needs. (Regione Emilia-Romagna, *Programma regionale triennale 2004–06 per l'integrazione dei cittadini stranieri*, 17)

Hence, the regional programs on immigrant integration approved in the first part of the decade (2000–2005) are those where the differences between the

Emilia-Romagna and Veneto are more pronounced: the former embraced what we have called the culture-friendly approach, while the latter an assimilationist one. In subsequent years, though, local labor needs in Emilia-Romagna, and pressures from the schools and civil society organizations in Veneto, seem somehow to have forced the two regions to commit to a more comprehensive integration policy. However, they continue to maintain their original, distinctive traits: the three strategic goals of the 2009–2011 Emilia-Romagna programs remain political participation, cultural intermediaries, and antidiscrimination, while Veneto's approach privileges employment, housing, and vocational training.

An important persistent difference between the two regions, revealed by an analysis of the indirect labels, are the different degrees of devolution to local tiers of government. Whereas Emilia-Romagna not only delegates policy implementation but also policy decision responsibility, since local authorities can choose which proposed policies to prioritize, the Veneto region has more of a steering role. This is consistent with the different traditions of welfare services organization in the two regions. In particular, Emilia-Romagna's tradition of local autonomy stands in opposition to Veneto's emphasis on the necessity of involving voluntary organizations, which is a recurrent recommendation to local authorities in this region's documents.

To sum up, our analysis shows primarily a trend toward a partial horizontal convergence between the two regions triggered, on the one hand, by local services and the concern of NGOs for immigrants' inclusion, and, on the other, by labor market needs. As for vertical convergence, this seems to have taken place in more of a bottom-up than top-down manner: given the pivotal role of the Northern League in the fourth Berlusconi government (2008–2011), which appointed party leader Roberto Maroni as minister of the interior, Veneto's policy approach seems to have been somehow uploaded at a national level. However, an element of top-down vertical convergence can be found in the national and, later, EU funding provided in order to carry out language and civic integration courses, which also led Emilia-Romagna to pay more and more attention to this kind of measures.

Conclusion

Theories of classical national inclusion models have long been under discussion, given the heuristic power of the model metaphor in accentuating differences among the various countries' policy approaches. More recently, and as a reaction to the debate on the presumed failure of the Dutch multicultural model (Koopmans 2003), various scholars have started to question the notion of model, while studies applying the well-established concept of *policy frame* to immigration policy making have emerged, providing a fresh perspective for the understanding of migration policy.

This chapter has assumed such an argumentative turn. Following Bleich (2003: 184), we maintain that frames matter in policy making, because they "shape the range of policy options considered, ruling out options in one country that seem natural and effective in another." Yet, rather than focusing only on policy frames at a national level, in this research we have attempted to gauge processes of policy framing from a multilevel governance perspective. In this respect, it is clear that national-level policy frames (including law and policy discourse), while relevant, account for just part of the story. Since the mid-2000s, the culturalist policy that characterizes the framing of immigrant integration policy at a national level in Italy, and that emphasizes issues of cultural identity and compliance with established rules, was actually forestalled by the Veneto region's integration programs and only partly reflected in Emilia-Romagna's ones.

As a consequence, various, and often also conflicting, policy frames are likely to be in play in the context of decision-making processes at different levels of government. This is especially true insofar as we move from the espoused theory to the theory in use, where regional policy narratives, forged by political factors such as ideology and power, have to confront practical issues such as pressures from local authorities for the intercultural adaptation of services and labor market necessities. Changes in national policy do not appear to represent the main factor of convergence, which seems to be linked primarily to the availability of specific funding for civic integration courses rather than to the new culturalist rhetoric.

This study can be considered a first attempt to investigate frames in a multilevel perspective, taking into account a case, that of Italy, which stands out for not being one of the classical immigrant integration models described by most of the literature on integration policy in Central and Northern European countries. However, more has to be done in order to find out how different frames travel across levels of government, which actors play a role in multilevel framing processes, and how they mobilize.

NOTES

1. The minister's gesture provoked violent protests against the Italian consulate in Bengasi, where eleven protesters were killed. The minister was forced to resign.

2. The charter was actually promoted as a reaction to the initiative of the UCOII (Union of Islamic Communities in Italy), a confederation gathering together some 104 local Muslim associations considered extremist, to publish advertisements in the main Italian newspapers that compared Israeli repression in the Palestinian territories to the Nazi Holocaust. This was perceived as an "integration crisis" (Caponio, Hunter and Verbeek 2015), signaling the potential disloyalty of the Islamic community to the democratic principles of the Italian constitution.

3. *Carta dei valori della cittadinanza e dell'integrazione - Introduzione*, 1–2. Decree of Interior Ministry, n.137/2007.

4. See also the document *Piano integrazione nella sicurezza. Identità e incontro* [Integration and security program. Identity and encounter], which was approved by the fourth Berlusconi government in June 2010.

5. In 2014 the governors of the two regions were Vasco Errani, of the Democratic Party in Emilia-Romagna, and in Veneto Luca Zaia of the Northern League, who was elected in 2010 also with the support of the People of Freedom Party, founded in 2009 with the merging of the previous House of Freedoms and National Alliance parties.

6. Espoused theory and theory in use are concepts used in organization studies. In particular, we refer to the notion of theory of action of Argyris and Schön (1978).

7. Direct and indirect labels are our original instruments that we introduce in order to better give an operational definition of concept of espoused theory and theory in use in our context of analysis.

8. Assemblea Legislativa della Regione Emilia Romagna, Delibera n. 260 del 16 Dicembre 2008, "Approvazione del programma 2009–2011 per l'integrazione sociale dei cittadini stranieri," 3.

9. Consiglio Regionale del Veneto, Deliberazione n.57, 12th July 2007, "Piano triennale di massima 2007–2009 degli interventi nel settore dell'immigrazione," n.189/2002.

10. From the 1860s through the 1970s Veneto was a region of Italian mass emigration. In most cases, Venetian emigrants or their children became third-country nationals, especially Argentinian and Brazilian. Some of them have returned to Italy, especially during the Argentinian economic crisis in 1999–2002, yet their number is far lower compared to that of new foreign immigrants: in 2011, neither Argentina nor Brazil were among the first fifteen countries of origin of foreigners living in Veneto (*Dossier Statistico* 2011).

11. See: http://fieri.it/2010/01/11/come-votano-gli-immigrati/.

II

Regions with Distinctive Histories of Cultural Diversity

3

Migrations, Language, and Social Mobility in Catalonia

AMADO ALARCÓN

The essays in Part I considered the role of local and regional governments in integrating immigrants in new destination countries. The chapters by Dobbs and Caponio and Campomori demonstrated that the commitment to and character of immigrant integration at the level of local bureaucrats and political parties varies considerably, depending, in part, on partisan ideology (Italy) and partisan self-interest (Ireland). This chapter continues the regional focus in examining the challenges associated with immigrant integration in the Spanish region of Catalonia. Wheras Ireland and Italy faced challenges associated with unprecedented diversity, in Catalonia, immigrant diversity overlays the preexisting position of Catalans as a distinct ethnic minority group in Spain. The adoption of bilingual Catalan education was not a response to immigration, but rather a policy to address indigenous cleavages. Nevertheless, Alarcón shows that it has important implications for patterns of immigrant integration.

The arrival of foreign immigrants and the bringing up of a second generation in officially bilingual communities provide special insight into the issue of the social promotion of immigrants in relation to the language or languages used as the vehicle for assimilation.[1] The theory of segmented assimilation has provided useful tools for dealing with linguistic adaptation processes, mainly in the case of the United States (Portes and Hao 1998).[2] This theory suggests that the children of immigrants do not necessarily assimilate into the norms of mainstream middle-class culture,

or experience upward mobility for that matter. Therefore, not all processes
of sociocultural assimilation are the same, nor do they produce the same
itinerary of socioeconomic integration (Ambrosini 2004; Mac Thomais
St. Hilaire 2001; Portes and Rumbaut 2001; Portes and Zhou 1993). The
incorporation of immigrants and their descendants into bilingual societies
raises new challenges, insofar as it is based on incorporation into a receiving
context already characterized by hybridity, or the combination of changing
identities and subjectivities, and often historically constructed out of antag-
onism and asymmetry.

Catalonia is an interesting space in which to analyze these dynamics,
since it is a receiving context of international immigration in which two
official languages, Spanish and Catalan, coexist with different local statuses
and functions. The benefits of learning Catalan and the improved status associated with it have been reported mainly in relation to Spanish-speaking
internal migrants in Catalonia (Badia i Margarit 1964, 1969; Rendon 2007;
Solé 1981; Woolard 1985, 2003). The issue now is whether immigrants and
their offspring assimilate in Catalan, Spanish, their mother tongue, or a combination of these languages. From a sociological perspective, it is important
to examine the causes and consequences of each type of linguistic assimilation in connection with different paths of social mobility. To what extent
are the use of and preferences for either Catalan or Spanish linked to the
strategies and constrictions for upward social mobility in the host society?

In collaboration with researchers of the GEDIME (Grup d'Estudis sobre
Minories Ètniques i Migracions, Autonomous University of Barcelona), we
have examined the relationship between socioeconomic variables and linguistic preferences and attitudes of children of international immigrants
using: (1) a qualitative basis of parents and descendants from Argentina,
Colombia, and Morocco (Alarcón and Garzón 2011, 2013); and (2) a quantitative basis of 3,578 descendants of immigrants between twelve and seventeen
years old (Alarcón and Parella Rubio 2013). In these studies we have examined
how the social and demolinguistic structure of Catalan society determines
different itineraries of linguistic adaptation among immigrants' teenage
children. Our hypothesis is that, given the context of extended diglossia (a
society with two languages with different functions and status for each one),
one would expect young people from families with greater economic and
cultural capital, high educational aspirations and expectations, as well as
academic success to achieve better knowledge of Catalan and to prefer Catalan over other languages (Newman 2011; Woolard 1985, 2003). Patterns of
linguistic integration will have repercussions on the types of itineraries of
adaptation that will be followed by immigrants' offspring in Catalonia as
well as their possibilities of upward social mobility.

The chapter is organized as follows: in the second section I proceed to a
contextualization of the sociolinguistic situation in Catalonia and its links

with bilingual educative policy. The third section reviews the scientific literature on the social status of languages in Catalonia. The focus of the fourth section is the qualitative results about the links of language and the integration of immigrants in different social spheres (labor markets, schools, neighborhoods). The fifth section contrasts the effects of the main predictors of the theory of segmented assimilation on language preferences and language skills among the second generation of immigrants in Catalonia. Finally, the chapter concludes with a review of the main relations between linguistic segmentation and migrations in Catalonia.

Sociolinguistic Context

Bilingualism in Catalonia can be explained mainly by previous political and immigration processes. After Spain's transition to democracy and various stages of prohibition and persecution, the Catalan language was legally established Catalonia's "own" language, jointly official with Spanish, Spain's official language. In the early 1980s, Catalan became the main language of the education system, giving rise to one of the most successful experiences worldwide of the recovery of the language of a stateless nation (Fishman 1991). However, there are still some areas (mass media; public institutions, like courts of justice, which depend on the central government; and urban concentrations of interior migrants), in which Catalan is used only by a minority.

Regarding migration processes, there have been two major immigration influxes into Catalonia during the last century. First, the internal migration of the 1950s–1970s, during which nearly 1.4 million internal migrants arrived in Catalonia. By 1971, 42.9 percent of Catalonia's residents had been born in other parts of Spain. Internal migrants were Spanish speaking and employed mostly in low-skill-level jobs. This meant an increase in the use of Spanish among the working classes in Catalonia (Solé 1981). Second, with an interal growth close to zero (birth minus deceased), from the 1990s onward, foreign migration increased Catalan population from 6.1 million inhabitants (3 percent of the population) in 1998 to 7.5 million (15.7 percent) in 2012 (IDESCAT 2009).

The 2008 Survey on Language Uses of the Population (EULP-2008, for its Catalan acronym) revealed the existence of two main language groups: mother-tongue Spanish speakers and mother-tongue Catalan speakers (55 percent and 31.7 percent, respectively; 3.6 percent declared both languages as their mother tongue).[3] Due to international immigration, 9.3 percent of Catalan residents also speak languages other than their mother tongue. Foreign-born residents represent 17 percent of the adult population of Catalonia. Forty-nine percent of them speak Spanish as a mother tongue (mainly Latin American immigrants), 1.5 percent speak Catalan (returning migrants), and 49.5 percent speak other foreign languages. Among foreigners, the main foreign language spoken in Catalonia is Arabic (15.3 percent).

Only 25.2 percent of the foreign-born population writes in Catalan, whereas among locals the figure is 85 percent (IDESCAT 2009). This low figure among the foreign born points to the relatively recent arrival of immigrant communities in Catalonia.

With the exception of some foreigners, the majority of Catalonia's population shares Spanish as a first or second language. More than three-quarters of Catalan residents can speak Catalan to some degree, and 99.7 percent speak Spanish. The periodic Survey on Linguistic Use in Catalonia (EULP) shown in 2013 that the percentage of people willing to learn Catalan has consistently increased in recent years. More than 40 percent of the population considers it their first language, while 53.5 percent consider it their main language upon reaching adulthood. This increased use of Catalan may be interpreted—as discussed below—as a consequence of institutional policies and the role of Catalan for social promotion in Catalan society.

In order to understand the linkage between immigration and language in Catalonia, it is important to consider that knowledge of Catalan has had an important effect on the social promotion of previous generations of Spanish-speaking internal migrants. The attractiveness of the Catalan language is evident in the intergenerational transmission of language. Children born in Catalonia who speak Spanish as their mother tongue (children of internal migrants) account for 41.3 percent of Catalans, but 29.2 percent of them consider Catalan to be their main language. Up to one-third of the children of internal migrants switch from Spanish to Catalan or adopt both languages as their own (IDESCAT 2009).

Delving into political factors, a key element in the bilingualization of Catalan society was the establishment in the 1980s of a bilingual model in the education system. The model was not originally conceived as a tool for integration policy, but rather as a way of restitution of Catalan identity and language to Catalan institutions targeted by nationalistic political parties. There was an important political debate in the early 1980s between the convenience of a segregated model, with different languages of instruction in different schools (advocated by right-nationalistic parties), and a generalized bilingual model for all students, also called a "conjunction model" (advocated by left parties worried about social and linguistic cleavages in the Catalan society) (Woolard 2003). The model of "school conjunction" was legally approved. This model educates students together, adopting Catalan as the main language of teaching, regardless of students' first language. As we have seen above, the model largely achieved the goal of bilingualization in the case of internal migrants. Indeed, the model contributed, as an expected outcome, to a de-ethnization of the Catalan language, since different ethnic groups share similar language competences.

Mastery of host society languages among immigrant-origin youths is an especially salient issue in the Catalan context, given the state policy of official bilingualism. Yet, since many immigrants to Catalonia originate from Spanish-speaking countries and are thus fluent in Spanish, there is increasing concern from native Catalans about the assimilability of foreigners into the distinct society and culture of Catalonia. Scholars, educators, and policy makers are concerned that a lack of fluency in either Spanish or Catalan would impede educational success. Given that Catalan is the main language of instruction in elementary and secondary schools, they argue that conversational ease in Catalan is a critical skill for excelling in one's studies. Indeed, research has shown that the children of immigrants, particularly those who arrive in Spain after the age of school entry, experience difficulty in becoming fully proficient in Catalan (Huguet Canalís and Navarro Sierra 2005; Oller 2008).

Social Status of Catalan and Spanish Languages in Catalonia

Research conducted in Catalonia has shown that the Spanish language accomplishes the functions of primary integration for internal migrants from other parts of Spain (Badia i Margarit 1964, 1969; Solé 1981). On the other hand, in spite of a national dictatorship (1939–1975) adverse to the recognition of linguistic diversity, Catalan has become a symbol of status and social promotion in the local context (Woolard 1985, 2003). Carlota Solé (1981) and Kathryn A. Woolard's (1989) research shows that in the late 1970s in Barcelona and its metropolitan area (the economic engine of the region and the main immigration reception area), immigrants perceived Catalan as the language of prestige at the local level and as a necessary language (in addition to Spanish, which is almost universal and widely used socially), for achieving upward social mobility. Subsequent research has found that the population expresses a significant consensus over the fact that knowledge of Catalan, together with Spanish, provides greater facilities for securing employment and promotion at work (Solé 1988). Moreover, recent years have seen written skills in Catalan increase the likelihood of being employed in Catalonia and of earning a higher income of up to 18 percent, ceteris paribus, in the case of those born outside Catalonia (Di Paolo and Raymond 2010; Rendón 2007). These data reflect a positive link between immigrants' knowledge of Catalan and upward social mobility. This would contribute to the fact that Spanish and Catalan are valued differently by immigrants' representations (Gore 2002; Pujolar 2010; Woolard 2003).

The social functions and prestige of the Catalan language in Catalonia must be viewed in relation to ethnic and social cleavages. Matched-guise tests, with a special focus on solidarity and social status, have been used in Catalonia over the last three decades to describe language attitudes (Newman, Trenchs-Parera, and Ng 2008; Woolard 1985, 1989; Woolard and

Gahng 1990). The assumption is that individuals will show greater solidarity with members of their own group while recognizing the prestige of privileged groups and their native languages (e.g., native Catalan speakers of Catalan). Research has shown that the social extension of language competences through the linguistic normalization policy after the dictatorship gave rise to a reduction in the classic in-group support/out-group rejection paradigm with regard to solidarity, which corresponds to the introduction of Catalan-medium education in Catalonia (Newman 2011). These studies show an interesting development in relation to status. Status scores show a decline in the value of Catalan, which can be understood as indicative of a weakening in the relationship between class and ethno-linguistic origin, where two languages are seen as variable alternatives for both communities (Newman Trenchs-Parera, and Ng 2008). Nevertheless, "based on cross-speaker comparison, there is evidence that the hierarchy that puts Catalan speakers above standard Spanish speakers, and both above Barriada speakers, remains intact" (Newman Trenchs-Parera, and Ng 2008).[4] Woolard (2003: 100), based on qualitative research, concludes that "with faint but growing echoes of the process Bourdieu described for French, the class meaning of the Catalan language is becoming accentuated as the ethnic symbolism recedes."

Together with these elements that show the value of the Catalan language at work, we should also consider the demographic importance of Spanish, its official nature in Spain as a whole, and its role in the world as an international market language. Therefore, when we refer to the instrumental value of Catalan in social mobility, we are referring to the local linguistic social rules and logic that have been historically acquired.

Immigrants, Descendants, Language, and Social Mobility in Catalonia

Our research group has examined the link between Spanish-Catalan bilingualism and social mobility among first-generation immigrants (pioneer cohorts who arrived in Catalonia in the late 1970s, the 1980s, and the early 1990s) and the children of immigrants raised in Catalonia and currently living outside the family home (Alarcón and Garzón 2008, 2011, 2013). The objectives of this research project were: (1) to identify the use, instrumental value, and symbolic value of official languages in the areas of education, the labor market, and housing;[5] (2) to identify the attitudes and preferences for Spanish and Catalan among our informants; and (3) to draw relationships between attitudes and dispositions toward languages in Catalonia and different trajectories of integration across generations. The empirical data are derived from forty-five biographical interviews with parents and their adult children living outside the family home from Argentina (parents who migrated in the 1970s and 1980s due to political reasons, who were frequently well-paid professionals in Argentina), Colombia (middle-class individuals who arrived in the 1980s and argue that they migrated to Catalonia because of violence and insecurity in Colombia), and Morocco (working-class speakers of Arabic and/or Tamazight language, who arrived in Spain during the 1980s and 1990s). The interviews in our research covered three issues central to processes of social mobility: education, housing, and the labor market. Our fieldwork was undertaken in the years 2007 to 2008 in industrial areas of Barcelona and Tarragona that had a high presence of working-class Spanish-speaking internal migrants. The interviews were conducted prior to the extension of the social effects of the 2008 economic crisis, which means that socioeconomic problems detected in our study have increased.

Neighborhoods and Schools

Catalonia has been proud historically of its "social elevator," which can be defined as the capacity to generate upward social mobility for the children of interior immigrants—although, critically, little academic research has been done to support or refute its claim.[6] Its success on this score has been made possible through Catalan immersion, or "school conjunction," since the 1980s. As explained in section two, in this model students are educated together, with Catalan adopted as the main language of teaching, regardless of students' first languages. Due to mandatory scholarization in Catalan and Spanish language, the descendants of immigrants in the study were mostly bilingual in Spanish and Catalan. However, their use of and proficiency in the two languages varied widely. Often their bilingualism was just passive (having only listening and reading comprehension in Catalan). The lack of use of Catalan outside of school is correlated with low proficiency, reduction of expressive capacity, and hence an infrequent use of the language, even when it is necessary. As for the effects of the "school conjunction model" for foreign immigrants, although the differences in competence levels are reduced in time, children of foreign immigrants, especially non-Spanish speakers, fail to catch up with their native peers linguistically (Huguet Canalís and Navarro Sierra 2005).

The results cast doubt on the widely held idea that second-generation students of immigrant origin do not have linguistic problems and can be treated as native speakers (Oller 2008). For the children of immigrants, particularly those of Hispanic origin, Catalan is the language of the classroom, whereas Spanish is the language of the playground. There is also linguistic segregation between areas with either a majority of Catalan speakers or Spanish speakers, which can largely be explained by social and residential segregation due to socio-economic reasons (Benito Pérez and González Balletbó 2009).

Some differences with the processes of internal migration made us think that it is likely that social mobility patterns of the second generation of foreign migrants will be different from that of the second generation of internal migrants. The main ways that external migrants differ from internal migrants are: (1) In most cases they do not have Spanish nationality, and there are differences in access to nationality according to country of origin. This may even create comparative grievances between young migrants from different countries. (2) Their mother tongue in the host society is only relevant in the case of Latin American children. For one-half of the immigrants' descendants, it is not possible for them to speak with teachers at school in their mother tongue. (3) There is an absence of shared cultural references and an asymmetry in knowledge of other cultures, both among young people and in relationship with teachers in the educational system. (4) The Spain-Catalonia (center-periphery) cleavage is perceived generally as something external.

In the case of internal migrants: (1) They and their children are already Spanish citizens. (2) Their language is also the official language of Spain, and the only one that had institutional and symbolic value in the first years of their settlement (prior to transition to democracy in 1975 Spanish was the only official language in Spain). (3) In the educational system both teachers (local) and migrants (from other regions) speak the same language, Spanish, whereas foreign migrants do not. (4) The cultural identity of internal migrants are also part of the Catalan culture, although they were not aware of the importance of Catalan language because its use and teaching were not allowed by Franco's Government. (5) They are part of the center-periphery cleavage in Spain, being migrants (or their descendants) from the center that went to live in a peripheral region.

In Catalonia, the district of residence determines the choice of school, and the predominant language in the neighborhoods of our sample is Spanish. Many of these neighborhoods have decayed in the last twenty years; the residents who have been able to flee have done so, and these areas have entered into a downward spiral. Growing up in Spanish-speaking areas has made these children differentiate between a "formal language" (Catalan) and a "street language" (Spanish). Spanish is a language that has been learned not only in the classroom but also in noninstitutional contexts, unlike Catalan, which is only learned in the classroom. Therefore, immigrant children perceive Spanish as more informal than Catalan. Spanish is perceived as "authentic" and a "street" language, in contrast to Catalan, which is seen as an "anonymous" and "official" language (Gal and Woolard 1995).

Immigrants perceive residential segregation between Spanish-speaking and Catalan-speaking neighborhoods, which is a key factor in attributing instrumental and symbolic value to the two official languages. The following quote from a Moroccan immigrant shows how changing neighborhoods and schools bring the higher social status of Catalan in Catalonia into focus. The increase in the knowledge and use of Catalan is dependent on the upward social mobility of the parents, something that goes in the inverse direction of causality in the human capital theory. There is a remarkable insistence on proficiency in the legitimate variety of Catalan. As there are no instrumental or communication problems among bilinguals, the discussion focuses on the symbolic value of the dominant variety of Catalan in integration and mobility in the host society.

> I changed schools and it was a radical change. . . . I saw a difference between Catalan-speaking people and Spanish-speaking people. And so I decided . . . to look Catalan, a little, you know?—what kind of difference?—People who spoke Spanish did not speak proper Catalan. It was not only that Catalan was not their mother tongue; it was that when they spoke Catalan they spoke a very broken Catalan. Then you saw the difference. You do not speak Catalan because you can't, I can, so . . . if I do not speak perfect Catalan I should make an effort to speak it, you know? To learn it, you know? And I decided, then, I don't know, I must learn Catalan. (Ikram, Moroccan, twenty-five years old, born in Catalonia, works in retail, university educated)

In the neighborhoods populated by a majority of Spanish, working-class, internal immigrants, we detect negative attitudes toward Catalan and minimal use of this language outside the regular institutional channels. These migrants have difficulty understanding why greater linguistic accommodation is expected of them, since they already speak "the language of Spain." In most of the neighborhoods in which migrants live, the language spoken in everyday life is Spanish, and the fact that Spanish is used not only at home but also in the street may contribute to a greater perception of informality of Spanish in contrast with that of Catalan, as the latter is mostly learned at school. Catalan thus becomes a language linked to educational insertion and acquisition of the officially sanctioned cultural capital. Children of immigrants who have attended university feel emotional attachment to both Catalan and Spanish. Moreover, they are aware that a successful career in Catalonia requires the ability to use Catalan.

Labor Market and Language

The most common situation among second-generation immigrants is that their parents' status in the labor market is carried over. Structural changes in the labor market affect young people, both immigrants and locals, more than adults. Many of the informants pointed to the difficulties linked to employment instability. This instability creates a barrier to upward mobility, which deeply affects the expectations of families that were upper-middle class in the country of origin, but who in Catalonia lack the social capital that played a key role in becoming professionals in their countries of origin. For this reason, downward mobility in the second generation is more common among Argentineans than among the other two groups.

Second-generation immigrants from Colombia and Argentina acknowledge the need for Catalan, even if during their daily lives they use very little of it. Catalan is considered a key requisite for accessing more skilled jobs, even if the job itself does not involve the use of Catalan on a day-to-day basis. Nevertheless, when applying for a job, technical skills, when these are scarce, often become more important than Catalan-language skills.

Our study detected cases of status inconsistency (high education levels and low-skill jobs) among Moroccan women. Specifically, three Moroccan women with a university degree working in retail have argued that there is widespread discrimination toward Moroccans in the Catalan labor market. Discrimination is then countered by adopting the symbolic markers of Catalan culture, such as language. Moreover, children have not had the early labor market insertion their parents had. The failure to cover the parents' expectations raised by insertion in the educational system of the host society may also contribute to further increases in the rate of school dropouts. There is little mobility, rather a reproduction of position with changes, most of them linked to structural changes in the Catalan labor market. Precarious and poorly paid jobs are the norm and become a barrier to upward social mobility.

This is especially traumatic for middle-class families (Colombians and Argentineans) who lost their social capital due to migration. Whereas in their country of origin, the networks of strong ties often provided support and assistance, in the host country the family is often disenfranchised. Children of migrants who suffer economic difficulties often fail at school, in part due to family troubles, which in the country of origin would have been lessened by the support of kinship ties.

Frequently, the experience of second-generation migrants is marked by an inconsistency of status. This is especially the case among Moroccan women. Although in many cases they seek to pursue higher education (a B.A., but not an M.A. or Ph.D.), often they work in low-skilled positions (e.g., as a customer service assistant). There is a strong perception of discrimination against Moroccans in the labor market. The strategy adopted by Moroccan informants is clear: adopt the symbolic values of Catalan culture, especially Catalan language, as a tool for surmounting the entry barriers to better-skilled employment.

Interethnic Relations and Attitudes toward Host Languages

Locals consider that learning Catalan is a positive indicator of immigrant integration. In Catalonia, young people from the second generation of immigrants, who have university diplomas, are perfectly bilingual, something that is instrumental for a better labor market insertion. In spite of the de-ethnicization of Catalan identity based on learning of Catalan language (Woolard 2013)—where anyone who can speak Catalan could be socially considered Catalan—during the last decades, according to our young informants of Moroccan origin, locals have yet to assume the bilingualism of second-generation Moroccan migrants. Locals single out people of immigrant origin who speak Catalan, even though education should make bilingualism the norm for the second generation. Therefore, second-generation Moroccan immigrants suffer a lack of recognition of their identity as Catalans. "It is like when they say, 'your Catalan is very good!' And you say, 'I was born here.' And they insist, 'your Catalan is very good.' But I was born here; *it has nothing to do with it!*" (Latyya, Moroccan, twenty-six years old, born in Catalonia, works in retail, university educated). Children of immigrants associate knowledge of Catalan with a higher cultural capital and improved integration in Catalonia. Young people of Moroccan origin who have done better in Catalan schools are looking forward to challenging discrimination against their community through the increased use of Catalan.

According to Woolard (1985: 744), adolescents in Barcelona reported that Castilian speakers "ridicule their peers who attempt to speak Catalan. Just as there is strong pressure to use exclusively the right language or keep silent in formal situations, so too are negative sanctions enforced in these domains. In these dominated markets, it is equally important to use only the right language; there is nothing 'relaxed' about them." In our sample, we observe that this social valuation of "good and correct" Catalan takes place not only in intragroup but in intergroup relationships as well, reinforcing linguistic cleavages. The three groups point out the need for appropriate proficiency in Catalan: "You must speak good and correct Catalan." The need to speak the dominant variety of language is not new. Some informants pointed out that locals who are older (that is, who are less habituated to migration in comparison to younger generations) are among those who give more importance to a correct pronunciation of the language.

Language Assimilation and Integration Paths

For the second-generation, the Catalan language has a symbolic value for integration within and acquisition of the national capital of the receiving country. Many of the informants we interviewed were bound to follow an illusory assimilation. Illusory assimilation underlines the tension between a paradoxically successful assimilation to the local lifestyle, with a strong component of acculturation and consumption of youth culture, and yet a persistent lack of opportunities for social and economic improvement (Ambrosini 2004). In our area of study this would mean the lack of correspondence between language and cultural assimilation (largely successful),

**TABLE 3.1   SOCIAL AND CULTURAL INTEGRATION OF CHILDREN
OF MIGRANT ORIGIN: THREE CASES**

	Moroccans	Colombians	Argentines
Languages	Can speak but not write the language of their parents. Bilingual in Spanish and Catalan (minor)	Bilingual in Spanish and Catalan, but use of Catalan is minor	Bilingual in Spanish and Catalan, but use of Catalan is minor
Education	Primary and secondary education	Secondary education mainly	Secondary and higher education
Employment	Low-paid jobs. Semiskilled jobs with expectations of improvement	Secondary and higher education jobs	Secondary and higher education jobs
Linguistic attitudes	Low value of mother tongue High social and instrumental value of Catalan Indifference in using Spanish or Catalan	High value of Catalan language to integrate in Catalan society Preference for Spanish	High value of Catalan to integrate Preference for Spanish
Remarks	Linguistic acculturation Dissonant acculturation, with ethnic consciousness Upward mobility	Certain ethnic consciousness Disenchanted with Spanish language Maintenance of status	No ethnic consciousness Disenchanted with Spanish language Consonant acculturation Downward mobility

Source: Alarcón and Garzón (2011). Based on forty-five qualitative interviews with parents and children from Argentina, Colombia, and Morocco.

educational success (mostly among Moroccan women), and the precariousness and frustration that they experience in their careers due to new Spanish internationally based ethno-stratification processes. An increase in the number of cases of downward assimilation (particularly among the descendants from Argentinean and some Colombian parents from the middle and upper classes in their origin countries) is also likely—in other words, children of professionals may manage to get only low-skilled service jobs. In these cases, the second generation experiences a broken link between cultural assimilation and socioeconomic integration.

The disaffection of children of immigrants is, therefore, a possibility in the future. In our fieldwork, we have detected some anomic cases among the Argentine community. The situation of children of immigrants may worsen if the Catalan labor market remains stalled (following the effects of the 2008 economic crisis) and if the salaries for university graduates do not increase. The crisis is already affecting the employment prospects of Moroccan girls schooled in Catalonia, who are often highly qualified but cannot find a suitable professional position and experience processes of downward assimilation.

However, there is no evidence among our informants of an "ethnic flight," or a tighter attachment to national belonging to the country of origin as a response to troubles in the host society. On the contrary, in the case of Moroccans and Colombians, their strategy for upward social mobility is to progressively incorporate the symbols of Catalan culture into their daily life and erase the features than can be more easily associated to migration by locals.

In Table 3.1, we summarize the main features of the relationship between language choice and social mobility among children of migrant parents in Catalonia.

Determinants of Linguistic Preferences and Language Skills of Immigrants' Descendants

Departing from the ILSEG sample (produced by the Center for Migration and Development at Princeton University and Universidad Pontificia de Comillas), Alarcón and Parella (2013) aimed to discover which factors help to determine the preference for the Catalan language (instead of Spanish and the languages of origin) and the acquisition of written skills in Catalan among these young people of immigrant origin.[7] Their sample was composed of 3,578 descendants of foreign immigrants aged between twelve and seventeen in the metropolitan area of Barcelona. The sample consisted mainly of foreign-born youths (the "1.5 Generation"), with only 15.8 percent having been born in Spain, reflecting the relatively recent nature of external immigration. A total of 70.6 percent moved to Spain after the age of six, with a median age of 9.7 at the time of arrival. An analysis of national origin—a variable recorded on the basis of the young person's country of birth for those not born in Spain and on the basis of the parents' country of birth for those born in Spain—shows a marked Latin Americanization of the sample. The majority of young people opt for Spanish as their preferred language (only 15.2 percent preferred another unofficial language, while Catalan was the first choice for just 5.3 percent of cases). At the skills level, the group as a whole had greater skill in Spanish than Catalan. Young people who were born in Spain or arrived before the age of six had a higher index of knowledge of both languages (index of knowledge of Catalan and index of knowledge of Spanish), as a result of having been taught in both official languages since their first entry into the education system.

Various multivariable logistic regression models were carried out on the basis of theoretically relevant predictors provided by the Segmented Assimilation Theory. The main predictors under this theoretical approach are linked to modes of incorporation and include: parental socioeconomic status, family composition, age at arrival, origin and birthplace, gender, and type of school (public or private), as well as correlates of integration (time devoted to study, academic expectations, feeling of belonging, and origin of peers). The results of the analysis show that there are different itineraries for linguistic adaptation among the teenage children of immigrants, reflecting a linguistic segmentation.

According to the results shown above in Table 3.2, the acquisition of written Catalan skills depends largely on age and the number of years in Spain, in other words, on when the young person was incorporated into the Catalan education system. Together with the aspects concerning the schooling process, one of the main factors that positively influence the acquisition of written skills is a family structure with two parents in the household. Conversely, negative factors include being of Latin American or Chinese origin and, albeit with a low level of significance, studying at a charter school once the family socioeconomic situation has been controlled for. Lastly, Catalan skills correlate positively with the expectation of pursuing a university degree, achieving good academic grades, feeling Spanish, and having friends, less than half of whom are foreign.

With regard to the preference for Catalan, having a high family socioeconomic status, mixed parentage—only one parent is foreign born—and number of years in Spain are determining factors in preferring Catalan. These determinants differ considerably from those that determine written skills. The variables concerning the parents' professional prestige and educational capital, expressed through the family socioeconomic status index, acquire greater significance and value in the coefficients, as shown by the bivariate analysis. The table shows a negative effect among young people of Latin American origin on the preference for Catalan. Conversely, Chinese and Moroccan groups adopt positive values in their preference for Catalan. However, the values are only significant in the case of those from the most developed countries in western Europe; preference for Catalan appears to be practically unrelated—or at least no significant links in the case studied were observed—to the linguistic root of the languages of origin of young people. Conversely, the fact of being students from more developed countries (Western Europe) has a significant effect on the preference for Catalan, even when family socioeconomic status has been controlled for. This points to the link between linguistic inequality—in our case, inequality of linguistic preferences—and the inequalities existing by level of wealth in young people's countries of origin. The subjective aspects associated with the preference for Catalan include the expectation of going to university, high academic grades, and having fewer than 50 percent of foreign friends. Causal relations between these variables and dependent variables are problematic, in that they reflect, like the dependent variables in our models, a successful

TABLE 3.2 DETERMINANTS OF PREFERENCE TOWARD CATALAN AND WRITING SKILLS IN CATALAN

	(a) Preference toward Catalan Categories: 1. Preference for Catalan; 2. Other Languages		(b) Writing Skills in Catalan Categories: 1. Poor; 2. Average; 3. Well or Perfectly	
	B	*Wald*	*Est.*	*Wald*
Constant	−4.358	9.88**		
Age	0.017	0.03	−0.198	25.69***
Years in Spain	0.024	0.77	0.208	192.67***
Female	0.141	0.55	0.096	1.14
Offspring of mixed parentage	1.216	22.34***	0.297	1.81
Two parents at home	0.098	0.22	0.183	3.60
Charter school	0.107	0.24	−0.283	5.78*
Family socioeconomic status	0.683	10.76***	0.027	0.05
Reference: other origins		25.66*		
Ecuador	−0.520	1.65	−0.513	7.03**
Morocco	0.264	0.47	0.175	0.46
Colombia	−0.361	0.55	−0.972	17.76***
Peru	0.033	0.01	−0.686	8.71**
Dominican Republic	−1.283	2.74	−0.671	7.56**
Bolivia	−0.981	1.60	−0.212	0.74
China	0.356	0.47	−1.316	24.59***
Philippines	−0.523	0.61	−0.721	5.77**
Argentina	0.230	0.30	−0.014	0.00
Pakistan	0.440	0.52	−0.183	0.30
Brazil	−0.494	0.51	−0.86	8.00**
Chile	−0.008	0.00	0.128	0.11
Romania	−0.995	0.82	0.356	0.73
Other: South or Central American countries	−0.226	0.21	−0.351	1.92
Other: Western Europe	0.900	6.17*	−0.079	0.04
Expectations: University	0.655	10.78***	0.41	13.04***
Studies over four hours a day	0.534	2.94	0.020	0.01
Grades above 7.5	0.425	4.28*	0.639	28.38***
Feels Spanish	0.323	2.21	0.276	5.60*
Fewer than 50% of foreign friends	0.636	9.23**	0.21	5.25*

Source: Drawn up by Alarcón and Parella (2013) on the basis of the ILSEG study microdata.

(a) Binary logistic regression n. 2.606 (3 578). Listwise deletion of lost data option.
Gl: 27; −2 log: 873.297, X: 232.166***; R: 0.247.
X: *Chi*-square; R: X. Nagelkerke R^2; −2 log: −2 log likelihood.

(b) Ordinal logistic regression. n. 2.606 (3 578) Listwise deletion option
Gl: 27; −2 log: 3525,298, X: 609.855***; R: 0.259.
***$p < .001$; **$p < .01$; *$p < .05$.

school career and the characteristics of their integration into the host society. The fact that these variables have high positive and significant values regarding preferences and written skills in Catalan, even after controlling for other variables, clearly indicates that they are associated with the upward mobility of the second generation in Catalonia. In alternative analyses (Parella and Alarcón 2015), we individually observed the choice of Spanish or another unofficial language (Moroccan, Chinese, Portuguese, etc.). Multinomial regression analysis shows that Spanish emerges as a language linked to low socioeconomic status, low academic expectations, and less dedication to study outside school. The quantitative analysis carried out shows that the tendency toward linguistic adaptation follows different patterns among new members of the second generation in Catalonia. These differences can be explained by variables linked to the year of arrival and length of residence, as one would expect. However, the fact that the parents' socioeconomic situation and the type of family structure are significant predictors enable one to interpret these results as future processes of segmented assimilation when these young people enter the labor market, unless proper compensatory mechanisms are implemented.

Both skills in Catalan and the preference for Catalan show a positive link with academic performance and the expectations of pursuing university studies in the future. However, the regression models indicate that the predictors of skills and preferences are very different. Skills acquisition is largely determined by age and number of years in Spain, in other words, by when a person enters the Catalan education system. Conversely, these variables no longer serve as determinants for explaining the preference for Catalan. In this case, the factors determining preference are socioeconomic, together with the fact of having at least one parent who was born in Spain. Moreover, national origin, unlike skills in Catalan, is unimportant when it comes to explaining the preference for Catalan.

These observations point to different types of linguistic incorporation into Catalan society. First of all, we have a relatively small subgroup in which a consonant process of acculturation is produced in terms of the theory of segmented assimilation. The Catalan language (preferences and skills) are introduced into a subgroup of young people characterized by having parents with high educational and professional levels, a family structure with two parents at home, good academic grades, higher educational expectations, and a small number of foreign friends. This casuistry must be understood within the framework of the processes of social reproduction in families with professional prestige and high educational attainment. Moreover, when one of the parents is Spanish or the parents are from Western Europe, linguistic preference for Catalan is reinforced.

Secondly, a third of the participants in the research stated that their Catalan skills were poor or average. This can largely be explained by their late incorporation into the education system, although other factors intervene, such as the fact of not belonging to two-parent households (single parent-hood). In these cases, preference for Catalan is virtually nonexistent. Given the high rates of academic failure, which mainly affect the immigrant popu-lation, it is extremely likely that young persons will finish their compulsory education without sufficient skills in Catalan. Given the possible link between the deficit in linguistic skills (linguistic integration) and future socioeconomic position, within the framework of the theory of segmented assimilation it is essential to analyze the ability of Catalan society to generate labor transitions that are not marked by frustration and do not relegate cer-tain groups of young people to the lowest levels of the labor market or even to marginalization. Since socioeconomic opportunities for young people who do not incorporate the Catalan language may be negatively affected, this must be corroborated through future longitudinal analyses.

A third, majority, group is characterized by satisfactorily evaluating lin-guistic skills, without showing a particular preference for Catalan. Most of the questions about their future socioeconomic incorporation will focus on this majority. Institutions in Catalan society—especially the education system—convey the centrality of the Catalan language as a common public language, capable of placing people on a level of equality and preventing the risk of exclu-sion (Pujolar 2010). That is why structural mechanisms must be guaranteed to ensure that immigrants' children do not have to subsequently face discrimina-tion at work similar to that of their parents, based on ethnic social markers, the color of their skin, their religion, or national origin, among other factors.

Conclusion

Although compulsory education in Catalan and Spanish has contributed to the deethnicization of language in Catalonia, hierarchies in the social status of languages remain. Catalan has receded as an ethnic attribute, but with the spread of bilingual competences through the educational system in the second generation, languages have become not only communicative compe-tences, but a form of symbolic capital in the social structure. As indicated by Richard Blot (2003: 95), we observe in our qualitative data regarding the second generation that Catalan is "a discursive tool mastered and used by middle classes, regardless of their ascriptive ethnicity." And it is socially "mastered" due to biographical trajectories within a linguistically segmented social structure observable in residential segregation (which implies school segregation) and in the labor market.

Social mobility in both the parents' and children's trajectories influences attitudes toward and the use of Catalan among immigrant communities. Proximity to Catalan may be explained by the opportunities for upward social mobility offered by the host society. Tendencies toward assimilation vary among members of the second generation. The daughters of first-generation Moroccan immigrants who attended university in Catalonia attempt to erase or soften the accent of the original language (in this case Arab and Amazigh) as a way to gain economic independence from the community of origin. The problem here is that the labor market does not reward this form of linguistic assimilation. Therefore, we found a lack of correspondence between linguistic integration and socioeconomic integration, leading to an illusory assimilation of fully integrated youth. In other cases, in particular among low-educated Latin Americans, the use of Catalan is consciously and voluntarily very low due to its lack of applicability in the workplace. They have little contact in the labor market with Catalan peers and clients, negatively affecting their expressive capacities in Catalan, in spite of the fact that their education in Catalan schools has provided them with basic knowledge of the language.

Herbert Gans (1992) anticipates the "decline of the second generation" in the sense that host societies no longer have the capacity to generate upward social mobility as in the past. Integration in the host society is now more complex than for interior migrants and their descendants, increasing risks of "getting stuck" for the children of immigrant families, especially those in the lower strata. Differences in the mobility processes of the descendants of immigrants are important. It is worth asking what the key factors will be in comparing the integration patterns of children of immigrants to those of internal migrants. The different nationalities of the parents, the incorporation of phenotype variables in discrimination, employment insecurity, and/or new patterns of residential segregation are among the factors that make us consider that bilingualism is no guarantee of social equality.

The current context of economic crisis, which manifested itself in all its rawness after our fieldwork, with youth unemployment rates above 40 percent within immigrant populations, will shape the rise of the new second generation in Catalonia. It will have important repercussions on the linguistic integration and social cohesion of later cohorts of the descendants of immigrants. In this sense, although the Latin American linguistic origin of migrants' young children is crucial to explaining their preference for Spanish and positive attitudes toward that language, in the long run, it will not be a sufficient reason. We must remember that after several generations in Catalonia a considerable part of the internal immigrants of Spanish-speaking origin have adopted Catalan as their own, or usual, language. The explanation for this phenomenon, which requires establishing a link between sociolinguistic and socioeconomic integration, is one of the main gaps in sociolinguistic research in Catalonia. It is therefore essential not only to undertake longitudinal research with the new generations of external immigration but also to carry out retrospective studies on the connection between language, status, and internal migrations.

NOTES

Acknowledgments: Empirical evidence used in this chapter is based on Alarcón and Garzón (2011, 2013) (research funded by Institut d'Estudis Catalans Research Program and Catalonia Government–ARAFI 00021) and Alarcón and Parella Rubio (2013) (in collaboration with Princeton University).

1. From the sociological perspective, according to Rogers Brubaker (2001: 543), "as a normatively charged concept, assimilation . . . is opposed not to difference, but segregation, ghettoization and marginalization." The actual use of the concept of assimilation involves a shift "from the automatic valorization of cultural differences to a renewed concern with civic integration. . . . A shift from . . . complete absorption, to abstract understanding of assimilation, focusing on a process of becoming similar (in some respect, to some reference population)" (542).

2. A major contribution of segmented assimilation theory is its recognition of the significant role of the broader societal context into which immigrants and their descendants are received—"context of reception"—and how the distinct characteristics of the ethno-immigrant groups interact with the conditions of the destination society in determining their adaption—that is, the "mode of incorporation." Depending on the availability of socioeconomic resources in the family, the existence of tightly knit co-ethnic communities, and the openness to immigrants of the reception context, different groups of immigrants and their descendants will experience varying forms of cultural assimilation and socioeconomic integration, producing different effects on social mobility, whether upward, downward, or stagnant (Ambrosini 2004; Mac Thomais St. Hilaire 2001; Portes and Rumbaut 2001; Portes and Zhou 1993).

3. These rates reflect the answers to the question: "Do you remember what language you spoke first, at home, when you were a child?" (IDESCAT 2009). The data for "Catalan" include "Aranès" (0.1 percent).

4. The term "Barriada," used by Newman Trenchs-Parera, and Ng refers to the working-class neighbourhoods in the outskirts of Barcelona. These neighborhoods were created in the 1960s to house the arriving cohorts of internal migrants from other parts of Spain. Recent years have seen these internal immigrants being replaced by foreign immigrants from a variety of countries, mostly Morocco and Latin America.

5. In only ten years, the children of external immigrants have become a large group in the education system. According to the Catalonia Department of Education, compared with 2 percent during the 1997–1998 school year, during the 2008–2009 school year, foreign students accounted for 15.1 percent of the total in elementary education (between the ages of six and eleven) and 17.5 percent in secondary education (between the ages of twelve and sixteen years). Most immigrants' children are still concentrated in the initial stages of the education system and mainly at state schools (84.4 percent).

6. Jordi Pujol, former president of the Catalan Government (Generalitat de Catalunya), in *La Vanguardia*, February 22, 2006.

7. The study aims to replicate the research design of the Children of Immigrants Longitudinal Study (CILS) in the United States.

4

The Difference a Decade
of Enforcement Makes

Hispanic Racial Incorporation and Changing Intergroup
Relations in the American South's Black Belt (2003–2016)

HELEN B. MARROW

Similar to the situation of new immigrants in Catalonia, Hispanic immigrants
in the American South join a minority group of long standing, in this case
African Americans. In Spain, the post-Franco revival of minority languages
and cultures created a necessary but not sufficient condition—the acquisition of
both Spanish and the regional language—for the socioeconomic integration
of immigrants in Catalonia. Marrow similarly finds that preexisting patterns
of race relations as well as changing popular attitudes toward immigrants in
North Carolina condition the emerging patterns of the incorporation of His-
panics. As in Catalonia, policies devised to address embedded ethnic divisions
are shaping immigrant integration outcomes. In Marrow's analysis, the chal-
lenges go beyond language to the class and racial statuses of Hispanic immi-
grants relative to African Americans and non-Hispanic whites. She finds that
the place of Hispanic immigrants relative to the traditional black-white color
line is being negotiated differently among elites and nonelites, with an outcome
that is as yet uncertain.

The southern color line has historically been drawn and policed specifically around *blacks*. In spite of dramatic growth in the region's
Hispanic/Latino population, in my prior work I described three
factors still upholding a black-nonblack color line in rural North Carolina in
the early 2000s. First, white southerners there demonstrated clear and strong
preferences for Hispanics over blacks—as workers, neighbors, and even as

intimate contacts—and Hispanic newcomers saw and internalized those preferences. Second, many Hispanic newcomers expressed their own anti-black stereotypes, whether they were brought from Latin America or developed in the context of American racial hierarchy, or both.[1] And third, whether true reflections of whites' and blacks' attitudes or not—and most likely they are *not*—many Hispanic newcomers perceived more "discrimination" in their daily interpersonal interactions to come from blacks than whites. Together, I argued that these three factors, each of which is intimately tied to perceptions about intergroup hierarchy and interaction, were coalescing in the early 2000s to produce a situation in which Hispanic newcomers—even many who were dark-skinned, poor, and unauthorized—had come to perceive the social distance separating themselves from whites as more permeable than the social distance separating themselves from blacks. And I showed that Hispanic newcomers were engaging in distancing strategies from blackness and African Americans that may well have been reinforcing such a distinction (Marrow 2011).

How well do those findings hold up a decade later? Anti-immigration sentiment rose throughout the nation after 2005, especially in new immigrant destinations, including many in the South (Hopkins 2010; Lippard and Gallagher 2011; Weise 2012). The issue of immigration became more salient, and the media took a decidedly more anti-immigrant tone (Akdenizli, Dionne, and Suro 2008). Restrictive laws and policies started to pass at the federal, state, and local levels—primarily at the hands of white politicians and legislators aiming to make life tougher for unauthorized immigrants in a variety of policy domains (Chavez and Provine 2009; Ramakrishnan and Wong 2010; and Varsanyi et al., Chapter 9 of this volume). Border and interior enforcement grew substantially after the mid-2000s, as well as the criminalizing and racializing of all Hispanics, not just unauthorized immigrants (Douglas and Sáenz 2013; N. Rodríguez 2012). And I even began to notice that whereas there had been very few black-brown coalitions in eastern North Carolina back in 2003 (Marrow 2011), more had cropped up throughout the state and region by 2010.

This new political landscape suggests that Hispanic newcomers and African Americans in the rural South may now be developing closer linkages than was the case a decade ago, if only because conditions have been worsening so much and so rapidly for Hispanics that the two groups may now have greater reason to recognize a shared minority status and experience. Perhaps a rising anti-immigrant tide could be leading Hispanic newcomers in eastern North Carolina to see themselves as more strongly discriminated against by whites, and thereby to develop a stronger sense of commonality with each other, as racialized Hispanics or Latinos (Okamoto and Ebert 2010; Sanchez and Masuoka 2010). Perhaps sharpening structural discrimination could be leading Hispanics to empathize more with the historical plight of another racial minority group, African Americans (San-chez 2008), and, conversely, it could be leading more African Americans to empathize with Hispanics as new targets of white ire, or to even see Hispan-ics as a parallel minority community (Jones 2012).

In this chapter I reconsider the state of interminority relations in the South a decade after my field research, in order to discuss their implications for ongoing theorizing about the southern color line. My purpose is not to strike down my prior documentation of black-Hispanic tensions, or my argument that a black-nonblack color line reigned in eastern North Carolina in 2003. Other scholars have also documented such tensions in the South (see McClain et al. 2007; McDermott 2011; Rich and Miranda 2005), as well as shown that the strongest and most consequential dividing line in Ameri-can society often still falls primarily between blacks and all others, not whites and all nonwhites (Kasinitz et al. 2008; Lee and Bean 2010; Parisi, Lichter, and Taquino 2011). And so we would not be surprised to observe blacks continuing to represent the primary racial "other" in the Black-Belt South—the region infamous, if not unique, for subjugating blacks as second-class citizens, and where immigration is still relatively new (Marrow 2011).

Rather, my purpose here is to acknowledge and integrate two points into my analysis as fully as possible: first, that Hispanics' location within the American color line has been "complex" for a long time (see Fox and Gug-lielmo 2012); and, second, that where the color line falls at any given point is determined by a complex mix of factors, all of which can vary over time, place, and institutional context (Fox and Guglielmo 2012; Gleeson and Gon-zales 2012; Marrow 2011). In this chapter I therefore distinguish between both *level* and *institutional domain* and use these distinctions to describe what I see as a recent divergence in elite versus nonelite black-Hispanic rela-tions in the South after 2005. Specifically, I argue that the increase in anti-immigrant policy making and immigration enforcement has united black and Hispanic political and civic elites—by whom I mean elected politicians and other formal community leaders and activists who are often themselves strongly civically engaged—thus creating feelings of interminority group solidarity that were either not there, or were at least not as strong or as visi-ble, in the early 2000s. I show that African American political and civic elites have increasingly come to view and empathize with Hispanic newcomers as parallel racial minorities who are also discriminated against by whites, and that some Hispanic political and civic leaders are now turning toward Afri-can American and civil rights organizations, models, and allies.

However, outside the formal realm of politics and down at the level of everyday life among nonelites—by whom I mean ordinary community resi-dents in workplaces, neighborhoods, and public spaces who are *not* formal leaders or activists—the research still suggests a messier and more ambiva-lent picture. At this level and in these domains African Americans' reactions toward Hispanics range all the way from quiet hostility, resentment, and active avoidance to friendliness, empathy, and cooperation, and research generally documents even more negative attitudes, feelings, and boundary-drawing behaviors among Hispanics toward African Americans. So, despite the existence and possible growth of white-Hispanic tensions, I argue here that patterns of black-Hispanic relations still belie a cohesive sense and feeling of togetherness as nonwhites. And I contend that such patterns, combined with those that characterize elites, may signal an emerging bifurcation in the state of the southern color line at the present time: perhaps a white-nonwhite color line is now developing in the elite domains of southern politics and civil society, while a potentially (though not necessarily) black-nonblack color line still characterizes intergroup relations among nonelites in other domains.

Political and Civic Elites: Parallel Minorities

In an overview of the current state and future prospects of black-Hispanic relations in the American South, Néstor Rodríguez (2012) argues that increased federal and local enforcement of immigration will play an important role, albeit one that could ultimately shape relations in several different directions. Southern states have played a key role in intensifying interior immigration enforcement, leading the way in the formal collaboration and cross-training of local and state law enforcement officers with federal immigration officials. The first such agreement, known as 287(g), was signed by the state of Florida in 2002, the second by Alabama in 2003. By October 2009, Virginia was home to the greatest number of agencies officially entered into 287(g) memoranda of agreement, followed by North Carolina, where seven county sheriff departments and the Durham City police had enrolled in 287(g) between 2006 and 2009. By 2010, all one hundred North Carolina counties had enrolled in Secure Communities, and a combination of aggressive political and law enforcement interests had generated a unique and direct relationship between the state's sheriffs and federal Immigration and Customs Enforcement (ICE) officials, which remains unparalleled today (M. Coleman 2012; see also Varsanyi et al., Chapter 9 in this volume).

By the 2010s, an increase in immigration enforcement, a shift from border toward interior enforcement, and the relatively indiscriminate targeting of criminal and noncriminal immigrants nationwide (see C. Rodríguez et al. 2010) had intensified the perceived threat and the danger of arrest throughout immigrants' workplaces, individual homes, and a host of public spaces connecting their spaces of work and leisure (M. Coleman 2012). In the South, this "penumbra" threat has generated enormous anxiety for many Hispanics, even those who are not undocumented, constricting their movement in public spaces and depressing their engagement in schools and religious organizations (Gill 2010; Jones-Correa and Fennelly 2009; Stuesse and Coleman 2014).

Simultaneously, southern states have played a leading role in expressing anti-immigrant sentiment through legislative activity. Omnibus bills aimed at punishing and repelling unauthorized immigrants have been passed in Alabama, Georgia, North Carolina, South Carolina, Tennessee, and Virginia. In my fieldsite of North Carolina, policy making in such diverse realms as employment, higher education, and driver's licenses became noticeably more restrictive over the 2000s (Gill 2010; Jones 2012). A state immigration court was established in 2006 to speed up the deportation of unauthorized immigrants (McClain 2006). Various bills appropriated money to the state sheriff's association's "Illegal Immigration Project" and accelerated the cross-deputization of state and local police. In 2013, debate was flaring over proposed House Bill 786, or the "RECLAIM NC" Act, which included a "papers please" clause that would authorize immigration status checks for anyone lawfully stopped, detained, or arrested, and effectively establish a second-class "restricted driver's license" for unauthorized immigrants, issued only upon self-disclosure of their illegal presence (ACLU 2013; General Assembly of North Carolina 2013).

The critical question here is how these trends toward heightened enforcement and restrictive policy making will ultimately affect intergroup relations in the South. One possibility, noted by Rodríguez (2012) and that I support here, is that they may promote greater solidarity between Hispanics and African Americans, especially if the two groups begin to view law enforcement as an institution that disproportionately targets and profiles both of their communities (see Rios 2011). Indeed, in a new research project on intergroup contact and relations in Atlanta, my colleagues and I have encountered at least two Hispanic advocacy and service organizations that acknowledge that African Americans and Hispanics both suffer from racial profiling and cite this as a basis for mutual organizing efforts.[2] A representative of one of these groups reported that the organization has "some" relationship with African American civil rights leaders and politicians who "support our marches" for immigration reform and against local traffic roadblocks in which Hispanics are being racially profiled, ensnared in the judicial system, and eventually deported. This representative also reported that Project South, a social justice organization working to dismantle systems of poverty, racism, and violence while also building community power (see http://www.projectsouth.org/), has a "younger" African American membership that is "very open" to talking and working with Hispanic organizations in the area. Similarly, a representative of the second organization reported that local historically black colleges (such as Morehouse) are among the universities that send them student volunteers, and that the area's African American civil rights leadership "sometimes works with us when we do advocacy. And we could do more with them if we tried—it wouldn't be resisted [on their part]" (Jones-Correa et al. 2013; Atlanta fieldsite visit, March 1–4, 2013).

Research in North Carolina also shows signs of increased black-Hispanic coalition building among formal political and community leaders. Amexcan—the state-level umbrella group of Mexicans in North Carolina—has strengthened its activities partnering with African American community leaders and organizations over the past decade, working hard to bring more members of both communities together to discuss their common interests and goals. In January 2013, Amexcan cosponsored a Martin Luther King Jr. birthday dinner in Archer Bluff (a pseudonym for a small town in Bedford county, one of my two original fieldsites from 2003 to 2004), in conjunction with the Opportunities Industrialization Center and Eastern North Carolina Latin-American Coalition. Just a few months earlier, Amexcan also convened a networking breakfast in Archer Bluff to help identify and discuss local Hispanics' needs in a public setting. Prominent invited guests and attendees included an African American Democrat in the U.S. House of Representatives, an African American Democrat in the North Carolina Senate, and an African American Democrat on the Archer Bluff City Council. And, on August 28, 2013, Amexcan organized still another special event in honor of Martin Luther King Jr. on the fiftieth anniversary of his "I Have a Dream" speech at the March on Washington.

To be sure, Amexcan has long worked to build coalitions with local and state African American organizations. Back in 2002, it had started sponsoring a Hispanic Leadership Course at Wilcox County Community College (in the second of my two original fieldsites) that was modeled on a similar course designed by the Wilcox County Center for Leadership Development to promote African American civic engagement. In 2003, Amexcan had also begun engaging in coalition building to promote long-term voter registration and education projects with the North Carolina Coalition on Black and Brown Civic Participation, a state-level subsidiary of the National Coalition on Black Civic Participation. But Amexcan's present efforts and activities cannot be viewed simply as expansions of those that preceded them. Its new workshops, meetings, and public demonstrations represent a serious and intentional ramping up of earlier efforts. And they are now taking place in parts of the state where the Hispanic population is relatively small and where I had documented very little formal interminority collaboration back in 2003 (Marrow 2011).

It is also notable that local, state, and even national African American politicians are now taking a more prominent and visible role in interminority coalitions. Back in 2003 only one Bedford county commissioner had mentioned black-Hispanic coalition building to me, and even then only to report that it was "on the agenda" of the county chapter of the NAACP. Fast

forward to a local newspaper writeup of Amexcan's networking breakfast in
2012, where one national African American congressperson specifically
highlighted a budding commonality between black and Hispanic *leaders*,
contrasting this relationship with different sentiments among whites as well
as both minority groups' respective nonelite constituencies: "We are a plu-
ralistic society and those of us in leadership understand the value of that,
[even though] there are a lot in the community that do not. . . . Let's come
together and stay together and work together" (*Archer Bluff Times* [a pseud-
onym], October 20, 2012).

Farther south in the United States, so too do Kim Williams and Lonnie
Hannon (2016: 146) find that Alabama's restrictive omnibus House Bill 56,
passed in 2011, served as a "turning point" that shifted the views of African
American civic and political leaders toward supporting immigrants and
viewing immigration as a civil rights issue when they had not done so before.
Williams and Hannon find that African American civic and political elites
in Birmingham back in 2007 felt little stake in the immigration debate
raging in Washington, DC; on balance, such elites "did not readily connect
the movement for immigrant rights with the state's ugly racial past" and its
historical fight to end Jim Crow laws. Several even argued the comparison
was "inappropriate" and "not respectful" (148–149).

But once Alabama state legislators—most of them white Republicans—
began targeting immigrants at the local level in 2010 and 2011, some of the
same black elites began to recognize immigration as more centrally connected to their own group's civil rights history and struggle. In follow-up
interviews in 2013, Williams and Hannon found that while black politicians
had not retreated entirely from their earlier position that African Americans
are descendants of involuntary slaves and therefore differ from Hispanic
immigrants in Alabama who are largely voluntary labor migrants, they now
exhibited a salient move to the left and had begun to "see the link" between
immigrant and civil rights. One respondent who had remarked that immigrant rights and civil rights were "totally different struggles" in 2007 reported
seeing a "loose connection" between them by 2013 (Williams and Hannon
2016: 148), particularly in relation to law enforcement. Consistent with my
argument and Rodríguez's hypothesis, Williams and Hannon argue that *immigrant marginalization*, not necessarily a broader perceived analogy between
immigrants and blacks, lies behind the shift. They point out that even though
black elites are often still scarce at immigrants' rights rallies in Alabama, such
elites have now symbolically and substantively opened the doors of the most
hallowed civil rights venues to immigrants, such that the overall balance of
interminority relations in Alabama now tips toward cooperation.

Additional evidence from Georgia, North Carolina, Florida, and Louisiana
(see Alvarado and Jaret 2009; Fussell 2010; Jones 2012; Stuesse, Odem, and
Lacy 2009) supports my claim that the intensification of black-Hispanic

cooperation at the upper echelons of regional politics and civic society may be occurring regionwide. It could even be occurring nationwide, although such a possibility is beyond the scope of this chapter. Kim Williams (2016) shows that national black public opinion toward immigration improved substantially after 2007, even among working-class blacks and even during a massive economic recession. In recent opinion polls, blacks have reported Hispanics to be the most discriminated against group in America and also expressed their deep dissatisfaction with the U.S. government's treatment of immigrants. So while Williams argues that African Americans may still feel ambivalent or economically threatened about immigration, especially if they continue to see blacks as discriminated against (see also Wilkinson and Bingham 2016), she argues that their feelings are now moderated not only by changing mass perceptions of how Hispanics and immigrants are treated, but also by a substantial shift in the tone and stance of national black political elites and organizations since the late 2000s. Today, Williams (2016: 254) describes a new "unified strategic message" from national black elites who refer to immigrant rights as civil rights and send out influential elite cues calling for a path to citizenship for undocumented immigrants, rejecting a states' rights approach to immigration, and arguing that exploiting immigrants is not in blacks' economic interest.

Of course, the evidence is more complex than these examples suggest. There are still plenty of fissures and internal arguments between black and Hispanic politicians and activists (see Alvarado and Jaret 2009; McDermott 2011), even ones engaged in interminority coalitions. And, according to a representative of one of the Hispanic advocacy and service organizations we spoke to in Atlanta, restriction and enforcement there have put so many Hispanics in such an "extreme position of vulnerability" that they feel physically unable to "give anything back" to African American civil rights organizations. This has resulted in a loss of collaborative opportunity, even though this organization is theoretically open to coalition building (Jones-Correa et al. 2013; Atlanta fieldsite visit, March 1–4, 2013).

Yet despite such complexities I agree with Rodríguez (2012) and Jennifer A. Jones (2012) that an important shift appears to be underfoot, one in which increased immigration enforcement coupled with heightened anti-immigrant sentiment and policy making is promoting greater feelings of solidarity and closeness between Hispanic and African American politicians and activists. To appreciate the full extent of this change, consider the political situation of Hispanics in Georgia back in 2002. There, African American legislators defeated a bill supported by the governor that would have broadened the state's minority designation to include Hispanics and allowed Hispanics to be included in tax breaks for companies that hire minority contractors. A member of the state's Legislative Black Caucus drew clear symbolic and material lines between African Americans and Hispanic newcomers during that debate, replying: "We are not comfortable amending laws that originally were passed to aid racial minorities, such as African Americans and Native Americans who have a long history of being discriminated against" (Glanton 2001; see also Schmid 2003). Only after continued discussion did Hispanics/Latinos get recognized as an official racial minority group in Georgia.

African Americans' hesitancy to see Hispanics as a parallel racial minority at that time may seem surprising from today's vantage point. Over the past decade, African American politicians and activists have increasingly shown signs of acknowledging and supporting Hispanics, both in word and action. In 2011, several prominent African American leaders in Alabama vigorously criticized the omnibus House Bill 56 as a vestige of the state's racist history against African Americans (WBRC 2011, quoted in Rodríguez 2012).[3] In 2008, Juan LaFonta, an African American–Creole representative from New Orleans in the Louisiana State House, reported that "all these arguments they're making against Hispanic folks are the ones they did against black people. That's not right" (quoted in Fussell 2010). Ten of the twenty-eight Democratic cosponsors of North Carolina's House Bill 1183 in 2005—a bill that would have granted in-state UNC-system tuition to the children of unauthorized immigrants, but ultimately failed—were African Americans (Luebke 2011). In Georgia, African American state legislators overwhelmingly voted against both the omnibus Senate Bill 529 in 2006 and the omnibus House Bill 87 in 2011 (Browne and Odem 2012). In a symbolic show of support, Reverend Joseph Lowery, a former lieutenant to Martin Luther King Jr., stated that "though we [African Americans and Hispanics] may have come over on different ships, we're all in the same damn boat now" (Lovato 2008; quoted in Lippard and Gallagher 2011). Indeed, Browne et al. (2013) show that between 2005 and 2012, African American Democratic legislators throughout the South were significantly less likely than white legislators of either party to support their state's restrictive immigration policies. They voted less anti-immigrant in every policy arena except health, and most strongly so in the two arenas most central to black civil rights: voting and law enforcement.

In sum, more African American political and civic elites appear today to perceive Hispanics as "getting treated like Black people used to get treated" (Alvarado and Jaret 2009: 30). Conversely, more Hispanic politicians and activists appear to be making use of African American civil rights–inspired groups, organizations, and institutions as their symbolic "proximate hosts" (Mittelberg and Waters 1992) and material "role models" (Waters, Kasinitz, and Asad 2014) for fighting what they see as intensifying racialized anti-immigrant discrimination. The heightened presence of prominent African American political and community leaders in Amexcan's recent breakfast workshop in Archer Bluff demonstrates this. African Americans are still a numerical and political majority in Bedford County, and so have little strategic need to ally with Hispanic newcomers compared to African Americans living in places where both they and Hispanics are in the minority (Marrow 2011). Today, their elites are doing so *despite* demographic and political insulation.

Unsettled Boundaries: Nonelites in Everyday Life

While I see convincing evidence of increased solidarity and coalition building among African American and Hispanic political and civic elites, when we turn to intergroup relations among nonelites outside these domains, a less certain picture emerges. Some new research finds that immigration enforcement and anti-immigrant sentiment and policy making have indeed contributed to budding comity and empathy between African Americans and Hispanic newcomers in workplaces, neighborhoods, religious institutions, and public spaces across the region. For example, Jones (2012: 71) argues that both Afro-Mexican and mestizo-Mexican immigrants in Winston Salem, North Carolina, have come to feel more strongly targeted and racialized as minority "others" since the "severe backlash" of the late 2000s, due to increased institutional discrimination by law enforcement and other governmental institutions. In turn, they have come to identify more strongly with local African Americans, whom they see treated as "second-class citizens" by whites (63) and whose experiences serve as their most immediate and proximate set of symbols, cues, and discourses in that area.

While these Mexican immigrants do not all necessarily identify as blacks themselves, immigration enforcement has clearly heightened their perceptions of discrimination by both legal status and race, and thereby contributed to their development of a stronger identity as racial minorities in North Carolina. Jones argues these immigrants also now speak of—in stark contrast to what I uncovered in the early 2000s (Marrow 2011: 73)—a more open reception by, and general sense of closeness with, blacks than whites. In this way, these immigrants' intensifying experiences of discrimination appear to be serving as a new foundation for intergroup understanding, sympathy, and identification with African Americans in Winston Salem.

Other scholars also find evidence of positive relations between Hispanic newcomers and African Americans in a variety of low-wage southern workplaces. In New Orleans, African American construction workers, even as they perceive some economic threat from Hispanic newcomers, sometimes temper it with memories of their own racial history. One construction worker interviewed for Elizabeth Fussell's (2010: 29) research drew a formative parallel, envisioning his Hispanic coworkers as new "slaves": "When I talk to the ones who are my friends, I tell them . . . 'Stop working for fucking nothing. Stop working like fucking slaves.'" Recalling African Americans' own history of racialized exploitation in the construction industry helps this man to resist the temptation to scapegoat his Hispanic coworkers when he

feels economically pressured. Similarly, in rural Mississippi's poultry processing plants, Angela Stuesse, Mary Odem, and Elaine Lacy (2009; see also
Stuesse 2016) found that some African American production lineworkers,
instead of blaming Hispanic coworkers for putting pressure on their salaries
or weakening their attempts at organizing around workplace issues, sometimes drew sympathetic parallels between the problems their Hispanic
coworkers face today and the conditions that gave rise to the civil rights
movement: "They's where we was at fifty years ago before we even knew our
rights." In Memphis as well, Barbara Ellen Smith (2009: 102) documented
Hispanic and African American warehousing and construction workers
voicing a sense of shared status when they saw both groups being treated
poorly by white bosses.

However, other evidence from studies of intergroup relations, public
opinion, and racial attitudes points to simmering tensions between African
Americans and Hispanics in southern workplaces, neighborhoods, and
public spaces. In Monica McDermott's (2011) ethnography of all three
domains in Greenville, South Carolina, which she conducted in 2005–2006,
lower-middle-class African Americans were often enthusiastic about
befriending Hispanics, learning more about their language and cultures,
and in some cases actively standing up for them at work and in their neighborhoods. But they were the exception. In contrast, working-class and
upper-middle-class African Americans demonstrated patterns of quiet hostility, subtle disrespect, passive resistance and resentment, and active avoidance toward Hispanic newcomers—patterns McDermott explains via
differential forms of threat: individual economic threat among the former
and collective cultural threat among the latter. For their part, the Hispanic
community also appeared distant from the black community in day-to-day
life. Most importantly, the initial confusion, curiosity, and uncertainty that
McDermott documented Hispanics provoking among natives in South Carolina prior to 2006 morphed into more tangible resentment by the end of
2006—the year ramped-up immigration enforcement triggered immigrants'
rights marches nationwide—especially among whites but also among some
blacks. Consequently, a group once diffusely considered "foreigners in need
of assistance" became overtly racialized as "Mexicans" or "illegals" who are
"economic threats" (McDermott n.d.).

This profound change may be significant for the future of the southern
color line. Prior to 2006, McDermott's (n.d.) data match my own (Marrow
2011), when she writes that whites' "comparisons between Hispanics and
blacks were almost entirely favorable to Hispanics." But after the immigrants' rights marches of 2006, whites' comments have more typically drawn
parallels between blacks and Hispanics, such as when a white man commented that they both "do what they want" and break the law, or when
whites have even compared Hispanics *negatively* to African Americans

(McDermott n.d.). To the extent that whites' new attitudes might endure, and that Hispanic newcomers and blacks might perceive a shared experience of discrimination, this may indeed signal a breaking in a prior black-nonblack color line in Greenville.

However, McDermott's fieldwork includes examples of Hispanics reacting to the new tense climate by withdrawing from their social interactions not just with local whites, but also local African Americans, in anticipation of potentially negative reactions from both. Moreover, her writing includes several examples of blacks—not just whites—feeling uncomfortable around, disrespecting and resisting, and generally viewing Hispanics as more "problematic" now that native resentment has intensified against them since 2006. Thus, there is also the possibility that Hispanic newcomers are becoming more strongly excluded from *both* the local white and black communities in Greenville—at least in the first immigrant generation, since McDermott's findings are more promising regarding South Carolinians' acceptance of the second generation.

In a separate domain of health care, Natalia Deeb-Sossa (2013) uncovered a painful picture of black-Hispanic tensions in one North Carolina community health clinic in the mid-2000s, among workers and between workers and clientele. Lower-status African American workers acted as gatekeepers against Hispanic clients, constructed them as unworthy people and "bad" parents who "abuse the system," and contributed to differential access to the clinic and health care outcomes. Lower-status African American workers also made use of seniority to withhold training and expertise from their Hispanic coworkers, acted in an authoritarian and dismissive way toward them, and labeled them lazy and less capable workers. In contrast, at the top ranks of the clinic, Deeb-Sossa documented both white and Hispanic providers constructing Hispanic patients as the "neediest of the needy," and positioning themselves as special defenders and protectors of this group (including vis-à-vis African Americans). While moments of conflict and perceived discrimination did emerge between the white and Hispanic workers, the clear take-away was that tensions and processes of "defensive othering" were by far most prevalent between African Americans and Hispanics.

Even the studies cited above that document interminority cooperation often include simultaneous evidence of tensions, albeit for different reasons. In Mississippi, Stuesse (2009) shows that many African American poultry-processing workers also made negative comments about and expressed resentment toward Hispanic coworkers, whom they perceived as too willing to work for low wages and as whites' preferred workers (see also Fussell 2010). In return, Hispanic workers expressed anti-black and anti-indigenous racism that Stuesse reports seriously challenged crossracial organizing efforts. She argues that they read African Americans' forms of workplace resistance (such as production slowdowns or taking long breaks) out of context as inherent laziness, and that they felt African Americans do not experience workplace discrimination and "are living in different worlds" from themselves, whom they perceived as the new and authentically exploited class of workers, largely due to their vulnerabilities in immigration and legal status. Altogether, Stuesse (2009: 100–103) argues, these antagonistic discourses were further promoted by industry practices that worked to obscure workers' abilities to find linkages in common experiences.

Similarly, Hispanic workers in Memphis perceived their position and vulnerability due to their precarious immigration and legal statuses as setting them apart from, not linking them to, their African American coworkers. Smith (2009) goes on to detail multiple tensions between the two groups that arose over the pace and intensity of work effort, language differences and struggles to communicate during the workday, and lack of knowledge of each other's structural histories. Smith is careful to qualify that some black workers' disdainful stance toward immigrants was "not one of superordinate or exclusionary claim to the available local jobs and other resources" like some white workers they interviewed, but rather stemmed from "the historical context of their own racial exclusion and exploitation" (313). This interpretation melds well with those of other scholars studying black-Hispanic relations. In New Orleans, African Americans' views of Hispanics in the late 2000s were not hostile overall (Wilkinson and Bingham n.d.). Rather, to the extent some did express negative feelings toward or about Hispanics, it was largely because they continue to feel racially subordinated vis-à-vis whites (see also Wilkinson and Bingham 2016, in a national analysis).

In her ethnography of intergroup relations on a North Carolina food-processing production line in 2009 to 2010, Vanessa Ribas (2016) expands on this explanation. She too draws on Lawrence Bobo and Vincent L. Hutchings's (1996) concept of *racial alienation* to explain tensions between African American and Hispanic workers. Defined as the degree to which group members feel oppressed or aggrieved, and produced by racial subordination, racial alienation is theorized to heighten the competitive threat that one group feels toward another, particularly when it perceives the other group as having (or shortly to have) higher status. In the aforementioned studies, some African Americans' continued feelings of racial alienation in various parts of the South do appear to undergird a sense of competitive threat from incoming Hispanics, even as other African Americans express more positive views, as some of their stances are empathetic and supportive (see McDermott 2011). But Ribas also argues, in line with Stuesse (2009), that Hispanic immigrants in this poultry plant feel that they, and *not* African Americans, are now the most oppressed and exploited group, due to their precarious immigration and legal statuses and intensifying immigration enforcement. Indeed, they feel they are in a position of relative disadvantage vis-a-vis African Americans, whom they see located farther up the hierarchy because they have greater rights.[4] These Hispanic immigrants perceive that African Americans get better positions in the plant, are treated more leniently and with greater preference by their supervisors and managers, and like to demean and "humiliate" Hispanics. Drawing on anti-black ideologies from their home countries plus racializing language they pick up from coworkers and neighbors in North Carolina, Ribas argues that Central American immigrants come to project such frustrations and racialized resentment *out onto* African Americans, rather than feeling competitively threatened by them.

In contrast, Ribas argues that the African American workers exhibit much less negative boundary work against Hispanics; they tend to talk about workplace disputes, language obstacles, and perceived slights by Hispanic coworkers in individual-level terms rather than the highly racialized group-level language that Hispanics use about them. While Ribas speculates that African American lineworkers probably do feel a strong degree of racial alienation vis-à-vis whites, she suspects that some may tacitly understand why many Hispanics now feel located in an inferior position to African Americans within this specific workplace context. And she argues that they apparently do not feel sufficiently aggrieved to contest their racialization in group terms against Hispanics—although McDermott's (2011; n.d.) research suggests that they do, just in segregated settings where they feel safe enough that they can, and where observational techniques deployed only in one shared workplace setting could fail to pick it up.

A pattern of simmering and perhaps even hardening negative black-Hispanic relations among nonelites also shows up in some public opinion surveys. In Durham, North Carolina, in the early 2000s, Paula D. McClain and colleagues uncovered a stronger perception of economic threat from Hispanic immigration among blacks than among whites (see also Vallas and Zimmerman 2007 for similar results in Virginia). They found that this pattern was intensified when African Americans held negative stereotypes of Hispanics, yet moderated when African Americans displayed a strong sense of group identity and linked fate with other blacks. In the other direction, McClain and colleagues (2006) found that Hispanics in Durham held more negative stereotypes of African Americans than African Americans held of Hispanics, and that Hispanics reported having more in common with whites than with blacks (a feeling whites did not reciprocate). Interviews with political and community elites added to this negative picture. One African American elected official spoke of his constituents not liking Mexicans, and other social services and community leaders talked of hearing complaints among their clientele about perceived job competition, perceived involuntary contact, and language difficulties with new immigrants (McClain et al. 2003).

Replicating their survey in Durham in 2007, and further extending it into Memphis, Tennessee, and Little Rock, Arkansas, McClain and colleagues (2011) later found that African Americans in all three cities perceived both economic and political threats from Hispanic immigration, whereas whites in all three cities perceived just political threat. The researchers also found that Hispanics in all three cities generally evaluated their relations with African Americans much more negatively than African Americans evaluated their relations with Hispanics. Most importantly, they suggest that something had "soured" in terms of Hispanics' perceptions of their relations with African Americans in Durham between 2003 and 2007, precisely the period when anti-immigrant sentiment and enforcement began to intensify. Whereas only a third of Hispanics (31.5 percent) saw their relations with African Americans as very or somewhat negative in 2003, almost half (45.3 percent) did so in 2007; conversely, whereas half (50.9 percent) of Hispanics thought that relations with African Americans were either somewhat or very positive in 2003, only 23 percent did so in 2007 (229–230). Finally, Hispanics in all three cities evaluated their relations with whites as better than their relations with African Americans. Hispanics' and whites' evaluations of their relations with each other in Durham even improved slightly between 2003 and 2007.

In sum, it is unclear whether immigration enforcement and restrictive policy making have contributed to growing interminority solidarity and coalition building among nonelite black and Hispanic southerners over the past decade—at least not in the same way or not to the same degree it appears to have done among political and civic elites. Some studies of intergroup relations do give reason to think immigration policies might have engendered new feelings of interminority solidarity, but others suggest the opposite, and still others suggest the continuing coexistence of solidarity and division. Studies of public opinion are likewise divided. While McClain and colleagues (2013) suggest that interminority tensions in the South may have even increased, recall that Williams (2016) shows evidence of national black public opinion toward Hispanics and immigrants *improving* in recent years, possibly because more African Americans are following their elites' shifting supportive cues. Still other studies suggest that anti-immigrant sentiment is not significantly associated with being black at all (O'Neil and Tienda 2010), but rather with being white and culturally and politically conservative (Chavez and Provine 2009; Ramakrishnan and Wong 2010; Vallas, Zimmerman, and Davis 2009; Weise 2012).

Conclusion

Recently, sociologist Herbert Gans (2012) has argued that the American color line is best described, at least for now and for the country as a whole, as a tripartite one consisting of whites and light-skinned Asians and Hispanics at the top; African Americans and others perceived by whites as black (including some Caribbeans and Hispanics) at the bottom; and a heterogeneous stratum of "non-white-but-non-black" Americans in the middle (see also Bonilla-Silva 2004). But Gans (2012: 271–272) also notes that African Americans most clearly made up the lowest strata *before* the "intense demonization of unauthorized Mexican immigrants began," and that "no single nationwide racial hierarchy exists that fits all regions of the country" because "positions in the hierarchy differ somewhat between regions." These qualifiers point to the tentative nature of any attempt to predict the future of the American color line, whether across geographic space or historical time. They also highlight the importance of the intense anti-immigrant backlash since 2005 (Marrow 2011: 231–266), particularly as it may be changing the relative standing of, and relations between, African Americans and Hispanics.

In this chapter, I have attempted to highlight the additional importance of *level* (e.g., elite versus nonelite) and *institutional domain* (e.g., politics and civic leadership versus workplaces, neighborhoods, and public spaces) of analysis. Retaining my primary focus on intergroup relations in the South—which is just one element, albeit a central one, in the larger study of racial boundary making and change[5]—I have shown that intergroup relations in the South are context dependent not only across geographic space and time, but also level and institutional domain.

Among political and civic elites, an important and substantive change appears to have occurred over the past decade. African American political and civic leaders have increasingly come to see and support Hispanic newcomers as parallel racial minorities, in part because intensifying anti-immigrant opinion and immigration enforcement have put Hispanics in such a weakened position that these African American political elites more clearly recognize them to be discriminated against, both interpersonally and structurally. In the other direction, Hispanic leaders and activists have increasingly come to view and accept African Americans as their political proximal hosts—looking to their civil rights history as a symbolic role model and instrumental source of strategies, tactics, and resources as they work to improve their declining condition. These trends suggest a fraying of the black-nonblack color line I found so much evidence to support in the early 2000s. And perhaps they even signal the emergence of a white-nonwhite color line at this level and in these domains today—one that is increasingly uniting black and Hispanic political elites and activists in feelings of intergroup solidarity, not just material conditions and treatment.

In contrast, down at the level of everyday life among nonelites in southern workplaces, neighborhoods, or public spaces, I argue that the overall state of intergroup relations appears messier, and its implications for the state of the color line are still unclear. Some research uncovers patterns not dissimilar from those I see occurring in elite politics and civil society, and may also suggest a new shift toward a white-nonwhite, or perhaps even tri-racial, color line. But other research continues to document ongoing black-Hispanic tensions, some of which are perhaps growing worse. And all too often, the same black political and civic elites who are actively engaged in coalition building openly admit that interminority tensions are more prevalent among their nonelite constituencies (see Alvarado and Jaret 2009; McClain et al. 2003; Williams and Hannon 2016). Indeed, some of these political and civic elites view such tensions as their raison d'être, in that their very existence provides the rationale for elite leaders' efforts to work to counteract them.

Thus, despite complex and at times contentious white-Hispanic relations, I argue that a cohesive sense and collective feeling of togetherness among African Americans and Hispanic newcomers at the nonelite levels of everyday southern society has not yet solidified. Perhaps in these domains immigration enforcement has had the primary effect of pushing Hispanics inward for survival and self-protection, lessening their contact with African Americans and reducing their potential to see African Americans as cooperative parallel minorities along the way (Rodríguez 2012). Or perhaps Hispanic newcomers' recognition of greater discrimination due to immigration enforcement has led them, instead of relating more closely to African Americans, to feel even more deprived relative to them, and thus more inclined to distance away from them to protect their own group (Uhlaner 1991).

Either way, the current bifurcation by level and domain suggests that there may well be several color *lines* still emerging and transforming in the contemporary U.S. South. The rigid and longstanding hierarchy between whites and blacks remains strong and tangible. But the relational as well as material place of Hispanic newcomers may indeed be moving closer to that of African Americans in some ways, perhaps staying closer relationally to that of whites in others (see Marrow 2011; Randall and Delbridge 2005); or, perhaps as McDermott's (n.d.) research suggests, coming to occupy a position even more ostracized and marginal, at least in the first, if not the later, generations. Some African American and Hispanic leaders and activists may well come together and begin to see more common cause in politics and community events, just as some African American nonelites may develop greater comity and begin to empathize more strongly with their Hispanic coworkers' and neighbors' plights. Alternatively, immigration enforcement may cultivate a sharper sense of relative deprivation among Hispanics as a group, which they may in turn project out onto African Americans in negative ways (Ribas 2016). From the other side, perhaps African American residents, despite coming into greater contact and connecting with Hispanics in some ways, may continue to feel a sense of unique historical deprivation as descendants of slaves and the South's great historical other, which may contribute to continued separation.[6] Perhaps these may all even occur simultaneously, such that rising anti-immigration sentiment, restrictive policymaking, and immigration enforcement may ultimately intensify trends toward both interminority cooperation *and* tension (see Jones-Correa 2011), just in varying combinations, depending on the time, place, level, and institutional domain.

As we await president-elect Donald Trump's inauguration, few scholars expect an alternative to continuing and deepening restriction. But one important question looking forward is what might happen to these trends if Congress ever passes a new immigration reform bill including provisions for unauthorized immigrants to legalize their status, or if immigration enforcement and policing subside in other ways. In new immigrant destinations, Dina Okamoto and Kim Ebert (2010) find that immigrants' political activity is reactive; immigrants mobilize largely in response to immediate threats, whereas immigrants in traditional gateways are more likely to mobilize in response to long-term political opportunities. Given the current context, it may not be surprising that we see southern African American and Hispanic political elites "reacting" and coming together today. But if threats to their status subside, might Hispanic elites stop looking to African Americans for political alliance, if such an alliance is no longer deemed necessary? Or might Hispanics possibly strengthen their relations with African Americans as they become a more central part of American society? Similarly, among nonelites, what new forms of collaboration and tension might arise between African Americans and Hispanics as legalization could potentially change the landscape of workplaces, neighborhoods, public services, and public spaces? Might some African Americans feel more threatened and anxious at the prospect of a new group becoming more formally incorporated? Or might legalization help to dismantle some of the structural features that create intergroup competition between them in the first place?

A second important question is how the trends among these two different levels may influence each other going forward, particularly in the elite-to-nonelite direction. Williams (2016) rightly notes that elite cue are considered to wield most influence over mass public opinion when the public is politically aware, when the issue at hand is complex, when elites express preferences already in line with the masses' worldviews, and when elites present a unified front in their messaging. Not only is immigration an extremely complex policy issue that generates substantial ambivalence and contradiction, opening up substantial room for elite cues to shape mass opinion, but, according to Williams, all four of the above conditions were also satisfied between 2006 and 2013 in Alabama as black leaders and institutions moved significantly to the left on the issue immigration. Thus, while we still see divided opinions and some tensions among nonelite black and Hispanic southerners, perhaps the new cooperative shift among their elite counterparts may engender more cooperation and greater affinity at the nonelite level in the near future, as elite cues and messaging filter down.[7] We wait and see.

NOTES

Acknowlegments: I thank Asad Asad, Bart Bonikowski, Natasha Kumar Warikoo, Monica McDermott, Vanesa Ribas, Nestor Rodríguez, Cinzia Solari, Angela Stuesse, Kim Williams, and the conference participants and volume editors for their careful readings and helpful comments.

1. Zamora (2016) argues that Mexicans who have never migrated to the United States learn anti-black stereotypes via *interactions* between anti-black messages already prevalent in Mexican society and media and anti-black stereotypes that get remitted home to them via their migrant friends and family members.

2. In this project, we are combining data from a representative survey of 2,000 U.S.-born whites, U.S.-born blacks, Mexican immigrants, and Asian Indian immigrants with follow-up interviews and observations. Our main goal is to investigate the impact of ethnic diversity on civic life in twenty-first-century America, particularly how intergroup contact in different social and institutional spaces may enhance or inhibit trust and civic engagement.

3. Rodríguez notes that the views of nonelite African American residents of Alabama regarding the new restrictive law "have yet to be assessed" (31).

4. Ribas argues that to the extent that these greater rights exist, it is because African Americans are U.S.-born citizens. However, her Hispanic respondents convey these rights in racialized terms—as advantages that accrue to being black.

5. According to Fox and Guglielmo (2013), to assess the properties of racial boundaries it is important to analyze the extent to which such boundaries are *recognized* and *institutionalized* by state and nonstate actors, as well as the extent to which such boundaries are deemed consequential in terms of *social closure* (i.e., how they are related to individuals' life chances and the accessibility of material and symbolic resources) and *social distance* (i.e., how they are related to individuals' subjective state of "nearness" to—as distinguished from physical contact or frequency of contact with—others).

6. Stuesse, Cheryl Staats, and Andrew Grant-Thomas (forthcoming) uncover several examples of coalition-building organizations that draw parallels between contemporary immigrants' migration histories and African Americans' twentieth-century migrations from the U.S. South to the U.S. North or West, as a mechanism to generate intergroup empathy. A separate parallel with African Americans' original trips to the United States as involuntary slaves or indentured servants is harder, though not impossible, to make, particularly for blacks who never out-migrated from the South.

7. Of course, if enforcement and restriction continue to take their toll on Hispanic advocacy and service organizations, as they have done in Atlanta, perhaps African American elites and organizations may have greater capacity to influence their constituencies' attitudes and behaviors than Hispanic elites and organizations may have on theirs.

III

New Destination Locales within Traditional Destination Countries

5

The Politics of Place

The Impact of Local Contexts in Immigrant Voting

CLAUDIO A. HOLZNER
MELISSA M. GOLDSMITH

Part III of this volume continues the regional focus of Parts I and II while turning its attention to new destination locales within traditional destination countries. Claudio A. Holzner and Melissa M. Goldsmith's chapter returns to the question of immigrants' political incorporation addressed by Dobbs in Chapter 1. It examines more broadly the conditions for political incorporation in municipalities of different sizes in a new destination American state, Utah. Through an analysis of several levels of data, they make the case that immigrants' local political experience can be a critical driver of the voter turnout of foreign-born citizens in presidential elections. While some might expect that small, rural new destinations would be isolating for immigrants, the authors instead find greater immigrant electoral participation in smaller cities, thus suggesting that these settings are not inherently demobilizing.

L ocal politics was vitally important for the political mobilization and incorporation of millions of European immigrants who arrived in the United States during the early part of the last century. The vast majority of these immigrants settled in urban areas, where they were mobilized by local party organizations and bosses, given assistance with naturalization and registration, and asked to vote in local and national elections (Wong 2006). The United States is now in the midst of a second great wave of immigration. Since 1990, more than twenty million new immigrants have arrived in the United States, raising the percentage of the foreign-born population to 13 percent in 2010—its highest level since the 1930s (U.S. Census Bureau 2010). One of the key features of this second wave of immigration is the dispersion of immigrants to states, cities, and towns with little or no prior history of international immigration. Although the country's six traditional receiving states—California, Florida, Illinois, New Jersey, New York, and Texas—continue to attract the most immigrants, the rate of growth of immigrant populations in states like Georgia, North Carolina, Tennessee, Nevada, and Utah is three to five times higher than the national average. Immigrants are also settling outside of the traditional metropolitan gateway cities like Los Angeles, New York, Miami, and Chicago and moving directly to new metropolitan gateways, to suburbs, and even to small towns and rural areas (Fortuny, Chaudry, and Jargowsky 2010; Hardwick 2008; Marrow 2011; Singer 2008).[1]

What impact do these demographic shifts have on the political engagement of immigrants? Does settling in smaller cities with weak party structures and fewer immigrants affect voter turnout? The dispersion of immigrants to new destination cities creates opportunities to deepen our understanding of how city-level variables affect the political behavior of immigrants (Marrow 2005). After all, immigrant political incorporation has long been a function of cities and local-level political institutions, which often provide immigrants and naturalized citizens their primary point of contact with U.S. government (DeSipio 2001). However, the current literature has failed to exploit this diversity of settlement contexts. Much of the early research on immigrant political behavior and incorporation emphasized the importance of immigrant specific factors, such as length of residence, education, and language skills, which fail to consider the possible effects of place. More recent studies have explored the powerful role that place-based political opportunities and constraints play in channeling immigrants in or out of the political process (Hochschild and Mollenkopf 2009c). However, the focus of these studies has been on national and state-level contexts. More needs to be done to understand how local contexts and institutions shape immigrants' political experiences, their political socialization, and ultimately their political behavior.[2]

A number of important studies have explored how features of cities affect the political behavior of immigrants. But the focus of this literature has been almost exclusively on traditional gateway cities like New York, Los Angeles, and Miami (de la Garza, Menchaca, and DeSipio 1994; Jones-Correa 1998a, 2001a; Lien, Conway, and Wong 2004; Mollenkopf, Olson, and Ross 2001; Mollenkopf and Sonenshein 2009; Ramakrishnan and Bloemraad 2008a; Wong 2006). This scholarship has identified a number of features of local contexts that have a positive effect on immigrant turnout, such as large concentrations of coethnics (Barreto, Segura, and Woods 2004; Gordon 1970; Ramakrishnan and Espenshade 2001), minority candidates in top-of-the-ticket elections (Barreto 2007), and a density of mobilizing resources such as

Spanish-language media and immigrant service organizations (Ayón 2006; Wong 2006). However, these supporting structures rarely exist in new immigrant cities. In these places, immigration is so recent that most immigrants are not yet citizens, so local and national-level campaigns or parties almost completely ignore the immigrant vote.[3] Other mobilizing resources, such as community organizations and the Spanish-language media, are also much weaker and fragmented. What if the places where immigrants settle exclude them from politics? Will this make them less likely to participate in national elections and slow down their incorporation into the broader political system?

To begin answering these questions, we analyze the impact that local politics has on the voting behavior of naturalized citizens in Utah, a new immigrant destination that has had one of the fastest growing immigrant populations in the country since 1990. While much of the literature on new destinations has focused on the American South, Utah deserves further attention, in part because the state has proposed some innovative legislative responses to addressing unauthorized immigration (Cook 2014). The state offers a unique opportunity for investigating new destination immigrant political incorporation, thanks to data the state collects on voting behavior, which allows us to identify naturalized voters and the cities where they live.

Cities and towns are important sites where immigrants learn about U.S. politics, gain experience with the political system, and begin the lengthy process of political incorporation. Although political theorists have long celebrated the power of local politics to create a democratic citizenry, enabling immigrants to acquire an interest in politics and learn democratic habits and skills (Barber 1984; Hamilton 1971; Pateman 1970), local contexts can also block the process of political incorporation if they fail to provide immigrants with meaningful opportunities to participate in politics. Therefore, we theorize that immigrants' political integration (or lack thereof) into the United States is directly related to their experiences with local political activity and local political institutions. Local-level institutions and political contexts that lower the costs of political participation and create opportunities for political engagement with local politics accelerate immigrant political integration, while contexts that discourage engagement with local politics delay it. We develop an explanation for immigrant voting behavior that combines insights from two different literatures: research on immigrant voting behavior and research on local turnout. Research on local turnout has found that contextual factors such as city size and the structure of municipal institutions, namely whether the executive is a professional manager or an elected mayor, matter a great deal for political participation at the local level. We propose that such local contexts also matter for turnout in national elections, but their effect on turnout is mediated by citizens' participatory resources: specifically how long they have lived in the United States and any experience with democratic politics prior to migrating. We also explore how experience with local politics—that is affiliating with a local party organization and voting in municipal elections—affects the likelihood that immigrants will vote in national elections.

We explore the relationship between local politics, immigrants' backgrounds, and voting using a unique dataset that combines official individual-level turnout data from Utah's Lieutenant Governor's Office with demographic data collected by the Utah Population Database (UPDB), and that is augmented with neighborhood- and city-level variables from the U.S. Census that allow us to estimate models of turnout for both native- and foreign-born citizens. The combination of individual-level and contextual information we collected gives us a powerful new resource with which to explore how city-level factors affect the political behavior of immigrant citizens.

Our results contribute new insights into the impact of place on immigrant voting behavior. First, we find that the place where immigrants settle matters for their political socialization and engagement. Immigrants' experiences participating in local politics are powerful predictors of voting in a national election. The participatory boost is much stronger for foreign-born citizens than for the native born, which suggests that immigrant political incorporation in the United States depends in large part on their experience with local political parties and elections. We also find that immigrants, particularly immigrants from authoritarian countries, are more sensitive to the impact of city size. While the size of a city has no effect on the turnout of native-born citizens in national elections, turnout among immigrants is highest in small- and medium-sized towns, suggesting that those places create the most welcoming environment for immigrant political incorporation. All in all, our analysis suggests that local politics in new immigrant destinations, particularly in smaller cities, can still serve as a pathway for immigrant political incorporation.

Local Politics and Immigrant Voting

Virtually all research that examines immigrant voting patterns has found that foreign-born citizens vote at lower rates than the native born (see, for example, Bass and Casper 1999; Jones-Correa 2001a). Most explanations of this pattern emphasize individual or immigrant-specific factors, such as income and education levels, English-language proficiency, and length of residence (Bass and Casper 2001; Bueker 2005; Marrow 2005; Ramakrishnan and Espenshade 2001). Whether an immigrant comes from an authoritarian country is another factor that influences the voting behavior of naturalized citizens.[4] A number of studies suggest that immigrants who come from a country with a long electoral history may have acquired meaningful political experiences with elections, campaigns, and political parties that facilitate their political incorporation into the United States. Once in the United

States, this prior democratic experience becomes a participatory resource that reduces the costs and increases the perceived benefits of voting (Bueker 2005; Wals 2011).

Though immigrant-specific factors are no doubt important, these explanations do not tell much about the process of immigrant political incorporation in new destination cities. Missing from these explanations is attention to immigrants' experiences with *local* politics. During the late nineteenth and early twentieth centuries, local political dynamics loomed large in the political incorporation experiences of immigrants. Political groups, parties, and urban machines needed immigrant votes and did their best to get them (Schier 2002; Wong 2006).[5] These early experiences fit the general expectation that local contexts serve as places where new citizens can learn about democratic politics and become empowered to participate in national elections. Indeed, immigrants' incorporation into their neighborhoods, towns, and cities happened before and was often a catalyst for political participation in national politics.

Political mobilization by parties and campaigns around election time is hugely important for political participation, particularly for the most resource-poor actors (Green, Gerber, and Nickerson 2003; Michelson 2003; Rosenstone and Hansen 2002). However, because immigrants vote less frequently than native-born citizens, political parties' interest in recruiting immigrants—even immigrants living in traditional immigrant gateways— has been limited in recent years (Andersen 2008; Jones-Correa 1998a; Wong 2006). This pattern is likely exacerbated in new gateways, where immigrant voters may be too few to attract the attention of political parties and campaigns, or whose inclusion might upset other core constituents. In addition, many new gateway communities in the Southeast and West are not located in battleground states, so national political parties and campaigns do not reach out to them during presidential elections. The result will be that immigrants settling in new immigrant destinations like Georgia, Utah, and Kentucky will find themselves on the periphery of the American political system (Wong 2006).

In the absence of mobilization by national party organizations and campaigns, perhaps immigrants' experiences with local politics can become a stepping-stone in the process of political incorporation. For recent arrivals, local politics may feel more accessible, less onerous, and more meaningful than voting in a national-level election. Even if they do not yet see themselves as "American" or feel like they have a stake in the outcome of national elections, or indeed even if they are not yet citizens, immigrants may care deeply about the quality of their schools, safety in their neighborhoods, clean parks, and other services that are under the control of local governments. The institutions of local communities such as schools, churches, and community and civic organizations provide additional arenas where immigrants can acquire civic skills, cultivate psychological engagement with politics, and become more likely targets for recruitment into politics (Verba, Schlozman, and Brady 1995; Wong 2006). City governments may be especially important, because they provide immigrants with meaningful opportunities for political participation even before they become naturalized citizens (Goldsmith and Holzner 2014). As DeSipio (2001: 88) points out: "It is these local governments and local political orders, often unconsciously, that train new citizens in how to participate and what to expect of American government and politics."

Thus, political experiences acquired locally can be catalysts for immigrant political incorporation. One such experience is voting in a prior municipal election, since any experience casting a ballot can be a powerful predictor of voting in subsequent ones (Niven 2004).[6] The majority of elections in the United States are held at the local level (Trounstine 2009), which means that local politics provides immigrants with many opportunities to practice democratic politics, have a voice in their local communities, and gain experience and confidence participating in the American political system. Moreover, compared to the national political system, local politics may offer immigrants relatively low-cost ways to become politically involved since local candidates, politicians, and government employees are often more familiar and accessible to residents (Hajnal and Lewis 2003; Trounstine 2010).

Another way immigrants can gain political experience is by affiliating with a local political party. Joining a party is often relatively easy to do and can lead to many new opportunities for political mobilization and participation.[7] Immigrants who have registered with a political party are more likely to be targeted for mobilization by campaigns and other political and civic organizations than immigrants who have not registered with a political party (Kaufmann and Rodriguez 2010). Moreover, the act of registering with a political party suggests that the individual has achieved a certain level of political engagement and a growing identification with the political system of the United States (Lien et al. 2001), two important predictors of political participation.

Yet, we should not underestimate the obstacles to political participation that can exist locally, particularly in new immigrant destinations. After all, turnout rates in local elections are about half that of national elections and have been declining for decades (Alford and Lee 1968; Bullock 1990; Caren 2007; Hajnal and Lewis 2003; Karnig and Walter 1983). The obstacles to local political engagement may be especially onerous in new immigrant gateways, since these places lack many of the conditions that are important for the political empowerment of immigrants (Goldsmith and Holzner 2014). Rapidly increasing racial, ethnic, and linguistic diversity in these destinations has also generated hostility against immigrants, often resulting in the passage of exclusionary anti-immigrant policies (Hopkins 2010).[8]

Which features of cities and towns matter most for foreign-born turnout in national elections? We test the effects of two city-level variables that the urban studies literature has shown to matter most for political participation: city size and the form of municipal government (Alford and Lee 1968; Bullock 1990; Caren 2007; Finifter and Abramson 1975; Hajnal and Lewis 2003; Karnig and Walter 1983; Kelleher and Lowery 2009; Oliver 2000). Because studies of immigrant turnout have focused almost exclusively on the country's largest metropolitan areas, it is unclear how city size affects immigrant voting behavior. One possibility is that larger metropolitan areas, because they have more immigrants, more mobilizational resources, and receive more attention by local and national get-out-the-vote campaigns, support higher levels of foreign-born turnout in local elections (Andersen, 2008; Kaufmann and Rodriguez 2010; Kelleher and Lowery 2009; Ramakrishnan and Bloemraad 2008b). Large urban centers with a long history as immigrant settlement sites also tend to have more immigrant and ethnic organizations that can serve as important nodes in mobilizing networks (Andersen 2008; Kaufmann and Rodriguez 2010). For Latino immigrants, the Spanish-language media has also proven to be a formidable mobilizing force for both local and national campaigns, providing Latino immigrants with valuable information and possibly also piquing their political interest (Ayón 2006).

On the other hand, large cities may discourage participation because they have more complex bureaucracies, greater spatial distance between city offices and citizens, and elected officials who represent more people (Oliver 2000). In contrast, residents of smaller towns are more likely to be familiar with candidates and local government officials, which makes gathering information about issues and candidates easier than in large cities. J. Eric Oliver also found that residents of smaller localities are more interested in local politics, are more likely to be asked to participate in political acts by friends and neighbors, and are much more likely to participate in a variety of nonelectoral civic activities than are people in large cities.[9] This kind of face-to-face recruitment may be particularly important for the political mobilization of the foreign born, who are often bypassed by traditional get-out-the-vote campaigns (Marrow 2005; Michelson 2003; Niven 2004; Wong 2006).

Local political institutions also shape the opportunities and costs of participation. Numerous studies have linked council-manager forms of local government, in which managers are appointed by the city council rather than elected by voters, with lower turnout in local elections (Alford and Lee 1968; Caren 2007; Hajnal and Lewis 2003; Karnig and Walter 1983; Wood 2002). Dispersed political power makes it harder for citizens to perceive a central political figure to identify with and hold accountable (Wood 2002). By weakening the power of the mayor and fragmenting political power, city-manager forms of government make it harder for voters to gather relevant information, reduce mobilization by political parties, and decrease the incentives for residents to vote. These costs associated with manager forms of government create barriers to participation that may be felt more acutely by immigrants, who have less familiarity with American politics. Though these studies explored the effect of manager forms of government on *local* turnout, to the extent that manager forms of government make it harder for immigrants to learn about politics in the United States and discourage participation in local politics, these institutions may also depress the turnout of naturalized immigrants in *national* elections.

Although the age of political machines is long gone, and local political party organizations often show little interest in mobilizing immigrants, we propose that local political institutions and immigrants' experiences with local-level political participation still matter for their political incorporation and for turnout in national elections. Positive democratic experiences at the local level may accelerate and deepen the process of political incorporation by spurring participation in additional local and national political activities. Alternatively, if local politics discourage immigrants from political activity, it may also hinder their political incorporation into the national polity. Thus, we expect turnout in presidential elections to be higher among immigrants living in smaller cities and towns, and in places governed by elected mayors rather than appointed managers.

By emphasizing contextual factors such as city size and form of government we are not underestimating the importance of individual-level factors. We still expect them to matter, but we argue that context shapes the way in which immigrant-specific factors influence political behavior (Gay 2001; Oliver 2000; Rosenstone and Wolfinger 1978). Since immigrants on average have less experience with democratic politics than U.S.-born citizens, we expect local politics and local political experiences (such as voting in local elections or affiliating with a political party) to have a stronger impact on the voter turnout of naturalized citizens compared to native-born citizens. Similarly, we do not expect that the politics of place will have a uniform effect across immigrants. Rather, our hypothesis is that immigrants from authoritarian regimes and who have lived in the United States for a short period of time will feel the negative effects of large cities and manager forms of government more strongly than immigrants from democracies or who have had more time to learn about how democracy works in the United States. The positive effect of prior local-level activism (e.g., voting in local elections or affiliating with a local political party) should also be more important for immigrants from nondemocratic countries who have had few opportunities to vote back home, or who may be turned off by the contentious party politics and elevated rhetoric characteristic of national elections. For these immigrants, local politics may provide a context in which to experiment with democratic politics and learn about the American political system, making engagement in national politics seem less daunting.

The Local Context in Utah

There is no doubt that Utah is unique in many ways, and we will be modest when generalizing to other cases. Nonetheless, Utah's context of reception shares key features with other new immigrant destinations that make it a good choice for focused study. Between 1990 and 2010, its immigrant population has increased by 280 percent, the tenth-fastest growth rate in the country. Though the growth has been rapid, only about 8 percent of the population (about 237,000 people) is foreign born; moreover, naturalized citizens account for only 3 percent of all citizens in the state.[10] This means, of course, that political parties and candidates have few incentives to mobilize the immigrant vote. Just like immigrants settling in other new destination states, immigrants to Utah are settling in a variety of places, including city centers, suburbs, small towns, and rural areas. This variation makes it possible to study the impact of these diverse local contexts on immigrant voting behavior. Additionally, Utah lacks many of the local conditions that foster political mobilization of immigrants in traditional gateways, including towns where immigrants or minorities constitute a majority of residents.[11]

Utah is also one of the most Republican states in the country. This fact, combined with the relatively small size of the Latino and foreign-born population, means that presidential campaigns typically dedicate little time or effort to getting out the immigrant vote. In this way, Utah is more similar to new immigrant destinations in the Southeast, where Republican presidential candidates also achieve victory easily. This pattern is in contrast to new immigrant gateway states in the West, such as Nevada, Colorado, and Arizona, which have recently become important battleground states.

With regard to local politics, Utah resembles western states whose electoral systems were shaped by Progressive era reforms that weakened local-level party systems. Local elections in Utah are nonpartisan contests, and roughly one-third of municipalities have city managers instead of elected mayors. This means that turnout in city elections has historically been very low by national standards because of reduced levels of political mobilization by parties.

Data and Variables

Because most studies that examine the political incorporation of recent immigrants have focused on major immigrant destinations or use national-level data that do not oversample new immigrant gateways, we know little about the process of political incorporation in these locales. To begin filling this gap, we constructed an original dataset that combines demographic information from the Utah Population Database (UPDB) with official voter records from Utah's Lieutenant Governor's Office. The UPDB is a rich source of information that was originally collected for genetic, epidemiological, demographic, and public health studies. A central component of the UPDB is an extensive list of demographic information about Utah residents, including address, birth country, ethnicity, age, and gender, which provides us with many of our key independent variables. In turn, the Voting and Elections database provides official voting records for all registered voters in the state, and includes data for state and local elections, general elections, special elections, and party primaries.

We linked the datasets using three unique identifiers: an individual's name, address, and age. Our linked dataset contains the vast majority of all of Utah's registered voters and includes information about voting in local and general elections, party affiliation, birth country, ethnicity, and length of residence in the state.[12] Given our interest in isolating the impact that local contexts have on the voting behavior of immigrants, we augmented the individual-level data with contextual information about all of Utah's 243 incorporated cities and towns using U.S. Census information, information from the Utah League of Cities and Towns, from the Lieutenant Governor's Office, and other sources. This includes information about each town's population, form of government, number and density of registered nonprofits, and whether it is located in an urban or rural context. Thus, we are able to improve on existing studies by analyzing the voting behavior of naturalized immigrants in a variety of settlement contexts.

Analyzing actual voter records has distinct advantages over using public opinion polls and even Current Population Survey (CPS) estimates of voter turnout, both of which have been used productively in recent years to study voting patterns among immigrants. Because public opinion polls have relatively small sample sizes, they are not well suited for studying the voting behavior of immigrants in new destination cities and states where the proportion of foreign born is still relatively small. Even the CPS, which includes large sample sizes for every state, produces impractically high margins of error for estimates of turnout by minorities and immigrants in new gateways.[13] The practical consequence is that the bulk of research on immigrant political incorporation has relied on national samples or on samples collected in traditional gateway states. Second, as Matt A. Barreto, Gary M. Segura, and Nathan D. Woods (2004) point out, official voter and registration records do not rely on self-reporting, so the overreporting of voting behavior common to polls is not a problem. Finally, because our data are derived from a census, not a probability sample, we are able to study the voting behavior of groups with relatively small populations, something that is difficult to do using traditional sampling techniques.

Our goal is to estimate the effect of local context and local political behavior on the likelihood that immigrants will turn out to vote in presidential elections. In all models, the dependent variable is whether or not an individual voted in the 2008 presidential election, and is coded 1 if an individual voted, 0 if not. Our two key measures of local context are *Size of city (x1,000)* (measured as a continuous variable and obtained from the most recent U.S. Census data),[14] and *Manager form of government*, which indicates whether the local executive is a professional manager (1) or an elected mayor (0) (Utah League of Cities and Towns 2010). We focus on the effects of two forms of local political involvement: *Voted in 2007 local election* is a dichotomous variable indicating whether an individual voted in the 2007 municipal election; and *Affiliated with Political Party* takes on the value of 1 if an individual affiliated with one of Utah's registered political parties and 0 if they did not.[15]

Of course, it is likely that people who voted in both the 2007 and 2008 elections are habitual voters who vote in most elections for which they are eligible (Gerber, Green, and Shachar 2003). To better isolate the effect of voting in municipal elections on turnout in presidential elections, we include the variable *Voted in 2004 presidential election*, which is coded 1 if an individual voted in the 2004 general election and 0 if they did not. This is an important control variable—usually missing in studies of voting behavior—because its inclusion in our models provides a better measure of the effect of other predictors such as socioeconomic resources and immigrant status.

We are interested in whether a registered voter was born in the United States or came here from another country. The UPDB contains detailed country-of-origin information for a majority of individuals in the dataset, which we used to construct the variable *Foreign born* (coded 0 if someone was born in the United States, 1 if born in a foreign country).[16] We also examine whether prior experiences with democratic regimes increase immigrants' likelihood of voting and their ability to overcome any participatory obstacles they encounter locally. Unlike most datasets that contain information about immigrants from a small number of countries, our data contain information about immigrants from more than one hundred countries. We used this detailed country-of-origin data together with the Freedom House classification of regime types to construct a dummy variable that indicates whether or not someone immigrated from a democracy or an authoritarian regime (*Free* = 1, otherwise 0).[17]

In addition to regime type, how long an immigrant has lived in the United States is an important factor that mediates the effect of local context on political behavior. *Length of residence* is measured as the number of years an individual has held a Utah driver's license. Though it is not a direct measure of actual length of residency, it is a good proxy because it establishes a minimum duration of residency in the United States. *Home ownership* is a continuous block-group-level variable obtained from the U.S. Census that indicates the percentage of the residences within a block group that are owner occupied.

The models also control for other variables that prior studies have shown to be important predictors of immigrant political participation (Bass and Casper 1999; Gordon 1970; Jones-Correa 2001a; Ramakrishnan and Espenshade 2001). *Income* is a measure of the median household income at the block-group level and is coded into three income categories: *Income less than $35,000, Income $35,000 to less than $50,000*, and *Income $50,000 or higher*, where the first category is the reference group. *Education* is a continuous variable measured using census data and refers to the percentage of residents in a block group who have at least some college education.[18]

To control for the effect of living in an area with a relatively large proportion of immigrants, we augmented our dataset with census block-group data that measure the proportion of foreign born living in each block group (*Foreign-born density*). This is a dichotomous variable that takes the value of 0 if immigrants make up less than 10 percent of the population in the block group, and 1 if immigrants account for more than 10 percent. To control for organizational density, which can be an important independent source of political mobilization, we constructed a variable called *Nonprofits per 1,000 inhabitants*, which is a measure of how many nonprofit organizations exist in each city or town per thousand residents.[19] The UPDB data contain several variables pertaining to ethnicity, which we used to identify whether a voter is Latino or Hispanic (*Latino*). The models also control for other key demographic variables, including sex (coded as *Male* = 1, 0 otherwise), *Age*, and whether someone lives in an urban or rural area (*Urban* = 1, 0 otherwise).[20]

Analysis and Results

We begin the analysis by estimating two logistic regression models that predict turnout in the 2008 general election using the full sample that includes both naturalized immigrants and U.S.-born citizens (Table 5.1).[21] Model 1, which represents a basic model of immigrant voting, demonstrates that immigrants are less likely to vote than native-born citizens, showing that Utah's immigrant population is not unique. Rather, their political behavior fits patterns others have found using national samples (Bass and Casper 2001; Ramakrishnan and Espenshade 2001). Also consistent with the findings of other studies, we find that Latinos turn out less often than non-Latinos; that income, education, length of residency, home ownership, foreign-born density, and age have positive and statistically significant effects on turnout; and that women are more likely to vote than men. Model 1 also shows that our two measures of local-level context (the city characteristics) do not affect the likelihood that citizens will vote in national elections.[22]

To further test the impact of local politics on turnout, Model 2 adds variables that account for prior political experiences at the local level, and we include voting in a presidential election. Again, city contextual factors have no effect on turnout, but Model 2 shows that direct experiences with political involvement at the local level provide a powerful boost to participation at the national level, even after controlling for prior voting in presidential elections. All else being equal, the model predicts that people who affiliated with a state-level political party were 5 percent more likely to vote in national elections than people who did not register with a party. More significantly, the predicted effect of voting in a prior local election is stronger than the effect of voting in a prior national election, a surprising result. On average, voting in the 2007 local elections boosted turnout in the 2008 presidential elections by about 25 percent, whereas voting in the 2004 presidential elections boosted turnout by 11 percent.[23] These results are meaningful because they reveal the importance of political experiences at the local level for encouraging participation in national-level politics.

In addition, a comparison of results from Models 1 and 2 reveals that once we include measures of prior political experience into the equations, the negative relationship between foreign-born status and turnout is eliminated, so that Model 2 predicts no difference in turnout between naturalized and native-born citizens. Lack of prior political experiences in the United States is one reason immigrants participate less than nonimmigrants. These results suggest that when immigrants are drawn into local politics, the political experience they gain boosts their activism much more than similar experiences by U.S.-born citizens living in similar places and possessing similar resources. This finding is a first indication that local politics can serve as a school for democracy, at least for those immigrants that enroll.

We next analyze the direct impact of local contexts on immigrants (Models 3 and 4). To do this we estimated logistic-regression models for a subsample of only naturalized citizens in order to identify the factors that best predict immigrant voting behavior. The models are almost identical to the previous ones, except that we include a dummy variable (*Free*) that indicates whether an individual immigrated from a democracy (1) or an authoritarian regime (0), instead of the dummy for *Foreign born*. As expected, the baseline model (Model 3) predicts immigrants from authoritarian regimes turnout at lower rates than immigrants from democracies with similar levels of education, income, length of residency, and other factors. Again, once we include variables that control for prior political activity (Model 4), that effect disappears. The results also confirm that the experiences with local politics of voting in a local election and affiliating with a political party provide the single most powerful boost to the likelihood immigrants voted in the 2008 presidential elections.[24]

We expect the effect of city-level factors on turnout will be stronger for foreign-born citizens than for the native-born because the former are more sensitive to the political opportunities and constraints that local contexts create. Though this was not the case for manager forms of government, it is for city size, which is negatively associated with immigrant turnout in both

TABLE 5.1   LOGISTIC REGRESSION MODEL PREDICTING VOTE IN 2008 PRESIDENTIAL ELECTIONS FOR NATIVE BORN AND IMMIGRANTS

	Model 1		Model 2		Model 3		Model 4	
City characteristics								
Manager form of government	0.036	(0.049)	0.061	(0.061)	−0.053	(0.066)	0.023	(0.076)
Size of city (x1,000)	−0.001	(0.001)	−0.001	(0.001)	−0.002**	(0.001)	−0.003**	(0.001)
Prior political experience								
Voted in 2007 local election			2.141**	(0.098)			2.225**	(0.128)
Affiliated with a political party			0.293**	(0.021)			0.362**	(0.048)
Voted in 2004 presidential election			1.563**	(0.057)			1.503**	(0.094)
Democratic experience								
Foreign born	−0.199**	(0.041)	0.050	(0.028)				
Free					0.372**	(0.074)	0.053	(0.058)
Length of residence	0.033**	(0.001)	0.022**	(0.001)	0.031**	(0.005)	0.012*	(0.005)
Nonprofits per 1,000 inhabitants	−0.001	(0.003)	0.002	(0.005)	0.002	(0.003)	0.005	(0.004)
Urban	0.051	(0.046)	0.057	(0.048)	0.104	(0.069)	0.060	(0.083)

	Model 1		Model 2		Model 3		Model 4	
Latino	−0.342**	(0.034)	0.006	(0.029)	0.011	(0.078)	0.254*	(0.066)
Income $35k–$50,000[a]	0.247**	(0.057)	0.284**	(0.066)	0.100	(0.057)	0.114*	(0.054)
Income $50,000 or higher[a]	0.382**	(0.078)	0.512**	(0.082)	0.288**	(0.085)	0.334**	(0.089)
Education	0.927**	(0.182)	0.163	(0.186)	0.897**	(0.222)	0.028	(0.214)
Foreign-born density	0.102*	(0.047)	0.114*	(0.049)	0.139	(0.086)	0.184	(0.098)
Home ownership	0.870**	(0.187)	0.666**	(0.169)	0.871**	(0.183)	0.860*	(0.195)
Male	−0.205**	(0.008)	−0.076**	(0.008)	−0.258**	(0.030)	−0.156*	(0.033)
Age	0.033**	(0.002)	0.013**	(0.002)	0.029**	(0.003)	0.012*	(0.002)
Constant	−2.585**	(0.119)	−2.971**	(0.129)	−2.768**	(0.204)	−2.629*	(0.183)
Number of observations	590,194		574,387		13,265		13,139	
Log likelihood	−338,517.479		−243,965.621		−7,977.997		−6,011.948	
Pseudo R2	0.093		0.324		0.091		0.307	

Source: Authors' data.

Clustered robust standard errors in parentheses

** p < .01, * p < .05

[a] The reference category for the income variable is *Income less than $35,000*.

Models 3 and 4. In other words, the results indicate that large cities depress the turnout of immigrants compared to smaller cities and towns. Moreover, a comparison of the results from Models 3 and 4 with Models 1 and 2 (that use the full sample) reveals that the negative effect of city size on turnout exists only for immigrants.

These results indicate that immigrant political behavior is more sensitive to the politics of the places in which they live than are U.S.-born citizens. To further test whether local politics has a differential effect on immigrants we include interaction terms between city-level variables and foreign-born status, shown in Models 5 through 8, shown in Table 5.2.

The first model in Table 5.2 shows that manager forms of government do not have a differential effect on immigrants. However, in Model 6, the coefficient for the interaction term between city size and foreign-born status is negative and significant, confirming that the negative effect of large cities on turnout is stronger for naturalized citizens compared to the native born. Figure 5.1 shows graphically how the size of the city affects the turnout of immigrant citizens differently than that of native-born citizens. The slope of the line predicting the turnout of immigrants is clearly steeper than the slope of the line predicting the turnout of U.S.-born citizens, which means that the negative effect of city size is stronger and only significant for immigrants. In numerical terms, the model predicts that turnout for U.S.-born citizens declines by about 2 percent between the smallest and largest cities, while turnout for foreign-born citizens declines by 5 percent. It is also telling that, after controlling for voting in a prior presidential election, immigrants living in towns with a population smaller than 75,000 are more likely to have voted in 2008 than native-born Americans living in similar-sized towns. This advantage disappears in cities larger than 100,000 inhabitants. This result supports our expectations but runs counter to the literature that immigrants are more politically active in large urban centers compared to smaller towns.

Models 7 and 8 test whether a direct experience with local politics—voting in prior local elections and affiliating with a state-level political party—provide a bigger boost to immigrants' turnout. The coefficient for the interaction terms are positive, as expected, but not statistically significant at the .05 level, so there is no evidence that these kinds of political experiences are more politically significant for immigrants than nonimmigrants. This does not mean that they have no effect. On the contrary, the earlier finding (Model 4) shows that participation in local politics is an important catalyst for immigrant participation in national elections, even in new immigrant destinations like Utah.

We also want to note one additional result: the coefficient for *Foreign-born density* is positive and significant in all of the models that include both native-born and foreign-born citizens, but it is not significant in models that examine only the voting behavior of immigrants. Places with greater density

TABLE 5.2 LOGISTIC REGRESSION MODEL ESTIMATING THE IMPACT OF LOCAL FACTORS ON VOTING IN THE 2008 PRESIDENTIAL ELECTION

	Model 5		Model 6		Model 7		Model 8	
City characteristics								
Manager form of government	0.026	(0.045)	0.023	(0.044)	0.061	(0.059)	0.023	(0.047)
Size of city (x1,000)	−0.001	(0.001)	−0.001	(0.001)	−0.001	(0.001)	−0.001	(0.001)
Prior political experience								
Voted in 2004 presidential election	2.016**	(0.065)	2.02**	(0.065)	1.604**	(0.056)	1.927**	(0.069)
Foreign born	−0.008	(0.053)	0.078	(0.040)	0.024	(0.032)	−0.032	(0.040)
Voted in 2007 local election					2.186**	(0.094)		
Affiliated with political party							0.552**	(0.023)
Interactions								
Manager*foreign born	−0.063	(0.065)						
City size*foreign born			−0.0013**	(0.000)				
Prior municipal vote*foreign born					0.116	(0.068)		
Party affiliation*foreign born							0.048	(0.035)
Length of residence	0.023**	(0.001)	0.023**	(0.001)	0.021**	(0.001)	0.026**	(0.001)
Nonprofits per 1,000 inhabitants	−0.001	(0.004)	−0.001	(0.004)	0.001	(0.005)	0.001	(0.004)
Urban	0.024	(0.041)	0.023	(0.041)	0.045	(0.048)	0.049	(0.041)
Latino	−0.149**	(0.031)	−0.15**	(0.031)	−0.004	(0.030)	−0.120**	(0.029)
Income $35k–$50,000[a]	0.231**	(0.061)	0.231**	(0.061)	0.275**	(0.066)	0.251**	(0.061)

(Continued)

TABLE 5.2 (Continued)

	Model 5		Model 6		Model 7		Model 8	
Income $50,000 or higher[a]	0.387**	(0.078)	0.39**	(0.078)	0.496**	(0.081)	0.422**	(0.081)
Education	0.617**	(0.173)	0.61**	(0.174)	0.236	(0.194)	0.465**	(0.158)
Foreign-born density	0.108*	(0.047)	0.11*	(0.047)	0.115*	(0.049)	0.106*	(0.047)
Home ownership	0.752**	(0.159)	0.75**	(0.160)	0.669**	(0.172)	0.743**	(0.155)
Male	−0.122**	(0.017)	−0.12**	(0.007)	−0.078**	(0.008)	−0.115**	(0.007)
Age	0.023**	(0.002)	0.023**	(0.002)	0.013**	(0.002)	0.023**	(0.002)
Constant	−3.101**	(0.116)	−3.103**	(0.115)	−2.87**	(0.126)	−3.28**	(0.116)
Number of observations	574,420		574,420		574,390		574,417	
Log likelihood	−281,627.03		−281,619.45		−244,760.75		−278,304.65	
Pseudo R-squared	0.220		0.220		0.322		0.229	

Source: Authors' data.

Clustered Robust standard errors in parentheses

** p < .01, * p < .05

[a] The reference category for the income variable is *Income less than $35,000.*

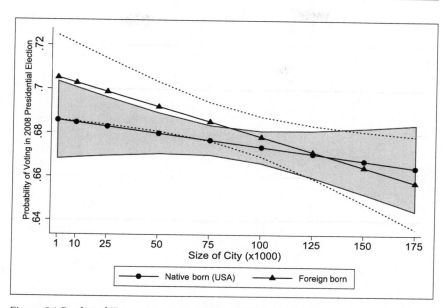

Figure 5.1 Predicted Turnout in 2008 Presidential Elections by Immigrant Status and City Size

of immigrants may boost immigrant political participation because those places have a larger concentration of mobilizing resources (e.g., organizations and native-language media) than places where immigrants are less numerous. Greater concentration of immigrants also gives local politicians more incentives to target them with mobilizing efforts. However, this dynamic probably only exists in traditional receiving cities and states with much higher concentrations of naturalized citizens. Most immigrants who settled in new immigrant destinations have not naturalized, and a substantial percentage of them probably reside illegally in the United States. This creates a political dynamic in which larger concentrations of immigrants do little to stimulate immigrant voting, but may motivate native-born citizens to go to the polls to express their opinions on immigration.[25]

Thus far the results show that the politics of place matters for the political participation of immigrants, and that city size matters more for immigrants than for U.S.-born citizens. We hypothesized that the effect of local context and local political experience varies because immigrants have fewer democratic skills and experience compared to U.S.-born citizens. If this is the case, then we should also see differences in the effect of place and local-level political experiences on immigrants from authoritarian regimes and with shorter lengths of residency.

To test this expectation, we estimated several models with interaction terms (Models 9 through 12 in Table 5.3) using only the subsample of foreign-born

TABLE 5.3 LOGISTIC REGRESSION MODEL ESTIMATING THE IMPACT OF LOCAL FACTORS ON VOTING IN THE 2008 PRESIDENTIAL ELECTIONS (IMMIGRANTS ONLY)

	Model 9		Model 10		Model 11		Model 12	
City characteristics								
Manager form of government	−0.166	(0.113)	−0.194	(0.147)	−0.038	(0.061)	−0.04	(0.062)
Size of city (x1,000)	−0.002**	(0.001)	−0.003**	(0.001)	−0.004**	(0.001)	−0.000	(0.001)
Prior political experience								
Voted in 2004 presidential election	1.879**	(0.081)	1.88**	(0.08)	1.88**	(0.082)	1.887**	(0.08)
Free	0.172*	(0.087)	0.233**	(0.062)	0.059	(0.114)	0.235**	(0.063)
Interactions								
*Manager*free*	0.158	(0.124)						
*Manager*length of residence*			0.011	(0.010)				
*City size*free*					0.002**	(0.001)		
*City size*length of residence*							−0.0002**	(.0001)
Length of residence	0.013**	(0.005)	0.009	(0.007)	0.013**	(0.005)	0.027**	(0.007)
Nonprofits per 1,000 inhabitants	0.0013	(0.003)	0.002	(0.003)	0.003	(0.003)	0.002	(0.003)

Urban	0.034	(0.072)	0.038	(0.071)	0.032	(0.071)	0.039	(0.071)
Latino	0.193**	(0.075)	0.194**	(0.075)	0.180*	(0.075)	0.195*	(0.077)
Income $35k–$50,000[a]	0.114	(0.059)	0.114*	(0.059)	0.114*	(0.059)	0.116*	(0.058)
Income $50,000 or higher[a]	0.310**	(0.089)	0.307**	(0.090)	0.305**	(0.089)	0.307**	(0.088)
Education	0.423*	(0.213)	0.423*	(0.216)	0.395	(0.212)	0.433*	(0.212)
Foreign-born density	0.145	(0.093)	0.143	(0.094)	0.148	(0.094)	0.142	(0.094)
Home ownership	0.795**	(0.173)	0.801**	(0.175)	0.804**	(0.170)	0.806**	(0.176)
Male	−0.195**	(0.031)	−0.195**	(0.030)	−0.196**	(0.031)	−0.195**	(0.031)
Age	0.019**	(0.003)	0.019**	(0.003)	0.019**	(0.003)	0.019**	(0.003)
Constant	−2.652**	(0.203)	−2.650**	(0.201)	−2.54**	(0.241)	−2.92**	(0.217)
Number of observations	13,139		13,139		13,139		13,139	
Log likelihood	−6,889.56		−6,889.21		−6,889.8		−6,886.16	
Pseudo R-squared	0.206		0.206		0.206		0.206	

Source: Authors' data.

Clustered robust standard errors in parentheses

** p < .01, * p < .05

[a] The reference category for the income variable is Income less than $35,000.

citizens to test whether the effects of *Manager form of government, Size of city, Voted in 2007 municipal elections,* and *Party affiliation* on turnout are mediated by length of residency or whether a person immigrated from a democratic country. The first result we note is that neither of the coefficients for the interaction terms between *Free* and *Voted in 2007 local election* and *Free* with *Affiliated with a political party* was significant.[26] Again, this simply means that direct experiences with local politics provide an equally powerful boost to the turnout of all immigrants. Similarly, the coefficient for the interaction terms for *Manager*Free* and *Manager*Length of residence* were not statistically significant. Only the coefficients for the interaction terms between *City size*Free* and *City size*Length of residence* were significant, which again is evidence that large cities have a meaningful effect on the political incorporation of immigrants, particularly those immigrants with fewer democratic experiences and time in the United States.

Specifically, the positive coefficient for the interaction term in Model 11 indicates that large cities especially depress the turnout of immigrants from authoritarian countries. The marginal probabilities show just how much stronger the effect of city size is on immigrants from authoritarian regimes. Between the smallest and largest cities, the probability that immigrants from a democracy will vote in national elections declines by about 7 percent, and for immigrants from an authoritarian regime, the likelihood of voting declines by 12 percent. Figure 5.2 further illustrates the effect of city size on the immigrant

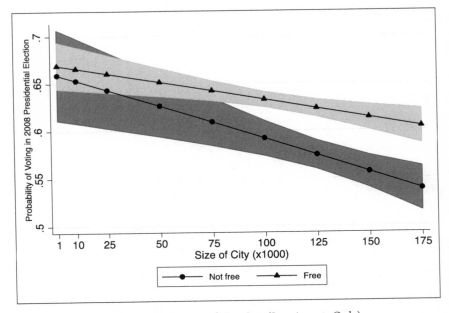

Figure 5.2 Predicted Turnout by Free and City Size (Immigrants Only)

vote. It is evident that immigrants from democracies and authoritarian regimes turn out at the same rates in small towns (under about 50,000 inhabitants), but a gap develops between the turnout levels of these two groups as city size increases, so that in the largest cities the turnout of immigrants from nondemocracies lags significantly behind that of immigrants from democracies.

The effect of city size also depends on the length of time that an immigrant has resided in the United States. Model 12 shows that the coefficient for *City Size*Length of residence* is negative and significant, which indicates that the negative effect of city size decreases the longer an immigrant resides in the United States. Figure 5.3 shows how the effect of length of residency works for immigrants who live in small (less than 100,000 inhabitants) and large (more than 100,000 inhabitants) cities. For both groups of immigrants, length of residency boosts turnout in presidential elections among those living in smaller towns, but the effect in large cities is negligible. In fact, turnout for immigrants who live in small towns and have lived in the United States for more than twenty-five years is approximately the level of turnout of immigrants from democracies who live in large cities. Immigrants from authoritarian countries living in large cities never match the turnout levels of those from democratic countries.

Previous research indicates that large cities dampen turnout of immigrants in *local* elections because they impose greater costs and provide fewer

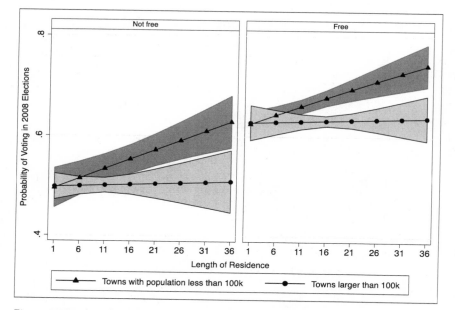

Figure 5.3 Predicted Turnout in 2008 Presidential Elections by Free, City Size, and Length of Residence

incentives for political participation (Goldsmith and Holzner 2014). But our results show that these barriers to participation also disproportionately discourage foreign-born citizens with relatively few participatory resources and little democratic experience from voting in *national* elections. Large cities slow the process of political incorporation of those immigrants (particularly those with few democratic experiences) who may find these contexts difficult to navigate. Immigrants with more abundant democratic experiences are hardly affected. Similarly, it appears that length of residency allows immigrants to learn how local *and* national institutions work in the United States, but only in smaller towns. In contrast, the barriers to political participation that large cities impose appear to hinder their political incorporation no matter how long they reside in the United States.

Conclusion

Study after study of immigrant political incorporation has found that foreign-born citizens are less likely to vote in general elections than native-born citizens. Some prominent scholars have worried that this relative political apathy might deepen among the millions of recent arrivals to the United States who will not be able to develop deep attachments to the American political system (Huntington 2004b), or who may see their political incorporation delayed because they settle in places with relatively small immigrant populations (Kaufmann and Rodriguez 2010).

We set out to test whether certain characteristics of new immigrant destinations influence the likelihood immigrants will become active in national elections. Our findings give us reasons to be cautiously optimistic about the prospects of immigrant political incorporation in new immigrant destinations. Indeed, *where* immigrants settle matters for the political lessons they learn, and is especially important for immigrants from nondemocratic countries who have to learn democratic politics from scratch. Most dramatically, it appears that the politics of large cities may discourage immigrants from engaging in local political activity, thus slowing their incorporation into national politics. This suggests that the gap in turnout rates that currently exists between native-born and foreign-born citizens is due in part to traditional settlement patterns in which the vast majority of immigrants settled in the largest metropolitan areas.

We also find that people's experience with local-level political activity, such as registering with a local political party and voting in a prior municipal election, is a powerful predictor of turnout—even more powerful than voting in a prior presidential election. One practical implication of these results is that political parties, campaigns, and interest groups that seek to mobilize the immigrant vote would do well investing more time and resources mobilizing immigrants around local issues and during local elections, instead of only every four years around presidential campaigns.

The biggest obstacle immigrants who have settled in new gateway states during the past twenty years face is voting in their first election. But once we take prior political experiences into account, our data show that immigrant turnout in presidential elections nearly matches that of native-born citizens. In addition, new settlement patterns may encourage rather than discourage the political incorporation of new arrivals. In recent elections, both Democratic and Republican presidential candidates have aggressively courted the vote of naturalized citizens in swing states with rapidly growing immigrant populations like Nevada, Colorado, North Carolina, and Virginia. Millions of recent immigrants have also settled in smaller cities and towns located in southeastern states where political parties are more active in local politics. Smaller towns provide more opportunities to experience and participate in local elections, which, in turn, accelerate the political learning and incorporation of all immigrants, but especially of immigrants who would otherwise be shut out from politics.

A broader conclusion of our analysis is that local contexts can empower immigrant citizens to participate in the larger political process, but to do so, local political institutions must be relatively open and provide numerous opportunities for political engagement at the local level. However, local politics can also discourage immigrant political activism. Turnout rates in municipal elections are very low (even by paltry U.S. standards) and have been declining for decades, so the overall impact of local-level activism on political activity may be small. Nonetheless, as new immigrants disperse to smaller cities, and as incentives grow for local-level campaigns and parties to mobilize immigrants in these new destinations, the voting patterns of immigrants in national elections may come to resemble that of other citizens.

NOTES

Acknowledgments: We would like to thank the Russell Sage Foundation and the Rockefeller Foundation for generous financial support, as well as Diana Evans, Tom Maloney, Anthony Messina, Irfan Nooruddin, and Carew Boulding, all of whose comments on earlier drafts refined our thinking and writing. Partial support for all datasets within the Utah Population Database was provided by the University of Utah Huntsman Cancer Institute and the Huntsman Cancer Institute Cancer Center Support grant, P30 CA2014, from the National Cancer Institute.

1. As recently as 1980, one-fourth of all immigrants living in the United States lived in the New York and Los Angeles metropolitan areas, and nearly 40 percent lived in the five cities with the largest immigrant populations. By 2007 these proportions had declined to 17 percent and 26 percent, respectively (Fortuny et al. 2010). By 2000, 48 percent of immigrants lived in suburbs, and another 8 percent lived in rural towns (Marrow 2005).

2. For examples of such research, see Bada, Fox, and Selee (2006) and Bada et al. (2010).

3. The Migration Policy Institute publishes state immigration data profiles that include estimates of the percentage of foreign born that have naturalized. The rate of naturalization in the ten fastest growing immigrant destinations ranges from 31 percent (North Carolina) to 47 percent (Nevada). By comparison, except for Texas, naturalization rates in traditional receiving states average about 50 percent (http://www.migrationpolicy .org/programs/data-hub/state-immigration-data-profiles).

4. The literature offers ambiguous expectations for the effect of regime type on voting. While S. Karthick Ramakrishnan and Thomas J. Espenshade (2001) find that experience with repressive regimes has no consistent effect on voting, Catherine Simpson Bueker (2005), among others, finds that immigrants from nondemocratic societies are less likely to vote (Portes and Rumbaut 1996).

5. Not all experiences were positive, and immigrants in many places were excluded from national politics by virtue of their exclusion from local politics. This negative dynamic reinforces the more general point that local politics matters in the process of national inclusion.

6. Certainly, voting in a prior presidential election is a powerful predictor of voting in subsequent ones, but that does not help us explain why someone voted in a presidential election in the first place.

7. Twenty-eight states plus the District of Columbia allow individuals to register with a political party when they register to vote or get a driver's license.

8. Though there is some evidence that anti-immigrant policies increase immigrant and Latino turnout in traditional gateways, it is not at all clear that the same dynamic will occur in cities and towns where there are fewer mobilizing resources for immigrants (Barreto and Woods 2005; Pantoja and Segura 2003).

9. But see Kelleher and Lowery (2009) for alternative viewpoints.

10. http://www.migrationpolicy.org/programs/data-hub/state-immigration-data -profiles.

11. The one exception might be the Mormon Church, which has vast resources and mobilizing networks that it uses to encourage its members to become civically and politically engaged. It is possible that immigrants who are members of the Mormon Church are mobilized more consistently into politics. However, there is no publicly available data that can tell us the religious background of immigrants.

12. Using these three pieces of information, we were able to uniquely identify and link about 75 percent of individuals from the voter registration dataset. The full, linked dataset contains 1,396,950 cases, which represents the total number of Utah residents who are registered to vote. The actual size of the sample analyzed is smaller because of missing values for some of the demographic variables.

13. For example, according to CPS data, 23.3 percent of Hispanic citizens voted in Utah, with a margin of error of 11.7 percent. In contrast, the CPS margin of error for Hispanic citizens in California and Texas is only 2.5 percent and 2.9 percent, respectively.

14. U.S. Census Bureau, Population Division (2011).

15. In addition to the Republican and Democratic parties, registered voters in Utah affiliate with several smaller parties, including the Green Party, Libertarian Party, and Constitution Party.

16. Since we linked the UPDB data with official voter records, we know that all individuals in the linked dataset are citizens of the United States who have registered to vote.

17. We coded immigrants' country of origin as a democracy (*Free*) if Freedom House categorized them as Free and as authoritarian (*Not free*) if Freedom House categorized them as Partly Free or Not Free.

18. Although block group socioeconomic data are less than ideal, our dataset does not have individual-level information about income or education. Some kind of control for socioeconomic factors is necessary, however, so we followed Barreto, Segura, and Woods (2004) who used the median household income and education level in a zip code as a measure of socioeconomic status (SES). However, our proxy measure is a better estimate of individual SES, because it estimates income at the block-group level, which is a much smaller level of aggregation than zip codes.

19. We built a database of nonprofit organizations in all Utah cities and towns using information from GuideStar and the IRS Publication 78. GuideStar provides information on 1.5 million nonprofit organizations in the United States, including specialized state lists of nonprofits derived from IRS 990 forms and the IRS Business Master File (Ramakrishnan and Bloemraad 2008b). We counted the number of tax-exempt organizations in each town, multiplied this number by one thousand, and divided that by the town's population. The number of nonprofits per one thousand ranged from zero to forty-three per thousand, with a mean of seven per thousand.

20. We used the U.S. Census Bureau's definition to construct the *urban* variable.

21. Our observations of individuals are naturally clustered within cities. To take into account the clustered nature of our data, we use robust clustered standard errors throughout. Using multilevel models is another strategy to deal with clustered observations, but given our very large sample size and the use of interactions, this strategy proved impractical. See Primo, Jacobsmeier, and Milyo (2007) for a detailed discussion of the tradeoffs of different analytical strategies.

22. We tested alternative specifications of the model that included a quadratic term for *Size of city (x1,000)* and saw no substantive changes in the results.

23. We estimate marginal effects by holding the variables city size, density of nonprofits, length of residency, income, education, homeownership, and age constant at their mean; in the case of dichotomous variables we hold them constant at the following values: *Manager* = 1, *Urban* = 1, *Latino* = 0, *Voted in 2004* = 1, *Voted in 2007* = 1, *Party affiliation* = 1, *Foreign-born density* = 1, and *Male* = 0.

24. Affiliating with a political party boosts turnout on average by 6 perecent among immigrants, while voting in the 2007 local elections boosted foreign-born turnout in the 2008 presidential elections by an impressive 29 percent.

25. We also tested whether the effect of foreign-born density is mediated by city size and found no statistically significant interaction.

26. Because of space constraints we do not show these results.

6

Religious Communities, Immigration, and Social Cohesion in Rural Areas

Evidence from England

RHYS ANDREWS

Just as Utah represents a new destination state within the United States, a traditional immigration country, rural English towns are becoming ever more diverse in the United Kingdom, the latter a significant site of immigration for more than a half century. In Utah, Claudio Holzner and Melissa Goldsmith find, among other things, that smaller towns provide immigrants with political experiences that accelerate their political incorporation beyond what they might experience in larger destination cities. In England, new rural destinations also offer unique opportunities. In this chapter, Rhys Andrews discovers that mainline Protestant churches assist the social integration of immigrants by engaging in activities that encourage the development of bridging social capital. Taken together, this chapter and the preceding one suggest that smaller towns may provide a level of both political and social contact that creates favorable conditions for immigrant incorporation.

A nalysis of the causes and consequences of variations in cohesion among members of communities has a venerable history within rural sociology (Sorokin 1928; Warren 1978; Wilkinson 1991). Much of this work reflected the notion that the population movements accompanying rural restructuring during the past century have seriously challenged the viability and cohesiveness of rural communities. In particular, beyond the problems associated with poverty, socioeconomic disadvantage, and social heterogeneity, the arrival of new immigrant groups within rural areas may disturb long-held norms of social interaction within an area as residents are confronted with newcomers who may look different and bring dissimilar social and cultural practices (Naples 1994; Neal 2002). Immigration may test long-term rural residents' psychological need for control over their social environment (Chavez 2005) by challenging existing preferences for living among the same type of people (Blau 1977) or, according to the "racial threat" hypothesis, prompting feelings of anxiety and insecurity (Blalock 1967), which can weaken perceptions of cohesion within a given area (Quillian 1995). At the same time, the "social contact" hypothesis suggests that immigration can stimulate cross-cultural interaction, leading to a corresponding reduction in out-group hostility, especially where social conditions are conducive to positive interactions (Allport 1954). Yet, despite a growing literature exploring immigrant integration in urban immigrant destinations, few researchers have studied the dynamics of the relationships between immigration and social sources of integration in rural areas. This study is intended to address this important issue by examining the recent historic movement of Central and Eastern European migrant workers into rural areas across England.

Social scientists agree that civil society is likely to bear a great responsibility for addressing the integration of immigrants within an area (Putnam 2007; Theodore and Martin 2007). In particular, the religious communities present within areas experiencing immigration may play a vital role in this process. The "moral communities" thesis developed by sociologists of religion suggests that religious groups and institutions build social cohesion within an area by fostering community integration and enhancing informal social control (Stark, Doyle, and Kent 1980; Welch, Tittle, and Petee 1991). However, subsequent developments in social science have led scholars to develop a more nuanced account of the contribution that different religious communities might make to social cohesion. Critically, Christian religious denominations often differ greatly in doctrine, and so adherents of those denominations might well have divergent attitudes toward the community beyond the congregation. As well as exhibiting important doctrinal differences, denominations also vary in the institutional support that they (are able to) offer to members and nonmembers, both in developed countries, such as the United Kingdom (Bruce 1995), and developing ones, such as Mozambique (Agadjanian 2001). One fruitful lens through which these denominational differences can be analyzed is the distinction between mainline (or mainstream) and evangelical religious communities (Moorhead 1999; Tipton 2008). Although many Christian denominations do not fall neatly into a single category (see J. Green 2005), it is possible to observe broad differences in doctrine and structure across the principal denominations in England, as well as in the United States.

Mainline Christian communities (Anglicans, Catholics, and Methodists in England) are associated with churches that have a long history and tradition.

These churches tend to have a formal organizational structure and arguably promote a commitment to social responsibility, which is elevated above the duties of church membership (Bruce 1995). Mainline communities are also often more embedded within the civil society of the countries in which they are found and can call upon a broader spread of funding sources than their evangelical counterparts. Core characteristics of the churches associated with evangelical communities include a certain degree of newness, frequently the result of some kind of revival movement. Such communities tend to place a great stress upon personal conversion (being "born again"), the authority of the Bible and the spiritual leader, and the importance of a religious foundation for social activism (Bebbington 2008). Evangelical communities may eschew mainstream social structures, and their churches are often entirely dependent on donations from their members. According to some social scientists, such variations in doctrine and institutional structure have important implications for how the different communities interact with the rest of society.

Robert Putnam (2000) claimed that mainline Protestants and Catholics within the United States were more likely to be involved in service to the wider community than evangelical Christians, who, by contrast, exhibit an inward focus on their own religious community. This, in turn, has led Kraig Beyerlein and John R. Hipp (2005) to consider adherence to mainline Christianity a direct measure of *bridging social capital* (interactions that connect diverse actors), and adherence to evangelical Christianity a measure of *bonding social capital* (interactions that connect like-minded actors). *Social capital*, defined broadly as "social networks and the norms of reciprocity and trustworthiness that arise from them" (Putnam 2000), is characterized by distinctive *bridging* (inclusive) and *bonding* (exclusive) aspects, which may embrace myriad diverse in- and out-group identities or reinforce exclusive in-group identities. While some scholars have focused on the benefits emerging from bridging interactions connecting many different actors as the source of social capital (e.g., Granovetter 1973), others emphasize the bonding nature of the shared norms that underpin group membership (e.g., J. Coleman 1994). The significance of Beyerlein and Hipp's argument is that whereas bridging social capital is thought to promote interconnectedness across the wider community and thereby generate social cohesion (Bellair 1997), bonding social capital may sometimes have the opposite effect by increasing group insularity and, in turn, social fragmentation (Sampson, Morenoff, and Earls 1999).

Based on these notions, it is possible to derive some broad expectations about the likely role that different Christian communities might play in the process of immigrant integration in rural areas. First, mainline denominations might have the institutional strength required to be able to coordinate opportunities for positive encounters between existing residents and newcomers, evoke political responses to the needs of immigrants, fund bespoke support services, or run community-awareness-raising events and work-shops. This, in turn, might advance the interests of immigrant groups in ways that contribute to their successful integration within the host area (J. A. Schneider 2007). Second, mainline religious communities may also be espe-cially well placed to assist in the process of integration because immigrants are often already affiliated to these communities in their home countries. For example, Catholic religious communities in the United States have a long history of providing support for and advocacy on behalf of affiliated immi-grant groups (Menjívar 2003). Third, on the face of it, evangelical communi-ties might seem less likely to take an interest in the welfare of nonmember groups. Nevertheless, despite the hypothesized insularity of these communi-ties, it is conceivable that their missionary zeal may actually drive them to reach out to immigrants as a source of potential converts (Menjívar 2003). Not only are there strong doctrinal reasons for individuals to pursue "salva-tion" in this way, but the hierarchical structure of evangelical communities may also prompt immigrant outreach work, especially where it is seen as a high priority by the spiritual leader. Indeed, community leaders from evan-gelical communities joined forces with mainline ones to mobilize congrega-tions to participate in the immigrant marches across U.S. cities in 2006 (Pantoja, Menjívar, and Magana 2008). Whether mainline religious com-munities are responding directly to the needs of immigrant groups or pro-viding platforms for collective action in their interest, their institutional strength and embeddedness could therefore hold the key to the social inte-gration of immigrants in rural areas, while the proselytizing fervor of evan-gelical communities too may play a vitally important role.

This chapter analyzes the separate and combined effects of religious communities and immigration on perceptions of social cohesion in rural areas across England using multivariate statistical techniques. The first part reviews the literature on the contribution of religious communities and immigration to social cohesion, and then I theorize their interactive effects within rural areas. I identify measures of social cohesion, religious commu-nities, immigration, and relevant control variables. I then present results of a statistical model of the separate and joint effects of religious community membership and immigration on residents' perceptions of social cohesion in rural areas across England and discuss their implications.

Religious Communities and Social Cohesion

According to many observers, industrial restructuring during the twentieth century prompted a series of population movements in and out of rural areas, which caused the reevaluation of existing social identities in ways that have often proved detrimental to people's well-being (Fraser et al. 2005; Nelson 1999). This, in turn, has placed great pressure on the key social and institutional bases of community strength within rural areas, such as schools, small businesses, and religious groups (Cotter 2004; Gray 1994). As rural communities have undergone a process of transformation, so these institutions have had to work hard to adapt to the changing social, political, and economic circumstances that they face. In particular, the religious communities within rural areas, though at risk of marginalization as population turnover inhibits their growth, remain a potentially critical source of social support for individuals (Halseth 1999). Indeed, such communities remain a vital touchstone for the lives of rural Americans (Elder and Conger 2000), and case study research in England too suggests that religious communities still make a vital contribution to community vibrancy in rural areas (see Furbey et al. 2006), albeit to a lesser extent than was the case in the past (King 2009).

In England, the Anglican community has occupied a central place within the life of country parishes for many centuries (Francis and Lanksheart 1992; Russell 1986), and, despite declining congregations, the Church of England continues to marshal more material and human resources than most other nonstate actors within rural areas. Similarly, the Catholic and Methodist communities have a long history of engagement with the wider community in rural England (Bruce 1995). While these mainline communities share many doctrinal and structural characteristics with their U.S. counterparts, they are, in some respects, more deeply embedded in the institutional structure of rural England. For example, the Anglican Church is a statutory provider of education in England and runs about a quarter of all elementary schools, including almost half of those in rural areas. The Catholic Church too is responsible for the provision of a small amount of elementary schooling, while a tiny number of Methodist-run schools are still in existence (Berkeley and Vij 2008).[1] Evangelical religious communities, such as the Baptists and Pentecostals, have fewer adherents within the rural areas of England than in the United States, and are less deeply embedded in the social and political structure of those areas than mainline communities. At the same time, they often rely solely on the financial contributions of members and have little institutional expression beyond the church. Thus, these communities arguably play less of a role in the wider community life of an area, preferring instead to focus on the spiritual concerns of the congregation.

Beyerlein and Hipp's (2005) social-capital thesis suggests that mainline religious communities are critical sources of the norms and networks that can underpin the growth of social cohesion in rural areas. Several studies in the United States indicate that mainline Protestant and Catholic communities encourage the development of bridging social capital across an area by organizing community activities, providing support to the needy, and volunteering to assist other organizations that serve local people (e.g., Wilson and Janoski 1995; Wuthnow 2004). A similar role has been identified for such communities within rural areas across England (Russell 2005). Mainline religious groups also play an increasingly important role as partners in the delivery of local public services in the United States (Chaves 2004) and in England (Church Urban Fund 2008), where in the latter case they are deeply involved in the provision of elementary and (to a lesser extent) secondary schooling in rural areas. Such engagement with and across the breadth of the community may strengthen the connections between religious adherents and nonadherents alike, adding to a perception of cohesiveness within the local area. By contrast, Beyerlein and Hipp (2005) argue that the inward focus of evangelical religious communities may weaken rather than strengthen community bonds.

In focusing their efforts on developing the cohesiveness of their own group, evangelical communities might restrict the growth of cross-group interactions and networks, thereby depriving rural areas of vital bridging social capital that might potentially be harnessed for the wider benefit of society (Iannacone 1994). Although the activist doctrine of evangelical communities may prompt them to engage in self-directed community-development work (Menjívar 2003), research in the United States suggests that they are less likely to participate in social programs or public-service delivery than mainline religious communities (Chaves 2004; Hoge et al. 1998). Evangelical religious groups may therefore be more prone to exhibiting the insularity sometimes associated with bonding social capital (Portes 1998). In England, while evangelical communities do participate in government-sponsored programs, the strength of their religious and (sometimes illiberal) social convictions can make it harder for them to develop links with out-group members (G. Smith 2002). Thus, we can anticipate observing a positive relationship between mainline religious communities and residents' perceptions of social cohesion, but a negative one for evangelical religious communities.

Immigration and Social Cohesion

Theories of social disorganization suggest that high levels of immigration are likely to disrupt social relations within an area (Shaw and McKay 1969). Because cultivation of the degree of interpersonal trust required to assimilate newcomers within communities requires substantial time and effort, sudden movements of population into an area represent a considerable challenge to residents' perceptions of control over their environment (Kasarda and Janowitz 1974; Sennett 1970). The arrival of new residents with observably different ethnic origins, linguistic practices, or cultural mores, in particular, can lead existing community members to feel (however unjustifiably) that they are becoming strangers in their own environment (Crowley and Lichter 2009). Thus, although population growth is often indicative of increasing economic prosperity within an area, it can also present a serious test of levels of social cohesion, at least in the short term (Bursik 1988). Indeed, immigration and the apparent fragmentation of social identities in advanced democracies have led to what some observers describe as "a new crisis of social cohesion" (Kearns and Forrest 2000).

Immigration poses a challenge for social cohesion in rural areas principally because of its impact on the perceptions of existing community members (Chavez 2005; Crowley and Lichter 2009). Anxieties about the arrival of new immigrant groups can be experienced by longtime residents of an area as a loss of control over the destiny of their current "imagined community" (Sennett 1970)—a perceived loss that is often resisted in more or less overt ways (Chavez 2005). In part, this anxiety may reflect the aversion to heterogeneity (Alesina and La Ferrara 2002) identified by social identity theorists (e.g., Tajfel and Turner 1979, 1986), which ties group positive self-image to the maintenance of a negative out-group identity. According to this perspective, people tend to like others who more closely resemble themselves. Such anxieties could also be a product of feelings of "racial threat," whereby ethnic and cultural prejudices are brought to the front when the size and visibility of new immigrant groups is much greater than anticipated (Coenders and Scheepers 1998; Quillian 1995)—what Fennelly (2008) describes as a "symbolic threat" that may or may not reflect reality.

Contradicting the racial-threat thesis, social-contact theory suggests larger population movements might actually prompt greater interaction between newcomers and existing residents, and thereby reduce residents' out-group hostility (Allport 1954; Pettigrew and Tropp 2006). Yet collective-action problems associated with influencing local affairs, such as the need for effective communication and coalition building, are also thought to be exacerbated by the introduction of diverse and potentially conflicting viewpoints on important community matters (see Walsh 2006). As a result, rural areas experiencing high levels of immigration may have to overcome not only the negative effects of prejudice on cohesion but also those associated with lower levels of political agreement (Alesina and La Ferrara 2000). Whatever its possible origins, a negative relationship between immigration and social cohesion has been corroborated by a number of quantitative studies at the state and metropolitan levels, suggesting that it weakens social bonds (e.g., Putnam 2007; Shumaker and Stokols 1982). This leads to the expectation that large movements of newcomers into rural areas will be negatively related to residents' perceptions of social cohesion.

Religious Communities, Immigration, and Social Cohesion

Rural restructuring has reinforced the role of key social and institutional bases of community strength involved in the process of social integration within rural areas, such as schools, businesses, and religious groups (Cotter

2004; Gray 1994). And some evidence suggests that the involvement of religious communities in the pursuit of integration can have important benefits for rural areas. In addition to providing opportunities for developing the bridging social capital that contributes to the growth of community cohesiveness more widely, mainline religious communities often participate in or coordinate activities that address the complex social problems experienced by immigrants (Farnell et al. 2006; Menjívar 2003). As a result, they are sometimes better able to integrate migrants than are local state institutions, especially where immigrants are able to participate in religious communities to which they may have belonged in their native countries (Romaniszyn 1996).

Research has shown that in areas with many mainline religious communities, immigrants may find that social integration is made possible by accessing the social support that such communities can provide (J. A. Schneider 2007). Indeed, the sheer numbers of sources of support in such areas is an important determinant of the rate and intensity of volunteer participation among immigrant groups (Handy and Greenspan 2009). Thus, areas with stronger mainline religious communities may be especially resilient to social problems associated with immigration, as they possess a large stock of appropriable human and material resources for social integration. Again, this may be especially important for immigrants who are affiliated with the mainline community in question. For example, Krystyna Romaniszyn's (1996) case study of Polish migrant workers in Athens, Greece, highlights the key role played by the Catholic Church there in enabling the immigrants to settle successfully.

In contrast to mainline religious communities, evangelical ones have sometimes been thought less willing to engage with issues of immigration, due to their inward focus on the concerns of the church with which they are associated (Hagan 2006). Nevertheless, although such communities sometimes exhibit less liberal and more conservative social attitudes in general in both the United States (Smith and Johnson 2010) and the United Kingdom (Francis 2008), there is growing evidence to suggest that evangelical communities are active in outreach to immigrants because they are seen (initially at least) as potential converts (Menjívar 2003). Not only are immigrants potentially members in the making, but the focus of existing members on individual salvation through participation in religious activities amplifies their commitment to building the community of the faithful. African Pentecostal churches, which emerged in response to migrants' needs, for instance, are growing in number and influence in England (Burgess 2009)—though these communities (and others like them) are typically located within urban rather than rural areas.

All of the above discussion leads to the expectation that rural areas with stronger mainline Christian communities will be able to moderate the negative relationship between immigration and perceptions of social cohesion. Areas with stronger evangelical religious communities might benefit from the missionary zeal of those communities, but this may be less likely to positively influence residents' attitudes than the efforts of their mainline counterparts. Hence, I anticipate that in rural areas with a large number of immigrants, those with more mainline Christian adherents will be likely to maintain a higher level of social cohesion than those with more evangelical adherents.

Methodology

The units of analysis are rural districts in England.[2] Using data on all such areas minimizes the likelihood of sample selection bias and enhances the potential for generalizing the findings (Heckman 1979). These areas are a highly pertinent context for investigating the relationship between religious communities, immigration, and social cohesion. Under the previous Labour national government, faith groups became regarded as vital partners in the drive to build strong and cohesive communities across England, especially within rural areas (Department for Communities and Local Government 2008a). This focus on the social benefits of faith is continuing under the current Conservative–Liberal Democrat coalition government's drive to promote what has been described as the "Big Society" (Stunell 2010). At the same time, the United Kingdom recently experienced one of the largest movements of population in its history, when migrant workers from several Central and Eastern European countries were accorded the right to work there following their entry into the European Union (EU).

Dependent Variable

Noah E. Friedkin (2004) suggests that social groups are cohesive when aggregate-level conditions "are producing positive membership attitudes and behaviors." I conceive social cohesion as an ideational construct that reflects individuals' perceptions of social life, rather than as a relational construct pertaining to the composition of their social networks (Moody and White 2003). Empirically, the two approaches are not mutually exclusive, but the specific question of relational cohesion is left in the background for this study and the cohesiveness of rural areas is considered in large part to be constituted by the attitudes of the people residing within those areas.

Quantitative data on citizens' perceptions of social cohesion can be drawn from the General User Survey conducted by local governments serving rural districts across England. The survey asked a representative sample of residents a series of questions about the quality of life in their area, focusing in particular on their experience of community solidarity. Fieldwork for the survey took place between September and November 2006. Researchers drew a random or stratified random sample of respondents from the Small Users Postal Address File. Local governments then collected data by using a standard questionnaire template, with the data independently verified by the Audit Commission, a central government regulatory agency. Each local government was required to achieve a sample size of 1,100, based on a confidence interval of +/−3 percent at the 95 percent confidence level. Researchers finally weighted the collected data by age, gender, ethnicity, and household size to ensure that the achieved sample was demographically representative.

The questions within the survey were all based on a five-point response scale, with the published figures used for the analysis showing the mean of responses for each district. The researchers calculated this mean as responses agreeing with the survey statements as a percentage of those responding to the question (see Department for Communities and Local Government 2007). An item assessing whether respondents believed that people from diverse backgrounds got on well together in the area was included in the survey specifically to gauge perceived levels of social cohesion. This question is the standard survey item used by the central government as an indicator of a cohesive society. It captures the overall degree of harmony between groupings based on social class and economic position, as well as those based on faith or ethnic identities (Department for Communities and Local Government 2008b).

Independent Variables

To ensure that temporal causality runs in the correct direction, I operationalized the independent variables at least one year prior to the dependent variables.

Religious Communities

Using data from a census of all Christian churches in England carried out by Christian Research in May 2005, I measured adherence to five broad Christian denominations to gauge bridging and bonding social capital effects. I captured the bridging social capital associated with mainline communities using variables measuring the number of Anglican, Methodist, and Roman Catholic adherents per 1,000 capita, and gauged the bonding social capital associated with evangelical communities by measuring the number of Baptist and Pentecostal adherents per 1,000 capita, since, unlike Anglicanism and Methodism in the United Kingdom, these denominations are not directed by a central church, but rather adhere to a principle of local autonomy for each congregation. Adherence to Christianity has been on the wane in the United Kingdom for some years now (Voas and Crockett 2005). Nevertheless, the proportion of adherents among the local population is a good proxy for social capital, since this measure captures the likely relative size and therefore social and political influence of such communities.

Immigration

I measured immigration using a proxy for the arrival of a large group of migrant workers within the United Kingdom: the numbers of European Union Accession (EU A8) citizens allocated National Insurance (NI) numbers in English local government areas during 2005. In the wake of the accession to the EU of the Czech Republic, Estonia, Hungary, Latvia, Lithuania, Poland, Slovakia, and Slovenia in 2004, the U.K. Home Office estimated an annual rate of immigration of 5,000 to 13,000 EU A8 nationals (Dustmann et al. 2003). Not only was worker migration associated with EU accession far greater than predicted (228,080 NI numbers were allocated to EU A8 citizens in 2005 alone), but its spatial distribution did not follow closely any established pattern of immigration from Central and Eastern Europe. In particular, the incidence of migrants was not limited to metropolitan areas, but was also high in rural locales across the country that previously had low levels of immigration (Drinkwater, Eade, and Garapich 2009).

EU A8 citizens constituted about 50 percent of the immigrant worker population in rural England in 2011 (Department for Communities and Local Government 2011). Of these, most work in business administration and management, agriculture, hospitality and catering, or manufacturing. In this distribution, the rural migration following the accession of the A8 countries to the EU mirrors that associated with new immigrant destinations in rural America, with many workers finding employment in industries such as food processing (Crowley and Lichter 2009). However, there is also divergence from those patterns of migration in terms of the numbers of migrants obtaining administrative positions, which perhaps reflects the fact that EU A8 citizens have the right to seek employment in England, unlike many of their undocumented counterparts in the United States.

All in all, the great scale of the worker migration to England following EU enlargement in 2004 represents a kind of natural experiment for testing the impact of immigration on social cohesion. It also offers an interesting case study of the relationships between religion and immigration, as all but one of the EU A8 countries (the Czech Republic) is predominantly Roman Catholic in religion, and so this group of migrant workers might be expected to integrate especially well in areas with stronger Catholic communities. I summed the number of allocations to EU A8 citizens and divided the resulting figure by the size of the resident population to ensure that the measure was not distorted by greater movement into larger areas.

Control Variables

Socioeconomic Disadvantage

I measured relative levels of socioeconomic disadvantage using the average ward score on the indices of deprivation in 2004. This is the population-weighted measure used by the central government constructed from indicators of income, employment, health, education, housing, crime, and living environment. Rural communities experiencing socioeconomic disadvantage arguably have fewer resources with which to resolve collective-action problems (Cloke et al. 1995), and tend to experience lower levels of community spirit as a result (Countryside Agency 2000).

Demographic Diversity

The multiplication of social identities in socially heterogeneous areas may affect levels of citizen engagement. For example, ethnically diverse rural areas can suffer higher rates of crime (Osgood and Chambers 2000), and the population is often more polarized between young and old and rich and poor in rural localities than in the city (Cloke et al. 1995). To measure demographic diversity, I squared the numbers of the age, ethnic, and social class subgroups identified in the 2001 U.K. national census (such as children ages zero to four, black African, and lower managerial and professional occupations) for each local authority area, then summed them and subtracted from 10,000, with high scores reflecting high diversity (see Trawick and Howsen 2006).

Social Alienation

Population size and density figures drawn from the national census control for the possibility that residents of smaller, less densely populated rural areas experience stronger social ties and correspondingly higher levels of social control (Wilkinson 1984). Moreover, areas with denser populations may offer greater opportunities for antisocial and criminal behavior to flourish. For instance, prior research indicates that crime rates are lower in less populous rural areas (Osgood and Chambers 2000).

Community Organizational Life

Community organizational life in rural areas is measured as the number of community, social, and personal-services organizations (such as voluntary associations, film societies, or sports clubs) per 1,000 capita registering for the value added (or goods and services) tax in 2005. This measure represents a good indicator of potential benefits for social cohesion of a larger number

TABLE 6.1 DESCRIPTIVE STATISTICS	Mean	Minimum	Maximum	S.d.
Social cohesion	80.59	38.00	89.00	7.21
Anglican attendance per 1,000 capita	27.57	10.13	61.05	9.24
Methodist attendance per 1,000 capita	8.16	0.95	29.05	5.57
Roman Catholic attendance per 1,000 capita	13.30	0.00	57.82	7.20
Baptist attendance per 1,000 capita	5.08	0.00	17.00	3.74
Pentecostal attendance per 1,000 capita	1.69	0.00	6.75	1.41
Recent immigration per 1,000 capita	3.53	0.41	33.00	3.64
Deprivation	14.51	6.20	32.57	5.66
Ethnic diversity	919.45	260.37	4,020.04	614.67
Age diversity	8,680.73	7,279.36	9,932.64	275.44
Social class diversity	8,763.09	8,051.43	9,837.77	151.07
Population	94,415.78	24,457.00	169,331.00	30,659.16
Population density	213.74	23.19	2,794.87	272.42
Community-based organization per 1,000 capita	2.85	1.14	8.56	1.10

Sources: Office of the Deputy Prime Minister 2004, 2006.

Age diversity, ethnic diversity, social class diversity: Office for National Statistics, 2003, *Census 2001: Key Statistics for Local Authorities,* London, England: TSO. Age diversity comprised twelve groups: 0–4, 5–9, 10–14, 15–19, 20–24, 25–29, 30–44, 45–59, 60–64, 65–74, 75–84, ≥85. Ethnic diversity comprised sixteen groups: white British, Irish, other white, white and black Caribbean, white and black African, white and Asian, other mixed, Indian, Pakistani, Bangladeshi, other Asian, Caribbean, African, other black, Chinese, other ethnic group. Social class diversity comprised twelve socioeconomic classifications: large employers and higher managerial occupations, higher professional occupations, lower managerial and professional occupations, intermediate occupations, small employers and own account workers, lower supervisory and technical occupations, semi routine occupations, routine occupations, persons who never worked, long-term unemployed, full-time students, non-classifiable.

Recent immigration: Department of Work and Pensions, 2006, *National Insurance Number Allocations to Overseas Nationals Entering the UK*, London, England: DWP/ONS.
Population, population density: Office for National Statistics, 2003, *Census 2001: Key Statistics for Local Authorities,* London, England: TSO.
Community-based organizations per capita: Small Business Service, 2005, *Business Start-Ups and Closures: VAT Registrations and De-registrations*, London, England: DTI. The measure comprised two VAT-registered enterprise groups: Public Administration; Other Community, Social and Personal Services.
Church attendance per capita: Peter Brierley, ed., UKCH Religious Trends No. 6 2006/2007, London, England: Christian Research.

of community-based organizations being active within local areas and has been used in previous studies incorporating rural areas (e.g., Lee 2008).

Table 6.1 presents the descriptive statistics for all the variables used in the modeling of social cohesion across rural areas in England. Skewness tests revealed that social cohesion, Roman Catholic adherence, immigration, ethnic diversity, social-class diversity, population density, and community organizations were not normally distributed across rural areas (test results of −2.63, 2.19, 4.89, 2.31, 3.21, 6.86, and 1.98). I used logged versions of the positively skewed variables in the analysis, as well as a squared version of the dependent variable—the results are the same for the uncorrected social-cohesion measure.

Findings

Table 6.2 shows ordinary least-squares regression models of the relationship between religious communities, immigration, and social cohesion.

The first model regresses the independent and control variables onto perceptions of cohesion. The second model includes interactions between religious communities and immigration to test whether bridging social-capital effects

TABLE 6.2   RELIGIOUS COMMUNITIES, IMMIGRATION, AND SOCIAL COHESION IN RURAL AREAS

	Model 1 Slope	S.e.	Model 2 Slope	S.e.
Anglicans (A)	14.216*	7.830	−8.708	9.668
Methodists (M)	32.113**	11.599	23.179	19.568
Roman Catholics (log) (C)	−145.784	392.437	−7,678.357**	2,494.623
Baptists (B)	−41.704*	18.156	−62,780	27.796
Pentecostals (P)	−68.073+	52.246	−48.702	65.878
Recent immigration (log) (I)	−772.158**	115.589	−9,230.077**	2,692.071
Interaction terms				
A x I			21.200*	10.312
M x I			8.411	14.542
C x I			1,260.608**	436.057
B x I			21.762	27.941
P x I			−23.508	54.707
Control variables				
Deprivation	−36.573*	16.676	−34.436	17.365
Ethnic diversity (log)	−286.662+	16.676	−142.038	152.421
Age diversity	.131	.229	.118	.229
Social class diversity (log)	27,462.58**	8,484.347	21,171.34*	8,962.708
Population	.008**	.003	.007*	.003
Population density (log)	−125.554	120.924	−171.642	120.192
Community-based organizations (log)	1,122.268**	289.835	939.361**	294.612
Constant	−10,1063.2**	33,620.58	−10,5880**	36,317.99
F statistic	8.37**		11.91**	
R²	.59		.64	
n = 138. + *p* ≤ 0.10; * *p* ≤ 0.05; ** *p* ≤ 0.01; S.e. (Standard Error)				

associated with mainline adherents extend to the social integration of immigrants, and whether the outreach orientation of evangelical adherents might
also be evident in this context. The findings are not distorted by multicol-
linearity, as the average variance inflation factor score for the independent
variables is about 1.6 (Bowerman and O'Connell 1990). Breusch-Pagan tests
for heteroskedasticity revealed the presence of nonconstant error variance,
so I carried out robust estimation of the standard errors.

The statistical results for the first model provide mixed support for the
anticipated relationships between the control variables and social cohesion.
The coefficient for deprivation has a negative sign and is statistically significant. The coefficient for ethnic diversity is negative, as expected, and has a
weak statistically significant association with residents' perceptions of social
cohesion. The results for age and social-class diversity, however, do not support the proposed argument on their relationship with social cohesion. The
expected relationship between sources of social alienation and social cohesion, too, receives no corroboration. When I controlled for other relevant
variables, I found that population density is not related to social cohesion,
and, contrary to expectations, population exhibits a positive relationship. It
is conceivable that residents in large communities may share a greater sense
of communal pride (Lekwa, Rice, and Hibbing 2007). Finally, areas benefiting from vibrant community organizational life have significantly higher
levels of cohesiveness. This finding on social cohesion in rural areas mirrors
evidence on the positive externalities associated with community organizational life across urban areas (e.g., Sampson et al. 2005).

Taken in combination, the religious community measures make a statistically significant addition to the explanatory power of the first model
(F ratio $= 3.54$, $p \leq .01$). Moreover, the anticipated distinction between the
bridging and bonding effects of mainline and evangelical Christian communities is largely confirmed. Perceptions of social cohesion are positively
associated with a higher proportion of Anglican and Methodist adherents
within an area, while a greater share of Baptists and Pentecostals is associated with lower cohesion. However, the coefficient for Roman Catholic
adherents, though positive, is statistically insignificant. It is possible to
derive the substantive effects of these variables from a model predicting the
nonsquared version of the dependent variable. The coefficients for this model
(available on request) suggest that a 10 percent increase in Anglicans within
an area would result, on average, in a 1 percent increase in the mean rate of
social cohesion in rural areas in England. For Methodists, a similar increase
in adherents would result in a 2 percent growth in cohesion, for Baptists, a
3 percent reduction, and for Pentecostal adherents, a 4 percent drop.

The immigration measure makes an extremely large statistically significant improvement in the explanatory power of the regression model
(F ratio $= 44.62$, $p \leq .001$). High levels of economic immigration therefore

appear to be having a detrimental effect on perceived social cohesion across rural areas in England, even when controlling for other relevant variables. In fact, interpretation of the substantive effect of this variable suggests that a 10 percent increase in the number of migrant workers entering an area would result in a 1 percent decrease in social cohesion—an effect that has great resonance in this case given that the migration of EU A8 citizens was about seventeen times greater than predicted. This finding corroborates case study research suggesting that residents in one rural English district experiencing a high rate of EU A8 immigration have been susceptible to feelings of "racial threat" (Dawney 2008). It also illustrates that the effects of prejudice and out-group hostility on perceptions of social cohesion include cultural as well as racial biases, mirroring the findings of studies that reveal the strains that white ethnic diversity can sometimes place on perceptions of community attachment (Rice and Steele 2001).

In sum, these findings highlight that the social integration of new immigrant groups in rural areas is likely to be very challenging. To explore the potentially positive role religious communities may play in immigrant integration, it is necessary to examine the extent to which they may moderate the negative relationship between immigration and social cohesion shown in the first regression model. This requires the entry of interaction terms in the statistical model.

The interactions between religious communities and immigration shown in Table 6.2 make a statistically significant addition to the explanatory power of the first regression model (F ratio = 4.15, $p \le .002$).[3] Two of the five interactions offer strong confirmation of the argument that mainline religious communities fulfill an important role in the social integration of immigrants: the coefficients for Anglican adherents and Roman Catholic adherents times immigration are both positive and statistically significant, with the latter appearing to have an especially strong relationship with social cohesion. None of the other interactions are statistically significant.

To fully explore the statistically significant interaction effects, it is necessary to calculate the marginal effects of immigration on cohesion at varying levels of the moderator variables (i.e., Anglican or Catholic adherents) (see Brambor, Clark, and Golder 2006). Graphing the slope and confidence intervals of the marginal effects is the most effective way to present this information. Accordingly, Figures 6.1 and 6.2 provide a graphical illustration of the moderating influence of Anglican and Catholic communities on the relationship between worker migration and social cohesion.

Figure 6.1 confirms that the strength of the Anglican community within an area is likely to have an important moderating effect on the relationship between immigration and social cohesion. In particular, as the number of adherents per capita moves from its minimum to maximum level (10.13 to 61.05), the negative effect of immigration clearly decreases. However, the point at which this negative relationship becomes statistically insignificant

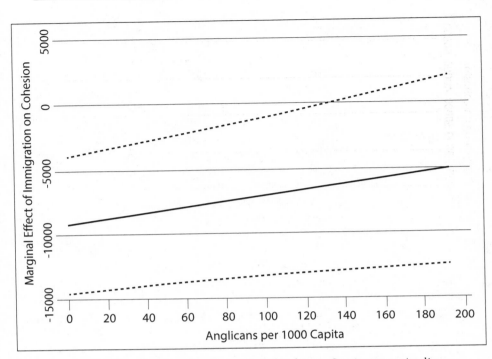

Figure 6.1 Marginal Impact of Immigration on Social Cohesion Contingent on Anglican Adherents within an Area (95% Confidence Interval)

(where the upper confidence interval meets the zero line on the graph) is beyond the range of the data (about 130 Anglicans per 1,000 capita). By contrast, Figure 6.2 indicates that as the number of Catholic adherents rises from its minimum to its maximum level (6.9 for the logged version of the measure used in the regression model), the negative relationship between immigration and residents' perceptions of cohesion is eventually eradicated.

On balance, the results presented in the figures support the conclusion that mainline religious communities have important moderating effects on the negative relationship between immigration and social cohesion—at least for this sample of rural areas in England. In particular, a greater share of Anglicans and (especially) Roman Catholics within an area is likely to enhance the prospects of immigrant integration within an area. However, no such moderating relationship was observed for rural areas with greater numbers of Methodist adherents, or for those with greater numbers of evangelical adherents. There are several possible explanations for these findings.

In addition to the bridging social-capital effects associated with its outward-looking focus, the Anglican community is able to draw on an especially strong base of institutional support for community-development activity. Although regular church attendance has declined in recent years,

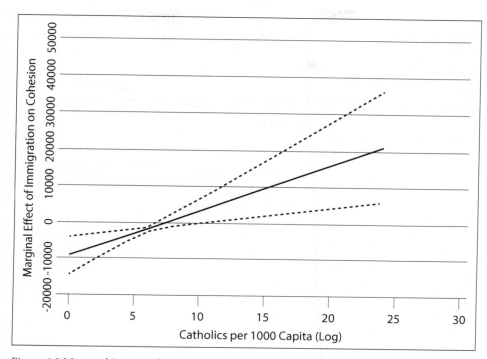

Figure 6.2 Marginal Impact of Immigration on Social Cohesion Contingent on Catholic Adherents in an Area (95% Confidence Interval)

the Church of England remains both the largest and best-resourced religious institution in rural areas across the country. Thus, despite comparatively small congregations by U.S. standards, the Anglican community is still a strong focus for civic activism and volunteering. Indeed, in many rural areas the resident Church of England priest and lay clergy may be the only non-governmental or nonprivate actors with access to resources, such as people and buildings, suitable to support such community-wide activities (Farnell et al. 2006; Russell 2005). The Anglican community is also likely to have strong links with or be actively involved in the schools within an area (Berkeley and Vij 2008), many of which may be attended by the children of migrant workers. In terms of sheer scale and capacity to assist in the process of incorporating immigrants within rural areas, the Anglican community may therefore be second only to the local state in its reach.

Although I did not observe a linear positive relationship with percep-tions of social cohesion for Roman Catholic adherence, a moderating effect on the impact of immigration on cohesion emerges very strongly. Like the Church of England, the Roman Catholic Church has the organizational presence and resources to support community activities across a wide range of geographical areas. However, the capacity supporting the outreach of the Catholic community is likely to be much more thinly spread than that underpinning the community service of the Anglican community. In this instance, then, it is likely that there is an additional factor at work that explains the strength of the interaction effect. That factor is almost certainly the religious adherence of the Central and Eastern European migrant workers. Apart from the Czech Republic, all the other EU A8 countries are predominantly Roman Catholic in religion. In particular, Poland, the country from which the vast majority of the migrant workers emanate, is overwhelmingly Roman Catholic, with very high rates of religious belief (almost 90 percent) and observance (over 50 percent) (European Commission 2005). The finding in the final regression model is therefore suggestive of distinctive bridging social-capital effects attributable to the values of Catholic adherents in the host country and within the new immigrant group.

Finally, it is noteworthy that the share of evangelical adherents neither strengthened nor weakened the negative relationship between immigration and perceived social cohesion. This indicates that while these religious communities may play little positive role in the integration of immigrants, neither do they appear to make integration more difficult. It is possible that the inward focus of the Baptist and Pentecostal communities in England leads them to take less interest in reaching out to immigrant groups than those in the United States, though it is also probable that they lack the organizational capacity to do such outreach work to the same degree as the mainline communities in rural England. Further research on the role of evangelical communities within rural areas could illuminate this interesting issue.

Conclusion

This chapter has provided quantitative evidence on the relationship between religious communities, immigration, and perceptions of social cohesion across rural areas in England. In keeping with the bridging and bonding social-capital hypotheses the article advances, mainline Protestant religious communities are associated with more cohesive communities, and evangelical ones with less social cohesion. At the same time, worker migration from Central and Eastern Europe has a strong negative relationship with perceptions of social cohesion. However, the strength of Anglican and (especially) Roman Catholic communities within rural areas may mitigate the negative relationship between immigration and perceptions of cohesiveness, thereby enhancing the prospects of social integration. These findings have important theoretical and practical implications.

The analysis presented here builds on existing theoretical and empirical work on religious communities in rural areas, providing a direct test of the links between those communities, immigration, and social cohesion. Prior studies have examined the separate effects of these phenomena using crime rates (e.g., Lee and Bartowski 2004) or residents' perceptions of community attachment (Brehm, Eisenhauer, and Krannich 2004; Brown, Dorius, and Krannich 2005). Until now, the combined effects of these phenomena have not been investigated within the same study, nor have their separate effects on residents' perceptions of the cohesiveness of their community been considered. What emerges from this analysis is a pattern of immigrant integration in rural areas that provides some support for both the "racial threat" and "social contact" hypotheses. In the first instance, higher rates of worker immigration are associated with weaker social cohesion, yet it appears that the presence of strong mainline religious communities can enable feelings of racial threat to be overcome. This suggests that there may be great potential for bringing together these two arguments about intergroup relations within a framework for empirical analysis that gives greater recognition to the complex temporal processes at work in immigrant integration in rural areas. It also points toward the need for more in-depth qualitative ethnographic research around this issue as well as longitudinal quantitative studies to explore the causal mechanisms associated with immigrant integration in greater detail.

Despite the strength of the findings, the analysis presented here has limitations. The statistical results may simply be a product of when and where the survey was conducted. Rural England has a very particular social structure, which may not map closely onto rural life elsewhere. Although Christian communities in England often play a similar role in supporting community activities to that of their counterparts in rural America, the salience of participation within those communities for rural residents has been in decline for some years now. The findings presented here may therefore speak to the ongoing institutional embeddedness of mainline communities rather than their doctrines or beliefs that they espouse, or the commitment and outreach work of their members. Thus, it would be important to examine in more detail how, and in what ways, that embeddedness influences the prospects of immigrant integration.

Similarly, evidence on the relationship between social cohesion and the arrival of other immigrant groups than those studied here would enable the dynamics of the immigration-cohesion relationship to be explored further. Although the sudden movement of large numbers of immigrants into rural areas is not common in England, such population shifts are more frequent in other countries, including the United States, where African American and Latino migration in nonmetropolitan areas is now extremely widespread (Donato et al. 2007). The relationships observed here between Central and Eastern European immigration and cohesion may take different forms for alternative immigrant groups. For example, the overwhelming whiteness of rural England is sometimes thought to make longtime residents especially hostile to nonwhite immigrant groups (Chakraborti and Garland 2004). How the process of integration occurs for different immigrant groups is a topic of vital importance for future research.[4] Finally, because of the focus on social cohesion at the aggregate level across rural areas, the findings are susceptible to problems associated with drawing inferences about individual attitudes from aggregated data (Blakely and Woodward 2000). Subsequent research could therefore build on this study by examining religious communities, immigration, and social cohesion using multilevel modelling.[5]

The findings presented here indicate that religious communities and recent immigration have an especially large statistically significant independent effect on perceptions of social cohesion. They also highlight that mainline religious communities can moderate negative externalities for social cohesion associated with the arrival of large numbers of newcomers in rural areas. Whether as a product of their embeddedness within the institutions of rural England, their doctrine of social responsibility, or their strong connections with affiliated immigrant religious groups, mainline communities seem to manifest bridging social capital, which offers the prospect of improved immigrant integration in this setting. This result implies that more should be done to understand how the role of these communities in promoting the integration of newcomers in rural areas could be supported. Future studies of the relationship between religious communities, immigration, and social cohesion in rural areas should therefore seek to include measures of the policy interventions and strategies designed to address this important issue.

NOTES

Acknowledgments: The research leading to these results was supported under the European Commission's Seventh Framework Programme under grant agreement No. 266887 (Project COCOPS).

1. Unfortunately, there are currently no data available at the rural district level on the religious character of elementary schools with which to explore the relationship between religious communities and this particular institutional structure in more depth.

2. To ensure that the analysis focused on rural areas, I entered only data from local governments serving rural communities (known as district councils) into the statistical models. These governments were selected on the basis of the urban-rural administrative-area classification used by the central government in the United Kingdom (see Office of the Deputy Prime Minister 2002). This classifies local government areas as rural or urban on the basis of an index of population density; overall employment; public-transport usage; agricultural employment; employment in mining, energy, and water production; and ethnic homogeneity.

3. It should be noted that the coefficients for the separate effects of religious communities and immigration shown in the second model can not be compared directly with those in the first one. The coefficients in the model, including the interaction terms, show the effects of each of these two variables when the other is set to zero (Jaccard and Turrisi 2003). For example, the significantly negative coefficient for Anglican adherence

in the interactions model is derived from an assumption that immigration is zero, which is beyond the range of the data (as shown in Table 6.1).

4. Repeating the analysis presented in this article for a measure of non-EU A8 immigration reveals similar results to those for EU A8 immigration, albeit with one important exception—the interaction between non-EU A8 immigration and Pentecostal adherence is negative and statistically significant. Systematic investigation of variations across alternative groupings of these non-EU A8 immigrants (e.g., nonwhite immigrant groups from former U.K. colonies) would constitute a research agenda in its own right, and so because of space constraints, that topic is not explored further in this study.

5. Unfortunately, the General User Survey and church attendance data are not available at the individual level.

IV

Early Migration Cycle Countries

7

The Challenges of Immigrant Incorporation in the Context of Multiple Transition Processes

The Case of Poland

ALEKSANDRA KAZŁOWSKA

MAGDALENA LESIŃSKA

The chapters in Part IV turn their attention to early migration cycle countries, which, unlike traditional destination countries such as the United States and Great Britain, are experiencing either sustained immigration for the first time in their modern history, as in the case of Poland, or immigration from different countries and under different conditions than previously, as in the case of Latvia. The focus in this section is on public policy responses at the national level, as opposed to the localized responses examined in Part III. Whereas Utah and rural English destinations have developed responses in the context of nations accustomed to immigration, Poland and Latvia are entirely unaccustomed to it, but nevertheless have developed policies in conformity with those of the European Union. Specifically, challenges stem from the EU's requirement that its member states adopt certain integration policies in the face of negative national attitudes toward immigration in Poland and Latvia. In this chapter, Aleksandra Kazłowska and Magdalena Lesińska discuss Poland's transformation from a country of emigration to one in which labor shortages and demographic issues have led to net in-migration. They show that although there is as yet no sense of political or policy crisis relating to the still-low levels of immigration, there is apprehension about the potential impact of immigration for Polish social cohesion. To date, integration policy making has been minimal and has been driven by the requirements of the EU, a supranational body, and by a desire to encourage temporary or circular migration.

This chapter analyzes Poland's response to immigration, with a focus on Polish immigrant integration policy. This is discussed in the context of the multiple transition processes related to the transformation of Poland's geopolitical position and changes in its migration profile after the EU accession in 2004. Poland is a country in which the consequences of systemic transition overlap with the intensive processes of modernization and EU integration. It has also been facing a change in its immigration status over recent years. Using Marek Okólski's (2012) concept of a *migration cycle*, which explains the complex relationship between migration and the state, Poland would appear to be in the transitional phase from an emigration state into an emigration-immigration one.

EU membership has had a powerful impact on Poland. Following the EU accession and the opening of their labor markets by some EU countries to citizens of new member states, Poland experienced a massive outflow of its citizens within a very short period. During the last few years, however, due to intensive economic growth and modernization processes, Poland has also become more attractive to foreign workers. As a result, the number of foreigners arriving in Poland and the diversity of their nationalities has increased. Nevertheless, the scale of these inflows and the size of the foreign population resident in Poland are still relatively small in comparison with other countries in Europe (foreigners constitute less than 2 percent of the resident population). According to the Register of the Office for Aliens on January 1, 2015, only 175,065 foreigners had documents giving them right for residence in Poland, mainly from Ukraine (40,979), Germany (20,200), the Russian Federation (10,739), Belarus (9,924), and Vietnam (9,042). Moreover, immigration has had a predominantly temporary and circular character (as opposed to settlement migration, which is slowly increasing), and the main groups of migrants come from the eastern neighboring countries, mostly from Ukraine.

To date, migration to Poland and consequent state immigration policy have been rather amorphous, reflecting the period of transition from the first to the second stage of the immigration cycle (Grzymała-Kazłowska and Okólski 2010). After the first stage of dynamic, irregular, and ephemeral inflows of the 1990s, Poland is currently entering the second stage, during which immigration is stabilizing and becoming more permanent and controlled.

Accession to the EU was also one of the milestones in Poland's transition processes. It brought not only a crucial change in its geopolitical status, but also—as an EU and Schengen area member state[1]—Poland has become part of the European immigration system, and, thus, it has been obliged to implement the *acquis communautaire* (European Union law) related to movements of EU citizens and third-country nationals. This required important changes in Polish national law and institutional arrangements, including changes in immigration and integration policies.

The main research questions this chapter addresses are:

1. How does a state with a long history of emigration and a highly homogenous society (in ethno-national terms) respond to immigration?
2. What approach has been adopted to integrate immigrants into state and society, and what legal and political institutional infrastructure has been developed to incorporate newcomers?

The main hypotheses related to these questions are:

1. Polish state immigration and integration policies as well as their implementation are a top-down process, driven mostly by pan-national forces, as the EU requirements are obligatory for all member states, in contradistinction to a bottom-up, uni-national process that originates from the reality of on-the-ground immigration patterns and immigrant population needs.
2. Polish political elites and authorities are anxious about permanent immigrant settlement given the experience of other immigration countries and, in particular, problems posed by the integration of foreigners, especially from culturally distinctive countries.

Thus, recent developments in immigration policy support circular or temporary immigration from neighboring countries, while the state's activities aimed at foreigners' integration are limited to the bare minimum required by the EU.

This chapter is organized into the following sections. First, it briefly introduces the dynamic of recent migration processes in Poland (both emigration and immigration) and their influence on the changing migration status of Poland, as it becomes a country of net immigration. The next section adopts a political perspective to discuss the state's response to challenges of immigration and the development of immigration policy. The final section focuses on recent developments and changes in immigration and integration policies of Poland. An emphasis is put on the practice of incorporation of foreigners within the state and society as well as legal and political factors influencing the implementation of these policies.

Becoming an Emigration–Immigration Country

Unlike other European countries that have already experienced the transformation from a net emigration to net immigration country, Poland retains its character as a country that still has substantial emigration, although, as an EU member and EU border country, it is an integral part of the European immigration system. The current transformation of the immigration status of Poland is shaped by a combination of factors, such as integration processes within the EU that are more significant than ever before accelerating globalization and transnational processes, the aging of the European populations, and the emergence of new migration phenomena such as *fluid migration* (Engbersen, Snel, and de Boom, 2010; Engbersen et al., 2013; Górny et al. 2009; Grabowska-Lusińska and Okólski 2009).

The massive outflows of Poles after the country's accession to the EU (on May 1, 2004), followed by the noticeable but not large return migration caused by the economic crisis in Western Europe, and increasing migration to Poland are processes that have also had a serious impact on Polish society and resulted in the profound transformation of immigration policy. In absolute terms, Poles are the leading group among migrants from the eight Central and Eastern European (CEE) countries that accessed to the EU in 2004. This is due both to Poland having the largest demographic potential related to the size of its population and to its traditions and culturally rooted patterns of migration. It is estimated that between May 1, 2004, and January 1, 2007, at least a million people emigrated from Poland. In general, emigrants constituted over 4 percent of the working-age population (Okólski 2012). According to the estimates of the Polish Central Statistical Office, in 2011, as many as 2.06 million permanent residents of Poland had stayed abroad for over three months, a large majority for over one year. Of these, 1.75 million people resided in EU countries, mainly in the United Kingdom, Germany, Ireland, and the Netherlands.

Compared to immigration in the transition period, postaccession migration could be characterized by not only higher intensity, but also a greater diversity of migrant strategies. Based on research on the Polish postaccession emigrants, a new form of emigration, originated from the strategy of intentional unpredictability, has been identified (Eade 2006). Godfried Engbersen and colleagues (2013) call this specific type of migration of "new Europeans" *fluid migration*, whereby patterns of migration are individualized, and migrants circulate looking for a place for themselves in different countries, taking advantage of open borders and free labor market access. Fluid migrants have, on the whole, weak ties with both sending and receiving countries (Engbersen et al. 2013). In contrast to the previous emigration, part of the postaccession emigration seems to consist of regular long-term and permanently settled migrants (often accompanied by their entire families). This intensive, long-term, and permanently settled migration is expected to lead to more serious and permanent changes in the sociodemographic structure of Polish society. Marek Okólski (2012) puts forward a hypothesis that the crowding-out and modernizing impact of contemporary emigration from Poland may allow for a permanent outflow of the structurally redundant population and, as a consequence, will accelerate development.

Poland is also becoming a country of net immigration. The influx of foreigners into Poland after the political transition in 1989 was a novelty for the relatively homogenous post–World War II Polish society.[2] From the beginning of the 1990s, thousands of Ukrainians, Bulgarians, and Romanians started to migrate in search of income to other countries in the CEE, including Poland (Kępińska and Stola 2004). Initially, most of these migrants were petty traders and irregular workers engaged in unskilled jobs. They were later joined by entrepreneurs, such as the Vietnamese, and then followed by contract workers from neighboring countries, mainly Ukraine. Asylum-seekers and repatriates constitute a separate contrasting category of newcomer that arrived in Poland. In 2012, there were 9,180 applications for refugee status submitted to Poland, substantially more than in any other CEE country. In recent years, applicants for refugee status in Poland have been mainly Russian citizens declaring Chechen nationality and Georgians. A minority of applicants receive refugee status or another form of temporary protection. However, most leave Poland and subsequently move to Western Europe. Between 1997 and 2010, over 7,000 migrants of Polish origin from the former Soviet Union arrived in Poland. Within the institutionalized repatriation system, recent statistics show a clear declining trend in repatriation immigration since 2001. The previously mentioned inflows have been complemented by intra-EU migration of highly skilled workers/expatriates from Western Europe and return migrants, especially from countries such as the United States, the United Kingdom, or Germany.

Immigration statistics for the past two decades show small numbers of registered, long-term foreigners living in Poland. The last National Census in 2011 showed that the number of foreigners with a permit for a fixed period or settlement in Poland still remains small, at just 63,000, although this number is perceived as underestimated, because it did not account for temporary migrants. According to the Central Population Register (PESEL), at the end of 2011 the number of temporary migrants who arrived from abroad and registered in Poland for a temporary stay of above three months was almost 66,000 (SOPEMI Report 2012). However, these data include not only foreigners, but also Polish nationals coming from abroad. The main countries of previous stay included Ukraine (18,200, 27 percent of all), Germany (5,500), Belarus (4,300), Vietnam (3,200), the Russian Federation (2,200), and China (2,700).

Another, probably more reliable source of data, is the Register of the Office for Foreigners. At the end of 2009, there were almost 93,000 foreign citizens recorded, which constituted approximately 0.2 percent of the population of Poland. Among them, immigrants from European countries (geographically and culturally close to Polish society) were found most frequently, with the highest number being that of Ukrainian nationals—almost 27,000 (29 percent). The most numerous non-European immigrants were the

Vietnamese—over 8,000, compared to almost 13,000 Russian citizens (half of them Chechen refugees) and almost 8,500 Belarusians. The data from the end of 2013 reveal a substantially larger number of foreign citizens registered to reside temporarily or permanently in Poland—almost 121,000. The largest groups were Ukrainians (37,600), Vietnamese (13,400), Russians (12,000), and Belarusians (11,100). This increase in numbers was partly a consequence of the last regularization (Kaczmarczyk 2014: 44–48).

Given their relative numbers and significance, Ukrainians and Vietnamese immigrants represent the two major types of economic immigrants to Poland (see Fihel et al. 2007; Górny et al. 2010; Grzymała-Kazłowska 2008). The Vietnamese are relatively new to Poland; their massive influx started in the late 1980s (not counting Vietnamese students coming on scholarships to communist Poland). After 1986, when a shift toward a market economy took place in Vietnam, it opened its borders for emigration, even though the communist political system remained in place. The Vietnamese began to come to Poland to take advantage of the economic opportunities during the transition period. They are clustered in Poland in two sectors: trade (most often) and catering. Very often they remain self-employed, working in companies established by themselves or with the help of other Vietnamese. The Vietnamese community is highly stratified in socioeconomic terms. It has formed a vibrant ethnic enclave with numerous ethnic associations and well-developed ethnic services. Even members of the first or second generation, regardless of their cultural and professional competencies and command of the Polish language, frequently remain in ethnic enclaves in the trade or restaurant sectors rather than search for employment in the wider primary market (Grzymała-Kazłowska 2008). In general, a strong Vietnamese identity and close in-group relations coexist in this group. It appears that the majority of the first generation of immigrants did not easily integrate into the Polish society at the individual level. On the contrary, a low level of Polish-language competency and a very high percentage of intragroup marriages are clearly visible. This adaptation strategy may have been reinforced by the surveillance attitude of the Polish state toward Vietnamese immigrants and the lack of integration policy aimed at this ethnic group. Moreover, the Vietnamese are perceived as immigrants who are highly distinct from the Polish society in cultural terms such as language, values, and social structures. Physical and sociocultural dissimilarity in the highly homogenous Polish society makes the Vietnamese particularly visible, and the cultural distance between them and the receiving society encourages strong in-group cooperation and self-reliance.

Ukrainians, on the other hand, represent an immigrant group perceived to be close to Polish society due to the past and present contacts between the two nations, language and cultural similarity, common history, similar experiences, as well as geographical proximity. The majority of Ukrainian immigrants who reside in Poland come from western Ukraine, which had historic connections with the Polish state, where a substantial Polish minority continues to live, and where there are the most widespread cross-border relations between Poles and Ukrainians. In general, the majority of Ukrainians work in the secondary sector (agriculture, construction, and household services). Ukrainians are the dominant group among migrants coming to Poland for seasonal, short-term work. They circulate between Poland and Ukraine following the scheme "earn here, spend there" and do not intend to settle in Poland. In the case of Ukrainians settled in Poland, cultural proximity, less sharply defined original national identity, and the pro-European and pro-Polish orientation of immigrants contribute to their individualization and assimilation in Poland in both structural and cultural senses.

To summarize, long-term immigrant settlement in Poland has not been on a large scale. However, it can be assumed that the number of immigrants in Poland will gradually increase. Due to Poland's geopolitical position, development, and modernization, as well as the influences of European integration and globalization, foreigners will flow into Poland, where the demand for their labor will grow, particularly in the context of Poland's aging population and the outflow of Polish workers to other European countries (Okólski 2010).

"Toward Controlled Opening Up": A Political Strategy to Incorporate Immigrants

In the 1990s, Poland had to transform itself from a state with a restrictive exit policy and forcibly repressed mobility characteristic of a communist regime (Stola 2001) into a democratic state with open borders, particularly for its citizens. This change was difficult, considering the fact that Poland has traditionally been a country of emigration with little experience in regulating migrant inflows. After 1989, Poland had a relatively liberal admission policy, but accession negotiations with the EU led to the introduction of new and stricter rules and regulations. The first Aliens Act of 1997 narrowed the possible legal channels of migrant entry and tightened border controls. The 2003 Aliens Act included even more restrictive legal provisions regarding border control, the visa system, and residence rights. The act introduced visa requirements for citizens of a number of countries (e.g., the Ukraine) who had previously enjoyed visa-free movement. An even stricter admission policy was generally implemented once Poland became a part of the EU (2004) and after the Schengen Agreement (2007).

There is no doubt that membership in the EU was a crucial milestone in the development of immigration policy in Poland (Kicinger 2005; Weinar 2006). The requirements, which Poland as a new member was obliged to fulfill, constituted the key impulse for the development of the current legal and institutional system. Moreover, this process has been top down, as a response to external EU administrative guidance and pressures rather than to local immigration processes (Duszczyk and Lesińska 2010). Many institutions and measures designed in western countries in response to the immigration phenomenon were transposed to Poland during the process of harmonization with the EU. This led to a paradox, with an attempt to create immigration policy before there was a real need for it, given the modest number of immigrants (Kicinger and Koryś 2011).

During the past few years, several important developments related to immigration policy have been noticeable. They all follow a trend, which could be summarized as an evolution toward slow and controlled opening up of Poland to foreigners' inflows. These developments, however, have some serious limitations: they promote a circular (as opposed to settlement) labor migration, incentives to migrate are directed only at EU citizens and nationals from eastern neighboring countries, and they are limited to the legal and economic spheres (rather than sociocultural or political spheres).

Of the developments that could be described as policy instruments assisting the immigrant incorporation process, the most important are presented below. The first important change was the simplification of the labor market entry system for foreigners. In 2007, in addition to the regular system of work permits based on the test of labor market conditions, a new, simplified preferential scheme based on employers' declarations was introduced. It allowed employers to hire foreign workers from six eastern countries (initially only from Ukraine, Belarus, Russia, and later also from Moldova and Georgia since 2012, and Armenia since 2014) for six months during twelve consecutive months. The procedures related to employing foreigners in this scheme are simple, fast, and low cost. The main aim was to encourage employers to hire foreigners on a regular basis and for immigrants to use the legal option to arrive and work in Poland. The number of employers' declarations of intent to employ a foreigner on the basis of this simplified procedure increased from almost 22,000 in 2007 to 260,000 in 2011 and since then remains at a stable level of over 200,000 declarations issued per year. Ukrainians constituted the vast majority of foreigners (more than 90 percent) using this scheme to come and work in Poland. Since its implementation, the scheme has evolved into the most significant (statistically) formula of employment of foreigners in Poland and has become one of the most popular corridors for foreign short-term (usually seasonal) workers (Kaczmarczyk 2015).

In the first half year of 2012, the third regularization program was implemented in Poland (following two similar programs which took place in 2003 and 2007), and was definitely the most extensive one, with more requirements in comparison to the previous programs. As a result, more than 9,500 people took this opportunity to apply for the legalization of their stay, and about 4,500 succeeded. The successful applicants gained permission to stay in Poland for two years. More than half of the applicants were Vietnamese and Ukrainian citizens.

Another development was the new naturalization rules implemented in 2012, when the Act of Polish Citizenship came into force. The most important changes in the new naturalization law include shortening the qualifying period of residence from five to three years (or two years in the case of privileged categories of foreigners, such as spouses of Polish citizens, stateless persons, refugees, and persons possessing a permit to settle obtained in connection with their Polish origin) and allowing dual or multiple citizenship. The waiving of the previous requirement to renounce citizenship of another country may induce more immigrants to naturalize in Poland. On the other hand, the new law introduced the Polish-language requirement for foreigners seeking naturalization. This follows a trend observed in other EU states for migrants to demonstrate their sociocultural integration before they are naturalized (Lesińska 2014).

Important progress has also been made in the development of state's migration strategy. In July 2012 the Council of Ministers adopted the policy document entitled "Polish Migration Policy—The Current State of Play and Proposed Actions." It includes an overview of the present migration policy and a normative base for further policy development, as well as practical recommendations related to law, institutions, and practice of immigration and integration policies. Growing migration to Poland is perceived by the authorities as an inevitable phenomenon due to the global processes occurring in Europe and in the world at large, as well as the growing need for a foreign workforce as a result of mass emigration and declining birthrates and population aging. Immigration is, however, also perceived as a possible threat to social cohesion mostly due to irregular migrant inflows and to problems with immigrants' integration—as a lesson drawn from the experience of the more mature immigration countries of Western Europe (Duszczyk and Lesińska 2010).

The inflow of foreign workers has been identified by Polish political elites as an inevitable occurrence, particularly in a time of the mass emigration of Poles, noticeable niches in the national labor market, and a growing demand for a foreign workforce in some sectors of economy. At the same time, however, settlement migration, especially of migrants of non-European origin, is perceived as problematic—if not undesirable. The experiences of Western European countries, especially related to problems with the integration of immigrants, constitute the primary reference point for the Polish authorities. The focus is on potential conflicts and the protection of state security and public order—phenomena that are characteristic of mature immigration countries, but that have not appeared in reality in Poland, yet.

In spite of the vigilant attitude of the Polish authorities and political elites toward immigration, the inflow of immigrants is not a hot social issue because of its small scale and the character of immigration. The *European Values Study* (as cited in Jasińska-Kania 2012) demonstrated that in 2008 far fewer people in Poland perceived the number of immigrants as too high compared to all other European societies (except Romanians and Bulgarians). Also, the level of insecurity linked to the presence of immigrants in Poland was among the lowest among all European countries (only Romania, France, Denmark, and Albania scored lower (Grzymała-Kazłowska 2012). Therefore, immigration is not an issue in any political or public debates (in contrast to the post accession emigration issue). Until now, immigration as a subject has been absent from the programs of the political parties, electoral campaigns, and politicians' struggles. In fact, the process of formulation and implementation of the policy could be described as a technocratic one, whereby the administration (the Ministry of Interior in particular) plays a primary role.

In summary, Poland is on the way toward controlled opening up to immigration, but in a rather restrictive way. The latest developments in immigration policy are limited to the promotion of legal stay and employment and better incorporation of foreigners in the labor market as a complementary workforce to Polish nationals. Moreover, the changes demonstrate a clear preference for newcomers from eastern neighboring countries, especially Ukraine, which is treated as the most desired source country for immigrants to Poland.

Integration Policy: Between Political Requirements, National Interests, and Immigrants' Needs

State policy toward immigrants, which has been implemented in Poland since the 1990s, could be described as incorporation "via abandonment" (Grzymala-Kazlowska and Weinar 2006). The limited institutional support from the state and NGOs, together with the marginally developed immigrant communities (with few exceptions) have made the adaptation of immigrants to life in Poland difficult, especially for those coming from culturally distinctive countries. The integration system has been very selective and small scale—there were only two special short-term integration programs for two particular categories of immigrants: people with refugee (or temporary protection) status, and repatriates and their families. The first program was enforced by international law requirements (e.g., Geneva Convention signed by Poland in 1991) and Poland's accession to the EU. The second resulted from a repatriation policy that has been adopted in Poland since the mid-1990s. The long neglect of integration policy has resulted from a failure to recognize the emergent ethno-cultural diversity in an otherwise homogenous country, and a belief that Poland is a transit country with "unproblematic" immigration, that is, dominated by immigrants of European origin (relatively close in cultural terms) and with a very limited scale of settlement immigration.

Still, the issue of integration of immigrants is a low priority on the Polish political agenda (Górny et al. 2010). The official justification for the narrow scope of the state's activity in this area is explained by the relatively small inflow of foreigners and its temporary (transit, circular) nature. Moreover, it is also stressed that there are only a small number of settled immigrants, most of whom come from neighboring countries (such as Ukraine) and have no serious integration problems due to their cultural and language compatibility. Other immigrant groups, such as the Vietnamese, are generally in-group oriented and are not perceived as a group requiring special assistance (Grzymała-Kazłowska 2015).

Thus, there is no complex, long-term, and systematic "national integration strategy" concerning the integration of foreigners in general. The legal and institutional framework created to address this issue has been created mostly in response to EU requirements and under EU guidance to align the Polish migration law with the relevant EU legislation, based on an obligatory *acquis* and a collection of recommendations and best practices that all EU member states should follow (via an open method of coordination introduced by the EU). For Poland, accession to the EU was a powerful determining impulse and accelerated the evolution of its immigration and immigrant integration policies. Institutions and measures designed by more mature immigration countries have been transposed, during the process of harmonization with the EU, to the new members. Initiatives related to integration have been very much triggered by the recent developments in the EU "soft law," particularly such as the Common Basic Principles of Integration and the European Agenda for the Integration of non-EU migrants, supported by the European Fund for the Integration (as the main financing instrument) and the Network of National Contacts Points on Integration (as an institutional structure established for exchanging and discussing best practices). To a much lesser extent, integration policy has been developed to solve specific problems that emerged in practice (to remove loopholes and avoid interpretational discrepancies). Therefore, the development of integration policy in Poland can be described as a reactive, centralized, and top-down process.

Until 2005, there was no official document detailing the issue of integration and its scope in a manner different than simple, general statements. In the "Proposals of Actions Aimed at Establishing a Comprehensive Immigrant Integration Policy in Poland" issued by the Ministry of Labor and Social Policy (officially responsible for integration policy), it is clearly confirmed that "at present, integrative actions in Poland, within special individual integration programs, are focused on one group of foreigners—those having refugee status" (Ministry of Social Policy, Poland 2005).[3] Since then, the scope of beneficiaries of the state's integration programs has not changed. Progress is only visible in the development of an institutional structure. In 2013, the Working Group on Integration of Foreigners was established within the Department of Aid and Social Integration (Ministry of Labor and Social Affairs). The main aim of the group has been to prepare the document "Polish integration policy of foreigners—assumptions and guidelines."

Concerning legislation related to incorporation of legal foreign residents into the social security entitlements system, Polish law meets European standards. Foreign nationals working legally in Poland possess the same bundle of social rights as Polish citizens, including an entitlement to pensions, medical care, and unemployment benefits. Taking into account the incorporation of foreigners into the legal-political system, Poland is still one of the most restrictive countries in Europe. According to current law, immigrants with temporary residence status may apply for a permit to settle after five years of legal stay in Poland. Foreign residents have no voting rights at any level (with exception of the EU citizens, whose right to vote and be elected at the local level is secured in the EU Treaty). Poland did not sign the fundamental document encouraging political participation of foreign nationals, namely the Council of Europe's *Convention on the Participation of Foreigners in Public Life at the Local Level*. Foreigners are not represented in any labor union or political party in Poland. This partly explains why these institutions do not include immigration-related issues on their agendas. Moreover, even if immigrants have the right to establish associations, their number and impact is very limited. They are not recognized as influential actors, and there is no institution—such as a consultative or advisory body—that could function as a communication forum between immigrants and authorities at the central level.

Despite the generally passive attitude of the state to the integration of foreigners, a more active approach to the integration of foreigners is noticeable in the NGO sector. The interest in the implementation of projects aimed at migrants and supporting their integration is spurred by the opportunity to apply for financial support by the EU (e.g., EIF—the European Fund for the Integration of non-EU immigrants, and ERF—the European Refugee Fund). Since 2007, diverse integration activities have been implemented by nongovernmental and local institutions following the best practices adopted in other EU countries (e.g., language and adaptation courses, information campaigns, intercultural education programs and training courses) using the support of the EU funds. It means that, in practice, NGOs partially substitute for the state when it comes to the implementation of integration policy. However, the scope of action of nongovernmental organizations is limited in time (the programs are funded for a maximum of a year's time) and space (located mostly in the biggest cities, where the organizations are placed), and therefore their practical impact is not very significant.

Conclusion

Poland is and has always been predominantly an emigration country, and its history has been marked by successive waves of emigrants. The last outflow after accession to the EU was a particularly momentous phenomenon in the post–World War II history of Poland, unparalleled with previous waves because of its magnitude, dynamics, and new destinations. At the same time, since 2006 the number of registered immigrants has been increasing, due first to the inflow of foreigners, and second to the return migration of Poles (those who left the country in the post accession period, in particular). The processes of migration to and from Poland have been linked to the multiple transitions taking place in Poland over the past few decades. In the context of the migration cycle, Poland at present is on the way toward the status of immigration-emigration country, when the stock of Polish nationals abroad becomes stable, and the number of foreign residents is growing (but still remains small in comparison with other countries).

Among the forces that shape the immigration and integration policies in Poland, three appear to be the most influential: (1) those related to the geopolitical location of Poland within contemporary migration space; (2) those linked to EU membership and its legal and political requirements; and (3) those based on beliefs of authorities responsible for immigration policy that growing immigration to Poland is an inevitable phenomenon that may eventually constitute a threat to social cohesion, which has been observed in more mature immigration countries in Europe.

Poland as an eastern border country of the EU has a specific position as a transit country for those migrating from East to West. As a result of the recent economic development and growing need for a labor force (also due to the mass emigration of Poles in recent years), Poland is increasingly attractive to foreign workers. Poland's immigration policy has shifted from protection against the inflows to facilitation for desirable groups of immigrants. The process toward opening up has been necessary, considering the aforementioned global changes on the one hand, and a negative demographic prognosis for Poland on the other. The current priority to have an immigration policy that encourages immigrants from neighboring countries to work in Poland will, however, have to be modified in the long run to take into account unfavorable demographics in preferred source countries such as Ukraine.

Poland's accession to the EU has been the main driver in the development of its immigration policy at its normative (migration doctrine) and functional (legal and institutional framework) levels. An almost linear interdependence between the EU and Polish policy is noticeable, particularly in terms of the conceptualization of integration (Polish documents closely follow EU recommendations). Additionally, integration programs that are carried out by NGOs directly follow the best practices recommended by the EU, and are funded from EU sources. Poland harmonizes its national law with EU legislation, and the obligatory participation of Polish authorities in EU consultative processes has also been an incentive to introduce similar approaches at the state policy level in Poland.

It is clear from the official documents and political statements that political elites and authorities are conscious of the fact that Poland is on its way to becoming a country of immigration. The growing inflows of immigrants have been identified as an inevitable occurrence, but immigration, in the case of settlement migration/immigration of foreigners of non-European origin, is perceived as problematic—if not undesirable. The experiences of Western European countries, especially related to problems with integration of immigrants, constitute the primary reference point for Polish authorities.

NOTES

1. Schengen area is composed of twenty-six European countries, which have generally abolished any type of control at their mutual borders.

2. According to rough estimates, the number of traditional national and ethnic minorities (nationals of non-Polish origin) is low (2 to 4 percent of the whole population in Poland), as confirmed by consecutive national censuses. In the 2003 census only 1.2 percent of the population declared a nationality different than Polish nationality (only one nationality could be declared). In 2011, when dual ethnic identification was allowed, the number of Poland's residents declaring non-Polish nationality increased to 3.9 percent (including 1.6 percent who declared only a non-Polish identity).

3. Immigrants coming with a repatriation visa automatically acquire Polish citizenship.

8

Political Participation of Migrants in Latvia

Lessons Learned?

DACE AKULE

In contrast to Poland, where immigration is unprecedented, contemporary migration to Latvia occurs in the context of conflict over historical Russian immigration and Soviet influence. In this sense, Latvia resembles the destinations discussed in Part II—Catalonia and the American South—where contemporary immigrant settlement occurs in an ethnically divided society. While Polish elites are concerned about the potentially negative impact of immigration on social cohesion, Latvian responses have been more adamantly opposed to immigration, as Latvian citizens have historically associated Russian immigration with their own repression. Akule argues in this chapter that Latvian attitudes toward immigration are highly negative and resistant to any policy change not absolutely required by the EU. As in Poland, the EU's influence has instantiated a baseline of immigrant integration policies in Latvia, although popular and elite political resistance to such policies remain significant.

Like several other new EU member states, Latvia is experiencing increasing but relatively low volumes of immigration. Despite the present firsthand experience as well as a long history of Latvian emigration, Soviet policies causing mass migration to Latvia have led to a very negative public opinion of immigration. The unwillingness or inability to provide a welcoming environment for newly arriving migrants has also been one of the reasons why a national immigrant integration policy was adopted only in 2011. This creates obstacles for the political participation of migrants, as the political discourse demonstrates a tendency to view them mainly as instruments for solving local problems—filling employment vacancies and ensuring the sustainability of the social protection system in the context of declining birth rates and ongoing emigration—instead of viewing migrants as humans who should have equal opportunities to fulfill their potential, including their contributions to Latvia's development via active civic and political participation.

Against this backdrop, this chapter will illustrate what the situation is like in Latvia with very practical examples, first providing an overview of the historic and current migration flows and the economic, social, and political rights of migrants, then moving on to details about naturalization, political representation, consultative councils, and nongovernmental organizations (NGOs). Finally, it will touch upon integration policy, public opinion, political discourse on migration, and referenda, concluding that more inclusive public attitudes and policies toward permanent residents of the country are issues that need to be addressed.

Historic Overview of Migration Flows

In the nineteenth century, the movement of residents in and out of the territory now called Latvia was very limited due to fact that most were indentured servants with limited legal rights to move, and, even after the end of indentured servitude, limitations on movement were enforced by the Russian Empire and the local aristocratic nobility. The liberalization of norms; the development of industry, urban construction, and transportation; as well as the increasing number of inhabitants were among the reasons why many people in the Baltic provinces left their birth places in the second half of the century, with Riga—now the capital of Latvia—becoming a regional metropolis. While in 1867 two-thirds of Riga's residents were born in the city, this number had decreased to one-third by 1913. The remaining two-thirds of residents came from other Baltic provinces or other Russian provinces. There were six major linguistic groups—Latvians (approximately 40 percent), Russians (21 percent), Germans (17 percent), and Jews, Lithuanians, and Poles (each 5 percent) (Zelče 2011).

At the same time, in the second half of the nineteenth century, many local farmers emigrated to acquire their own land in other provinces of the Russian Empire, as very few had that opportunity under the governance of the Baltic nobility. Educated persons, blue-collar workers, sailors, and other specialists joined farmers in looking for professional development opportunities—many headed west, with most settling in the United States. As a result, it is presumed that approximately 200,000 Latvians (or approximately 15 percent of the population) lived abroad prior to World War I.

Later, the mass emigration of Latvia's residents was driven by other political factors and repressions—Jews began emigrating because of anti-

TABLE 8.1	IMMIGRATION AND EMIGRATION, 1951–1990		
	Immigration	**Emigration**	**Migration Balance**
1951–1960	*639,888*	*459,832*	*180,048*
1961–1970	*476,934*	*335,872*	*141,062*
1971–1980	*548,643*	*428,235*	*120,408*
1981–1990	*506,576*	*423,953*	*82,623*
Source: Central Bureau of Statistics, Latvia, n.d.			

Semitism, leaders of Latvian national movements emigrated to pursue political aims in the safety of a foreign land, people emigrated to escape repression or the war zones. During World War I, the imperial government of Russia deported many residents—including Latvians, Jews, and Germans—to other parts of the empire. The country lost approximately one million people, or 37 percent of its prewar population during the war, with only 300,000 people returning to Latvia after 1918, when the country established independence. Although Latvia saw the immigration of Russians fleeing the Soviet regime and many Jews departing the country, the external migration during the interwar period did not have a significant impact on Latvia's demographic situation.

This changed in the 1940s when the USSR and Nazi Germany set up a partnership (the Molotov-Ribbentrop Pact) that led to the emigration of approximately 60,000 Germans from Latvia (when the country was still independent and also after it was already incorporated in the Soviet Union). In addition, the Soviet and Nazi regimes conducted mass deportations of Latvia's residents, and many others fled the return of Soviet powers to go to the West. After the war, the Soviet regime facilitated the return of displaced people, while people from the other Soviet Republics immigrated to Latvia to flee more devastated territories. As a result, Latvia's ethnic composition changed, with the German and Jewish communities being replaced by Russians, Ukrainians, and Belarusians, who moved to Latvia due to its comparatively higher standard of living, its shortage of labor for developing industries, and the USSR's need for military control as well as its policy to Sovietize or Russify Latvia. A total of four million people moved to Latvia between 1951 and 1990, while 1.82 million left the country, despite the fact that the regime did not allow free mobility (Zelče 2011). The local government managed to interrupt immigration only in 1989, when the percentage of Latvians in the population had already decreased to 52 percent and the great influx of Russian speakers had already resulted in the dominance of the Russian language in governance, public life, and workplaces (Table 8.1).

Current Migration Tendencies

When Latvia regained its independence in 1991, many people who had set-tled there during the Soviet period left the country, including Soviet military personnel and others who lost their Soviet citizenship and were uncertain about their status and future in Latvia. Although during the independence movement the Latvian People's Front had promised automatic citizenship to all residents (without a legal right to do so), the country introduced the status of noncitizens in line with the principle of the continuity of the Latvian state, thus only granting citizenship to pre-1940 residents and their descendants. Approximately 700,000 people had to wait until 1995 for their citizenship status, when the law on noncitizens was adopted, and two more years until noncitizens' passports started being issued.

The peak of this phase of emigration was in 1992, when more than 50,000 people (mostly Russians, Ukrainians, and Belarusians) left (Heleniak 2006). Compared to 1989, the Russian population in Latvia in 2000 had declined by 22 percent, Belarusian by 19 percent, and Ukrainian by 31 percent. At the same time, only a few thousand Latvians who had emigrated prior or during occupations returned, as many were too old to move, while the second- and third-generation exiles had settled permanently.

As Table 8.2 demonstrates, emigration was robust after Latvia regained its independence. In the late 1990s, emigration was limited, due to the hope for a better life in Latvia and the high costs of mobility (residence and work permits, costs of finding a job abroad, as well as costs of traveling and keep-ing in touch with relatives). Although Latvia's noncitizens needed a visa to travel to most EU countries, their comparatively less favorable situation in the local labor market (partly due to the requirement of Latvian language proficiency in many professions) created a push factor for them to emigrate. Thus, many of those who emigrated were not Latvian citizens or ethnic Lat-vians, and many were highly educated, possessing the skills and courage for mobility despite the many obstacles (Hazans 2011).

The situation changed when Latvia joined the EU in 2004, and Sweden, Ireland, and the United Kingdom opened their labor markets to the citizens of new EU member states. The "open doors" policy of these (and later also other EU) countries, the decreasing costs of mobility, and the availability of European employment services made emigration possible for many low-skilled workers. In addition to the higher salaries and better social security services, the economic crisis that hit Latvia in 2008 created many push factors for emigration—unemployment or decreasing income, as well as instability and insecurity about future prospects in the country. Although official statistics on the subject are scarce,[1] researchers estimate that approx-imately 160,000 to 200,000 Latvians—approximately 9 percent of the coun-try's population and 14 percent of its economically active population—have

TABLE 8.2 IMMIGRATION AND EMIGRATION, 1991–2013			
	Immigration	Emigration	Migration Balance
1991	14,684	29,729	−15,045
1992	6,199	59,673	−53,474
1993	4,114	36,447	−32,333
1994	3,046	25,869	−22,823
1995	2,799	16,512	−13,713
1996	2,747	12,828	−10,081
1997	2,913	12,333	−9,420
1998	3,123	8,874	−5,751
1999	1,813	5,898	−4,085
2000	6,483	22,911	−16,428
2001	5,376	24,539	−19,163
2002	6,642	15,837	−9,195
2003	4,063	15,647	−11,584
2004	4,844	20,167	−15,323
2005	6,691	17,643	−10,952
2006	8,212	17,019	−8,807
2007	7,517	15,463	−7,946
2008	4,678	27,045	−22,367
2009	3,731	38,208	−34,477
2010	4,011	39,651	−35,640
2011	10,234	30,311	−20,077
2012	13,303	25,163	−11,860
2013	8,299	22,561	−14,262

Source: Central Bureau of Statistics, Latvia, n.d.

emigrated since 2000 (Hazans 2011). Compared to emigration, migration to Latvia is less significant, although approximately 66,000 people possessed either a temporary or a permanent residence permit in 2013.

As Table 8.3 shows, most of the foreigners residing in Latvia possess permanent residence permits, the majority of them being Russian citizens who have lived in the country for several decades as Soviet citizens and Latvian noncitizens and who recently obtained Russian citizenship while keeping their residence status.[2] Other top countries from which migrants are moving include former Soviet republics (Ukraine and Belarus), with geographic, cultural, and linguistic proximity (ability to use Russian in their everyday life) among the main pull factors for immigration (see Table 8.4). Over half of all immigrants register their residence in the capital.

TABLE 8.3 NUMBER OF PERSONS WITH PERMANENT AND TEMPORARY RESIDENCE PERMITS, 2002–2013

	Permanent Permits	Temporary Permits
2002	23,527	6,676
2003	24,516	6,886
2004	25,466	7,547
2005	26,976	7,429
2006	29,487	8,003
2007	30,820	9,656
2008	33,055	12,815
2009	34,354	14,715
2010	36,249	13,785
2011	42,054	13,557
2012	44,328	15,957
2013	47,391	18,716

Source: Office of Citizenship and Migration Affairs, Latvia, n.d.

As for the purpose of their stay in Latvia, most foreigners with temporary residence permits list employment, followed by family ties and studies. While family reunification used to be the top reason for migration to Latvia some years ago, employment has become a more popular reason for residence in the country (40 to 45 percent of residents with temporary permits in 2008–2010). This may be surprising, given the relatively low income levels of the country (compared to the EU average), as well as the fact that access to the Latvian labor market depends on various factors like the purpose of immigration, the type of residence permit, as well as knowledge of the Latvian language.

The employment of migrant workers became more visible during the period of economic growth after the country's accession to the EU, when emigration led to labor shortages. For example, while only two thousand foreigners acquired a work permit in Latvia in 2005, the number exceeded four thousand in 2007. While the economic crisis decreased the need for migrant labor, the shortage of skills for specific sectors among the local population still motivates employers to recruit workers from abroad. Data show that in recent years the most popular sectors for migrant employment are manufacturing, transport, and logistics, as well as trade and repair. The biggest drop in demand for migrant workers was in the construction sector (36 percent of working permits in 2007, and only 3 percent in 2010). Most migrant workers come from Russia, Ukraine, and Belarus (these nationali-

TABLE 8.4 STOCK OF FOREIGNERS, 2013 (MOST SIGNIFICANT GROUPS)	
Russia	44,586
Lithuania	4,031
Ukraine	3,735
Belarus	2,318
Germany	1,536
Estonia	1,025
Bulgaria	698
Sweden	564
Poland	527
United Kingdom	518
United States of America	505
Kazakhstan	466
Uzbekistan	444

Source: Office of Citizenship and Migration Affairs, Lavia, n.d.

ties account for three-fourths of all work permit holders in Latvia). Latvia also has a bilateral agreement with Ukraine on recruiting welders for ship-building, as this qualification is not taught in Latvia.

However, in 2013 the most popular reason for immigration to Latvia—with the highest number of new residence permits issued to this group of migrants—has been due to investments in Latvia.[3] According to information from the Office of Citizenship and Migration Affairs (OCMA), 6,749 residence permits have been issued to investors and their family members since July 2010, with most of the investments being in the form of real estate purchases, mostly in the capital or the sea resort town of Jūrmala.[4] The highest demand (approximately 95 percent of all permits issued) comes from the citizens of post-Soviet countries like Russia, Ukraine, and Kazakhstan. Among the top ten countries of origin, only China, Israel, and the United States are not post-Soviet countries. It should be noted that investors and their family members have the right to work for any employer.[5]

As for foreign students, they form approximately 2 percent of all university students in Latvia. According to the Ministry of Education and Science, out of the approximately 2,000 foreign students in the 2010–2011 academic year, most came from Russia (358), Lithuania (231), Ukraine (215), Germany (152), and Georgia (96), and medicine and engineering were among the most attractive study programs. Since July 2010, student third-country nationals can (while their student residence permit is valid) apply for another type of residence permit (for family reunification or employment) while still residing

TABLE 8.5 CITIZENS, NONCITIZENS, AND FOREIGNERS IN LATVIA, 2000–2013				
	% Citizens	% Noncitizens	% Foreigners	Total Persons
2000	74.27	24.6	1.1	2,387,468
2001	75.43	23.3	1.2	2,360,434
2002	76.34	22.4	1.3	2,339,928
2003	77.01	21.6	1.4	2,331,467
2004	77.79	20.8	1.4	2,317,454
2005	78.86	19.6	1.5	2,302,932
2006	80.07	18.3	1.7	2,290,765
2007	80.99	17.2	1.8	2,284,871
2008	81.60	16.4	2	2,276,282
2009	82.04	15.8	2.2	2,267,886
2010	82.51	15.3	2.2	2,254,654
2011	82.91	14.6	2.5	2,236,910
2012	83.36	13.8	2.8	2,207,716
2013	83.46	13.5	3.1	2,201,277
Source: Office of Citizenship and Migration Affairs, Latvia, n.d.				

in the country.[6] This amendment is aimed at facilitating the recruitment of highly skilled workers and removing bureaucratic obstacles for university graduates to stay in the country.

Latvia receives a few asylum applications—only 367 persons applied for asylum in the period of 1998–2010, with 29 persons having obtained the status of refugee, and 45 persons having been granted alternative status.[7] Latvia also attracts a modest number of undocumented migrants. In 2008, the greatest number—approximately 1,600 persons—was detained either by border guards or in the territory of Latvia. In addition to foreign residents in the country, Latvia's noncitizens formed approximately 13.5 percent of the country's population in 2013, thus approximately 16 percent of the country's inhabitants did not possess Latvian citizenship (see Table 8.5)

Naturalization

A third-country national can apply for naturalization after having lived in Latvia for at least ten years (five years with a permanent residence permit, which can be granted [after passing a Latvian language test] after at least five years of temporary residence). However, until October 2013, Latvia's citizenship legislation included a ban on dual citizenship, that is, a third-country national had to refuse his or her original citizenship to become a Latvian citizen, which is a serious obstacle for naturalization (Zepa et al. 2009). Citizenship law amendments (which entered into force on October 1, 2013) allow limited dual citizenship for persons coming from other EU, NATO, or European Free Trade Association countries, as well as New Zealand, Brazil, and Australia. This exception also applies to citizens of countries that have concluded bilateral agreements with Latvia on the mutual recognition of dual citizenship, or persons having obtained permission from the government to keep their native citizenship. This may result in better conditions for integration, including political participation rights, for some of the foreigners living in the country. However, this is a very small step toward dual citizenship for most third-country nationals living in the country because the citizens of Russia, Ukraine, andBelarus (the top countries of origin of immigrants) are not covered by them (Akule 2012).

Naturalization is seen as the only key to the acquisition of all political participation rights, therefore opening up new opportunities for participation—like granting the right to vote in local elections to all permanent residents—and is not supported by most political parties currently represented in the Parliament, nor by the public.[8] This indicates the perception that providing more political rights to migrants would decrease their motivation to naturalize, although it is not confirmed by a recent study indicating that only 45 percent of citizenship applicants (Latvia's noncitizens) noted voting rights as a very significant reason for naturalization (Office of Citizenship and Migration Affairs 2013). Debates on granting more political participation rights to third-country nationals are also inevitably linked to a discussion of the political rights of Latvia's noncitizens, who do not have the right to vote or stand for election in municipalities. Thus, the conceptual framing of political participation within the context of citizens and noncitizens arguably has had a side effect of creating obstacles to participation by third-country nationals (Brands-Kehris 2010).

Since 1995 (when naturalization started) through April 2013, 140,473 persons have acquired Latvian citizenship (including 14,153 children of noncitizens).[9] Ninety-eight percent of naturalization candidates are Latvia's noncitizens (Krūma 2010). Since 2009, the number of naturalized persons has decreased, with young people (ages eighteen to thirty) being the top applicant group (47 percent of applicants in 2011), and the elder generation (over the age of sixty) being the smallest (under 6 percent of applicants) (Latvian Centre for Human Rights 2013). Table 8.6 shows the changing pace of naturalization due to both internal and external factors:

- Heated discussions about the rights of former Soviet Union citizens and the policy to limit the number of naturalization applicants led to implementation of a regulation (in place during 1995–1998) providing so-called windows of naturalization when persons of specific age groups would be allowed to naturalize, ensuring that not too many of them would acquire citizenship quickly. This order was canceled in a 1998 referendum, also leading to the granting of citizenship to newly born children of noncitizens, hence increasing the number of naturalized persons in 1999 and 2000.

- An increase in naturalization is also visible in the first years of Latvia's EU membership as the rights and opportunities of EU citizens—including the free movement of labor—were a strong motivating factor.
- In 2007–2008 the visa-free regime for noncitizens within all EU countries decreased motivation for naturalization, in addition to the visa-free regime for noncitizens to travel to Russia (in place since 2008).

According to an OCMA study, the most frequently mentioned factor driving naturalization in Latvia is a person's willingness to get rid of the shame or discomfort of being the only one in the family without Latvian

TABLE 8.6 NUMBER OF NATURALIZED PERSONS IN LATVIA, 1995–2012	
	Persons
1995	984
1996	3,016
1997	2,992
1998	4,439
1999	12,427
2000	14,900
2001	10,637
2002	9,844
2003	10,049
2004	16,064
2005	19,169
2006	16,439
2007	6,826
2008	3,004
2009	2,080
2010	2,336
2011	2,467
2012	2,213

Source: Office of Citizenship and Migration Affairs, Latvia, n.d.

TABLE 8.7 DISCOURAGING FACTORS FOR ACQUIRING LATVIAN CITIZENSHIP, 2012 (IN PERCENTAGES)	
Latvian citizenship should be granted automatically	24.8
Can't pass naturalization exams	21.3
Waiting for easier procedures	17.2
Ease to travel to post-Soviet countries	13.5
No time to naturalize	9.4
Satisfaction with the current status	8.2
Other reasons	3.9
Not willing to naturalize	1.7
Source: Office of Citizenship and Migration Affairs, Latvia, n.d.	

citizenship. The most frequently mentioned discouraging factor is also emotional, namely the feeling of resentment about the division of population between citizens and noncitizens after the country regained independence in 1991 (see Table 8.7). Many also criticized the social and economic policies implemented by governments during the last twenty years and the fact that a person needs to pay a fee for the naturalization procedure (OCMA 2012). The study also shows a range of rational reasons considered relevant by third-country nationals and noncitizens of Latvia. Among the motivations to naturalize are the right to include the length of one's working life accumulated in a third country into the calculation of one's retirement pension in Latvia, as well as the right to purchase land and participate in the political life of the country.[10] In turn, precluding factors are also the costs of visa processing for traveling to Russia, costs of renunciation of former citizenship, and costs to prepare for the naturalization exam (e.g., language and history courses).[11] Qualitative research on the reasons why Latvia's noncitizens do not apply for Latvian citizenship show that many believe that citizenship should be granted to them automatically.

It should be stressed that an increasing number of Latvia's citizens have given up their citizenship and opted for Russian citizenship beginning in 2009 in order to enjoy better retirement benefits, as the retirement age in Russia is much lower than in Latvia. Over eleven thousand of Latvia's noncitizens applied to rescind this status, as they had become Russian citizens in 2009–2011, with most of them retaining their residence in Latvia.

Economic and Social Rights of Migrants

The rights extended to immigrants in Latvia (third-country nationals, not Latvia's noncitizens) depend on the type of residence permit they hold. With regard to the right to work, unlimited access to the labor market is available to family reunification immigrants (who joined a spouse who is a Latvian citizen or noncitizen or a migrant with a permanent residence permit), students (working no more than twenty hours per week), and highly skilled migrants (like scientists, sportsmen, and artists). On the other hand, access to the local labor market is restricted for migrant workers, who have obtained a temporary residence permit. These individuals are linked to the employer who invited them to Latvia, with no option to freely change employers or their employment position within the company. If a migrant worker who stays in Latvia on the basis of a temporary residence permit becomes unemployed, his or her residence permit and work permit is canceled and the migrant has to leave the country, with no right for unemployment benefits or services.[12] In addition, access to the Latvian labor market also depends on knowledge of the Latvian language, because many occupations require a certain level of language skills by law, which is the reason why there are almost no migrants employed by state or local government institutions or commercial companies, where the majority of capital shares are owned by the state or the local government. This policy is in line with the agenda to strengthen the status of the Latvian language in Latvia (Ķešāne and Kaša 2008).

As for immigrants' social welfare rights, persons holding a temporary residency permit are vulnerable. These people are not eligible for state-guaranteed health care, legal and social aid, or unemployment benefits. A third-country national who has arrived on the basis of an employment contract is subject to the same income tax and national insurance taxes as local employed inhabitants from the day they arrive. However, all the health care and social and legal services must be paid by immigrants themselves (via an individual health insurance policy that is a requirement for residence in Latvia). With the exceptions of Ukrainian citizens and pensioners with Russian citizenship, the state does not even cover medical emergencies for this group of migrants.[13]

The same applies to the children of migrants holding temporary residence permits—they are not eligible for free public health care, or social and judicial aid. Moreover, until recently (March 2010), they did not have access to free education, which was contrary to Latvian and international legislation requiring that all children have equal and free access to compulsory education.

The situation improves once an immigrant is eligible for a permanent residency permit or for long-term resident status of the European Community in Latvia, as then the person is given the same rights as Latvian noncitizens. They can receive state-provided health care services and unemployment benefits. In order to receive unemployment benefits, payments into the national insurance system must have been made for at least one year during the previous eighteen months. If this condition is satisfied, the spouse of the permanent resident or the long-term resident in Latvia can receive the unemployment benefits as well (Ķešāne and Kaša 2008). The social and economic rights of Latvia's noncitizens are closer to those of citizens than those of resident foreigners and third-country nationals (Brands-Kehris 2010).[14]

Political Participation Rights

Third-country nationals (citizens of non-EU countries and Latvia's nonciti-zens) in Latvia enjoy minimal political rights, as they cannot:

- Vote and stand for election in parliamentary and local elections
- Be members of a political party and form political associations
- Establish nongovernmental organizations (NGOs), or engage in already existing civil society organizations and trade unions
- Take part in marches and protests

According to Latvian law, fully taking part in the democratic life of the country is reserved only for Latvian citizens, though in some cases this right is extended to the citizens of other EU countries residing in Latvia. Only Latvian citizens have the right to vote and stand for election in national elec-tions, while Latvian citizens and EU citizens residing in the country have the right to vote and be elected in local elections.[15] Just like Latvian citizens and EU citizens residing in the country, Latvia's noncitizens are allowed to be members of political parties. However, no political party can be established without a significant number of Latvian citizens, since the law requires that in a party with four hundred members, at least two hundred of them should be Latvian citizens.[16]

As for civic participation, any person has the right to establish and be a member of an NGO. The leaders of NGOs must be at least eighteen years old and have a declared residence in Latvia, while there are no restrictions on membership.[17] Every inhabitant of Latvia working and studying in the coun-try can take part in a trade union.[18] In addition, every inhabitant of Latvia has the right to participate in assemblies, marches, and protests. At the same time, third-country nationals with a temporary residence permit do not have the right to organize or lead such events. Only Latvian citizens, Latvian non-citizens, and persons with permanent residency permits are allowed to be the organizers, leaders, leader assistants, and guardians of meetings, marches, and protests.[19] Thus, the citizens of other EU countries residing in Latvia with a temporary residence permit cannot be among the official organizers of such events.

Political Representation

Traditional ethnic minorities are noticeably present, at both the national and local levels, but their proportion of the population depends on whether the entire population or only the population who are citizens is used as the base line (Brands-Kehris 2010).[20] According to the census data, 62 percent of Latvia's population identified themselves as Latvians in 2011, which shows an increase of approximately 5 percent compared to the data of 2000 (57.7 percent). At the same time, the size of largest group of ethnic minorities in the population has slightly decreased (see Table 8.8).

The representation of ethnic minorities in the parliament, the Saeima, has slightly improved if one analyzes the decreasing percentage of parliamentarians who have identified themselves as Latvian. If, in the one-hundred-seat Saeima, eighty-four parliamentarians were Latvian in 1998, the current parliament has only sixty-seven Latvian parliamentarians, which is slightly more than the representation of ethnic Latvians among the population. At the same time, the number of parliamentarians who have identified themselves as Russian (the largest ethnic minority in Latvia) has remained stable in the period since Latvia regained independence (see Table 8.9).

The presence of minority representatives actively working to make claims for minority rights in the Saeima is visible, mainly due to the representatives from the political parties For Human Rights in a United Latvia (represented in the Saeima until 2010) and from Harmony Center (currently representing the largest political group in the Saeima). Although these parties have been trying to put several issues on the political agenda (like strengthening the status of minority languages, increasing the rights of noncitizens, and designating Russian Orthodox Christmas and Easter as official holidays), these proposals almost never have a long life, as they are introduced

TABLE 8.8 MAIN ETHNIC MINORITIES IN LATVIA IN 2000 AND 2011 (IN PERCENTAGES)		
	2000	2011
Latvian	57.7	62.1
Russian	29.6	26.9
Belarusian	4.1	3.3
Ukrainian	2.7	2.2
Polish	2.5	2.1
Lithuanian	1.4	1.2
Others, including no data	2	2.2
Source: Central Bureau of Statistics, Latvia, n.d.		

TABLE 8.9 ETHNIC IDENTIFICATION OF PARLIAMENTARIANS, 1922–1934, 1993–2011 (IN PERCENTAGES)

	1922– 1925	1925– 1928	1928– 1931	1931– 1934	1993– 1998	1995– 1998	1998– 2002	2002– 2006	2006– 2010	2010– 2011	2011–
Latvians	84	84	80	83	88	no data	84	79	78	76	67
Poles	2	2	2	2	1	no data	10	1	no data	no data	no data
Russians	4	4	7	6	6	no data	3	14	15	13	13
Lithuanians	no data	no data	no data	no data	no data	no data	1	no data	no data	no data	no data
Jews	0	0	5	3	no data	no data	no data	no data	1	no data	no data
Germans	6	5	6	6	1	no data	no data	no data	1	1	1
Karelian	no data	no data	no data	no data	no data	no data	no data	1	1	1	1
Other ethnicities/ no information provided	4	5	no data	no data	4	no data	no data	4	4	9	18

Source: Central Bureau of Statistics, Latvia, n.d.

and briefly debated, but either voted down in plenary or sent off and buried in committees. In addition, political parties have a strong tendency to consist of either exclusively majority or minority parliamentarians (Brands-Kehris 2010).

It should be stressed that political parties representing ethnic minorities have never been in power, even in the role of a minority partner in the governing coalition. The formation of the current government—following extraordinary elections after the Saeima was dissolved in a referendum—attracted some criticism among a part of the population, as the winner of the election, Harmony Center (pro-Russian, seen as representing the interests of Russian-speaking voters), was not invited to join the coalition. This political force is increasingly popular among Latvia's citizens, as the party won the municipality elections in Riga and is the political affiliation of the current mayor of the capital. Hence, one could argue that the increasing popularity of Harmony Center is also a result of the ongoing attitude of the majority to deliberately ignore some issues important to minorities and to disregard their positions on issues that affect all inhabitants of the country.

There are no official ethnically disaggregated data on minority participation in elections, but survey data about the intention to participate and reported participation, as well as attitudes toward elections does not show significant differences among citizens of different ethnic and linguistic groups (Brands-Kehris 2010). At the same time, "passivity and the tendency to ethnic self-segregation in organizations and public activities are the most significant risks to integration through political participation" (121–122).

Research on parliamentary and media debates in Latvia, analyzing the discourses of Latvian politicians and the media about nation, citizenship, cultural diversity, history, and the nation-state, also reveals that opinion leaders and major printed media in Latvia sometimes propose "shrinking citizenship"—supporting arbitrary limitations to the public visibility, participation, or citizenship[21] of a number of groups whom they deem "suspect"—noncitizens, new immigrants, LGBT individuals, and activists working within NGOs that receive international funding (Golubeva, Kažoka, and Rozukalne 2007). An analysis of the parliamentary debates of the current Saeima reveals that delegitimizing strategies are still being used and often framed in terms of "us" and "them," constructing the illusion of two opposed, clear-cut camps, each with its own goals and values that are incompatible with the goals and values of the other "camp." Although some parliamentarians often condemn delegitimizing strategies and proposals that would cause rifts in society, there is an increasing tendency to exalt Latvian values and identity and emphasize the needs of the "constituent nation."[22]

Consultative Councils

Various advisory bodies focus on promoting the exchange of views between state or local authorities and ethnic groups traditionally residing in Latvia, that is, the national minorities. Among them is a council for national minorities reestablished under the President's Chancellery in 2008, but it is unclear what functions and competencies this council has, considering the president's own limited constitutional role (Brands-Kehris 2010).[23] There is also a National Minority Organizations Council on Participation. It was established in 2006 under the Secretariat of the Special Assignment Minister for Social Integration, and continues working under the leadership of the Ministry of Culture.[24] Experts point out the lack of assessment of the use of such bodies or stress their formal nature, unclear principles of operation, and lack of set membership criteria, as a result of which consultative councils have not enabled national minorities to influence decision-making processes on issues affecting their interests and rights (Brands-Kehris 2010). The few representatives of immigrant associations that have been involved in such consultative bodies admit that sometimes their participation was seen only as a formality (Kaša and Ķešāne 2008).

Nevertheless, two promising developments took place in 2013:

- The National Consultative Council for the Integration of Third Country Nationals was established. The council is chaired by the minister of culture, and includes representatives from state and municipal institutions, as well as representatives of employers' confederations, trade unions, and five NGOs working in the field of immigrant integration.[25] The objective of the council is to enhance discussions and cooperation among institutions in the field of integration of third-country nationals, and enhancing the participation of third-country nationals and their representatives in policy making in the area of integration.
- A council to oversee the implementation of country's integration policy—as defined in the policy document "National Identity, Civil Society and Integration Policy Guidelines 2012–2018" and its action plans—was established. The main aim of this council is to manage the processes of policy implementation as well as to exercise its advisory power to propose amendments to legislation. Consisting of representatives and experts of different state institutions, NGOs, and academia, the council is also chaired by the minister of culture, as the ministry oversees integration policy (European Website on Integration 2013).

NGOs Fostering the Political Participation of Immigrants

There are no representative data on the members of NGOs. However, only a few organizations directly represent the interests of immigrants or provide services to third-country nationals in Latvia. Some of them—like Afrolat, an Arab cultural center, and the Latvian-Lebanese society—have worked to combat intolerance and discrimination, while state funding priorities have inclined them toward cultural activities (Zankovska-Odiņa 2009). They have also been engaged in consultative political discussions, which indirectly affect the issues of immigration. However, overall the self-organization of the NGOs dealing with immigration is rather weak, and their political and social participation is not noticeable (Kaša and Ķešāne 2008).

Most of these organizations were established rather recently, and their membership is small. Most do not have any or a significant representation of third-country nationals among their members. The only exception is Afrolat—twenty-six out of thirty members of this organization are third-country nationals—while the rest (four members) are naturalized first-generation immigrants. For most of the organizations, work with immigrant integration is among other areas of activities. Although it may not be included in their statutes or NGO mission statements, most of them work with providing assistance to immigrants, organizing cultural events, and representing their interests in policy-making processes.

As for the constituency of the NGOs, they are defined by different criteria. Some focus on third-country nationals from one country of origin or one ethnic/linguistic group; for example, Afrolat mainly works with migrants from African countries, while Dialogi.lv has worked with third-country nationals from Ukraine and planned to extend their activities to Russian-speaking third-country nationals. For others, the target group is linked to the location of the NGO—Shelter Safe House works with migrants based in or close to the capital. Workshop of Solutions works with third-country national students. The Latvian Centre for Human Rights serves a wide constituency, from the general public to decision makers and state and municipal workers. The center works with groups that face discrimination and intolerance, including third-country nationals.

In addition to NGOs that work with third-country nationals, approximately two hundred ethnic minority NGOs also exist (e.g., Russian, Ukrainian, and Moldovan culture NGOs). However, there is little cooperation between ethnic minority and other NGOs.

Integration Policy

Latvia's immigrant integration policy has been cited as the least favorable among thirty-one European and North American countries by the

Migrant Integration Policy Index. It stresses that Latvia has projects, "but no coherent strategy" for immigrant integration (British Council and Migration Policy Group 2011). This has not been among the highest priorities of the country because the number of foreign residents and newly arriving third-country nationals is relatively small, but at the same time the integration of third-country nationals is inevitably linked to the general social integration policy in a country with a sizeable Russian-speaking population that arrived during the Soviet era. This connection is strengthened by immigration statistics showing that most immigrants come from countries with Russian-language knowledge.

Recognizing the importance of integration policy, a special institution—the Secretariat of the Special Assignment Minister for Social Integration—was established in 2003, but due to austerity measures and the need to decrease the size of the public administration, the secretariat was closed in 2009. Since then, the function of immigrant integration policy has been shifted between four ministries, finally landing at the Ministry of Culture as of April 2011. As a result, the state failed to adopt an integration strategy until October 2011, when the "National Identity, Civil Society and Integration Policy Guidelines 2012–2018" were approved by the government.

An advisory council was set up for the establishment of this policy paper, but the involvement of most of the council members in drafting the document was formal—many proposals and objections submitted by representatives of state or NGOs (including minority NGOs) were disregarded (Latvian Centre for Human Rights 2013).

The document focuses on civic participation and civic education, naturalization, and Latvian language, culture, and "social memory." The goal is to establish a strong Latvian nation—a national and democratic community that ensures the conservation and enrichment of its unifying foundations—Latvian language, culture, and national identity; European democratic values; and a unique cultural space—for the balanced development of the Latvian nation-state. According to the policy document, every person has the possibility to become Latvian and can choose whether to have multiple identities.[26] The document says that Latvia has a number of "new immigrants"—third-country nationals who live in Latvia with a temporary or permanent residence permit and who have arrived in Latvia after 1991, when it regained independence. At the same time, it stresses that a more considerable number of persons living in Latvia are "long-term immigrants"—citizens of the former Soviet Union who came to Latvia during Soviet occupation, live in Latvia permanently, but have not acquired Latvian citizenship or have become the citizens of a third country, living in a "parallel world."

One of the concerns raised in the discussions of the policy paper regarded the controversial definition of the *constituent nation*, which "was perceived as placing ethnic Latvians in a privileged position," and the strong ethnocentric

approach of the conceptual framework. The use of the term *immigrants* for
the Russian-speaking population in Latvia that has not managed to naturalize and fully integrate was an additional reason for harsh criticism from a
part of the society. Several minority NGOs also pointed to the "overly politicized" nature of the program that aimed at "total assimilation of national
minorities," stressing its alienating and insensitive character, which would
cause rifts in society rather than promote consolidation. As a result, some
NGOs expressed their intention to ignore this project, which seems to have
materialized, for example, in the fact that the Ministry of Culture had to
prolong the open call for candidates from NGOs and academic institutions
to work in the consultative council overseeing the implementation of this
document.[27]

Although until October 2011 the Latvian government had failed to adopt
a policy document outlining the immigrant integration policy of the country, regular activities in the field had taken place since 2009 via the European
Fund for the Integration of Third Country Nationals. This is the main public
funding source for immigrant integration in Latvia, and it has put immigrant integration on the national agenda. However, the driving force for
work in this area seems to be the available funding, pressure from NGOs,
and European commitments (the need to implement the EU's basic principles on integration). Latvians do not support an immigrant integration
policy—60.9 percent of respondents did not support budget spending on integration policies in 2008, and it is safe to assume that this figure is even higher
in the current economic and budgetary crisis (Sociālās Alternatīvas Institūts
2008). Moreover, until now, the political participation of third-country
nationals has not been among the priorities of the fund. The majority of the
funding has been dedicated to either providing services to migrants or help-
ing to build the capacity of the country (institutions, service providers, and
NGOs) to work with migrants. Only some projects have addressed the civic
and political participation of migrants, and most of them have aimed to
inform third-country nationals about the existing opportunities.

In addition to the national policies, several larger municipalities (Riga,
Jelgava, Daugavpils, Jūrmala, Ventspils, and Liepāja) have elaborated society
integration programs at the local level and/or have created a department for
the promotion of integration and support for integration projects (Latvian
Centre for Human Rights 2013).

Public Opinion

Immigration is a very sensitive topic for most Latvians due to their experience with Soviet immigration policy.[28] While emigration is perceived with
understanding, immigration is viewed with dislike and denial (Karnīte and
Karnītis 2009). In a 2009 opinion poll, 65 percent of respondents said that

TABLE 8.10 PREFERENCES OF NATIONALITIES FOR MIGRANTS, 2012 (IN PERCENTAGES)	
Thinking of the dramatic demographic problems (low birth rates, emigration, shrinking population size, and aging population) and expected labor shortages, in your opinion, from which countries or groups of countries would it be desirable to let in immigrants from?	
Immigration should not be allowed under any circumstances	43.4
EU countries	28.9
Russia, Belarus, Ukraine	26.1
Difficult to say/no answer	11.1
Other countries of NIS	9.7
Countries of Middle East	2.1
China	1.8
India	0.8
African countries	0.7
Other countries	0.6
Source: SKDS Public Poll Institute 2012.	

the possibility of an additional influx of migrant workers in Latvia was "completely unacceptable," while 24 percent said it was "rather unacceptable." Only 2 percent of respondents said it was "very acceptable," with another 4 percent saying it was "rather acceptable" (Ķīlis 2009).[29] When asked in a more recent poll about the most preferred countries of immigrants' origin, more than 40 percent of respondents said that immigration was not be to allowed under any circumstances. One-third supported immigration from other EU countries, followed by Russia, Belarus, and Ukraine in preference (see Table 8.10).

As Table 8.11 shows, Latvians see many negative consequences from immigration—taking away jobs that could otherwise be filled by local workers, increasing the pressure on the social budget, and threatening the existence of Latvian culture.[30] At the same time, one-fifth of the respondents also agreed to the statement that every individual has the right to move for a better life.

Attitudes toward immigrants differ based on the ethnic background of respondents. Latvians are slightly more likely to think that immigrants increase crime rates, and less likely to think that immigrants bring benefits to a country's economy. At the same time, Russian respondents are more likely to agree that immigrants make Latvia more open to new ideas and cultures (Table 8.12).

A similar tendency is also evident in the attitudes toward the statement that "in general, people should live in their historic homeland (Latvians in

TABLE 8.11 OPINIONS ABOUT THE IMPACT OF IMMIGRATION, 2011 (IN PERCENTAGES)	
What is your attitude toward the willingness of people from other countries to come to work and live in Latvia?	
Migrants create problems by taking over jobs from the locals	*38*
I don't think that migrants would be interested to live in Latvia—living in other countries would be more beneficial for them	*32*
I think that every person has the right to go to live and work in another country, including Latvia	*22*
Migration was, is, and will always be, it is an inevitable process	*22*
Migrants create problems by increasing the burden on the social budget	*22*
I would personally not like it if people from different races come to live in Latvia	*21*
Migrants endanger the existence of Latvian culture	*17*
Only inhabitants of other EU countries should be allowed to live and work in Latvia	*11*
Migration would solve the problems that have been caused by the decreasing number of inhabitants of Latvia like shortages of labor	*7*
Migration would bring benefits to Latvian culture and life by increasing diversity, e.g., cuisine, fashion	*4*
Source: SKDS Public Poll Institute 2011.	

Latvia, Russians in Russia, etc)." Persons from families communicating in the Russian language are more likely to disagree, while persons from families communicating in the Latvian language are more likely to agree to this statement (see Table 8.13).

These opinion polls are in line with earlier studies indicating that the majority of Latvians are intolerant of other nationalities and religions, and that they resist the emergence of a multicultural society (European Union Agency for Fundamental Rights 2005).[31] Analyzing these patterns, researchers have found that in general, ethnic Latvians feel and act like "the endan-

TABLE 8.12 ATTITUDES TOWARD MIGRANTS' IMPACT ON SOCIAL AND ECONOMIC PROCESSES, 2010 (IN PERCENTAGES)*		
	Latvians	Russians
Migrants take away jobs from people born in Latvia	65.6	54.9
Migrants increase crime rates	47.7	28.9
Migrants make Latvia more open to new ideas and cultures	33.4	49.3
Migrants bring benefits to the country's economy	21.1	40.7
Source: University of Latvia, Faculty of Social Sciences, 2010.		
N = 1,004 Latvia's inhabitants * "absolutely agree" and "rather agree" answers were added together.		

TABLE 8.13 PEOPLE SHOULD LIVE IN THEIR HISTORIC HOMELAND (LATVIANS IN LATVIA; RUSSIANS IN RUSSIA; UKRAINIANS IN UKRAINE; THE IRISH IN IRELAND, ETC.), 2012 (IN PERCENTAGES)

	Completely Agree	Rather Agree	Neither Agree nor Disagree	Rather Disagree	Completely Disagree	No Answer
All respondents	10.1	17.1	22.7	19.4	25.7	5.1
Family communicates in Latvian	15	23	24	19	14	5
Family communicates in Russian	4	9	21	20	41	6

Source: SKDS Public Poll Institute 2012.

gered majority," which can be largely attributed to the consequences of Soviet migration policy (Šūpule et al. 2004). This argument is further supported by surveys showing that ethnic Latvians, in comparison to other nationalities living in Latvia, are more hostile toward immigrants from post-Soviet countries (Indāns 2004). Asked which of the named factors pose the most serious concerns for the country's future, respondents named emigration, the loss of economic independence, as well as various factors linked to immigration (see Table 8.14).

TABLE 8.14 THREAT PERCEPTIONS, 2012 (IN PERCENTAGES)

In your opinion, how large of a threat do the following aspects pose Latvia and Latvia's population?	Very Large	Small	No Threat at All	Difficult to Say/No Answer
Latvia's inhabitants emigrate	76.1	13.8	6.8	3.2
Latvia loses its economic independence since large foreign companies take over and force locals out of business	60.5	25.1	9	5.5
People from other countries come to Latvia to look for a better life	38.7	38.9	17.2	5.2
Traditional moral standards change due to standards that come from other countries and regions	27.9	39.4	22	10.7
Arrival of different (untraditional to Latvia) religions	27.9	37.4	27.2	7.5
Arrival of different cultures and traditions	18.8	40.9	35.7	4.6
Mixed marriages between Latvia's inhabitants and people of different ethnicities and skin color	17.5	35.7	41.2	5.6

Source: SKDS Public Poll Institute 2012.

Political Discourse on Migration

The negativity of public opinion has for many years made immigration policy a taboo topic and one to be avoided by the media, general public, or politicians. The first time immigration-related issues were addressed in platforms of political parties was in the 2004 European Parliament elections, when the conservative People's Party (Tautas Partija) promised it would not permit uncontrolled immigration, and the nationalistic party, For Fatherland and Freedom/LNNK (Tēvzemei un Brīvībai/LNNK), said that Latvia could not take on the responsibility for hosting and integrating "new immigrants" following the floods of immigrants arriving in the country as a result of Soviet migration policies (Zankovska-Odiņa 2005). In the national elections of 2006, the majority of parties already focused on the ways to repatriate those Latvians who had emigrated, as the negative effects of emigration became more visible in the form of labor shortages. Still, this did not stop the nationalistic party from using slogans that revealed its incomprehension of the need to appreciate all human resources available in the country. For Fatherland and Freedom/LNNK promised to help people "not loyal to Latvia" leave the country in its platform for the 2006 elections.

In recent years public discussions have increasingly turned to immigration, as it is linked to the bigger question of who is going to live in Latvia as it faces serious demographic challenges due to the shrinking and aging population, low birth rates, and high volumes of emigration. Discussions have mainly focused on enhancing birth rates, stopping emigration, and hoping for the mass return of Latvian emigrants. Thus, the platforms of political parties participating in the 2010 national election included slogans about Latvia as the "superpower of large families" and allegations that "Latvia would only exist if every family would have at least two children." The platforms of all parties elected in the 2011 extraordinary elections included a similar focus on increasing birth rates, while some also talked about facilitating the return of Latvian emigrants.[32] For example, the Reform Party, one of the current coalition parties, stressed facilitating the return of Latvian emigrants as a "better alternative to immigration from other countries that is difficult to avoid" (Akule 2010).

One of the current governing parties, the nationalistic alliance All for Latvia! For Fatherland and Freedom/LNNK, is the most visible party when it comes to immigration. The party has promised to "exclude guest workers from former Soviet republics . . . to stop maintaining the self-sufficiency of Russian language at the cost of state [Latvian] language," and to exclude immigration from "countries with radically different understanding of values and behavior" (Akule 2010). It has also on several occasions attempted to stop the issuing of residence permits to persons having purchased real estate in Latvia, calling them "fake investors."[33] The nationalistic alliance wants to cancel this policy, as they believe that foreigners from Russia, China, and other countries who buy real estate in Latvia continue what was done to the country during the Soviet occupation—suppression of the ethnic Latvian state with foreign languages and cultures. The party included this issue among a few things it wanted to see changed in return for supporting the state budget for 2014 in a vote in the parliament in October 2013. After heated discussions, the parliament in October 2013 adopted amendments to the immigration law that would introduce quotas, limiting the number of residence permits issued to third-country nationals for purchasing real estate to 350 to 700 per year.[34] This would result in a dramatic decrease, since 3,409 permits were issued to these investors in 2013.[35] In addition, this might increase corruption, as emphasized by the local Transparency International.[36] Latvia's president also pointed out the contradictory elements of the amendments, and sent the legislation back to the parliament. At the end of May 2014, the parliament adopted improved amendments, according to which, as of September 2014, the minimum value of real estate that will allow individuals to acquire temporary residence permits will be doubled: instead of 71,000 to 140,000 EUR, now the value of a property has to be at least 250,000 EUR in any place in Latvia. In addition, when acquiring the permit for the first time, the person will have to pay 5 percent of the real estate value to the national budget.[37]

With the nationalistic alliance represented in the governing coalition, the government also worked on a first migration policy paper, with a deadline of October 2014 set in the government's action plan. According to the plan, the aim of the policy is to establish a balanced system for the entry of foreigners into the country, which is in line with Latvia's interests and facilitates economic growth. Based on the concept paper, new immigration legislation was also to be adopted by the end of 2014.[38]

The last previous attempt of the government to adopt a migration policy document was in 2007. It suggested three differnet scenarios for migration policy:

1. Not changing the strict immigration policy, under which the procedure to invite workers from third countries was long and expensive
2. Decreasing state fees and easing the bureaucratic procedure for inviting migrant workers
3. In addition to easier procedures and smaller fees, laying out criteria for "emergency" situations, when quotas of specific professions could be filled using easier conditions. However, these migrants would be able to stay only for a short term, with no family reunification rights. (Ministry of Interior 2007)

Although the document awaited discussion in the government, it was never approved, as one of the coalition parties in the government was the

nationalistic alliance, which was strongly against the liberalization of migration policy. Instead, a part of the proposals were put in place via amendments to country's immigration law or other regulations (for example, the
easier procedure to recruit third-country nationals).[39]

At the same time, due to the broad consensus on the need to facilitate the
return of Latvian emigrants, the government adopted the proposals for measures to facilitate return migration in June 2013.[40] This initiative is linked to
the estimates of the Ministry of Economy that approximately 120,000 jobs
would be created by 2030 as a result of economic growth, with an additional
100,000 vacancies becoming available due to the older generation leaving the
labor market.[41] According to the ministry, the objective of the return migration plan is to ensure that the majority of these vacancies are filled by Latvians who have returned to the country, instead of immigrants. However, as
the majority of emigrants (65 percent) do not plan to return to Latvia in the
next five years (Diena 2012), in March 2013 the government also adopted a
wider cooperation program covering consular support, support for Latvian-
language learning, cultural activities, as well as political participation of the
Latvian community abroad.[42]

Referenda

Due to Soviet-era immigration and the consequently sizeable community of
Russian-speaking residents in Latvia, the country has had firsthand experience
of the close connection between immigration and immigrant integration,
with heated discussions on specific integration aspects—like citizenship,
education, and language—having taken place on a regular basis since Latvia
regained independence. Large protests took place in 2004 in connection to
minority education reform and the transition to an increased share of Latvian instruction in the publicly funded Russian-language schools.[43] But the
most recent event that increased the public focus on these issues was the
February 2012 referendum—initiated by NGOs—on granting the status of
second official language to the Russian language. Although approximately
75 percent of participants voted against this proposal, the referendum urged
wide reassessment of the successes and failures of the integration policy. A
special parliamentary committee on social cohesion was established, and the
government granted additional funds for integration.[44] The referendum also
spurred intense discussions among academics and lawyers about the need to
reassess the requirements for initiating a referendum (increasing the minimum number of signatures needed to put any issue on the public agenda via
a referendum and defining a list of issues that could not be questioned in a
referendum) and the need to clarify the currently unwritten core of the Latvian Constitution.[45] The referendum also revealed a lack of inclusive policy
discourse toward Latvian citizens, with several politicians hinting at the dis-

loyalty of citizens or incomprehension of the "core values" of Latvia's Constitution if they had voted in favor of Russian as the second official language of the country.

In 2012, the movement For Equal Rights attempted to initiate a referendum on amendments to the Citizenship Law and envisioned granting Latvian citizenship to all noncitizens.[46] Even though the required number of signatures was collected, the Central Election Commission—following the opinions of various state institutions and universities—stopped the referendum process by ruling that the draft law should not be considered as fully elaborated, as it not only did not comply with the provisions of the constitution, but would also have put into doubt the continuity of the Republic of Latvia. According to many experts, the Central Election Commission—by evaluating the content of the draft and subsequently rejecting it—created a precedent "which in the future could restrict any initiative of the voters, which causes controversies among the public and politicians" (Latvian Centre for Human Rights 2013).

The automatic citizenship issue was also one of the focuses of the Congress of Non-Citizens that was established in 2013. The congress—functioning as an NGO and representing the interests of Latvia's noncitizens (members of this forum were chosen in an online and offline "election" process)—wants to liquidate the institution of noncitizenship in Latvia and serve as an effective channel for the civic participation of noncitizens.[47] Although the predominant position of the governing political elite toward this establishment seems to be critical,[48] some experts have suggested that recent discussions are linked to the problems of a democratic deficit in a country where approximately 15 percent of permanent residents (noncitizens and third-country nationals) are excluded from the political discussions on any (even a local) level.

It should be stressed that one of the events leading to these heated discussions was the initiative of the nationalistic alliance to phase out state-funded education in minority languages. In January 2010, the nationalist For Fatherland and Freedom/LNNK party started to collect signatures to initiate a referendum on constitutional amendments that would lead to all publicly funded schools teaching solely in the Latvian language.[49] The required 10,000 signatures were submitted to the Central Election Commission in March 2011. To be submitted to the parliament, the draft required the support of more than one-tenth of the total number of citizens eligible to vote in the previous parliamentary elections (153,232 voters), but only 120,433 voters signed, thus falling short of the required number and revealing the position of the majority of the public on this proposal.[50]

The heated discussions on the status of the Russian language, the status of noncitizens, and the language of teaching in public schools reveal a lack of capacity or willingness to engage in a pragmatic discussion on necessary improvements to create a more inclusive society. In addition to the focus on "who is to blame," the developments were not evaluated in the context of the last twenty years—as a result of the decisions and actions taken in the past that have created feelings of being unwelcome, insulted, endangered, or not represented in a part of the population. Therefore an attempt was made to change the discourse and reveal the pragmatism of Latvian society by supporting and practicing participation in finding sustainable solutions to shape a more inclusive society. In an NGO initiative, representatives of the general public via online and offline methods drafted ideas for ten priority areas that would make Latvia's society more inclusive. The participants in the initiative also defined their visions for the ideal inclusive society as having:

- No division of people based on their ethnic backgrounds
- A state that is listening to all the members of the society
- A common identity and cultural events
- An ability to agree on a common future
- An understanding between people no matter what language they speak

Some of the examples of the obstacles that prevent Latvian society from being more inclusive are:

- Living in two parallel cultural worlds
- The heritage of the past and inability to let go
- Divided media space—printing and broadcasting in Latvian and Russian
- Language barrier
- Division of people between the founding nation and "the others"
- Sensitive topics being used to retain political capital
- Inability to identify with the government where people with different ethnic backgrounds are not represented
- Noncitizens not able to take part in decision-making
- Lack of individual responsibility—an individual does not believe that he or she can make a difference

Conclusion

As we have seen, more inclusive public attitudes and policies toward the permanent immigrant residents of Latvia are still problems that need to be addressed, as the positions of the political elite, negative public opinion, negative coverage of immigrants in the media, and the weak capacity of immigrant NGOs pose many challenges to the political and civic participation of third-country nationals in Latvia. In line with these positions, there are several legislative obstacles to participation, including not having voting rights in local elections and not having the right to be a member of a political association. Legislation allows civic activism in the form of participation in or the establishment of NGOs and trade unions. However, effective consultative mechanisms that would engage NGOs in representing immigrants' voices and NGOs' working with migrants in decision making on issues that directly affect them still remains to be achieved. Moreover, the lack of strong NGOs representing immigrants (via third-country nationals among their members and leadership) leads to NGOs working with migrants and speaking for them, instead of migrants speaking for themselves.

The current political elite is not open to broadening political participation opportunities for third-country nationals, as they consider the current routes—consultative bodies, meetings with authorities, and participation in NGOs—as sufficient. According to the dominant conviction, naturalization is seen as the way to receive all political participation rights, assuming that providing more political rights to permanent residents would decrease their motivation to naturalize. A serious obstacle to naturalization is the country's citizenship policy. Although the recent limited dual citizenship is a significant improvement, most third-country nationals living in Latvia will still need to renounce their original citizenship to become a Latvian citizen and enjoy full political rights.

The considerably high volume of emigration, paired with considerably low birth rates and an increasing proportion of the population becoming older in recent years has contributed to an increasing—and at times desperate—public awareness about one of the main challenges of the country: a shrinking population. As competition for human capital takes place among EU countries and beyond, the availability of human resources in Latvia may create an obstacle for the country's economic growth and welfare in the future. Moreover, the country faces a trade-off between a more liberal approach to immigration or having a small population living in a half-empty country with a national park surrounding a few cities and either very high taxes to sustain the public services or a weak provision of public services as a consequence of this lack of human resources.

Although there is a general consensus on the need to facilitate the return of Latvian emigrants, this development is highly dependent on the general economic and social conditions within the country. Moreover, the society needs to realize that return migration is very likely to further increase the diversity of the local population, with spouses and children with different backgrounds joining their Latvian partners or parents. But a significant part of the population is not tolerant toward diversity, with negative opinions on immigration as one of the consequences of the Soviet migration policy. This has also created a certain unwillingness or incapability to provide a welcoming environment for newly arriving migrants. Thus, one of the main challenges for Latvia is building a more inclusive society with an increasingly diverse population.

NOTES

Acknowledgments: This chapter is based on the original work of Dace Akule, referencing previously published as well as unpublished material, including *Political Participation of Third Country Nationals on National and Local Level: Latvian Country Report* (2011), the unpublished article "Migration in the New Member States of the EU: Latvian Report" (2013), as well as data from ongoing research carried out by the author.

1. Many Latvians fail to register their intention to be absent from the country for longer than six months, thus remaining in the population registry.

2. As they had become Russian citizens in 2009–2011, 11,353 persons applied to rescind the status of noncitizen, with most of them retaining their residence in the country. One of the reasons why Latvia's noncitizens choose Russian citizenship is the lower retirement age (fifty-five for women and sixty for men in Russia, while it is sixty-two for both genders in Latvia).

3. Since July 2010, Latvia issues temporary residence permits to those who have invested in Latvia either in a company, in a credit institution in the form of subordinated capital, or by purchasing real estate according to specific criteria set in immigration law (Immigration law at: www.likumi.lv).

4. OCMA data quoted in "Trīs gados pret uzturēšanās atļaujām investēti 419 miljoni latu" [During three years 419 million Lats invested in return for residence permits], *Financenet*, September 17, 2013.

5. Cabinet of Ministers, Regulation No. 553 on work permits for foreigners, with amendments of July 29, 2011.

6. Prior to this amendment in the Immigration law, these students could only apply for a new residence permit in a Latvian embassy outside of the Schengen area.

7. Office of Citizenship and Migration Affairs, http://www.pmlp.gov.lv/lv/sakums /statistika/patveruma-mekletaji.html.

8. The only exception to this rule is the opposition center-left Harmony Center, which advocates for more political participation rights for noncitizens and would, presumably, also be in favor of granting these rights to third-country nationals. Forty-three percent of respondents from the general public were negative about granting voting rights in municipalities to noncitizens, 27 percent supported this proposition, 24 percent were neutral on this issue, and 8 percent said it was difficult to answer (Makarovs and Dimitrovs 2009).

9. OCMA website, http://www.pmlp.gov.lv/lv/sakums/statistika/naturalizacija. html.

10. Foreigners cannot purchase land in border areas, nor agricultural or forest land (this limit also applied to EU citizens until April 2014).

11. Latvia's citizens need a visa to travel to Russia, however, since 2008, noncitizens can travel there visa free.

12. If the migrant changes his or her employer in Latvia, they should receive a new work permit and the procedure is repeated. If the migrant faces unemployment in Latvia, it is essential that he or she find a new employer quickly and begin again the procedure to receive work and residence permits.

13. Medical emergency services are provided by the state to Ukrainians and Russians due to bilateral agreements with Ukraine and Russia. For others, these services are provided via compulsory health insurance that the migrant needs to have to apply for a temporary residence permit (Zepa et al. 2009).

14. Some discriminatory provisions have been gradually removed, but some still remain today, for example, differences in the right to pensions for the time worked in the Soviet territory outside of Latvia and the right to own land in the border areas.

15. The Law on the Election of City, County and Rural Councils (Article 5, Article 8) and the Saeima Election Law (Article 1, Article 4). All laws available at: www.likumi.lv.

16. The Law on Political Parties, Article 26.

17. The Law on Nongovernmental Organizations and Their Associations says that members of these organizations should be sixteen years old or—if they are younger than sixteen—they should have written parents'/guardians' approval (Article 5, Article 6). The Society and Foundation Law says that any individual has the right to establish and be a member of such an organization (Article 23).

18. The Law on Trade Unions (Article 2).

19. The Law on Assemblies, Marches and Protests (Article 3, Article 4).

20. In 2009, approximately 28 percent of citizens were minorities, compared to 40 percent of the whole population.

21. The authors of the study used *citizenship* in the broader sense of the word, including having access to policy debate.

22. From the unpublished report "Shrinking Citizenship—Monitoring of Parliamentary Debates and Legislative Initiatives Concerning Civic Participation and Citizenship in Latvia," PROVIDUS, 2013.

23. See the website of the President's Chancellery: http://www.president.lv/pk/content/?cat_id=6407&lng=en.

24. The leadership of this council has been shifting along with changes in social integration policy. First the function of the Secretariat of the Special Assignment Minister for Social Integration was moved to the Ministry of Children and Family Affairs (January 2009), then to the Ministry of Justice (May 2009), and then to the Ministry of Culture (January 2011).

25. The NGOs were selected after an open call for applications from organizations registered in Latvia and active at least for two years in representing the interests of Latvia's noncitizens, refugees, persons with alternative status, and third-country nationals, and those having expertise in the area of immigrant integration.

26. The document (in Latvian) is available on the website of the state newspaper: http://likumi.lv/doc.php?id=238195.

27. The open call for NGOs and research institutions to apply to work in the council was repeated three times in spring 2013. The first meeting of the council was held only on September 20, 2013. Ministry of Culture, September 25, http://www.km.gov.lv/lv/jaunumi/?news_id=3807.

28. In 1989, these immigrants accounted for more than 77 percent of the population (Vēbers 1994).

29. These figures from Ķīlis (2009) are based on public opinion data from SKDS. Just 52 percent of the population were ethnic Latvians, while before the occupation, Latvians accounted for more than 77 percent of the population (Vēbers 1994).

30. A representative sample of over one thousand respondents ages eighteen to seventy-four were surveyed by the public opinion and market research center SKDS for

the "DnB NORD Latvian Barometer." Respondents could agree to several statements. See: https://www.dnb.lv/sites/default/files/dnb_latvian_barometer/documents/2011/290 .dnb-nord-latvijas-barometrs-nr35.pdf.

31. Forty-five percent of Latvians and 41 percent of minority representatives don't want to live next to Muslims, 52 percent of Latvians and 59 percent of non-Latvians supported the statement that Muslim opinions and traditions can be dangerous for Latvia's population (Šūpule et al. 2004).

32. Extraordinary elections were held after the parliament was dissolved in a referendum initiated by Latvia's president.

33. Program of the nationalistic alliance in the national elections of 2010.

34. According to the amendments, 700 applications would be accepted in 2014 from persons having purchased real estate for at least 150,000 EUR, and having paid an additional fee of 25,000 EUR. In 2015 the quota would be 525, with 350 applications in 2016. An additional 100 applications would be acceptable for persons having invested in real estate valued at at least 500,000 EUR.

35. Data from the Office of Citizenship and Migration Affairs.

36. Transparency International-Latvia Statement of October 31, 2014, http://delna .lv/en/.

37. Amendments to the Immigration law came into force on September 1, 2014, http://likumi.lv/doc.php?id=266619.

38. Government's action plan, February 2014, http://www.mk.gov.lv/lv/mk/darbibu -reglamentejosie-dokumenti/straujumas-valdibas-ricibas-plans/.

39. One-stop agency for the issuing of work permits and residence permits, decreasing fees for work permits and residence permits, as well as decreasing the length of the procedure to recruit a third-country national were included in the plan to improve the business environment in 2008, under the responsibility of the Ministry of Economy.

40. The plan includes appointing a one-stop agency for questions linked to return migration; improving labor market information (available vacancies and approximate salaries); subsidizing the recruitment of highly skilled workers for the introduction of innovations; supporting the returnee and his or her family members in learning Latvian; cooperating with the diaspora; reassessing the support for pupils and their parents returning to the Latvian education system; assessing the requirements for foreign-language knowledge; and providing integration support for persons and their family members who have lived abroad for at least ten years. "Reemigrācijas atbalsta pasākumu plāns 2013. –2016.gads" [Action plan for the support of return migration, 2013–2016], June 2013, http://www.em.gov.lv/em/2nd/?cat=30791.

41. Press release of the Ministry of Economy, December 13, 2012, www.em.gov.lv.

42. Press release of the Ministry of Foreign Affairs, March 5, 2013, http://www.am .gov.lv/lv/Jaunumi/zinas/2013/marts/05-2/?print=on.

43. Approximately 20,000 people gathered in a protest on May 1, 2004.

44. Parliament's website, April 14, 2012, http://www.saeima.lv/lv/aktualitates /saeimas-zinas/19557-saeima-darbu-sak-sabiedribas-saliedetibas-komisija. Approximately 300,000 EUR were invested in 2012 in intensive Latvian-language courses, training for language instructors, and measures facilitating discussions about Latvia's history and cooperation among people with different ethnic backgrounds. Cabinet of Ministers' website, http://www.mk.gov.lv/lv/mk/tap/?pid=40252274&mode=mk&date=2012-05-29.

45. Among the issues discussed was a possibility of adding a preamble to the Latvian Constitution defining what constitutes the Latvian nation, the goals of the Latvian state, and the values that the state is based on.

46. The NGO suggested that, beginning January 1, 2014, those noncitizens who had not submitted an application to retain noncitizen status should be deemed to be citizens of Latvia.

47. See the website of the Latvian Noncitizens' Congress: http://www.noncitizens.eu/about.

48. For example, the prime minister's advisor on integration issues, Sarmīte Ēlerte, has said that this initiative is a pro-Russian political project that has nothing to do with attempts to really improve the lives of people who have not obtained Latvian citizenship Ēlerte 2013).

49. In the academic year 2011–2012, Latvia had 641 schools with Latvian as the language of instruction, 99 schools with Russian as the language of instruction (implementing bilingual education programs), and 65 schools had two language sections (solely in Latvian and also Russian with bilingual curriculum). Four schools carry out instruction partially in the Polish language, one in Polish/Latvian, one in Ukrainian, and one in Belorusian. In Estonian, Lithuanian, and two Jewish schools some subjects are taught in the minority language (Latvian Centre for Human Rights 2013).

50. See the website of the Central Election Commission: http://web.cvk.lv/pub/public/29863.html.

V

New Destinations in Comparative Perspective

9

Immigration and Policing Practices in New Destinations

Monica W. Varsanyi
Paul G. Lewis
Doris Marie Provine
Scott Decker

The chapters in this volume have focused thus far on the extent and nature of integration policies in particular new destination localities and countries. Part V introduces an explicitly comparative perspective, with chapters that examine the question of differences and similarities among old and new immigration destinations. In this chapter, Varsanyi and her colleagues look at public policy toward immigrants through the lens of policing. Their national surveys of police departments find that there is little difference in public policy toward immigrants across the United States in communities with significant Hispanic populations, with new destinations being no more likely to help with federal enforcement of immigration law than traditional ones, for example. The finding that variation in the policies and practices of policing is not explained by the newness of the destination reflects findings in other chapters that in some locales, even in small communities, efforts are often made to incorporate immigrants. Such attempts seemingly depend on the attitudes of certain elites and institutions, including bureaucrats (Ireland, Chapter 1), politicians/political parties (Italy, Chapter 2), and churches (England, Chapter 6). As in Ireland, where municipal bureaucrats preceded political parties in advocating for immigrants, Varsanyi and her colleagues find local police leading the way in U.S. new immigrant destinations.

The passage of (and battles against) state and local immigration policies, such as Arizona's SB1070, Alabama's HB56, and Hazleton, Pennsylvania's Illegal Immigration Relief Act, have received a great deal of media and scholarly attention in recent years. Indeed, the recent explosion of state immigration laws and local immigration ordinances has marked a compelling shift in the national immigration law and policy landscape. However, it is also crucial to highlight the actions of state and local bureaucrats, who, while one step removed from the policy-making process, arguably play an important role as policy *implementers*. Not only are these bureaucrats at the local frontlines of receiving and incorporating immigrants, but their agencies frequently act as policy incubators, generating practices that later become policy (Epp 2010; Lewis and Ramakrishnan 2007; Marrow 2011). In short, if we are to have a full and nuanced understanding of the experiences and incorporation of immigrants in the United States, it is essential to complement a study of state and local policy making with an exploration of the practices of state and local bureaucracies, such as schools, police/law enforcement, and social services.

This is particularly the case in new destinations, meaning places that have experienced a rapid increase in immigrant settlement in the past two decades and that have had little prior experience with foreign-born populations. In traditional gateway cities such as Los Angeles, New York City, Chicago, Houston, and San Francisco, foreign-born residents and their children are the norm, not the exception, and city governments—including local bureaucracies—have significant experience engaging with these populations, occasional tensions notwithstanding (de Graauw 2008). In new destinations, local bureaucrats lack such experience, and yet they often engage new immigrant communities and develop practices to assist them long before local government officials on the city council, or in the state legislature, have understood the extent of local demographic change (Jones-Correa 2008; Lewis and Ramakrishnan 2007).

Among bureaucracies in new destinations, local law enforcement is a prominent point of contact between recent immigrant settlers and the local state. Recent changes in federal (and some state) laws are adding further complexities to the already-challenging relationship between local police and these growing immigrant communities. Increasingly, local police are finding themselves facing decisions about their role in implementing and enforcing shifting and sometimes contradictory laws developed on the local, state, and federal levels. Elsewhere, we have analyzed quantitative data from three national surveys to determine the reasons local law enforcement executives, including police chiefs and sheriffs, choose particular enforcement regimes (Lewis et al. 2012; Lewis et al. 2013). In this chapter, we explore similar themes, but in the context of new destination dynamics. How are local police in new destinations engaging—or choosing not to engage—with expanding immigrant communities and increasing calls for their participation in immigration enforcement? Which factors play the most important role in the decisions made by police departments in developing policy and practices? How does policing in new destinations differ from policing in traditional Latino destinations? To answer these questions, this chapter draws upon both quantitative and qualitative data—namely an in-depth case study conducted in Allentown, Pennsylvania—from our multiyear study of immigration enforcement at the local level.

In the first section of the chapter, we set the stage for our analysis by discussing both the evolution of the new destination phenomenon, as well as the changing landscape of local immigration policing. We then review the salient literatures and highlight the theoretical and empirical contributions of this chapter, in order to provide scholarly context for our survey and case study data. We next offer a quantitative look into our data from our national surveys of police chiefs that highlight common policing practices and dynamics in new destination communities across the United States. We find, in terms of immigration policing practices, that new destinations do not differ significantly from more traditional immigrant destinations, other than being laggards in developing official immigrant-related policies. Finally, we present the case study of Allentown, which, as we discuss below, can be taken as both a typical, and yet in some important ways unique, example of policing in a new destination.

Setting the Stage

New Destinations

As many have now documented (Goździak and Martin 2005; Lichter and Johnson 2006; Marrow 2011; Massey 2008a; Singer et al. 2008), the last several decades have witnessed a sea change in the settlement patterns and growth of immigrant populations in the United States. In the decades before 1990, the majority of immigrants settled in the "big five" states: California, New York, Texas, Florida, and Illinois. In the 1990s, however, a growing proportion of immigrants began to settle outside of these traditional destinations. For example, the share of immigrants settling in California fell from 35.5 percent to 21.1 percent over the course of the decade. Rather than settling in so-called "second-tier" states (states that had also served as traditional destinations for immigration, albeit at lower levels), immigrants were now moving toward entirely new destination states such as Georgia, Arizona, Michigan, North Carolina, and Pennsylvania (Massey and Capoferro 2008: 36). This trend was even more pronounced among Mexican and other Latin American immigrants. As Daniel T. Lichter and Kenneth M. Johnson (2009: 497) describe, in 1990 approximately nine out of ten Latinos lived in ten states, with 54 percent of all Latinos living in California and Texas alone. Following the trend of all immigrants, broadly considered, this started to change dramatically in the 1990s, with 28 percent of Mexican immigrants settling in California in 2000, as compared to 63 percent in 1990 (Massey and Capoferro 2008: 39).[1] These trends have continued into the present.

In addition to regional shifts, immigrants—and in particular, immigrants from Mexico and Latin America—are increasingly choosing rural, suburban, and smaller city destinations over traditional big city life (Díaz McConnell 2008; Kandel and Cromartie 2004; Marrow 2011; Singer et al. 2008). This trend in Mexican migration to rural new destinations, particularly in the Midwest and South, has been pronounced enough that demographers have started calling these places "offset counties" or "counties that grew in population only because of gains in the foreign-born" (Donato et al. 2008).

Importantly, the new destinations phenomenon is not solely about immigrants. This fact is easy to overlook because of the demographic realities of immigration into the United States. Mexicans make up the majority of foreign-born persons residing in the United States, and much research has justifiably addressed the dispersion of, for example, first-generation and often undocumented Mexican immigrants to new destinations (see Zúñiga and Hernández-León 2005a). But this Mexican immigration pattern exists alongside a much more broad-based dispersion of Latinos, a group that includes immigrants, naturalized citizens, and the native born.

As a result of both trends, the Hispanic landscape of the United States has changed quite dramatically in the last several decades. First, the absolute number of these residents has increased significantly: in the 1990s, for example, the Latino population of the United States expanded by nearly thirteen million (a 58 percent increase) due both to immigration and natural increase (Lichter and Johnson 2009). And second, the pattern of settlement—the so-called new destinations dynamic—has evolved in dramatic ways.

Demographers tend to discuss new destinations in the United States not only as an immigrant phenomenon, but also as Hispanic dispersion, broadly speaking (see Johnson and Lichter 2008; Kandel and Cromartie 2004). Highlighting the multigenerational nature of immigrant dispersion, Douglas Massey and his contributors (2008) frame new destinations in the context not only of first-generation arrivals, but also of post-1965 immigration to the United States, a population that would now include both first-generation immigrants and their native-born children (and possibly their native-born grandchildren).

New destination settlement also transcends immigration in another way. Population growth in new destinations is the result of three dynamics: immigration, in which individuals choose new destinations as their first stop in the United States; in-migration, in which individuals who have first settled in one location then later move to new destinations; and natural increase. While new destinations certainly attract many immigrants who have just arrived in the United States, as Lichter and Johnson (2009) demonstrate, traditional destinations continue to remain attractive. In fact, immigration tends to drive population growth more heavily in traditional gateways. In new destinations, on the other hand, approximately half of settlement is the result of immigration from outside the nation and the other half is in-migration/domestic migration. In other words, a significant proportion of population growth in new destinations is the result of settlement not by newly arrived immigrants, but by those who first settled elsewhere in the country. We return to this dynamic in the Allentown case study below.

Local Immigration Enforcement

As Hispanic and immigrant communities continue to expand in new desti-nations, state and local governments have sought new tools and strategies with which to engage these communities, ranging from the inclusionary and incorporative to the exclusionary and enforcement oriented. On the enforce-ment end of the spectrum, local police now play a prominent role. This rep-resents a significant departure from the past. Local police played only a minimal official role in immigration enforcement in the United States from the 1880s through the 1990s because the federal government was under-stood to hold plenary power over immigration policy making and enforce-ment. It was not until 1996, when Congress passed the Illegal Immigration Reform and Immigrant Responsibility Act (IIRIRA), that a space opened for enforcement of civil immigration law by local law enforcement. Among other things, IIRIRA created a program whereby state and local police forces were invited—but not required—to partner with the federal government to enforce the civil provisions of immigration law. By signing what came to be called 287(g) agreements and undergoing federal training, local law enforcement officers could investigate the "alienage" (or noncitizen) status of individuals they encountered in their daily work, whether that be in the jails ("Jail Enforcement" agreements), or in the community ("Task Force" agreements).

Though created in 1996, no 287(g) agreements were signed until 2002, a change prompted by the post-September 11 environment. At the program's peak in 2010, approximately seventy state and local law enforcement agen-cies had signed agreements with the federal government and had officers trained to enforce immigration law. There are currently thirty-four active 287(g) agreements, but the program has been targeted for retrenchment and phase out, as new federal programs—first, Secure Communities, and more recently the Priority Enforcement Program (PEP)—have been implemented nationally (Department of Homeland Security 2013, 2014). Secure Commu-nities and PEP establish information sharing between all local jails across the United States and federal immigration databases, so that individuals who are arrested by local law enforcement are automatically screened for civil immigration violations. Whether under 287(g) agreements, Secure Communities, or PEP, however, the role of local police in immigration enforcement has been growing.

At the same time as 287(g) agreements between localities and the federal government were growing in number in the mid-2000s, states and localities across the country were introducing some of their own laws on immigration. If 287(g) agreements could be considered a "top-down" initiative, enabled by devolution and with the goal of engaging local law enforcement agencies as "force multipliers," the grassroots were taking action as well, particularly after congressional immigration reform efforts failed in 2006 and 2007. Both states and localities jumped into the immigration policy-making fray. Some of the most prominent anti-immigration laws passed at the state level included Arizona's SB1070 and Alabama's HB56, both of which include provisions requiring local police to check the immigration status of individuals they encounter; a provision that was to a large extent upheld by the U.S. Supreme Court in *Arizona v. United States* (2012). But SB1070 and HB56 were just a prominent tip of the iceberg. The Immigrant Policy Project of the National Conference on State Legislatures has been keeping track of immigration-related policy making in the state legislatures since the mid-2000s (www.ncsl.org). In 2005, 300 immigration-related bills were introduced in state legislatures, with 45 adopted. The number of bills becoming law has remained high since that time, with 222 laws passed by state legislatures in 2009, 306 in 2011, and 437 in 2013.

Importantly, while state and local anti-immigration laws tend to receive the lion's share of media attention, many local immigration laws have actually been integrative and pro-immigrant in nature. States and localities have extended health services and insurance to immigrants and their children, passed living-wage campaigns, extended in-state tuition benefits to undocumented college students, and more (Mitnik and Halpern-Finnerty 2010). In the realm of immigration policing and enforcement, since the 1980s a number of cities across the country, including many of the largest cities in the United States (New York City, Los Angeles, San Francisco, Chicago), have passed "noncooperation" ordinances that prevent city employees, including police, from seeking or reporting immigration status to federal authorities.

Literature Review

This chapter engages with, and seeks to make contributions to, three related literatures: local immigration policing, bureaucratic incorporation, and new destinations. All three are relatively nascent, reflecting the recent nature of the phenomena under study.

Local Immigration Policing

As local immigration policing took off in the mid-2000s, a number of professional associations, think tanks, and advocacy organizations issued reports that provided comprehensive information to police chiefs across the country about the changing nature of police-immigrant community relationships, documented best practices in developing positive relationships between police and immigrant communities, and outlined the legal boundaries around local immigration enforcement (Appleseed n.d.; International Association of Chiefs of Police 2007; Khashu 2009; Police Executive Research Forum 2008; Saint-Fort, Yasso, and Shah 2012). Legal scholars also became involved relatively early on, exploring the constitutionality of local immigration policing (Hethmon 2004; Pham 2004; Wishnie 2004). Social science scholarship on the phenomenon followed closely behind.

This scholarship has taken two forms: studies that have surveyed the phenomenon from a national or comparative perspective; and in-depth case studies, particularly of localities in which the police have taken on immigration-enforcement duties. In the first mode, we have conducted and analyzed three national surveys of policing practices at the local level (Lewis et al. 2011; Lewis et al. 2013). Our analysis has demonstrated inter alia the way in which localities—sometimes neighboring and overlapping—have diverged greatly on the question of immigration policing, despite being faced with a uniform federal government context, a phenomenon we have called the "multilayered jurisdictional patchwork" (Provine, Varsanyi, Lewis, and Decker 2016; Varsanyi et al. 2012). In another comparative study, Ingrid Eagly (2013) also documents the way in which divergent local outcomes can emerge out of a uniform federal context. She carefully explores how the criminal justice systems in three prominent immigrant destinations engage in quite divergent ways with noncitizens despite a common federal legal framework. Eagly categorizes the criminal justice system in Maricopa County (Phoenix, AZ) as having an "illegal alien punishment" model, Los Angeles County as an "alienage neutral" model, and Harris County (Houston, TX) as having an "immigrant enforcement" model.

Among the case-study-oriented analyses, we find nuanced explorations of the dynamics of local immigration policing and the engagement of local law enforcement with Immigration and Customs Enforcement (ICE), the federal agency in charge of immigration enforcement in the interior of the United States. Echoing Eagly, Mathew Coleman's exploration of immigration policing in North Carolina's Wake and Durham Counties highlights how federal laws and programs become indelibly shaped by "specific political, legal, policing, and biographic contexts" (Coleman 2012: 159) at the local level. Though neighbors, the immigration enforcement regimes in Wake and Durham Counties have developed in highly divergent ways, with Wake taking an enforcement orientation, and, in contrast, Durham County police operating under a general order that prohibits officers from investigating immigration status or contacting ICE. In a different vein, Amada Armenta (2012) explores the ways in which local police officers, deputized as agents of ICE through a 287g agreement, view their newfound role as agents in the immigration enforcement regime. In arguing against Michael Lipsky's (1980) well-known work on the exercise of discretion by "street-level bureaucrats," Armenta claims that these deputized local officers, who are indeed the street- and local-level face of ICE, do not on the whole exercise much discretion in their daily duties. In contrast to being policy makers à la Lipsky, they are policy implementers. Further scholarship details a variety of other dynamics related to local-level immigration enforcement (Leerkes, Varsanyi, and Engbersen 2012; Licona and Maldonado 2014; Waslin 2010).

Our exploration of Allentown in this chapter offers new empirical evidence to this growing body of scholarship. Whereas the in-depth studies discussed above explore the dynamics in communities in which federal-local immigration enforcement agreements are already in place, Allentown is a city in which the police and local government have no official policies on local immigration enforcement, either for or against. Allentown's profile thus contrasts with more settled immigrant and Latino destinations in which police and local governments have established practices and policies in place, and with places where such policies are newly established or in flux. Thus, in contrast to other sites that have been studied in depth, the Allentown Police Department (APD) and the city's local government are in the process of "catching up" with demographic change. Given their position on the frontlines of engagement, the police have necessarily developed a set of widely understood *practices* for engaging with their immigrant and Latino communities, though at the time of the research, these practices hadn't become official city policy.

Bureaucratic Incorporation

This chapter also seeks to shed light on the expanding "bureaucratic incorporation" literature. As discussed in the introduction, local street-level bureaucrats (Lipsky 1980) such as police officers, teachers, librarians, and social service providers are often on the frontlines of engagement with recently arrived immigrant communities, in both new destination communities and elsewhere. Various studies have explored the immigrant incorporative role of local bureaucracies, including local nonprofits (de Graauw 2008), public school teachers and administrators (Brettell 2008; Griffith 2008; Jones-Correa 2008), health care workers (Griffith 2008), librarians (Brettell 2008), police (Marrow 2011), and other local government workers (Brettell 2008; Marrow 2011).

As Paul G. Lewis and S. Karthick Ramakrishnan (2007) and Michael Jones-Correa (2008) discuss, local government bureaucrats are often aware of the challenges presented by rapidly shifting demographic realities before local government officials are, making these local bureaucracies an important site of policy innovation. Not surprisingly, as Jones-Correa's (2008) study of suburban Washington, DC, school districts and Marrow's (2011) study of two rural counties in North Carolina demonstrate, bureaucrats often find themselves in the position of negotiating intergroup relations, or tensions between long-settled, nonimmigrant community members and emerging immigrant communities. Reflecting this literature, this chapter situates local police in Allentown on the frontlines of both immigrant incorporation and intergroup tensions.

New Destinations

The Allentown case study also contributes to the new destinations literature. Like the scholarship on local immigration policing, this literature divides loosely into national-level and case-study-level camps. The national-level demographic studies explore the dispersion of Mexican immigrants or Latinos/ Hispanics away from traditional settlement gateways and to new destination communities (Díaz McConnell 2008; Lichter and Johnson 2009; Lichter et al. 2010; see the chapters in Part I of Massey 2008c). The case studies explore the reception of immigrants and intergroup tensions in new destinations (Benjamin-Alvarado, DeSipio, and Montoya 2009; see the chapters in Part II of Marrow 2011; Massey 2008c; Zúñiga and Hernández-León 2005b).

The focus in both types of new destinations studies is often on Mexican immigrants. As R. S. Oropesa and Leif Jensen (2010: 275) have argued in their work on Dominican immigrants in Reading, Pennsylvania: "At risk of overstatement, the emerging literature on new destinations tends to focus disproportionately on Mexican migrants in the South and Midwest." In this regard, Allentown differs. First, unlike many of the places explored in the new destinations literature, it is located in the Northeast of the United States. Second, the immigrant mix in Allentown is much more diverse, including many Dominicans and others (see also Oropesa 2012; Oropesa and Jensen 2010). And finally, the new destination dynamic in Allentown involves not just immigrants, but nonimmigrants. It is a place where a new Latino population—both immigrant and nonimmigrant—has settled in the last several decades. In other words, it is a new *Hispanic* destination, not just a new *immigrant* destination. As we see in the case study below, however, nativist tensions regarding broad demographic change have opportunistically jumped on the anti-immigrant bandwagon, despite the fact that many of the targeted individuals were not immigrants. Anti-immigrant animus, in short, has been directed against many native-born and naturalized Latinos, including Puerto Ricans.

Survey Evidence on Immigration and Policing Practices in New Destinations

Before delving into the Allentown case study, we take a broad empirical look at the types of policing practices found in new destinations, especially in comparison to more established Latino destinations. For evidence, we turn to two national surveys of police chiefs that we undertook in recent years. These surveys asked law enforcement executives or their designees a detailed set of questions about the policies and practices operative in their communities with respect to immigration policing and interactions with possibly unauthorized immigrants. Our first survey, conducted in 2007–2008, was sent to all municipalities with populations of 65,000 or higher that have their own local police departments. We began with a list of all U.S. cities and towns listed in the Census Bureau's American Community Survey (ACS) in 2005, which, according to the U.S. Census Bureau, was limited to cities above that size threshold (a few cities had slightly lower populations but were retained in our analysis). We dropped from this list several communities that contract with other local governments for police services, or which otherwise do not have a self-governed police department. These criteria yielded a sample of 452 municipalities—essentially the universe of large-city police departments—which we call our "large city" group. After several rounds of contacts, we ultimately received responses from 237 of these police departments (52.4 percent). Although most of these communities have substantial numbers of immigrants—the average proportion of foreign born was 16 percent in 2005—the share of immigrants ranged widely from 1 percent to 60 percent of the population. Some cities, as we describe below, fit the bill as new destinations for Latinos.

The new destination phenomenon, however, is often described as being especially prevalent in smaller communities in suburban and rural areas, where, until recently, there has been less of a history of immigrant—and specifically, Hispanic immigrant—settlement. To determine the policing practices of such places, in 2010 we conducted a survey of police chiefs in communities below the 65,000 threshold. This required a sampling strategy, because there are a huge number of U.S. municipalities that fall into this size category—more than 18,000, many of which are tiny communities that have very few immigrant or Latino residents. To maximize our chances of hearing from localities in which immigration policing might be a salient issue, we selected a survey sample of 450 small municipalities, all of which were located in counties of 20,000 or more residents and where at least 6 percent of county residents were foreign born at the time of the 2000 Census. To further ensure that the sample was nationally representative of this set of cities, we stratified the sample both by population size and by region of the country.[2] We again omitted localities that lacked their own locally controlled police department, replacing them on a one-to-one basis with other municipalities of the same size category and region. Coincidentally, we again received responses from 237 communities, for a response rate of 52.7 percent. The average small municipality responding to the survey had a population of 27,850. In both surveys, the ultimate sample of respondents was quite representative of the initial sample of communities that received surveys, except that police chiefs from large cities in the Northeast region were less likely to return surveys than their large-city counterparts in other regions.

In this analysis, we are most concerned with possible differences in immigration policing practices between new destinations and more traditional Latino receiving places. We examined a range of prior literature on new destinations in which scholars have attempted to create typologies or statistical delineations of these types of places (Lichter and Johnson 2009; Singer 2008) and then adapted these approaches in a way that made sense for our sample of municipalities. Following the convention in much of this literature, we think of new destinations as places that were largely "off the map" as places of Latino settlement prior to 1990, but which added Latinos at a rapid rate in the 1990s and 2000s, such that Latinos are now a significant and noticeable (if not necessarily huge) presence in the local population. New destinations scholarship tends to focus on growth in local Latino populations, rather than the foreign-born population more generally, probably because that growth has been at the center of the debate about illegal immigration and rapid demographic change in the United States.

To operationalize this thinking statistically, we include as new destinations the municipalities in our samples of respondents that meet both of the following criteria:

- *Had a Hispanic proportion of the population that was below 5 percent at the time of the 1990 Census.* The Hispanic share of the national population was 8.74 percent in 1990, so these are communities that were considerably below the national average, in many cases less than half that figure.
- *Had a Hispanic proportion of the population that then increased by at least five percentage points from 1990 until 2005* (for our 2007–2008 survey of large cities) *or until 2008* (for our 2010 survey of smaller municipalities).[3]

For example, a community that grew from 0 to 5 percent Latino after 1990 would meet these criteria, as would a community that grew from 4.9 to 9.9 percent Latino. Five percentage points is the *minimum* threshold for growth in Latino share, however, and many new destinations in our samples had Latino components that grew far more than that. Indeed, the average new destination community in our large-city dataset increased its Latino share of the population from 2.5 percent in 1990 to 11.2 percent in 2005; for the average small municipality, the equivalent figures were 2.6 percent (1990) and 13.3 percent (2008).

Below we compare our new destinations in each of the two samples to a set of *traditional Latino destinations*. We define traditional destinations as communities that met or exceeded the national proportion of 8.74 percent Hispanic in 1990. With these definitions in place, the large-city sample includes 25 new destinations and 107 traditional destinations. The much larger incidence of traditional destinations reflects the fact that larger cities have generally tended to draw significant numbers of Hispanics for some time, although there are some notable exceptions, as evidenced by our large-city group of new destinations. Among small communities (even despite the survey's minimum threshold of 6 percent Hispanic in 2000 for the *county* in which the municipality is nested), there is a higher proportion of new destinations and a lower proportion of traditional destinations, reflecting the more recent movement of Latinos into suburbs and rural areas. The small-municipality sample includes forty-one new destinations and sixty-four traditional destinations. In any event, there are sufficient observations to make some basic comparisons across the new destination/traditional destination dichotomy in each dataset. Because of the different years of our surveys, different sampling frame, and slightly different questionnaire format, we provide separate comparisons of new/traditional in the large cities and the smaller municipalities.

Policing Practices in New and Traditional Destination Localities

So, are new destination communities substantially different from traditional destinations in the ways that their police departments interact with immigrants or the priority given to immigration enforcement? Much of the previous literature, especially that in the case-study tradition, suggests that rapid demographic change in new destinations raises local anxieties (as well as challenges for local government), and thus may tend to provoke backlash in local public policy, or in our case, police practices. If this hypothesis is true, one might anticipate that in new destinations unauthorized immigration will be viewed as more controversial and destabilizing; that local governments and police departments will be more oriented toward active engagement in immigration enforcement; and that police practices will be less supportive of immigrants and less cognizant of the special needs of immigrants.

Our survey results suggest that differences in policing exist between new Latino destinations and traditional receiving communities, but that the differences are quite limited and do not always operate in the direction anticipated by the community anxiety/backlash hypothesis. If anything, there is some evidence that police departments in new destinations are somewhat behind the curve in adapting to the increased presence of Latinos in their communities. However, new destinations, for the most part, do not embrace policy approaches that are significantly more draconian or punitive toward immigrants.

Table 9.1 compares new destinations and traditional destinations for each of the two sets of communities, examining a range of perceptions by police chiefs about attitudes in their own department as well as in the broader community. Instances where the average response of new destination chiefs is significantly different from the average response of traditional destination chiefs are underlined.[4] The four pairs of rows in the table report average responses for each statement along a five-point scale, from "strongly disagree" (a score of 1) to "strongly agree" (a score of 5). Although we might anticipate that unauthorized immigration is a more controversial topic in new destination communities and police departments, the differences in scores in the top pair of rows are small and insignificant. The same is the case regarding agreement with the second pair of statements—that "people believe that it is relatively easy to determine who is in this country without authorization."

Regarding the third pair of statements, as to whether "gaining the trust of unauthorized immigrants is a priority" for the department and for the locality, differences are generally in the anticipated direction, but only one of the sets of differences is significant. Specifically, among the small municipalities, police chiefs from new destinations are less likely to agree that gaining the trust of unauthorized immigrants is a priority for their locality. The fourth pair of statements concerns whether chiefs believe that their department and their community agree that immigration enforcement is a federal, rather than local, responsibility. In this case, there are significant differences between new and traditional destinations. However, the differences for small municipalities indicate that new destination police chiefs are more likely to agree with the statement than their counterparts in traditional destinations. The pattern is the opposite in the large-city sample. Regarding the local community's sense of agreement with the statement, the differences are insignificant. Thus, looking across all of the agreement scores in the table, one must be circumspect in describing new destinations as distinctive.

Table 9.2 examines policies and practices, rather than perceptions. The first pair of rows examines municipal policies set by the mayor and council (as reported by the police chief). Cell entries in the first row show the percentage of communities that have what we call "supportive" local policies—which either declare the community a sanctuary for immigrants or establish

TABLE 9.1   AGREEMENT OF CHIEFS WITH STATEMENTS ABOUT DEPARTMENTAL AND CITYWIDE ATTITUDES TOWARD IMMIGRATION

	Large Cities		Small Municipalities	
	New Destinations	Traditional Destinations	New Destinations	Traditional Destinations
Unauthorized immigration is a controversial topic in my department	3.08	3.03	2.80	2.77
Unauthorized immigration is a controversial topic in this locality	3.92	3.72	3.27	3.52
People believe that it is relatively easy to determine who is in this country without authorization in my department	2.60	2.58	2.85	2.83
People believe that it is relatively easy to determine who is in this country without authorization in this locality	3.32	3.32	3.46	3.38
Gaining the trust of unauthorized immigrants is a priority in my department	3.46	3.77	2.98	3.39
Gaining the trust of unauthorized immigrants is a priority in this locality	3.00	2.96	_2.17_	_3.02_
Immigration enforcement is considered the responsibility of the federal government in my department	_3.63_	_4.17_	_4.04_	_3.58_
Immigration enforcement is considered the responsibility of the federal government in this locality	3.36	3.62	3.39	3.39

Note: Cell entries are average agreement scores on a scale ranging from 1 (strongly disagree) to 5 (strongly agree). Underlining indicates statistically significant differences ($p < .05$).

a "don't ask, don't tell" approach to dealings with unauthorized immigrants. The row immediately below shows the percentage of cities with "enforcement-oriented" policies, which either commit the police department to cooperating with federal authorities on certain immigrant-related law-enforcement issues or require that the police take on a proactive posture for detecting unauthorized immigrants in all their activities. All of the pairs of differences are in the anticipated direction—with new destinations less supportive and more enforcement oriented than traditional destinations—but none of the differences reach standard levels of statistical significance. And as the next

TABLE 9.2   CHIEFS' REPORTS OF LOCAL POLICIES, PRACTICES, AND CONDITIONS RELATED TO IMMIGRANT/POLICE RELATIONSHIPS

	Large Cities		*Small Municipalities*	
	New Destinations	**Traditional Destinations**	**New Destinations**	**Traditional Destinations**
Percent with supportive city policy (sanctuary or don't-ask-don't-tell)	16.7	25.2	9.8	23.4
Percent with enforcement-oriented city policy (cooperation with feds or proactive enforcement)	41.7	27.1	17.1	15.6
Percent with 287(g) MOU for investigation and arrests	4.0	1.9	7.3	4.7
Number of scenarios enforced, of seven possible	3.12	3.21	3.27	3.09
Percent with written departmental policy regarding interactions with immigrants	<u>20.0</u>	<u>51.4</u>	29.3	35.9
Percent with training for officers regarding interactions with unauthorized immigrants	32.0	41.1	29.3	34.4
Percent with personnel policies favoring bilingual speakers	88.0	72.9	<u>34.1</u>	<u>65.6</u>
Percent accepting Mexican consular cards as valid ID in at least some circumstances	76.0	79.2	87.8	85.9
Percent that "have enough officers proficient in foreign languages" to serve community	<u>17.4</u>	<u>53.8</u>	<u>41.5</u>	<u>65.6</u>
Percent holding regular meetings with immigrant-advocacy organizations	63.6	51.5	29.0	45.2
Percent saying immigrants are less likely than other residents to contact police as victims/witnesses	80	68.2	85.4	71.9

Note: Cell entries are average agreement scores on a scale ranging from 1 (strongly disagree) to 5 (strongly agree). Underlining indicates statistically significant differences ($p < .05$).

row reports, the differences in the percentage of municipalities that had signed Memoranda of Understanding with U.S. Immigration and Customs Enforcement (ICE) under its Section 287(g) program are also not significant (and the number of communities participating was very small in any event).

How about what police officers are actually doing in their day-to-day interactions with individuals they suspect might be undocumented? We asked police chiefs about seven possible scenarios—ranging widely in seriousness—and had them report which of these situations would typically lead officers to check an individual's immigration status or report the person to ICE.[5] The fourth row of Table 9.2 shows the average number of scenarios in which chiefs said their officers would likely pursue such contacts with federal immigration authorities. Here the differences between new and traditional destinations are very slight (and statistically insignificant), with each category of police departments pursuing, on average, slightly more than three of the seven scenarios. Thus, in the types of police-immigrant encounters that may matter most to the disposition of unauthorized immigrants, police in new destinations do not appear to be behaving much differently from their counterparts in localities with a more longstanding Latino presence.

The remaining rows of Table 9.2 relate to various procedural and personnel issues that may be important in how police departments relate to local immigrants. While most (though not all) of the pairs of relationships differ in the anticipated direction, the size of the differences is generally insignificant, with a few exceptions. These exceptions suggest that police departments in new destination locales may be somewhat slow to adjust to the increased presence of newcomers in their communities, which should not be surprising, given the rapidity of demographic change in many of these places. Among large cities, for instance, new destination police departments are significantly less likely than traditional destinations to have a written departmental policy regarding officer interactions with immigrants. Such lack of policy direction from the chief suggests that officers in these departments may be left somewhat more to their own devices in deciding how to handle such interactions (e.g., whether to call ICE after a traffic stop when the driver speaks little English and fails to produce a driver license).

Among the small municipalities, new destinations are considerably less likely than traditional destinations to have personnel policies that reward bilingualism among police officers (such as pay differentials or bonus "points" in the hiring or promotion process). The analogous difference, however, is not apparent for the large cities, where in fact new destinations are slightly more likely (though not significantly more likely) to have pro-bilingualism policies. The other instance of significant differences between new and old destinations also relates to language proficiency: police chiefs in new destinations are less likely to say that they have enough officers proficient in foreign languages to adequately serve their local communities. This is true both for large and small cities. Here we see that chiefs in new destination communities appear to be well aware that their departments will need to play catch-up in order to adjust to the rapid demographic change in their communities; a finding that leads us to Allentown.

Immigration Policing Practices in Allentown

Allentown is the third-largest city in Pennsylvania, considerably smaller than Philadelphia (which has 1.5 million people) and half the size of Pittsburgh (which has just over 300,000 inhabitants), but is a significantly sized metropolis nonetheless, with approximately 118,000 people in Allentown proper, and approximately 350,000 people in Lehigh County, in which the city is located. For many years, Allentown's population was dominated by the "Pennsylvania Dutch," descendants of settlers from Germany and Switzerland who settled in the area in the seventeenth and eighteenth centuries. During the twentieth century, the city became increasingly diverse, with significant Puerto Rican, Syrian, African, Irish, Italian, Arab, Ukrainian, and Polish American neighborhoods developing.

Allentown's location has played an important role in its shifting demography: the city is ninety miles due west of New York City and sixty miles northwest of Philadelphia. In the last several decades, two events played a role in significantly reshaping Allentown's current demographics: the completion in the 1980s of Interstate Highway 78 (I-78), running from New York City through Allentown and beyond, and the terrorist attacks on New York City in September 2001. With housing prices skyrocketing in the New York City metropolitan area, I-78 provided the means by which Allentown and its environs became, in essence, a commuter suburb of the greater New York City region (despite the two-hour one-way commute). And after September 11, seeking affordable housing and a sense of peace and safety, an even larger group of households made the move from New York City and its suburbs to Allentown and the broader Lehigh Valley. Many of those who settled in Allentown over the last two decades are of Latino origin, such that the city now boasts a diverse population of individuals with Mexican, Dominican, Puerto Rican, Venezuelan, and Colombian heritage, as well as first-generation immigrants from those nations.

In 1980, only 5.1 percent of Allentown's population was Hispanic. In the ensuing decades, the number of Hispanics living in the city rapidly expanded. In 1990, Allentown was 82 percent white and approximately 12 percent Hispanic. According to the 2010 Census, the proportion of white Allentown residents has fallen to 43 percent, whereas the city is now 25 percent Hispanic and 10 percent foreign born. These numbers are particularly significant when we consider that 4 percent of Pennsylvania's total population is Hispanic and that 5 percent of the state's total population is foreign born. The Latino population of Allentown is also relatively young: the Allentown public school district, once predominantly non-Hispanic white, is now approximately 75 percent Latino.

Tensions precipitated by the city's shifting demographics started to emerge after the Allentown City Council passed a nonbinding resolution in

1985 declaring the city a sanctuary for Central American refugees. Within a few months, Emma Tropiano, a controversial member of the city council, began raising concerns about immigration in Allentown. Though Tropiano had initially voted for the sanctuary resolution, she reversed course and tried to have it rescinded, stressing the fact that the city had no legitimate role in passing judgment on foreign affairs, and that actually enforcing the sanctuary resolution would violate federal law: "However laudable the goals of the Lehigh Valley Sanctuary Support Group and the Lehigh Valley Friends Meeting might be, the attainment of those goals, i.e., the provision of sanctuary to illegal aliens, nevertheless involves the violation of federal criminal statutes and a determination by some that the end justifies the means" (as cited in Mellin 1986).

Her attempt to repeal the sanctuary resolution failed in 1986, two votes to four, but she again revisited the sanctuary policy in 1991, this time expressing her concern that the city's sanctuary status might hasten the spread of the AIDS virus throughout the community (as cited in Shields 1991), as well as stating: "We have to start worrying about native Allentonians who have lived here all their lives, not the people who come here from New York and New Jersey." In 1988, she also publicly accused Hispanics of being responsible for 99 percent of the crime in the city (as cited in "Boycott Tropiano Hearing" 1991). Finally, in her waning years on the city council, in 1993, she proposed a local ordinance banning the "outdoor" use of "indoor" furniture. This was widely understood to be a protest against Hispanic families in Allentown who sat and socialized on sofas on their front porches, and hence another remonstration against the changing demographics of the city. Tropiano died in 2002. Many residents interviewed for this project viewed her as the public face of nativism during her tenure on the city council, and a voice for intergroup tensions simmering in the community.

As documented here and elsewhere (Varsanyi 2010b), the mid-2000s witnessed a huge jump in immigration policy activism at the local and state levels across the United States. A full explanation for the reasons behind this policy explosion is beyond the scope of this chapter, but suffice it to say, Pennsylvania and North Carolina were national leaders in the number of anti-immigrant local ordinances passed and 287(g) agreements signed. Hazleton, Pennsylvania, approximately fifty miles northwest of Allentown, was one of the birthplaces of the Illegal Immigration Relief Act, an anti-immigrant local ordinance that went on to be considered and adopted by 140 localities across the United States (Fleury-Steiner and Longazel 2010; Varsanyi 2011). In 2008 several white teenagers were accused (though later acquitted, controversially, by an all-white jury) of fatally beating an undocumented Mexican immigrant in Shenandoah, a Pennsylvania town near Hazleton and Allentown.

As anti-immigrant sentiment took root in the region, the state, and nationally, the Allentown City Council again became a space for the local articulation of nativism, responding to the city's shifting demographics. This time, the Allentown Police Department (APD) was brought into the fray. In 2006, Lou Hershman, a city council member, proposed an ordinance that would have required the APD to sign a 287(g) agreement with the federal government and to train two APD officers in enforcing immigration law. In the debates over the ordinance, Hershman recounted that he had talked with constituents who complained of long waits in the hospital emergency room, union members who complained of cuts to wages and benefits, as well as unemployment, and teachers who mentioned how the schools were increasingly overcrowded, so he decided to take on the issue in order to look out for "the residents of Allentown . . . the *legal* residents of Allentown" (interview July 22, 2009).

According to some members of the police force, immigration had reduced public safety in Allentown, as gang violence and drug-related crimes had also been on the rise in the city in recent years. Members of the police force with whom we talked linked this increase directly to the completion of I-78 in the 1980s and the easy connection between New York City and Allentown. By the time of our research, the connection between the NYPD and the APD was so tight that officers from one force would regularly spend time in the other city in pursuit of suspects.

Despite attempts to connect immigration with crime rates, hospital and school overcrowding, and economic hardship, council members defeated the 287(g) proposal. The proposal caused much controversy but ultimately did not garner support from the broader community, local government, or police force. As Assistant Police Chief Joe Hanna reported to one of the authors: "We work with all agencies equally and we assist them, but it's not one of those things where we have campaigns . . . that we need to 'clean up the city of illegal immigrants,' you know? We have a lot of things that, quite frankly, are more pressing" (interview July 23, 2009). The mayor of Allentown, Edward Pawlowksi—a former community organizer with left-leaning politics—also opposed the measure.

As Assistant Chief Hanna's statement indicates, however, the practice (though not policy) of the Allentown police department was not one of "noncooperation," or an unwillingness to cooperate with federal immigration authorities. The Allentown police regularly share information about national origin and alienage of arrestees (as best they can determine) with ICE, though it should be noted that even this practice is informal and ad hoc, evolving as it did from a long-standing professional relationship between members of the police force and former Immigration and Naturalization Service agents who had been stationed in Allentown in the past (interview,

July 23, 2009). Furthermore, the department has no policy or informal practice of seeking information about the immigration status of individuals
stopped but not arrested. When asked about his opposition to Hershman's
287(g) proposal and the broader question of police involvement in immigration enforcement, Police Chief Roger Maclean stated:

> I thought, you know, if we're breaking down doors looking for immi-
> grants, how in the world are we going to get information on the bad
> guys? You know? A lot [of immigrants] don't trust us to begin with,
> and then if we're starting to kick doors down and looking for green
> cards, you know, it makes it even harder. So, my thought process was,
> "Wait a minute, this is a federal issue. We'll continue to do *our* job and
> let the federal government do *their* job" (interview August 27, 2009).

This said, during the latter years of the 2000s, despite the absence of
police department policy or official directives, and insistence by police leadership that frontline police officers were not targeting immigrants, a number
of community leaders voiced concern that some Allentown police officers
practiced racial profiling. As one respondent complained, "driving while
brown" was a real problem in the city (interview, July 22, 2009). On the other
hand, another prominent Latino community leader downplayed this concern and argued that the police did follow an immigrant-neutral protocol,
and that community fears were based more strongly on what was happening
regionally and nationally at the time (interview, July 23, 2009).

The story in Allentown, then, has been one of shifting demographics as
well as periodically flaring tensions over this demographic change. As the
city's population changed, the APD developed a set of practices regarding
engagement with these new communities. And more recently, as we discuss
in the conclusion, city policies have been put into place. While this process
is somewhat in line with the policy process in new destinations around the
country—from no policy, to informal practices, to official policies—the
Allentown case study also offers something unique. While a number of
the migrants to the Allentown region are, indeed, first-generation immigrants,
many are actually legal permanent residents and citizens, albeit of a variety
of diverse ethnic groups. It should not be surprising then that, while the
anti-immigrant constituency in the city has tried to capitalize on tensions surrounding demographic change, all of these attempts have fallen flat, as the
majority of the city's population is uninspired by nativist rhetoric. As Alan
Jennings, a local community activist, told us: "I don't really think immigration is a big issue for the vast majority of people in the Lehigh Valley. I
think there are a lot of ignorant people who think that Puerto Ricans are
illegals; they don't understand that Puerto Ricans are Americans. There is
a lot of that but not nearly enough to prevail on the policy-making structure

and the law enforcement agencies to stand up and fight back" (interview July 8, 2009).

Conclusion

The quantitative analysis of our survey data highlighted the fact that, by and large, police forces in new destinations have been no busier in devising strategies to deal with immigrants than their counterparts in traditional destinations. If anything, police (and by extension, local governments) in new destinations tend to be behind the curve in developing formal policies regarding interactions with immigrants, "playing catch-up" with communities that have had longer histories of immigrant and Latino settlement. Allentown is a perfect example of this dynamic. Throughout our interviews with the APD, we heard frustrations that the police department was having difficulties recruiting people of color, as well as those who spoke foreign languages, into the police force and city government, despite rapid demographic change in the community. We believe that similar issues exist in a large number of smaller jurisdictions that have been slower to address the needs of new immigrants. While larger jurisdictions and those closer to the Mexican border have long faced and dealt with such challenges, the new immigration patterns present challenges for emerging immigration destinations.

The Allentown case study also indicates how communities can catch up. The informal practices of the police force—mainly the desire to avoid local immigration policing, and a recognition of the importance of strong relationships with immigrant and Latino communities—have recently begun to be reflected in official city policy. By 2013 the city had opened a Mayor's Office of Immigrant Affairs. As stated on its website, the office "promotes the well-being of immigrant communities by providing information and programs that facilitate successful integration of immigrants into the civic, economic, and cultural life of the City" (www.allentownpa.gov). The opening of this office follows a small, but growing, nationwide trend (de Graauw, personal communication, 2013) in which local governments recognize the value of an office dedicated specifically to fostering the incorporation of immigrants into their communities. More recently, the Allentown City Council has taken this a step further and passed a resolution calling for federal action on immigration, given that eleven to fourteen million immigrants "contribute to our communities, the economy and the country—yet are denied essential rights" (as quoted in Kraft 2014).

Therefore, on the one hand, we could say that, in light of the sizes of their foreign-born populations, these cities are slightly lagging in developing policies and practices. On the other hand, as the expanding number of local immigrant affairs offices demonstrates, these new destination localities may be gaining ground quickly—and perhaps even developing innovative, forward-thinking practices—with bureaucracies such as the police leading the way. It remains to be seen, however, the extent to which new policies influence or lead to new practices by law enforcement. Implementation, particularly in the face of rapidly changing demographics, remains a challenge for law enforcement and other bureaucracies.

Lastly, an important finding of this research is that Allentown and other new destination cities differ enormously from each other, and that they craft their responses to immigration in ways that are closely tied to local conditions. As Coleman (2012: 159) argues, "specific political, legal, policing, and biographic contexts" all impact and influence the policies and practices of law enforcement, local bureaucracies, and local legislators.

There is a debate about whether new destinations or other factors such as political partisanship are more important in predicting local legislative output such as local anti-immigrant ordinances (Chavez and Provine 2009; Hopkins 2010; Lewis et al. 2011; O'Neil 2010; Ramakrishnan and Wong 2010; Walker and Leitner 2011). This chapter extends that debate into the realm of local bureaucratic practices. As our work shows, at least in the case of policing, the new destinations dynamic—rapid demographic change— might not offer a way to satisfactorily explain changing practices and policies, except to demonstrate that new destinations tend to be late to the game in engaging with this change. While this chapter looks only at policing, a similar thesis is tested for schools (and similar conclusions are reached) by Melissa Marschall in Chapter 10 of this volume, and further research could test this thesis in other bureaucratic settings such as health care and social and family services. From a theoretical perspective, therefore, while the new destinations literature does a good job of documenting demographic change and offering richly textured case studies of social and political dynamics in specific locales, the power of demographic change to broadly explain local politics and bureaucratic practices is still unclear.

NOTES

Acknowledgments: The material in this chapter is based upon work supported by the National Science Foundation under Grants SES-0819082 and SES-0921202. Any opinions, findings, and conclusions or recommendations expressed are those of the authors and do not necessarily reflect the views of the National Science Foundation. Portions of this chapter have been revised from material originally appearing in chapter 5 of Doris Marie Provine, Monica W. Varsanyi, Paul G. Lewis, and Scott Decker, *Policing Immigrants: Local Law Enforcement on the Front Lines* (Chicago: University of Chicago Press, 2016).

1. A discussion of the factors leading to this demographic shift is beyond the scope of this chapter. For a full discussion, see Massey and Capoferro (2008).

2. Beginning with a list of all municipalities with populations of less than 65,000 in the counties that meet our criteria, we assigned each community to its region (Northeast, Midwest, South, or West) and to its population size range (0–4,999; 5,000–9,999;

10,000–19,999; 20,000–34,999; 35,000–49,999; 50,000–64,999). We then determined what percentage of the total population of the overall set of cities lived in each stratum (i.e., region by size range), and randomly selected the correct number of cities in each stratum to attain this percentage within our sample. Because we focused on "where the population is" within the overall set of small cities, larger-population communities were more likely to be selected for the sample than smaller ones. If we had instead randomly selected municipalities from the total universe, we would have ended up with a plethora of tiny (less than 5,000-resident) communities.

3. The differing endpoint years reflect the timing and source of demographic data for the communities in the two different surveys. We used the 2005 ACS to tabulate demographic data for the large-city survey, as it was the most recent systematic data source available at the time of the survey's distribution. We used the 2006–2008 or 2005–2009 ACS releases to tabulate demographic data for the smaller cities, which are not covered in the one-year ACS releases. The very smallest municipalities are only included in the five-year ACS releases, while somewhat bigger communities are included in the three-year ACS. For simplicity, we refer to these as "2008" data.

4. We tested for significance using a two-sided t-test of the difference in means with a p-value of .05 or less. Even relaxing the p-value to .10 does not add any instances of significant differences.

5. The seven situations included finding a suspected unauthorized immigrant who was: (1) suspected of a violent crime; (2) suspected of a nonviolent crime (e.g., shoplifting) with no prior criminal record; (3) implicated in domestic violence; (4) violating parole; (5) violating a traffic ordinance; (6) a victim of human trafficking; or (7) a victim of or witness to a crime.

10

Immigrant Incorporation in Local Schools

Policy and Practices in New versus Established Destinations

MELISSA MARSCHALL

Monica Varsanyi's and her colleagues' finding that policies and practices in new destinations differ little from those in traditional destinations prove not to be unique to police departments. Marschall similarly discovers that in schools across the United States, those in new destinations respond to the challenges of immigrant students very similarly to those in traditional destinations and counties on the Mexican border, despite the growth in public and political sentiment against bilingual education. Similar to Erica Dobbs's findings concerning municipal elections in Chapter 1 and Varsanyi's concerning policing, Marschall argues that school officials, in their role as street-level bureaucrats, enjoy some discretion in how they respond to immigrants, even when public policy is not supportive of immigrants. As her survey analysis shows, schools in new destinations are as likely to try to accommodate the needs of immigrant students and parents as those in more traditional destinations, thus laying important groundwork for the social and economic incorporation of immigrants.

T he United States is a nation of immigrants. It has and continues to be defined by the contributions of different ethnic groups who have built culturally diverse communities and shaped the social, political, and economic fabric of American society. Immigrant incorporation involves the full participation of immigrants in the host society and their exercise of corresponding rights and obligations. It can be measured by socioeconomic and political participation, upward mobility, and the ability to communicate in English. Incorporation, however, is not automatic, but is instead shaped by many factors. In particular, the process of immigrant incorporation relies critically on the participation of both immigrant groups and the host society, their engagement and interaction with one another, and ultimately the relationships they build together.

This chapter focuses on the process of immigrant incorporation in the context of schooling. Schools provide a primary venue for interactions between immigrants and governmental institutions. As with all individual-government interactions, these exchanges convey information—in this case, about how nonimmigrants in the United States perceive immigrant groups, the degree to which they value or fear cultural diversity, and what immigrants can and should expect from their government in terms of programs, services, and responsiveness (Newton 2005; Schneider and Ingram 2014; Soss 2000). At the same time, schools are a primary vehicle through which the second generation develops the human capital necessary to advance. Thus, the educational process and the specific ways in which schools organize and deliver educational programs and services to the children of immigrant families plays an important role in the process of incorporation.

The educational challenges confronting children in immigrant families are many. One of the most significant of these is the lack of English proficiency. Though immigration has slowed in the past several years, children with limited-English proficiency (LEP) continue to enroll in American schools (McDonnell and Hill 1993). Between 1995 and 2006 the enrollment of English Language Learners (ELLs) grew 57 percent, far outpacing total enrollment (Terrazas and Fix 2009). By 2008 roughly 10 percent of all public school students were classified as LEP (Jost 2009; Pandya, McHugh, and Batalova 2011). The most significant growth in ELLs occurred in nontraditional immigrant gateways such as South Carolina, Indiana, Nevada, Arkansas, and North Carolina. Particularly in these new immigrant destinations, schools are faced with increasing demands for teachers who have been trained to work with ELLs and children from diverse cultural backgrounds.

This chapter investigates the extent to which schools situated in immigrant gateways, including new and more established destinations, make adjustments in curriculum, parent outreach, and school organization to meet the increasing demands that immigrant populations place on them. Focusing on school-level practices with regard to staffing, instruction, and outreach for LEP students and their families, I examine how institutional and contextual factors shape the ways in which local schools deliver language and other educational services to immigrant and ELL constituents. Building on the work of Melissa J. Marschall, Elizabeth Rigby, and Jasmine Jenkins (2011) and Marschall, Paru Shah, and Katharine Donato (2012), I examine three sets of dependent variables drawn from the National Center for Educational Statistics Schools and Staffing Surveys (1987–2007): (1) English language and subject matter instruction; (2) staffing to accommodate LEP students; (3) school outreach to LEP parents.

Building the case for why school-level practices with regard to staffing, instruction, and outreach for ELL students and their families are so critical begins with demographics. In recent decades the United States has witnessed large-scale immigration that is more diverse than in earlier decades. The number of foreign born in the United States began to sharply accelerate in the 1980s, increasing by 46 percent from 1970. By 2007, the foreign-born population reached 38 million and accounted for 12.6 percent of the total U.S. population (Migration Policy Institute 2008). Although immigration to the United States continues to be most concentrated in traditional gateway cities and their metropolitan areas, it is increasingly being felt in new destinations. Indeed, Latino immigration in regions where Latino settlements and communities have previously not existed has exploded in the past decade (Massey 2008c). Nowhere is this demographic shift more apparent than in the American South, where growth in Latino immigration has outpaced any other part of the country (Kochhar, Suro, and Tafoya 2005).

Given the age structure of immigrant families, the effects of demographic changes are felt more strongly in schools. Children of immigrants—both foreign and U.S. born—represent a dramatically rising share of the school-age population: increasing from 6 percent to 19 percent between 1970 and 2000 (Fix, Passel, and de Velasco n.d.). This growth is most evident in the Latino population (C. Chen 2011; Zhou and Logan 2003). Today more than one in five children in U.S. public schools is Latino (C. Chen 2011). These trends are accompanied by a dramatic increase in the number of LEP children in U.S. schools (McDonnell and Hill 1993; Terrazas and Fix 2009).[1] Between 1998–1999 and 2008–2009, the number of ELLs in grades pre-K through 12 increased 51 percent (from 3.54 to 5.35 million) (NCELA 2011). Further, whereas schools in traditional gateways continue to have the largest concentrations of ELLs, new destinations have experienced the highest rates of growth. Between 1998–1999 and 2008–2009, eleven states (Alabama, Georgia, North Carolina, South Carolina, Virginia, Kentucky, Tennessee, Indiana, Missouri, and Delaware) experienced ELL enrollment growth of over 200 percent (NCELA 2011).

Apart from being the most rapidly increasing segment of the public school population in the United States, LEP and Latino students have the additional "distinction" of having consistently poor academic performance in comparison to non-LEP and Anglo students. For example, the Latino-white achievement gap in reading has remained virtually unchanged over nearly two decades, dropping only two points for both fourth- and eighth-graders. In math, the Latino-white gap grew one point between 1990 and

2009 for fourth-graders and three points for eighth-graders (Aud et al. 2010). The achievement gap between Latino and non-Latino students continues to grow as students progress through the educational system. When it comes to overall educational attainment, Hispanic students lag furthest behind, with less than 70 percent of twenty-five- to twenty-nine-year-olds attaining a high school credential and only 12.2 percent obtaining a bachelor's degree (compared to 89 percent of African Americans and 95 percent of non-Hispanic whites earning a high school credential in 2008 and 19 percent and 37 percent, respectively, attaining a bachelor's degree) (Aud et al. 2010).

Increasingly Hostile Political Climate

While the needs of poor and minority children in low-performing schools are many, children of immigrant parents often have an additional set of difficulties that stem from their family's nativity status and migration experiences. As the institution at the frontline of meeting newcomers to this country, schools are faced with the challenge of providing services and outreach for immigrant children and their parents. Although many districts and schools are implementing innovative programs and services (see Jones-Correa 2008; Marrow 2009a; Terrazas and Fix 2009), they are often constrained by the intergovernmental political context in which they operate (Marschall, Rigby, and Jenkins 2011). Particularly when it comes to language and instructional policy, immigrant rights, and general service provision for the undocumented, the political environment has become increasingly nativist and, in many cases, downright hostile.

Looking back in history, language policy has always been contentious, posing issues of identity, citizenship, and even patriotism. Though the United States has never had an official language policy, federal laws have tended to promote linguistic assimilation and English monolingualism rather than multiculturalism and bilingualism. This tendency can be observed at least as far back as the turn of the last century, when the first wave of foreign immigration to the United States reached its pinnacle and Congress passed legislation that not only reduced the flow of immigrants, but also made English proficiency a requirement for citizenship. By the middle of the twentieth century, linguistic assimilation had taken root and the notion that immigrants should assimilate as quickly as possible to English had become powerfully entrenched (Linton 2004).

In the 1960s and 1970s, immigration reform and the civil rights movement created some space for minority groups to articulate their identities and lobby for language policies promoting linguistic diversity and multiculturalism.[2] However, the policy gains made during this period were relatively short lived, and by the 1980s a growing nativist movement had resurfaced with renewed commitment and a new agenda. Beginning with Virginia in

1981, a number of states adopted official English or English-only laws (Tata-lovich 1995), and today the majority of states (thirty) have such laws on their books. The 1990s witnessed other important developments embracing the ideology of language assimilation. California's "Save Our State" movement, which supported three nativist ballot initiatives targeting immigrants and their educational opportunities, is a prime example. One of these, Prop 227, or the "English Language Education for Immigrant Children" initiative, essentially did away with most bilingual education and English-language development programs in California (Contreras 2002: 144). Since 2000, voters in two other states have also passed ballot initiatives ending bilingual education (Arizona in 2000 and Massachusetts in 2002).

For the most part, federal education policy has followed the nativist trend of state ballot initiatives and legislation. For example, Title III of the No Child Left Behind Act (NCLB) eliminated federal support of innovative bilingual programs such as dual-language immersion and developmental bilingual models that seek not just English acquisition but bilingual compe-tence (Katz 2004: 144). In its place, it endorsed the acquisition of English only. Several other provisions of NCLB also had direct implications for lan-guage instruction. First, the act required that all teachers who instruct ELL students in academic content and English language be "highly qualified" in both fields. NCLB's shift toward English acquisition and the reduction in funding for bilingual teacher training aggravated the already limited supply of bilingual teachers in the United States. Second, under NCLB, schools must report the academic progress of all students, including ELLs. If schools fail to demonstrate that ELL students have made progress in both English and other subject matter, they may be subject to sanctions that range from staffing reassignments to state takeovers (Terrazas and Fix 2009).

Context of Reception and School Policy toward Immigrant Parents and Students

Against this backdrop, local schools and districts make decisions about how to meet the needs and preferences of their students and families. While local school actors confront explicit directives, regulations, and symbolic mes-sages from state and federal policy makers, they can and do act in ways that are sometimes at odds with federal and state policies. Why do they do this? Part of the answer to this questions lies in a closer examination of the con-text in which immigrant families and schools interact and the nature of the relationship between the two. Where and when immigrants enter the United States and the sociopolitical features of the communities in which they reside play an important role in shaping their expectations and interactions with schools and other institutions. In other work I have focused on how two aspects of the receiving community influence the extent to which schools address the concerns of immigrants: resources and demand (Marschall, Shah, and Donato 2012). On the one hand, a community's ability to generate adequate resources hinges on its experience with immigration and the subsequent historical development of institutions and structures to assist with the assimilation of newcomers. On the other hand, immigrants' demands for services and accommodations rest on the size of their population, both historically and contemporaneously, and fluctuations in population demographics over time. Three contexts of reception seem particularly salient for the study of immigrant incorporation: communities along the U.S.-Mexico border; established destinations (communities with a long history of receiving immigrants); and new destinations (communities with no prior experience as immigrant gateways that are now experiencing rapid or dramatic increases in their foreign-born population).

Established destinations such as New York, Chicago, and Houston have historically served as the primary entry point for immigrants. While school districts in these destinations have often struggled to accommodate newcomers, their extended history with Latino and other immigrant populations, as well as the fact that they have large native-born Latino and Asian populations, place them at a distinct advantage for addressing immigrant issues. For example, compared to newly arrived immigrants, second- and third-generation Latino and Asian residents have the experience and social networks to find employment, adequate housing, and social services (Suro and Passel 2003). Established destinations are also more likely to have advocacy groups or institutions that promote immigrant interests and provide resources and assistance to immigrants (Singer 2004). Consequently, they have made progress when it comes to political incorporation. Although the political climate in some established destinations has grown increasingly anti-immigrant in recent decades, local groups in many of these places have learned to effectively mobilize and utilize demand-protest strategies to combat this hostile environment and effect positive policy change.

In contrast to established gateways, new destinations have witnessed tremendous growth in their foreign-born population in the last twenty years (Chapa and De La Rosa 2004). They have thus had less time to adjust and adapt to incoming populations than have established destinations. The presence of new immigrants is particularly evident in suburban areas, where, according to U.S. Census data, four in ten immigrants are now moving. These trends have an impact on the process of immigrant integration given that many new gateways have limited experience, infrastructure, and resources (e.g., bilingual training, legal support, community organizations) for accommodating a culturally and ethnically diverse population. The incorporation process is considerably more complex in some places as well. For example, the influx of a young, mainly Spanish-speaking, population has challenged the traditional black-white racial dynamics of many new destination locations

(Marrow 2009a). Although some studies report that the U.S.-born in some small towns have positive sentiments about immigrant newcomers, and many residents show a significant degree of acceptance because they associate immigrants with renewed economic vitality (Fennelly 2008), without organizational support and advocacy structures, immigrants in new destinations are likely to be initially disadvantaged in ways that adversely affect the schooling and educational outcomes of their children.

Although border communities share many of the characteristics of established destinations, their location and distinctive historical development suggest that the process of immigration incorporation may be quite different. First, the Latino and foreign-born populations are significantly higher in border communities than in established destinations, and they have not experienced the influx of immigrants from multiple countries of origin as most established destinations have. In this respect, border communities are dominated by Spanish-language and Mexican cultural traditions and are not multicultural in the way that many communities in established destinations are. Second, because Latinos (Mexicans) lived in the border states Arizona, California, New Mexico, and Texas prior to annexation by the United States, many residents cannot be considered "immigrants." And, unlike other destinations and gateways, these locales make up the "heartland" of second- and third-generation Latinos, who are most equipped to handle Latino issues socially and politically. Indeed, of the 5,928 Latino elected officials in the United States in 2012, 4,911 (83 percent) were in the four border states (NALEO 2012).

Given these differences in immigration history and subsequent institutional response, schools in border communities and established destinations are likely to be better equipped to provide programs and services to meet the educational needs of immigrant and LEP families than are schools in new immigrant destinations. Community support for devoting scarce resources to programs more narrowly targeting ELL students may also be greater in these contexts of reception than in new destinations. After all, immigrant groups in border and established communities have a longer history of organizing and a potentially stronger voice and presence in local decision making. Presumably, they have established relationships with institutions, groups, and individuals within the host society. These schools may therefore be more likely to implement policies, such as bilingual education, even if such policies are explicitly or symbolically proscribed by state-level legislation such as English-only laws. Of course, this argument is premised on the assumption that schools have actors and mechanisms in place to formulate and implement such policies and decisions. As I explain below, the literature on bureaucratic responsiveness and "cultural brokers" provides a useful framework for understanding how this might work.

Bureaucratic Responsiveness and Cultural Brokers

While the broader context in which schools operate shapes the supply and demand features of local programs and policies, policy implementation rests squarely on school-level actors. Under the bureaucratic politics model, school officials, like other street-level bureaucrats, operate in a relatively autonomous environment that provides considerable discretion and thus power when it comes to policy implementation (Marschall, Rigby, and Jenkins 2011; see also Elmore 1979; Lipsky 1980). This model suggests that school-level actors, and principals in particular, serve largely as their own guides, making decisions about things like language accommodations and staffing based on their own expertise, priorities, and values.

Building on this framework, recent work by Michael Jones-Correa (2005b, 2008), Helen B. Marrow (2009a), and Paul G. Lewis and S. Karthick Ramakrishan (2007) develops a model of bureaucratic incorporation of new groups and immigrants in particular. These authors argue that under certain circumstances, administrators (acting out of a sense of mission, professional norms, or personal ethos) may create de facto policies that advance the interests of groups who are otherwise marginalized by local politics. Most relevant for the present analysis is Marrow's 2009 study of Hispanic newcomers in two rural North Carolina counties. She found that the beliefs of local educational bureaucrats about fairness and appropriate action toward their clients led them to view themselves as advocates for these clients, rather than for the system. This led school administrators and teachers to sometimes go around restrictive government policies in order to provide "more-than-routine" services for newcomer clients (Marrow 2009a: 759). For example, these rural districts hired bilingual/ESL staff despite substantial costs and established policies to encourage Latino parent involvement in their children's education.

Findings from an earlier study that looked at whether and how state English-only laws might constrain local schools' implementation of bilingual and ESL instruction provided evidence supporting not only the bureaucratic responsiveness model but also the role of "cultural brokers"—coethnics and colinguists in bureaucratic positions of relative power that act on behalf of those like them who are in need specific programs or resources (Marschall, Rigby, and Jenkins 2011). Cultural brokers are typically defined as school personnel who have important connections to their racial or ethnic origin group whether through mutual history or shared sociocultural experiences (Achinstein and Aguirre 2008). While they are often teachers or administrators of color, this need not be the case, since those who share religious, country of origin, or other culturally relevant characteristics can also serve in this capacity.

In addition to shaping school-level policy regarding instruction and staffing, cultural brokers may improve the school-parent-community environment in a number of ways. For example, teachers of color are often better equipped at recognizing and addressing cultural differences that manifest themselves in parental attitudes and behaviors that might be misinterpreted as disengagement or indifference. For example, schools with larger shares of language minority and immigrant parents often face challenges because these parents may be unfamiliar with school procedures and expectations and/or intimidated by school administrators. Without linguistically and culturally sensitive school personnel, parents may view school-based activities as less welcoming (Daniel-White 2002). Studies have found that having racial/ethnic minorities present as school administrators and teachers does indeed foster more supportive relations and stronger ties between schools and parents (Marschall 2006; Shah 2009).

Putting these two streams of literature together, we might expect a greater incidence of policies and programs targeting the needs of immigrant students and families in established destinations and border counties compared to new destinations. Similarly, schools with larger shares of Latino teachers or the presence of a Latino principal may be more likely to implement policies that serve immigrant students and families compared to schools with fewer Latino teachers or a non-Latino principal. Though the literature does not provide definite direction regarding the possibility that cultural brokers might function differently depending on the context of reception, this is a key empirical question for the present study. On the one hand, research suggests that the need for cultural brokers to act as representatives for immigrant families may be greater in new destinations given the absence of existing institutions and the relative unfamiliarity with immigrant needs, cultural values, and expectations among existing residents in these locales (Marrow 2009a). New destinations may provide a stronger impetus for coethnic teachers and administrators to play the role of cultural brokers and representative bureaucrats. However, their numbers are smaller in new destinations, and they too may be less familiar with how to advocate for or provide services to immigrant populations. They may lack the confidence to speak on behalf of the immigrant community or even prefer not to be spokespersons at all (see Ferris 2012).

At the same time, the greater familiarity with and number of immigrants in established destinations and border counties might lead coethnic teachers and principals to feel that they need not stand in for immigrant students and families. They may assume that other groups or actors will play this role. Yet the expectation more in line with the literature would be for cultural brokers to be particularly empowered in the contexts where they are more incorporated and thus have more access to and influence over the distribution of local public goods and services. Examining these competing explanations is one goal of the empirical analysis of this study.

School Language Accommodation Policy and Practice: A Descriptive Look

Data for this study come from the NCES Schools and Staffing Survey (SASS) (1987–2007), a national survey administered roughly every four years to a representative sample of all public U.S. elementary and secondary schools. These surveys include a variety of measures on school practices with regard to language instruction, staffing, and outreach for LEP students and parents. In this study, I rely on three sets of dependent variables to measure: (1) classroom language instruction; (2) staffing for language instruction for ELLs; and (3) outreach and accommodations to LEP parents.

To operationalize language instruction I construct two measures. *Language Instruction 1* includes separate categories for schools with no special instruction for ELL students ($Y = 0$), ESL programs or services where ELL student are provided with intensive instruction in English ($Y = 1$), and bilingual/native-language education in which the native language is used to varying degrees in instructing ELL students ($Y = 2$). Since the ESL/bilingual questions were combined starting in 1999–2000, I relied on a question that asked whether ELL students were taught subject-matter courses in their native language to code for bilingual/native language instruction for the 1999–2000 and 2003–2004 survey waves. The second indicator, *Language Instruction 2*, is a binary variable where 0 corresponds to no bilingual or native-language instruction and 1 includes any type of bilingual or native-language instruction.[3]

The second set of indicators focuses on staffing and includes three variables. The first measures the percentage of school staff dedicated to ESL/bilingual education. It was constructed by dividing the total number bilingual/ESL aides (full and part time) by the total number of staff across all staff categories included in the survey. The second measures whether the school had a vacancy for ESL/bilingual instruction in the prior school year (1 = yes; 0 = no), and the third measures the school's difficulty in filling this vacancy (1 = very or somewhat difficult or unfilled; 0 = otherwise).

The final indicator focuses on language accommodation for parents. *Outreach to LEP parents* is an additive index constructed from three survey questions that asked: (1) whether the school provided interpreters for LEP parents at meetings or parent-teacher conferences; (2) whether translations of printed materials, such as newsletters, school notices, or school signs are provided by the school; and (3) whether the school provided outreach to LEP parents (1 = yes; 0 = otherwise). The index was rescaled from 0 to 1 and can be interpreted as the percentage of LEP parent outreach activities offered by the school.[4]

Since relatively little attention has been paid to what schools across the country and in different contexts of reception are doing with regard to this set of policies and practices, I begin with a descriptive look at the data collected by NCES, using six of the SASS survey waves (1987–2007). In addition to looking at the data over time, I compare schools situated in the three distinct contexts of reception: (1) established immigrant destinations; (2) communities along the U.S.-Mexico border; and (3) new immigrant destinations.

Established destinations include schools in the metropolitan areas identified by Singer (2004) as *continuous* and *post–World War II* gateways.[5] Border communities include twenty-five counties in the four U.S. states that border Mexico: Imperial, San Diego (CA); Arizona Conchise, Santa Cruz, Pima and Yuma (AZ); Lea, Eddy, Otero, Dona Ana, Luna, Hidalgo (NM); and Cameron, Hidalgo, Starr, Zapata, Webb, Maverick, Val Verde, Terrell, Brewster, Presidio, Jefferson Davis, Hudspeth, El Paso (TX). Finally, new destinations are coded using a modified definition based on Singer (2004) that focuses on growth of the foreign-born population between 1990–2000 (> 100 percent), a relatively low proportion of foreign-born residents in 1990 (< 5 percent), and a minimum proportion of foreign born in 2000 (≥ 5 percent). This definition yields 151 new destinations counties (out of 3,196 counties total), with an average percent foreign born of 2.32 percent in 1990 and 8.19 percent in 2000, and an average change in foreign born of 447 percent from 1990 to 2000. Table 10.1 reports the distribution of schools across the three contexts of reception for each of the six NCES Schools and Staffing Survey waves.

Figures 10.1 to 10.3 report the three categories of language instruction over time and across the three contexts of reception.[6] Figure 10.1 includes the percentage of schools offering no language accommodation to LEP students. Because federal law requires school districts, not individual schools, to offer programs that educate LEP children, schools with LEP students do not necessarily provide instruction specifically designed to address the

TABLE 10.1 DISTRIBUTION OF SCHOOLS ACROSS GATEWAY TYPE AND TIME						
District Type	1987	1990	1993	1999	2003	2007
New destination	287	327	352	331	300	291
	(94)	(121)	(167)	(198)	(203)	(214)
Established destination	135	150	154	128	118	109
	(64)	(70)	(90)	(76)	(84)	(84)
Border counties	95	113	117	119	109	94
	(61)	(70)	(105)	(107)	(105)	(89)
Nongateway districts	8,334	9,242	9,352	9,106	8,420	7,850
	(2,466)	(2,915)	(4,115)	(4,773)	(4,862)	(4,843)
* Numbers in parentheses are the schools with LEP populations > 0.						

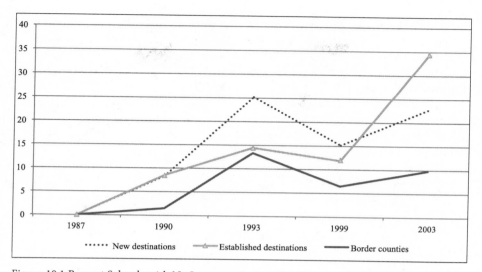

Figure 10.1 Percent Schools with No Language Instruction Program for LEP Students, by Year and Gateway Type

needs of these students. In most cases, the instructional program is likely offered at another school in the district. Regardless, we would expect the percentage of schools offering no instructional programs for LEP students to be relatively small, particularly in districts with a longer history of receiving immigrants.

As Figure 10.1 shows, the percentage of schools in border counties offering no language accommodations is relatively low, ranging from 0 percent in 1987 to 13 percent in 1993. A similar pattern obtains in established destinations, where typically less than 15 percent of schools offered no language accommodations (the exception was in 2003, when the percentage reached 35). Finally, as we might expect, new destinations have, on average, higher percentages of schools offering no language accommodations. Interestingly, the percentage of schools offering no language accommodations increased across all three immigrant destinations.

Although federal law does not require a particular educational approach, these laws can and do influence what type of language instruction program local districts pursue. Figures 10.2 and 10.3 depict the percentage of schools that offer ESL and bilingual/dual-language programs. As these figures show, schools in new destinations are much more likely to offer ESL than bilingual/dual-language programs, whereas the opposite is true of schools in border counties, at least up until 1999. Striking is the significant decline in the percentage of schools offering bilingual or dual-language programs—a trend that is consistent across all three contexts of reception.

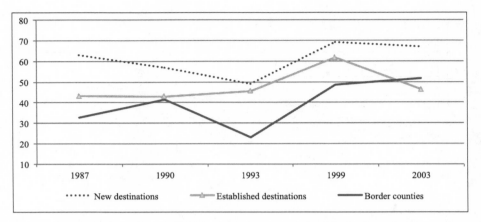

Figure 10.2 Percent Schools with ESL Language Instruction for LEP Students, by Year and Gateway Type

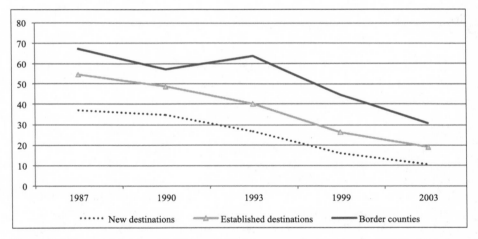

Figure 10.3 Percent Schools with Bilingual/Dual Language Instruction for LEP Students, by Year and Gateway Type

Given the increase in LEP students, we might expect to see an increase in staffing for these ESL/bilingual education programs. As Figure 10.4 indicates, this is indeed the case. Across all three contexts of reception the percentage of staff serving as ESL/bilingual aides has increased over time, with schools in border counties maintaining the highest percentages and registering the sharpest increase. Again, somewhat surprisingly, schools in new destinations have slightly higher percentages of ESL/bilingual aides than schools in established destinations.

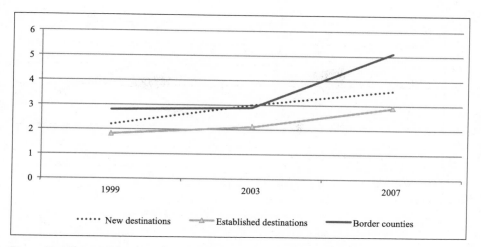

Figure 10.4 Percent Schools with ESL Staff, by Year and Gateway Type

For some schools, recruiting or retaining qualified teachers has been a challenge. Figure 10.5 reports data on the percentage of schools with teaching vacancies in ESL, English for Speakers of Other Languages (ESOL), or bilingual education. Particularly in border and established destinations, vacancies increased in the early 1990s, declined between 1993 and 2003, and increased again in 2007. In new destinations, fluctuations were more modest, and the overall trend was declining. By 2007, 27 percent of schools in new destinations reported vacancies, compared to 23 percent in established destinations and 39 percent in border counties.

Having a vacancy does not necessarily imply a shortage of qualified teachers or a problem with retention or recruitment. However, vacancies that go unfilled or that are difficult to fill might. Figure 10.6 reports the percentage of schools with unfilled or difficult-to-fill vacancies for ESL/ESOL or bilingual education teachers. While schools in border counties have typically had more difficulty filling these vacancies, over time the percentage of schools with difficulties declined—from roughly 50 percent in 1990 to about 30 percent in 2007. In new and established destinations there is considerably more variation over time, with a significant increase in the percentage of schools with difficulties in 1999 and an especially dramatic drop in established destinations in 2003. Overall, established destinations have the smallest percentage of schools with difficulties filling their vacancies (from 12 percent in 1990 to 21 percent in 2007).

Finally, turning to school policies and practices regarding outreach to LEP parents, Figure 10.7 indicates that schools in border counties score highest on the index of school outreach to LEP parents and provide consistently

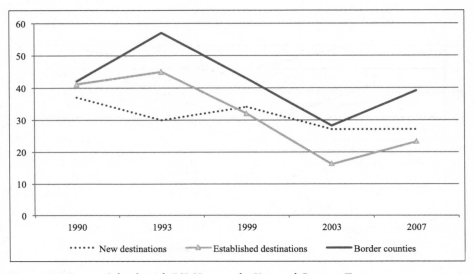

Figure 10.5 Percent Schools with ESL Vacancy, by Year and Gateway Type

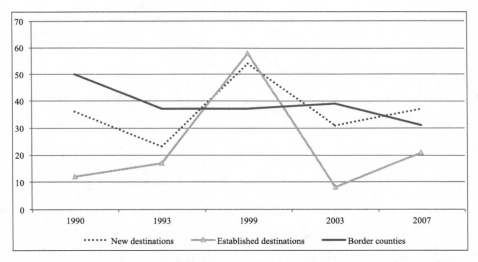

Figure 10.6 Percent Schools with ESL Vacancy Unfilled or Very/Somewhat Difficult to Fill by Year and Gateway Type

more programs for LEP parents than do schools in new and established destinations.

Taken together, the data presented here roughly conform to expectations, showing that schools in border counties tend to offer greater accommodation and programming in the area of instruction, staffing, and outreach

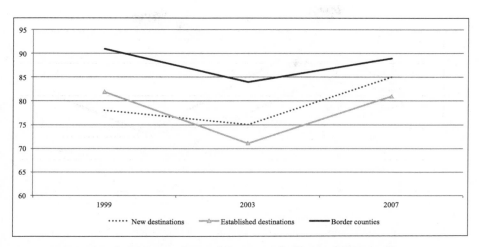

Figure 10.7 Percent of LEP Parent Outreach Programs, by Year and Gateway Type

to limited-English proficient students and parents. When it comes to new and established destinations, it is not the case that schools in new destinations always trail behind in their programs and policies. Indeed, schools in established destinations are less likely to engage in outreach to LEP parents than new destinations, and, in some years, are equally or more likely to offer no language accommodations to LEP students.

Multivariate Analysis and Findings

Since it is not clear that the differences over time and across context of reception hold up once other covariates are controlled, the next step is to estimate multivariate models of each of the three sets of dependent variables. I model school policies and practices as a function of both state and local factors. At the state-level, I include a binary variable that measures whether an English-only law was in place at the time the survey was conducted (1 = yes) (see Marschall, Rigby, and Jenkins 2011 for more detail). Other state-level indicators are included primarily as controls and capture states' political, sociodemographic, representation, and policy-making contexts. These include sociodemographic factors that might affect the state's proclivity toward a particular language policy, state wealth (drawn from the U.S. Census and adjusted to reflect constant 2008 dollars), the percentage of foreign-born residents, the percentage of residents with a bachelor's degree or more, and the percentage of non-Hispanic residents in the state (U.S. Census). Finally, I include the number of Latino state legislators (NALEO) to measure the level of Latino political incorporation in the state.

At the local level, I include a set of dummy variables measuring the context of reception: border counties, new destinations, and established destinations. The excluded category is schools not located in any of these three immigrant-receiving areas. At the school-level, I employ variables that measure the racial/ethnic makeup of the teaching faculty and principal(s) as proxies for "cultural brokers" for a representative bureaucracy. Specifically, I include the percentage of teachers who are either Latino or Asian, since these groups represent the largest immigrant groups in the United States (percent black is included as a control). I also include a set of dummy variables indicating the presence of minority (Latino, Asian, black) principals (1 = yes, 0 = otherwise), since they may not serve only as cultural brokers but also have authority over defining language instruction, staffing, and parent outreach programs.

Finally, I include variables measuring the racial/ethnic composition of students in the school (percent Asian, black, and Hispanic), as well as measures of students' socioeconomic status (percent free lunch) and language instructional needs (percent LEP students). In addition, controls for school size, charter schools, and elementary schools (1 = yes; 0 = otherwise) are also included.

Analytic Strategy

Since the dependent variables for the empirical models range from dichotomous to categorical to continuous, I estimate ordered logit (*Language instruction 1, Ease of filling vacancy*), logistic (*Language instruction 2, ESL vacancy*), and regression (*Percent ESL staff, LEP parent accommodation*) models with year-fixed effects. In addition, because schools are clustered in districts, which might influence school-level resources and programs, I report robust standard errors for all models. Finally, I estimate models only for schools that enroll LEP students. In addition to the baseline models, I also explore interactions between the context of reception and the indicators of bureaucratic responsiveness/cultural brokers. These interactions allow me to test whether school-level actors in different contexts are more likely to represent the needs of immigrant and LEP students and parents.

Baseline Models

I begin with findings from the two language accommodation models (Table 10.2). The dependent variable in the first model includes three categories: no language instruction (0), ESL instruction (1), and bilingual/dual-language instruction (2). The dependent variable in the second model is binary, measuring whether or not a school offers bilingual/dual-language instruction (1 = yes; 0 = otherwise). What these findings show is no real effect

	Language Instruction 1 (O Logit)	Language Instruction 2 (Logit)
TABLE 10.2 LANGUAGE INSTRUCTION MODELS		
English-only law	−0.108	−0.278**
	(0.058)	(0.104)
State wealth (2008 constant $)	−0.005	−0.016
	(0.010)	(0.013)
Percent state population w/bachelor's or more	0.015	0.018
	(0.009)	(0.013)
Percent state foreign born	0.022	−0.029
	(0.017)	(0.022)
Percent state non-Hispanic white	−0.001	−0.007
	(0.003)	(0.005)
Number Latino state legislators	−0.003	0.005
	(0.004)	(0.005)
New destination	0.070	−0.104
	(0.096)	(0.173)
Established destination	0.202	0.313
	(0.155)	(0.196)
Border county	−0.390*	−0.409
	(0.186)	(0.233)
Elementary school	−0.060	−0.058
	(0.048)	(0.074)
Charter school	−1.955**	0.260
	(0.706)	(1.185)
Percent LEP students	2.397***	1.755***
	(0.252)	(0.267)
Percent free lunch	−0.307**	0.266
	(0.107)	(0.148)
Percent Asian students	0.809**	−0.203
	(0.253)	(0.825)
Percent black students	−0.366**	0.122
	(0.119)	(0.301)
Percent Hispanic students	2.774***	2.601***
	(0.182)	(0.226)

(Continued)

TABLE 10.2 *(Continued)*	Language Instruction 1 (O Logit)	Language Instruction 2 (Logit)
Percent Asian teachers	0.339	−0.140
	(0.261)	(0.755)
Percent black teachers	0.974***	0.784*
	(0.261)	(0.383)
Percent Hispanic teachers	1.567***	1.445***
	(0.317)	(0.324)
Asian principal	0.043	0.339
	(0.118)	(0.243)
Hispanic principal	0.006	−0.250
	(0.110)	(0.152)
Black principal	0.239**	0.161
	(0.079)	(0.116)
1990	−0.326***	
	(0.059)	
1993	−0.676***	1.285***
	(0.068)	(0.078)
1999	−1.860***	0.458***
	(0.068)	(0.075)
2003	−2.138***	
	(0.068)	
Constant		−2.326***
		(0.529)
Cut1	−2.842***	
	(0.340)	
Cut2	1.056**	
	(0.329)	
N	15868	10051
chi2	3017.252	862.713
* $p \leq 0.05$, ** $p \leq 0.01$; *** $p \leq 0.001$		

for the context of reception. While the border county coefficient is significant in the first model, it is primarily picking up the opposite trends for ESL versus bilingual education over time. In other words, schools in border counties are increasingly more likely to offer ESL but less likely to offer bilingual education. No significant effects were found for new and established destinations. On the other hand, the results show strong effects for the percentage of Latino and black teachers and also the presence of a black principal. And, schools with larger concentrations of LEP, Hispanic, and Asian students are also more likely to offer ESL and bilingual language instruction. Consistent with the bivariate results, the effects of time are also significant and negative, reinforcing the declining incidence of bilingual education programs in U.S. schools over the past two decades. Finally, the presence of English-only laws also decreases the likelihood that schools offer bilingual instruction, a finding consistent with prior research as well.

Moving on to the resource/staffing for ELL instruction models (Table 10.3), most of the factors expected to increase the likelihood of a vacancy for ESL/bilingual instruction matter (column 1). In particular, schools in new destinations are more likely to have vacancies, as are schools with higher proportions of LEP, Asian, Hispanic, and black students. And, schools with a greater percentage of Asian teachers are less likely to have a vacancy. In addition, the likelihood of an ESL vacancy increases over time. For schools with ESL/bilingual teacher vacancies, there appear to be no differences in the ease with which schools in different contexts of reception fill them, despite the fact that the supply of candidates with the requisite skills and training is likely to vary (column 2). In fact, it is the characteristics of the student body that matter most. Schools with more Asian students are more likely to easily fill the vacancy, while schools with more Hispanic students face greater difficulties. At the same time, schools with more Hispanic teachers are more likely to easily fill their ESL vacancies.

Finally, when it comes to ESL/bilingual staffing levels in the schools more generally (column 3), border counties have a significantly smaller percentage compared to schools not located in border or gateway areas. Though this might seem somewhat counterintuitive, given the higher degree of bilingualism in these areas, the need for dedicated ESL/bilingual staff may be lower. On the other hand, schools with larger shares of LEP, Asian, and Hispanic students have significantly higher proportions of ESL/bilingual staff. This suggests that greater demand by these students yields greater supply. And, while the model indicates no effects for teachers, the effect for Hispanic principals is significant and negative. Again, this finding appears counter to what the bureaucratic responsiveness and cultural brokers research would suggest. The negative effects of time are also surprising. Despite the increase in LEP students over time, the percentage of ESL/bilingual staff is decreasing with time.

Finally, looking at the results of the school outreach to LEP parents model (Table 10.4), there are strong effects for the contexts of reception. The estimates indicate that schools in new destinations engage in significantly more outreach (providing translation, interpreters, and general outreach) to LEP parents than schools in nonimmigrant gateways. While the assumption

TABLE 10.3 RESOURCES/STAFFING FOR LEP STUDENT INSTRUCTION			
	ESL/Bilingual Vacancy (Logit)	Ease of Filling Vacancy (O Logit)	Percent ESL/ Bilingual Staff (OLS)
English-only law	0.006	0.223**	−0.001
	(0.047)	(0.074)	(0.001)
State wealth (2008 constant $)	−0.011	0.037***	−0.000
	(0.006)	(0.011)	(0.000)
Percent state population bachelor's or more	−0.001	−0.013	0.001
	(0.007)	(0.010)	(0.000)
Percent state foreign born	0.038***	−0.025	−0.000
	(0.011)	(0.018)	(0.000)
Percent state non-Hispanic white	0.006*	−0.003	0.000***
	(0.003)	(0.004)	(0.000)
Number Latino state legislators	−0.003	−0.001	−0.000*
	(0.003)	(0.005)	(0.000)
New destination	0.243**	−0.083	0.001
	(0.085)	(0.155)	(0.002)
Established destination	−0.050	0.439	−0.006
	(0.127)	(0.266)	(0.004)
Border county	−0.098	0.234	−0.011*
	(0.140)	(0.211)	(0.005)
Elementary school	−0.305***	0.227***	0.006***
	(0.038)	(0.067)	(0.001)
Charter school	−0.224	0.198	0.017
	(0.334)	(0.556)	(0.011)
Percent LEP students	1.098***	0.438	0.071***
	(0.139)	(0.274)	(0.009)
Percent free lunch	−0.269**	−0.250	0.003
	(0.089)	(0.156)	(0.002)
Percent Asian students	1.903***	1.539*	0.029**
	(0.334)	(0.618)	(0.010)
Percent black students	0.366*	0.250	−0.006*
	(0.150)	(0.259)	(0.003)
Percent Hispanic students	1.644***	−0.613**	0.032***
	(0.133)	(0.228)	(0.006)
Percent Asian teachers	−0.735*	−0.682	0.002
	(0.335)	(0.611)	(0.007)

Percent black teachers	0.021	0.684	0.000
	(0.232)	(0.367)	(0.004)
Percent Hispanic teachers	−0.070	0.771*	−0.004
	(0.200)	(0.305)	(0.006)
Asian principal	−0.008	−0.090	0.006
	(0.121)	(0.174)	(0.004)
Hispanic principal	−0.088	−0.056	−0.006*
	(0.089)	(0.137)	(0.003)
Black principal	0.058	−0.055	0.001
	(0.075)	(0.133)	(0.001)
1990	0.758***	0.175	
	(0.066)	(0.121)	
1993	1.033***	0.242*	
	(0.059)	(0.098)	
1999	0.474***	−0.263**	−0.003**
	(0.056)	(0.095)	(0.001)
2003	−0.012	−0.074	−0.006***
	(0.060)	(0.088)	(0.001)
Constant	−1.916***	0.000	0.000
	(0.281)	(.)	−0.001
Cut1		−2.510***	
		(0.437)	
Cut2		−0.065	
		(0.431)	
Cut3		1.456***	
		(0.431)	
N	17916	3749	12214
chi2/R2	1016.435	482.876	.15
* p ≤ 0.05, ** p ≤ 0.01; *** p ≤ 0.001			

has traditionally been that new destinations lack the experience, cultural understanding, resources, and know-how to identify and address the needs of newcomers, perhaps the novelty of these newcomers and their lack of experience with the U.S. school system provides the impetus and urgency for new destination schools to engage in greater outreach to these parents. In addition, schools in new destinations may not be able to rely on the community or other parents to engage these parents due to language and cultural

TABLE 10.4 OUTREACH TO LEP PARENTS	
English-only law	0.011
	(0.009)
State wealth (2008 constant $)	−0.006***
	(0.001)
Percent state population w/bachelor's or more	0.001
	(0.001)
Percent state foreign born	0.019***
	(0.002)
Percent state non-Hispanic white	0.002***
	(0.000)
Number Latino state legislators	−0.001
	(0.000)
New destination	0.062***
	(0.015)
Established destination	0.002
	(0.023)
Border county	−0.065**
	(0.022)
Elementary school	0.040***
	(0.006)
Charter school	−0.046
	(0.039)
Percent LEP students	0.057
	(0.033)
Percent free lunch	0.008
	(0.016)
Percent Asian students	0.407***
	(0.077)
Percent black students	0.202***
	(0.028)
Percent Hispanic students	0.531***
	(0.025)
Percent Asian teachers	−0.032
	(0.062)
Percent black teachers	−0.125**
	(0.041)

Percent Hispanic teachers	−0.122***
	(0.032)
Asian principal	−0.055**
	(0.019)
Hispanic principal	−0.048***
	(0.013)
Black principal	−0.002
	(0.012)
1999 (excluded)	
2003	−0.003
	(0.009)
2007	0.098***
	(0.009)
Constant	0.530***
	(0.050)
N	12,091
R2	.14
* p ≤ 0.05, ** p ≤ 0.01; *** p ≤ 0.001	

barriers. At the same time, schools in border counties engage in significantly less outreach to LEP parents (compared to schools not located in the three contexts of reception). Perhaps these schools can rely more on other parents and the community for translation, interpreters, and general outreach due to higher rates of bilingualism in border communities. Also, contrary to expectation is the negative effect of cultural brokers: schools with larger shares of Hispanic teachers and Asian or Latino principals offer significantly fewer outreach programs for LEP parents. Perhaps the same logic applies here. Schools with cultural brokers rely less on formal policies and strategies and more on informal outreach and engagement than do those without cultural brokers.

Interactive Models

To test for the conditional effects of bureaucratic representation/cultural brokers on school policies and practices, I focus here on the presence of Latino principals and the percentage of Latino teachers in the schools. Given that new destinations are primarily being settled by Hispanic immigrants, this focus makes sense. The question then is whether school policies are

TABLE 10.5 CONDITIONAL MODELS			
	Language Instruction 2 (Logit)	ESL/Bilingual Vacancy (Logit)	LEP Parent Outreach (OLS)
English-only law	−0.252*	0.013	0.012
	(0.105)	(0.047)	(0.009)
State wealth (2008 constant $)	−0.011	−0.011	−0.006***
	(0.013)	(0.006)	(0.001)
Percent state population w/bachelor's or more	0.014	−0.002	0.001
	(0.013)	(0.007)	(0.001)
Percent state foreign born	−0.027	0.039*	0.019***
	(0.021)	(0.011)	(0.002)
Percent state non-Hispanic white	−0.006	0.006*	0.002***
	(0.005)	(0.003)	(0.000)
Number Latino state legislators	0.004	−0.003	−0.001
	(0.004)	(0.003)	(0.000)
New destination	−0.386	0.206*	0.065***
	(0.219)	(0.092)	(0.018)
Established destination	0.458*	0.104	0.025
	(0.209)	(0.123)	(0.031)
Border county	0.201	−0.132	−0.053
	(0.219)	(0.190)	(0.033)
Elementary school	−0.061	−0.304*	0.040***
	(0.074)	(0.038)	(0.006)
Charter school	0.490	−0.183	−0.042
	(1.124)	(0.325)	(0.038)
Percent LEP students	1.784*	1.110*	0.057
	(0.265)	(0.140)	(0.034)
Percent free lunch	0.266	−0.276*	0.007
	(0.147)	(0.089)	(0.016)
Percent Asian students	−0.230	1.901*	0.406***
	(0.825)	(0.334)	(0.077)
Percent black students	0.100	0.360*	0.202***
	(0.300)	(0.152)	(0.028)
Percent Hispanic students	2.572*	1.656*	0.533***
	(0.225)	(0.134)	(0.025)
Percent Asian teachers	−0.093	−0.728*	−0.031
	(0.762)	(0.335)	(0.062)

Percent black teachers	0.800*	0.036	−0.124**
	(0.383)	(0.235)	(0.041)
Percent Hispanic teachers	1.782*	−0.003	−0.101**
	(0.354)	(0.227)	(0.038)
Asian principal	0.338	−0.010	−0.055**
	(0.239)	(0.121)	(0.019)
Hispanic principal	−0.261	−0.126	−0.045**
	(0.184)	(0.112)	(0.014)
Black principal	0.169	0.059	−0.002
	(0.116)	(0.075)	(0.012)
1990		0.757*	
		(0.066)	
1993	1.287*	1.034*	
	(0.078)	(0.059)	
1999	0.455*	0.472*	−0.003
	(0.076)	(0.056)	(0.009)
2003		−0.011	0.099***
		(0.061)	(0.009)
2007			
Constant	−2.451	−1.935***	0.529***
	(0.536)	(0.282)	(0.051)
New dest*percent Hispanic teacher	3.195*	1.103*	0.076
	(1.450)	(0.438)	(0.089)
New dest*Hispanic principal	−0.097	−0.400	−0.104*
	(0.465)	(0.284)	(0.048)
Established dest*percent Hispanic teacher	−1.066	−1.149	−0.168
	(0.826)	(0.663)	(0.110)
Established dest*Hispanic principal	0.013	0.146	−0.009
	(0.685)	(0.355)	(0.069)
Border*percent Hispanic teacher	−2.033*	−0.514	−0.124
	(0.734)	(0.411)	(0.077)
Border*Hispanic principal	0.227	0.477*	0.065
	(0.397)	(0.239)	(0.037)
chi2/R2	1115.500	1113.766	.36
N	10051	17916	12091

* $p \leq 0.05$, ** $p \leq 0.01$; *** $p \leq 0.001$

more favorable toward the needs and preferences of Latino immigrants in new versus established destinations or border counties when Latinos are more represented in the school faculty and administration. In three of six models, there were significant effects of the interaction terms, however, these were not always in the hypothesized direction. Table 10.5 reports estimates from these three models, but here I focus only on the substantive interpretation of the interactions.

Interacting the context of reception dummies with the percentage of Latino teachers and the presence of a Latino principal yields some different results. First, whereas the baseline model found the percentage of Latino teachers positively and significantly related to bilingual instruction, here the results show these effects are variable. In new destination schools, larger shares of Latino teachers increase the likelihood of bilingual instruction, while in border counties the relationship is negative. Second, cultural brokers in the form of Latino teachers and principals also matter for ESL/bilingual teacher vacancies. In new destination schools, teacher vacancies are more likely when the percentage of Latino teachers is greater, while in border counties the presence of a Latino principal increases the probability of a vacancy. Third, whereas schools in new destinations engaged in more outreach with LEP parents, in the conditional model, this relationship is attenuated with the presence of a Latino principal. Overall, there are no conditional effects of Latino teachers or principals in established destinations.

Conclusion

Overall, the findings of this study indicate that schools in new destinations are responding to the needs of immigrant and LEP populations. Though they have historically been less likely to offer bilingual education than schools in established immigrant gateways or border areas, once other covariates are controlled, there is no difference in the type of instructional programs offered across the three contexts of reception. Second, schools in new destinations do have significantly more teacher vacancies in ESL/bilingual education. However, these schools were not more likely to face difficulties filling these vacancies compared to schools in established/border areas or schools in nonimmigrant gateway locations. Thus, it may be that in new destinations ESL/bilingual teacher vacancies signal a heightened priority of this position and/or the likelihood that these schools may be hiring ESL/bilingual teachers for the first time. Though it is typically assumed that school districts in new destinations face shortages in ESL/bilingual education, the findings here suggest that this shortage is either no worse than in other parts of the country, or that these districts have been relatively successful in their recruitment efforts.

Schools in new destinations were also found to have slightly higher percentages of ESL/bilingual staff than schools in established immigrant destinations or border areas, and these effects remained after controlling for other covariates. As noted above, this may be because schools in new destinations cannot rely on a set of more established, second-generation immigrant parents to provide language and cultural support and assistance since these parents do not exist in many new destination communities. Thus, schools in new destinations may need to hire dedicated staff aides to serve in this role. In contrast, schools in established destinations and border communities typically have a large pool of second- and even third-generation immigrant parents on whom they may rely for more assistance and support. In this case, these schools may elect not to devote scarce resources to hiring dedicated staff personnel to serve as ESL/bilingual aides. Similarly, schools in established/border communities may be able to count on existing teachers to fill ESL/bilingual teaching positions, since more teachers on their faculty may have the requisite training and certification. On the other hand, they may also have no vacancies at all, since these schools may already have ESL/bilingual teachers with long tenures. In fact, this same logic can be applied to the finding that schools in new destinations engaged in significantly more outreach to LEP parents. The need to formalize these programs and activities often results from the absence of more informal activities or norms that make formal policies unnecessary. Schools in new destinations may need to formalize their outreach activities to LEP parents to a greater extent than schools located in established/border areas.

The presence of cultural brokers generally had the expected effects on school language, staffing, and outreach policies. In particular, regardless of the context of reception, schools with more Latino teachers were more likely to provide ESL and bilingual education programs. In these schools, filling teacher vacancies in ESL/bilingual education was also easier. The presence of cultural brokers in new destination schools also made a difference. In particular, their presence increased the likelihood of bilingual education and also increased the likelihood of ESL/bilingual teacher vacancies. As discussed above, this increase in teacher vacancies could signify that Latino teachers are advocating for instructional programs and staffing to meet the needs of the growing number of LEP students in new destination schools. At the same time, the negative relationship between cultural brokers and outreach with LEP parents was unexpected. One possible explanation is that outreach with these parents is already occurring on a more informal basis in schools with cultural brokers, thereby making formal outreach efforts unnecessary. However, further investigation with more micro-level data is warranted in order to understand better this dynamic.

Given the macro-level nature of the data reported here, the findings only suggest potential causal mechanisms. This said, the empirical analysis provides a rare and valuable overview of what schools across the United States have been doing in the area of language, staffing, and outreach for ELL students and their families over the past twenty years. On the whole, the findings of this study suggest that lack of experience with immigrant and LEP populations in new destinations (compared to established and border counties) has not hampered the ability of schools to implement programs that target the needs of these populations. This is encouraging news.

NOTES

    1. LEP and ELL are used interchangeably.

    2. For example, *Lau v. Nichols* (1974) and the Equal Educational Opportunities Act required schools to take appropriate action to ensure ELLs had the basic English skills needed to participate in instructional programs. In 1980 the Carter administration proposed regulations requiring bilingual education, and in 1981 a federal appeals court established a means for evaluating bilingual education programs (Jost 2009).

    3. For this measure, the 1999–2000 and 2003–2004 questions combining ESL and bilingual instruction were coded as 1.

    4. $\alpha = 0.81$.

    5. Continuous: Boston-Cambridge-Quincy, MA-NH; Chicago-Naperville-Joliet, IL-IN-WI; New York-Northern New Jersey-Long Island, NY-NJ-PA; San Francisco-Oakland-Fremont, CA. Post–World War II: Houston-Baytown-Sugar Land, TX; Miami-Fort Lauderdale-Miami Beach, FL; Riverside-San Bernardino-Ontario, CA; San Diego-Carlsbad-San Marcos, CA; Los Angeles-Long Beach-Santa Ana, CA.

    6. All descriptive graphs include only those schools where the LEP population was > 0.

11

Civic and Political Engagement by Immigrant-Background Minorities in Traditional and New Destination European Cities

KATIA PILATI
LAURA MORALES

The previous two chapters found that street-level bureaucrats in new immigrant destinations are not necessarily disinclined to support immigrants. In the case of education, for instance, new destinations are about as likely as traditional destinations to help incorporate students with limited English proficiency. In this chapter, Katia Pilati and Laura Morales return the focus to Europe, as they examine immigrant engagement in civic organizations across new and traditional destination cities. Civic organizations serve as a potential bridge to political engagement, just as faith-based associations facilitate immigrant integration in rural England. Pilati and Morales used surveys of immigrants in nine European cities during two time periods to examine the importance of the receiving context for immigrant integration. They find some systematic differences between new and traditional destination cities in both civic and political engagement, but, consistent with the findings reported in other chapters, these differences are less extensive than one might expect. New destination context is not an obstacle to immigrant integration. In those circumstances in which the receiving context affects engagement, we see that once again, the local context has importance that transcends national public policy.

A debate has developed in recent scholarship around the distinction between new and traditional immigrant destination cities (Lichter and Johnson 2009; Marrow 2005). According to such studies, immigrants' social, economic, and political integration is expected to be different depending on whether migrants have settled in new or traditional countries and cities of immigration. In Europe, the focus on how contexts shape migrants' civic and political integration has been centered on how different degrees of openness in immigration policy and legislation affect such integration (Ireland 1994; Koopmans et al. 2005; Morales and Giugni 2011). Less discussion has been devoted to the differential impact of opportunities for civic and political integration associated with new and traditional destinations of migration. This chapter tries to fill in this gap by exploring the patterns of civic and political engagement in nine European cities, including both new and traditional destinations. In order to achieve this goal, the chapter analyzes the factors affecting engagement in ethnic, native, and pan-immigrant organizations as well as immigrants' political engagement in mainstream and immigrant-related activities in Budapest, Barcelona, Geneva, Lyon, London, Madrid, Milan, Stockholm, and Zurich.[1]

To address our main research question, focusing on the impact of the type of destination on immigrants' civic and political involvement, we draw on the literature that has discussed the role of the degree of openness of political contexts on immigrant integration, and on the political behaviorist scholarship with specific reference to studies applied to migration. The latter has offered important insights on the importance for immigrant-background individuals to get organized in order to be better represented and to mobilize in the political sphere.

Since the pioneering work of Sidney Verba and several of his colleagues (Almond and Verba 1963; Nie, Powell, and Prewitt 1969a,b; Verba and Nie 1972), scholarship on political engagement has afforded a central role to associational engagement as a critical resource to mobilize citizens into political attentiveness and action. Associations are also crucial in the political mobilization of immigrant-background minorities. In the late 1990s a few groundbreaking studies led by a group of Dutch scholars suggested that organizational structures played a critical role in shaping the political integration of immigrant-background individuals.[2] These scholars underscored the role of ethnic organizations—that is, organizations mainly composed of people of the same ethnic group—and of membership and engagement in such organizations, claiming that ethnic organizational networks encourage higher levels of political participation. In other words, the larger the "ethnic civic community"—and by that they meant the ethnic organizational network— the higher the levels of political participation among immigrant-background residents (Fennema 2004; Fennema and Tillie 1999).

Other work has emphasized that these positive benefits are not restricted to single-group ethnic associations. When immigrants from multiple ethnic groups organize together in pan-immigrant associations, pan-ethnic identities sustain mobilization in the residence country (Okamoto 2003; Okamoto and Ebert 2010). Thus, pan-immigrant organizations also act as vehicles for the political participation of immigrant-background individuals in the settlement country. Finally, findings on the impact of immigrants' engagement in native-based organizations suggest that these organizations foster their political involvement as well (Berger, Galonska, and Koopmans 2004; Lee, Ramakrishnan, and Ramírez 2007; Mollenkopf and Hochschild 2009; Ramakrishnan 2006; Ramakrishnan and Bloemraad 2008a; Wong 2006).

Such scholarship has, however, overlooked how contextual aspects may affect engagement in organizations and, therefore, engagement in politics too. The integrative effect of ethnic organizations may, for example, vary depending on whether migrants have settled in traditional or new countries of destination. In fact, in new countries of destination, migrants' organizational structures may be much weaker than in traditional destinations. Or the integrative capacity of new and traditional destinations may vary depending on whether immigrant organizations are afforded a dominant role in the immigrant organizational field and in immigration policies and therefore are differently positioned to provide the resources and political cues that will help immigrants engage in public affairs. This chapter looks at these expectations in some detail.

Understanding Immigrants' Civic and Political Engagement

Political engagement is at the center of the concept of the democratic state as it contributes to the equal protection and representation of groups' interests, it implies the possibility to take part in public affairs, and it increases governments' legitimacies, the acceptance of a democratic form of government, and the sense of collective responsibility and civic duty.

In turn, organizations are important services providers. In addition, the study of organizations as mobilizing structures in the political sphere has been widely acknowledged, particularly within the political-behavioral perspective, by the "civic voluntarism model" (CVM) (Verba, Schlozman, and Brady 1995). In this perspective, organizations are conceived, together with workplaces and places of worship, as intermediary structures between the socioeconomic positions of individuals and their political participation. While still emphasizing the importance of the socioeconomic status (SES) model—and of the resources individuals derive from their socioeconomic positions—for citizens' political participation, the CVM underscores the role of organizational resources. According to the CVM, political participation is deeply rooted in social institutions such as the family, the school, the workplace, voluntary associations, and churches. Citizens' affiliations to formal and structured groups—such as associations—as well as their interpersonal connections and embeddedness in informal social groups, are the key to facilitating political recruitment and participation. In particular, they enable the accumulation of resources, such as civic skills, which are the communication and organizational abilities needed in order to employ other kinds of resources—particularly, time and money—efficiently in political life (Verba, Schlozman, and Brady 1995: 271, 304). Involvement in all sorts of formal and informal groups contributes to gaining the knowledge and skills that facilitate access, recruitment, and participation into the political sphere (McClurg 2003). Social connections also create the reciprocal expectations that encourage participation and collective action by facilitating the expression of shared identities (Diani and McAdam 2003).

In immigration studies scholarship, the importance of political engagement by immigrants and of the role of organizations for the political incorporation of immigrants has also been widely acknowledged (Hochschild and Mollenkopf 2009a; Morales and Pilati 2011; Ramakrishnan and Bloemraad 2008a). Jennifer L. Hochschild and John H. Mollenkopf argue that highly organized and politicized local communities in the United States help immigrants learn about the political system and that immigrant incorporation turns out to be substantially fostered by networks of nonprofit organizations (Hochschild and Mollenkopf 2009b: 19; Mollenkopf and Hochschild 2010: 32). The U.S. scholarship has also repeatedly shown that ethnic organizations are important means for immigrants to engage in transnational politics and that transnational politics is not a zero-sum game with mainstream politics (Portes, Escobar, and Arana 2008, 2013).

Single-case studies in Europe have further addressed the impact of ethnic and cross-ethnic organizations on immigrants' political involvement. Dirk Jacobs, Karen Phalet, and Marc Swyngedouw (2004) and Jean Tillie (2004) find a positive effect of ethnic associational involvement on political engagement. Yet, other studies have shown that this relationship is not as clear-cut. A study in Denmark on second-generation immigrants from the former Yugoslavia, Turkey, and Pakistan showed that the impact of involvement in ethnic organizations for political participation depends on the ethnic group (Togeby 2004). In Berlin, immigrants involved in ethnic organizations are more politically active but show no greater interest in German politics than those not involved in ethnic organizations (Berger, Galonska, and Koopmans 2004). The few existing comparative studies suggest that the effect of engagement in ethnic associations on mainstream political engagement across European cities is either negative or nil (Morales and Pilati 2011). Other scholarship shows that, even if immigrants usually occupy a peripheral position in the participatory structure—see, for instance, S. Karthick Ramakrishnan (2006) on Latinos and Asians in the United States—their involvement in civic institutions such as trade unions and other types of voluntary organizations, often mostly composed of natives, systematically fosters their political engagement (Lee, Ramakrishnan, and Ramírez 2007; Ramakrishnan and Bloemraad 2008a). Maria Berger, Christian Galonska, and Ruud Koopmans (2004) show that engagement in German organizations promotes the political integration of immigrants, and similar research in Milan showed that the effect of engagement in native organizations on political incorporation is greater than engagement in ethnic organizations (Pilati 2010).

The scholarly literature that has analyzed immigrant organizations and the mechanisms of mobilization at work has suggested some reasons why pan-immigrant and native-based organizations should foster immigrants' political engagement more consistently than ethnic organizations do (Pilati and Morales 2016). Sometimes, language barriers affect some ethnic organizational leaders who lack linguistic skills, and this hinders their capacity to mobilize members into local politics and can result in important differences in the impact that ethnic and native organizations have on immigrants' political engagement (Aptekar 2009). Equally, differences in the public visibility of ethnic and mainstream or native organizations may lead to different mobilizing effects because the information cues and shortcuts that they provide to their respective members will differ. In turn, native organizations are likely to sustain many and more structured links to political institutions of the country of residence and play a central role in the associational field. Consistent with this, Ramakrishnan and Irene Bloemraad (2008b) show that mainstream organizations in six Californian cities have considerably higher levels of political presence vis à vis local government officials and policy makers than ethnic organizations.

Consequently, the additional resources that immigrants obtain from joining mainstream organizations—and which they do not necessarily obtain from ethnic organizations—are manifold. Native organizations will be more likely to successfully mobilize immigrants into mainstream political engagement because they accumulate more organizational resources and contacts than ethnic organizations. For instance, natives have much greater political knowledge and information, socioeconomic resources, and social capital than immigrants across all European countries (Messina 2007). Therefore, native organizations may more easily provide such resources to immigrants. Native organizations can also offer their immigrant members symbolic resources that legitimize political action. They can, for instance, secure the political recognition that many immigrants lack when they are not national citizens. For all of these reasons, native organizations are regarded as key *bridging actors* between immigrants and mainstream political institutions, sometimes even crowding-out ethnic and pan-immigrant organizations in providing this linkage function (Caponio 2005).

Migrants' Organizations in Traditional and New Destinations

Recent scholarship, mainly in the United States, addresses the impact of contextual conditions in new destination cities on immigrants' integration. This scholarship has explored how migrants settled in new destinations may encounter different conditions of integration compared to migrants settled in traditional destination cities and countries. New destinations tend to be characterized by rapid growth of the foreign-born migrant population, and therefore have overall lower rates of citizenship acquisition. Immigrants in new destinations have lower language proficiency as well as fewer resources—both individual and collective—such as the multiple relationships and social capital immigrants progressively accumulate in the place of settlement. New destinations may be also less prepared for immigration flows, with political elites having less know-how on best practices, policies, and experiences to face immigration-related challenges, and with extremely different approaches to including or excluding the new arrivals (Hall 2013; Marrow 2005; Okamoto and Ebert 2010).

For these reasons, immigrants settling in new destinations may have more difficulty joining voluntary associations and getting involved in political action than immigrants settling in traditional destination cities where the organizational structure and broader political context is more prepared for immigrant flows. For instance, immigrants' collective rights (cultural, educational, religious, rights related to equal access to media for all ethnic groups, labor, and so on) may be more easily recognized in traditional than in new destinations. The same may be expected for individual rights (access to residence permits and citizenship, family reunion, welfare, antidiscrimination, and so on), leading to more inclusionary approaches toward immigrants in the civic and political spheres. Therefore, following the literature that argues that more open political contexts in terms of individual and collective rights foster migrants' political integration compared to closed political contexts (Cinalli and Giugni 2011; Koopmans et al. 2005), immigrants in traditional destinations are expected to be more likely to engage in civic and political activities than in new destination ones (general hypothesis).

In addition, ethnic and pan-immigrant organizations in new destinations may be less adept than those in traditional destinations at *bridging* immigrants and local political institutions, primarily because of the limited size of the migrant population and its recent arrival. Therefore, organizations might provide dissimilar resources across different contexts depending on their position in the immigrant organizational field and their engagement in the policy-making process. Furthermore, previous research suggests that whereas ethnic organizations are afforded a dominant role in the social organization of multicultural policies of diversity accommodation in certain traditional destination countries—such as in the Netherlands, the United Kingdom, or Canada (Bloemraad 2006a; Ramakrishnan and Bloemraad 2008a)—ethnic organizations are often marginalized in terms of the resources they have at their disposal and in terms of the recognition of their potential contribution to the political process in less accommodating or "closed" political contexts, such as Italy and Spain, which are new destination countries in Europe (Morales and Ramiro 2011; Pilati 2012). In such contexts, ethnic organizations are unlikely to have much leverage in the public arena and will have a difficult time incorporating immigrants into mainstream politics. In contrast, in traditional destination countries such as the Netherlands or Belgium, for example, where the historical and institutional roots of ethnic minority recognition derive from the system of "pillarization" that organized various institutions (newspapers, radios, trade unions, schools, and so forth) along political or religious affiliations (Post 1989), ethnic organizations have a better chance to become powerful mobilizing structures that contribute to the political incorporation of immigrants (Fennema and Tillie 2001; Pieterse 2001). In these contexts, immigrants are encouraged to organize in ethnic associations that are then capable of conveying many political resources to their members because of their well-established structure and connections with the local authorities. Consistent with this, some results in these countries suggest that the magnitude and structure of the ethnic civic communities are closely related to the levels of political participation and trust in local political institutions of immigrants (Fennema and Tillie 1999; Vermeulen 2006).

Therefore, there are reasons to expect that there is a partial overlap between the type of destination and the receptivity of the policy approaches, such that traditional destinations are likely to be the most open ones, whereas new destinations—which tend to be characterized by more restrictive integration policies—might be less welcoming and less prepared for the immigration flows.[3] Thus, drawing on the literature on the impact of the openness of political contexts, we expect that contextual conditions related to new destinations will hinder immigrants' engagement in native, pan-immigrant, and ethnic organizations as well as their involvement in different types of political actions (specific hypothesis).

Data and Variables

The empirical evidence presented in this chapter derives from survey data collected between 2004 and 2008 from representative samples of individuals of immigrant background in nine European cities: Budapest, Barcelona, Geneva, Lyon, London, Madrid, Milan, Stockholm, and Zurich.[4] Whereas Barcelona, Budapest, Madrid, and Milan can be classified as new destination cities, Geneva, Lyon, London, Stockholm, and Zurich are traditional destination cities. Indeed, while postwar immigration characterized the Swiss cities, London, and Lyon, and migration to Stockholm developed a bit later (primarily since the early 1970s), most immigration flows to the Spanish cities, Budapest, and Milan have taken place only since the late 1980s, with considerable peaks happening in the 1990s and 2000s in the three Southern European cities.

In each city the survey focused on either two or three different ethnic groups: in Budapest—Chinese, ethnic Hungarian immigrants, and a mixed group of immigrants originating from Muslim countries; in Barcelona and Madrid—Ecuadorians, other Latin American Andeans, and Moroccans; in Geneva—Italians and Kosovars; in Zurich—Turks, Kosovars, and Italians; in Milan—Filipinos, Egyptians, and Ecuadorians; in Lyon—Algerians, Moroccans, and Tunisians; in London—Bangladeshis, Pakistanis, and Indians; and in Stockholm—Chileans and Turks. The groups were selected according to their size in relation to the overall immigrant population, and they included in each city at least one group of long-standing immigration, one of more recent arrival, as well as one of Muslim religious background.

In most cities, the immigrant population makes up between 10 and 30 percent of the total local population, and the groups surveyed represent the major groups of immigrants present in the cities studied. The total immigrant samples in each city are random samples stratified by ethnic origin and composed of at least 250 individuals for each immigrant group. They include immigrants and second-generation members of the immigrant group. All the individuals selected had to have been resident in the cities for at least six months prior to the interview, and to be at least fifteen years of age.[5] The whole sample we employ includes 6,632 individuals of immigrant background.

Dependent Variables

While the definition of civic engagement is inconsistent across studies, we consider civic engagement as engagement in voluntary organizations. In turn, political involvement can be expressed in various forms: in electoral behavior; in extra-electoral activities—such as contacting officials; or in expressing an interest and attachment toward political affairs (Lane 1965; Sigel and Hoskin 1981). In this chapter we focus our attention on several types of civic and political involvement that are key indicators of the degree of civic and political incorporation of immigrant-background individuals in the societies where they live. With regard to civic engagement, we consider engagement in at least one ethnic association, engagement in at least one pan-immigrant organization, and engagement in at least one native organization.

The questionnaire included a detailed battery of questions on associational engagement in relation to a list of eighteen types of organizations (see the Appendix reporting the full list of organizations). Respondents were probed about the membership composition of each organization to which they belonged or had participated in in the previous twelve months.[6] One question asked whether half or more members were of immigrant background, and another whether half or more members were of their same ethnicity or country of origin. Thus, each organizational involvement was classified as relating to an ethnic, pan-immigrant, or native organization.

Consequently, we employ three dichotomous variables for civic engagement: engagement in ethnic organizations, engagement in pan-immigrant organizations, and engagement in native organizations.

We defined political engagement as consisting of participants' involvement in at least one mainstream extra-electoral activity and at least one immigrant-related extra-electoral activity in the previous twelve months. Political engagement in extra-electoral activities includes actions such as contacting, donating, and lobbying.[7] Following the approach of the American Citizen Participation Study, the surveys asked those respondents who had participated in any form of action: Who is affected by the issue that motivated the action? Whenever a respondent indicated that the issue fundamentally concerned the family or a few other individuals, the city, the country of residence, or the world, we considered this as indicative of mainstream political action. When a respondent indicated that the issue related to immigrants, we considered this indicative of immigrant-related political action. We thus excluded from these indicators actions that the respondents suggested were related to the country of origin of the respondents or of their parents, which are more likely indicators of transnational political action not specifically referring to the country of settlement.

Independent Variables

Traditional versus new destination cities are operationalized by using a dichotomous variable assigned a value of 1 for the new destination cities of Barcelona, Budapest, Madrid, and Milan and a value of 0 for traditional destination cities, namely Geneva, London, Lyon, Stockholm, and Zurich. The impact of factors related to the context of settlement (new versus traditional destination) is contrasted with the effect played by other variables thought to be important in shaping political involvement by classical behavioral perspectives as well as by theories emphasizing the characteristics related to the process of immigration. We thus include as control variables both sociodemographic and socioeconomic characteristics of immigrants, as well as attitudinal, and immigration-related correlates. The Appendix reports the detailed coding for all independent variables.

Results

Table 11.1 reports the descriptive statistics of the independent as well as dependent variables analyzed—civic and political engagement. Levels of civic engagement vary across cities. In Barcelona, Stockholm, and Lyon immigrants are active mostly through native organizations. In Milan, Madrid, and Zurich levels of engagement in native organizations are very similar to those in ethnic organizations, and only migrants in London are

TABLE 11.1 DESCRIPTIVE STATISTICS OF DEPENDENT AND INDEPENDENT VARIABLES BY CITY (MEAN)										
	BAR	BUD	GEN	LON	LYO	MAD	MIL	STO	ZUR	Total
Dependent variables										
Engagement in at least one native organization	0.228	0.060	0.200	0.090	0.346	0.112	0.112	0.783	0.167	0.203
Engagement in at least one pan-immigrant organization	0.099	0.006	0.190	0.043	0.206	0.069	0.027	0.197	0.079	0.092
Engagement in at least one ethnic organization	0.139	0.035	0.148	0.131	0.087	0.126	0.113	0.193	0.171	0.124
Engagement in at least one mainstream extra-electoral activity	0.200	0.064	0.205	0.046	0.332	0.075	0.037	0.581	0.086	0.155
Engagement in at least one immigrant-related extra-electoral activity	0.126	0.030	0.111	0.046	0.183	0.065	0.036	0.057	0.057	0.076
Independent variables										
Male	0.557	0.611	0.539	0.523	0.444	0.493	0.524	0.486	0.665	0.543
Age	38.970	33.846	43.985	33.750	36.366	34.998	35.398	38.006	44.625	37.712
Married	0.611	0.510	0.701	0.483	0.535	0.543	0.628	0.598	0.773	0.597

In paid work	0.789	0.561	0.535	0.599	0.535	0.776	0.731	0.665	0.559	0.641
Educational level attained	0.566	0.747	0.571	0.722	0.592	0.485	0.636	0.630	0.495	0.604
Interest in residence country politics	0.539	0.611	0.600	0.423	0.719	0.439	0.374	0.619	0.569	0.533
Proportion of life living in the country	0.232	0.279	0.589	0.756	0.797	0.203	0.272	0.604	0.554	0.458
Social trust	0.484	0.596	0.508	0.492	0.337	0.523	0.472	0.450	0.494	0.488
Second and third generations	0.008	0.019	0.134	0.502	0.484	0.003	0.022	0.173	0.111	0.155
Has no country of residence citizenship nor permit	0.109	0.079	0.200	0.021	0.057	0.157	0.207	0.000	0.176	0.117
Has country of residence citizenship	0.201	0.180	0.156	0.764	0.799	0.161	0.057	0.800	0.118	0.336
Has country of residence permit to stay	0.690	0.741	0.644	0.215	0.145	0.682	0.737	0.200	0.706	0.547
Speak host language fluently	0.874	0.538	0.708	0.825	0.930	0.743	0.165	0.886	0.381	0.648
Muslim	0.285	0.314	0.440	0.439	0.703	0.342	0.288	0.292	0.513	0.402
New destination city	1	1	0	0	0	1	1	0	0	
N	741	823	649	886	705	866	900	508	902	6,980

Note: All dependent variables are measured on a 0–1 scale and, hence, represent the proportion of all respondents engaged in the given type of association or political activity.

active mostly through ethnic organizations. Involvement in native organizations is extremely high in Stockholm due to the very high number of affiliations in trade unions—typical of all Scandinavian societies and also, in this case, extended to migrant populations—although engagement in ethnic organizations is also the highest in Stockholm. Concerning political engagement, the table shows that immigrants in Lyon and Stockholm manifest the highest levels of political engagement in mainstream issues, while Barcelona and Geneva show the highest levels of engagement in immigrant-related politics. In contrast, there are cities where immigrants are hardly engaged in any political activity, like Milan and Budapest.

Figures 11.1 and 11.2 show, respectively, the rates of civic engagement in at least one ethnic, pan-immigrant, and native organization (Figure 11.1), and political engagement in mainstream and immigrant-related activities (Figure 11.2) by city of settlement, specifically distinguishing between types of destination. If we take a look at Figures 11.1 and 11.2, a few interesting patterns emerge. There are considerable differences between new and traditional destinations with regard to engagement in native organizations as well as engagement in mainstream politics. This is especially clear if we consider the city of Stockholm, one of the European cities with the most open political contexts in terms of migrants' integration among the ones we study (Cinalli and Giugni 2011) and, as we show elsewhere (Morales and Pilati 2011), the degree of openness may have significant effects on the way migrants eventually engage in host country politics. However, other types of civic and political engagement do not seem to manifest a different pattern between new and traditional destination cities. In particular, engagement in ethnic organizations and engagement in immigrant-related political activities seem hardly affected by immigrants' city of settlement.

The multivariate analyses presented in Table 11.2 partially confirm such relationships.[8] While the coefficient testing the impact of the type of destination is always negative—indicating a smaller probability to engage in each type of organization or political activity in new destinations—only models 1 (native organizations), 2 (pan-immigrant organizations), and 4 (mainstream actions) show that the type of place of settlement significantly affects the probability of engaging in the respective form of civic and political engagement studied. Overall, these models show that migrants settled in new destination cities are less likely to engage in some types of organizations and political actions than migrants settled in traditional destination gateways, and that this difference reaches standard statistical significance in the case of engagement in pan-immigrant organizations (model 2).[9]

With regard to civic engagement, these results imply that new destinations may be less prepared in terms of providing the means for migrants to join pan-immigrant organizations. The latter is likely to be affected by the

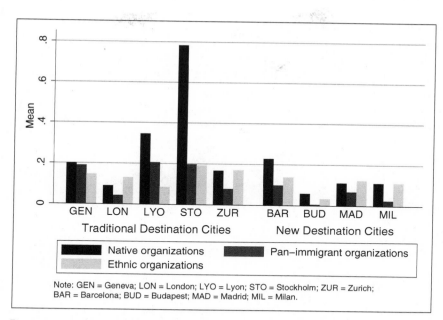

Figure 11.1 Associational Engagement by City and Type of Destination
(Source: Localmultidem, 2007–2010)

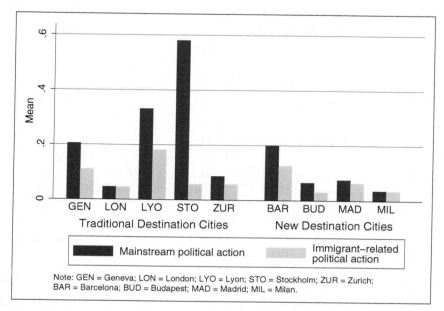

Figure 11.2 Political Engagement by City and Type of Destination
(Source: Localmultidem, 2007–2010)

TABLE 11.2 CORRELATES OF CIVIC PARTICIPATION (MODELS 1 TO 3) AND OF POLITICAL PARTICIPATION (MODELS 4 AND 5). LOGIT MODELS (DATA CLUSTERED BY GROUP-CITY)

	Model 1 Engagement in Native Organizations		Model 2 Engagement in Pan-immigrant Organizations		Model 3 Engagement in Ethnic Organizations		Model 4 Engagement in Mainstream Nonelectoral Activities		Model 5 Engagement in Immigrant-related Nonelectoral Activities	
	b	se	b	se	b	se	b	se	b	se
Male	−0.03	(0.08)	0.17+	(0.10)	0.20+	(0.10)	0.09	(0.07)	0.08	(0.10)
Age	0.05*	(0.02)	0.02	(0.04)	0.02	(0.02)	0.09***	(0.02)	0.05**	(0.02)
Age squared	−0.00*	(0.00)	−0.00	(0.00)	−0.00	(0.00)	−0.00***	(0.00)	−0.00*	(0.00)
Married	−0.08	(0.12)	−0.18	(0.13)	0.30**	(0.09)	−0.10	(0.09)	−0.06	(0.13)
Education	0.50	(0.32)	0.13	(0.28)	0.14	(0.23)	0.85***	(0.26)	0.62*	(0.24)
In paid work	0.22**	(0.08)	0.27**	(0.10)	0.12	(0.13)	−0.16+	(0.09)	−0.12	(0.10)
Interest residence country politics	0.59***	(0.10)	0.72***	(0.14)	0.23*	(0.10)	1.14***	(0.12)	0.91***	(0.16)
Social trust	−0.20	(0.15)	−0.13	(0.24)	−0.25	(0.21)	0.11	(0.20)	−0.42*	(0.20)
Proportion of life living in the country	0.34	(0.49)	0.27	(0.39)	−0.13	(0.31)	0.20	(0.39)	0.32	(0.32)

	Model 1		Model 2		Model 3		Model 4		Model 5	
Second and third generation	−0.83***	(0.23)	−0.32+	(0.19)	−0.16	(0.15)	−0.77**	(0.25)	−0.05	(0.18)
Home country language proficiency	0.74***	(0.15)	0.84***	(0.21)	0.18	(0.23)	1.30***	(0.15)	0.63**	(0.21)
Muslim	−0.62+	(0.36)	−0.10	(0.22)	−0.22	(0.22)	−0.65+	(0.36)	0.04	(0.18)
Legal status: Has no country of residence citizenship nor permit (REF)										
Has country of residence citizenship	1.17**	(0.36)	−0.40	(0.30)	−0.07	(0.30)	0.23	(0.33)	−0.43+	(0.24)
Has country of residence permit to stay	0.45**	(0.17)	−0.47*	(0.20)	−0.17	(0.26)	−0.42*	(0.18)	−0.42*	(0.18)
New destination city	**−0.93+**	**(0.49)**	**−0.96****	**(0.31)**	**−0.40**	**(0.24)**	**−1.02***	**(0.43)**	**−0.08**	**(0.25)**
Constant	−3.60***	(0.62)	−3.20***	(0.54)	−2.68***	(0.58)	−4.80***	(0.59)	−4.31***	(0.37)
ll	−2834.99		−1840.43		−2389.19		−2275.78		−1650.65	
chi2	450.60		228.29		190.46		662.51		190.75	
N	6,350		6,350		6,350		6,350		6,350	

+ p < .10
* p < .05
** p < .01
*** p < .001

policies of integration adopted and, consequently, by whether the places of settlement are new or traditional destinations.

Engagement in political activities is not significantly affected by the context of settlement in terms of new versus traditional destination. Indeed, model 4 suggests that a significant difference concerns mainstream political activities only. However, this result is not robust (see model 4A in Table 11.A in the Appendix). Our findings suggest that while immigrants settled in new destinations seem to find obstacles to engaging in pan-immigrant organizations, they seem to have similar opportunities to participate in political activities as immigrants settled in traditional destinations. Indeed, such political activities may include all those issues related to migrants' need to contact, for instance, political authorities for questions related to housing, employment opportunities, and health issues which migrants in new destinations also require and on which they have pressing needs.

In contrast to what we expected in our core hypothesis, traditional destinations are not consistently more likely to provide greater opportunities to become politically integrated into mainstream civic and political actions. However, this does not necessarily mean that the political context plays no role. Prior research shows that contextual characteristics linked to different policies of integration in European countries are of utmost importance in shaping migrants' chances to become integrated into the civic and political sphere (González-Ferrer and Morales 2013; Koopmans et al. 2005; Morales and Pilati 2011). What our findings suggest is that the factors related to the relative novelty of immigration waves and the preparedness of recipient societies as well as their reactions to unexpected waves are not the main driving factors.

In addition to the results related to the contextual characteristics in terms of new versus traditional destinations, Table 11.2 further illustrates that there are several key individual characteristics that are highly significant in shaping immigrants' engagement in the different types of civic and political activities. Most standard SES and attitudinal predictors of political engagement for natives apply to civic and political engagement by immigrants as well. However, their effect is not equally significant across the different types of civic and political actions looked at. Being a man tends to positively affect immigrants' chances of civic engagement in pan-immigrant and ethnic organizations, although this relation does not reach standard levels of statistical significance. Having attained a higher education level positively affects political activities of any type, while being employed positively affects civic engagement in both native and pan-immigrant organizations. In contrast, being in paid work decreases immigrants' chances to engage in political nonelectoral activities in general, although this relation does not reach standard levels of statistical significance.

Age shows a curvilinear inverted-U-shaped relationship with civic engagement in native organizations and political engagement, showing that as immigrants become older they show higher probabilities to join civic and political activities, but after a certain age this positive trend is reversed.

Another common correlate of political engagement—being married or in a stable partnership—shows a positive relation to engagement in ethnic organizations. As immigrants are more likely to marry conationals instead of individuals from other ethnic groups, the marital status might not provide the same resources for migrants' political engagement as for the majority population. Having a spouse from the same ethnic group may contribute to sustaining ethnic loyalties and attachments, and therefore it is reasonable that it leads to higher probabilities of joining ethnic organizations.

Across all models, people who are interested in politics are more likely to engage in any type of civic and political activity. Interestingly, the level of social trust is not significant for most types of engagement, but it significantly decreases immigrants' chances of engagement in immigrant-related nonelectoral activities. This result suggests that social trust, that is, higher levels of trust in others, may favor cross-ethnic loyalties to natives, therefore alienating migrants from ethnic and pan-ethnic bonding ties and sustaining engagement in immigrant-related nonelectoral activities.

Turning our attention to the variables relating to the immigration experience, their impact also differs across forms of participation. On the one hand, the native-born descendants of immigrants (second and third generations) show significantly lower probabilities of engaging in native and pan-immigrant organizations, as well as mainstream nonelectoral political activities. Being a Muslim is not significantly or consistently related to either civic or political engagement. On the other hand, language proficiency is highly significant. More specifically, the better migrants speak the language of the country and city of residence, the more they engage in the civic and political activities examined. The only type of activity that is not affected by language skills is engagement in ethnic organizations, and this is a reasonable finding, given that the language of the country of origin is likely to be commonly used within these associations.

On the other hand, the length of time spent in the country has no effect on civic and political engagement, whereas holding the nationality of the country of residence and a permit to stay considerably increases the chances of involvement in native organizations. This is likely due to the attachments and loyalties toward issues relating to the residence country that holding citizenship may bring with it, as migrants are more likely to feel greater attachments to the national community once they have obtained citizenship. This is consistent with those studies showing that the citizenship regime affects electoral participation in the residence country of immigrants and ethnic minorities (González-Ferrer and Morales 2013).[10] For similar reasons, holding citizenship of the residence country decreases the chances of migrants' engagement in immigrant-related nonelectoral activities as compared to being in an unauthorized situation. In turn, having a permit to stay provides a less consistent result as it increases engagement in native organizations but it decreases the chances of engaging in any type of political activity as well as involvement in pan-immigrant organizations.[11] This may be due to the volatile and unstable situation experienced by migrants who hold a fixed-term permit to stay.

Conclusion

In this chapter we analyzed the impact of specific characteristics of the context of settlement, namely settlement in a new or in an traditional destination city, on various types of civic and political engagement of immigrant-background individuals in nine European cities. In particular, we analyzed how settling in a new or traditional destination city may affect the involvement of immigrant-origin individuals in ethnic, pan-immigrant, and native organizations as well as their engagement in mainstream and immigrant-related activities (cf. Pilati and Morales 2016). Our core hypothesis is that traditional and new cities of destination are likely to implement different integration policies and have different legislation concerning individual and collective rights granted to migrants and their descendants. Therefore, these characteristics are expected to affect civic and political engagement. In particular, traditional gateways are expected to provide more "open" political opportunity structures for immigrants' integration and participation whereas new ones are expected to be more restrictive because of a slower implementation of political integration policies, less know-how by political elites, less preparedness, and less experience with immigration flows.

Our first contribution is conceptual. We use a more fine-grained distinction among types of organizations depending on the ethnic composition of the membership and among types of political engagement. Thus, we distinguish between native, pan-immigrant, and ethnic organizations with regard to civic engagement, and between mainstream and immigrant-related activities concerning political engagement. This distinction has proved very insightful, as our results show that the contextual effect of new and traditional destinations changes depending on the type of civic and political engagement studied. In particular, the type of destination mainly significantly affects engagement in pan-immigrant organizations. This is of utmost importance. On the one hand, this is likely to have negative effects on the mobilizing impact of organizations on political engagement of migrants, as migrants are eventually going to have fewer resources for mobilization derived from pan-immigrant organizations. On the other hand, it shows that migrants, with the exclusion of pan-immigrant organizational engagement, have equally important organizational and political resources at their disposal in new and traditional destinations. However, as mentioned, this does not mean that other contextual characteristics may not be significant in shaping migrants' opportunities to participate in the civic and political sphere, in line with prior research arguing that the context of policies and legislation that afford migrants varying individual and group rights actually matters for their political inclusion (Bloemraad 2006a,b; Koopmans et al. 2005; Morales and Giugni 2011; Ramakrishnan and Bloemraad 2008a). Future research may specifically look at how other contextual conditions affect migrants' civic engagement, as this has been less studied when compared to their political engagement. Indeed, the context is not only relevant to understanding to what extent migrants engage in politics, but it also determines how useful certain resources—in our case, the multiple skills and social capital provided by associational involvement—are for political engagement. Given that involvement in associations is quite low for immigrant-background individuals across most European societies (see, e.g., Strömblad, Myrberg, and Bengtsson 2011: fig. 6.3), lack of access to these organizational resources might prove to be a considerable source of political inequality.

NOTES

1. The literature usually refers to either ethnic or cross-ethnic organizations indistinctly. Yet, because our data enable us to do fine-grained classifications, we distinguish between ethnic, pan-immigrant, and native organizations. Note that by ethnic organizations we do not mean only ethnic advocacy organizations or homeland organizations but also all other types of associations—no matter their goals—mainly composed of immigrant-background people of a single ethnic group. The latter includes sport clubs, cultural activities groups, religious associations, and so forth.

2. For the sake of language economy, we refer to "immigrants" in a general sense to include both first generations (immigrants in a proper sense) and their immediate native-born descendants, who are not immigrants but immigrant-background individuals.

3. Of course, traditional destinations vary so that those most open to collective rights—such as the multicultural contexts of Great Britain and the Netherlands—are very different from the more assimilationist France.

4. The data we employ were collected at the local level, yet we do not have enough variation between cities within single countries. Consequently, differences of contextual indicators across cities match differences across countries with the exception of Zurich and Geneva, and Madrid and Barcelona, and we cannot systematically test the effect of country-level indicators versus the impact of local-level indicators.

5. Further details on the sampling methods used in the different cities and methodological issues are found in Morales and Giugni (2011), and the technical description of the surveys is available in Palacios and Morales (2013).

6. In the few cases where respondents were involved in more than one organization of the same type (e.g., more than one environmental organization, or more than one sports club), the probing was in relation to the organization in which they were more active or to which they devoted more time.

7. See the Appendix for the detailed coding of the variables.

8. In order to accurately estimate predictors, given the multistage design employed in the survey, we estimate logit models and specify that the data are clustered by groups within cities.

9. Given that the city of Stockholm may bias the results due to the unusual high levels of involvement in native organizations (model 1) and in mainstream political action (model 4), we also run the same analyzes identifying this city with a dummy variable (see Table 11.A). The results indicate that, as suggested by Figures 11.1 and 11.2, migrants living in Stockholm have significantly higher probabilities to become involved in native organizations and in mainstream political activities, and that once this is taken into account, the difference between traditional and new destination cities ceases to be statistically significant. In any case, with a restricted number of settings, results are bound to be sensitive to individual cases when they are outliers.

10. Most of these findings, with a few exceptions, are confirmed by the separate analyses provided in Table 11.A.

11. We recognize the possibility that different immigrant groups' participation might be influenced by cultural factors specific to their countries of origin. We have maximized the variation in those origins by choosing groups for each city that have been in the country for a longer period of time, recent arrivals, and one group of Muslim religious background. While the number of countries of origin is too large to include a control variable for each, the variable that may make the largest difference in this regard—Muslim origin—is included. The small effect of this variable lends confidence to the conclusion that characteristics of particular national origin groups do not unduly influence our results. Moreover, it is unlikely that our findings are accounted for by the possibility that the mix of immigrants in traditional destination cities is systematically different from the mix of immigrants in new destination cities. In traditional destination cities we have Italians (two cities), Kosovars (two cities), Turks (two cities), Algerians, Moroccans, Tunisians, Bangladeshis, Pakistanis, Indians, and Chileans. In new destination cities we have Chinese, Hungarians, mixed Muslim nationality groups, Ecuadorans (two cities), other Latin Americans, Moroccans, Filipinos, and Egyptians. Thus, the nationality groups differ more across individual cities than between traditional versus new destination cities.

Appendix: Coding of Variables

OUTCOME VARIABLES

Engaged in at Least One Political Activity

Participation in at least one of the following extra-electoral political activities in the previous twelve months: contacted a politician; contacted a government or local government official; worked in a political party; worked in a political action group; wore or displayed a badge, sticker, or poster; boycotted certain products; deliberately bought certain products for political reasons; donated money to a political organization or group; contacted the media; contacted a lawyer or a judicial body for nonpersonal reasons.[1]

Whenever a respondent indicated that the issue fundamentally concerned the family or a few other individuals, the city, the country of residence, or the world, we considered this as indicative of *mainstream political action*. When a respondent indicated that the issue related to immigrants, we considered this indicative of *immigrant-related political action*.

Engagement in Ethnic Organizations

Engagement in at least one organization for which the respondent was currently/in the past a member of, or participated in, during the prior twelve months and in which half or more of members are of the respondent's ethnic/national origin.

Engagement in Pan-immigrant Organizations

Same as above but half or more of members are of multiple immigrant origins.

Engagement in Native or Mainstream Organizations

Same as above but half or more of members are of the majority native group in the country.[2]

TABLE 11.A   CORRELATES OF CIVIC PARTICIPATION (MODEL 1) AND OF
POLITICAL PARTICIPATION (MODEL 4). LOGIT MODELS WITH CLUSTER
OPTION (DATA CLUSTERED BY GROUP-CITY) CONTROLLING FOR THE CITY
OF STOCKHOLM

	Model 1A Engagement in Native Organizations		Model 4A Engagement in Mainstream Nonelectoral Activities	
	b	se	b	se
Male	−0.01	(0.09)	0.11	(0.08)
Age	0.05*	(0.02)	0.08***	(0.02)
Age squared	−0.00*	(0.00)	−0.00***	(0.00)
Married	−0.05	(0.11)	−0.07	(0.06)
Education	0.69***	(0.19)	1.02***	(0.20)
In paid work	0.20*	(0.09)	−0.21*	(0.09)
Interest residence country politics	0.63***	(0.09)	1.21***	(0.12)
Social trust	−0.19	(0.18)	0.11	(0.23)
Proportion of life living in the country	1.10***	(0.29)	0.86**	(0.33)
Second and third generation	−0.63***	(0.14)	−0.59***	(0.16)
Home country language proficiency	0.67***	(0.15)	1.23***	(0.17)
Muslim	−0.38+	(0.22)	−0.43+	(0.23)
Legal status: Has no country of residence citizenship nor permit (REF)				
Has country of residence citizenship	0.53**	(0.18)	−0.33	(0.24)
Has country of residence permit to stay	0.29+	(0.15)	−0.55***	(0.16)
New destination city	**−0.17**	**(0.28)**	**−0.33**	**(0.31)**
Stockholm	2.54***	(0.20)	1.94***	(0.27)
Constant	−4.52***	(0.53)	−5.64***	(0.56)
ll	−2616.43		−2155.07	
chi2	4509.61		777.33	
N	6,350		6,350	

+ p < .10
* p < .05
** p < .01
*** p < .001

PREDICTORS

Political context: 1 = new destination cities (Barcelona, Budapest, Madrid, Milan);
    0 = old destination cities (Geneva, London, Lyon, Stockholm, Zurich).
Gender: Dichotomous in which 1 = male.
Age: Continuous variable, range 15–94.

Education: The highest level of education achieved; an ordinal variable ranging from 0 to 1 (0 = not completed primary education to 1 = first and second stage of tertiary education).

In paid work: A dichotomous variable distinguishing between those in paid work, assigned a score of 1, from others.

Married: A dichotomous variable for which 1 is assigned to people who are married or live in partnership.

Social trust: An ordinal variable ranging from 0 to 10 (0 = "you can't be too careful in dealing with people"; 10 = "most people can be trusted") recoded into a 0–1 range. Given the high number of missing values, these were imputed with the mean value.

Proportion of life spent in country: The number of years since arrival is divided by the age of the respondent, and a value of 1 is assigned to all those who were born in the country.

Second and third generation: A dichotomous variable for which 1 is assigned to people born in the country identifying second and third generations.

Legal status: Categorical variable for which 1 is assigned to all respondents who have the citizenship of the country of residence, 2 to those respondents who have a permit to stay and 0 otherwise.

Muslim: Dichotomous variable for which 1 is assigned to people declaring to be of Muslim religion.

Language: A dichotomous variable for which 1 is assigned to people who speak fluently the host country language.

NOTES

1. We follow the classification proposed by Teorell, Torcal, and Montero (2007) and exclude the more contentious forms of protest, namely signing petitions, participating in demonstrations, and joining strikes.

2. List of types of organizations: A. Sports club or club for outdoor activities; B. Organization for cultural activities, tradition preserving or any hobby activities (musical, dancing, breeding, etc.); C. Political party; D. Trade union; E. Business, employers, professional or farmers' organization; F. Organization for humanitarian aid, charity, or social welfare; G. Organization for environmental protection or animal rights; H. Human rights or peace organization; I. Religious or church organization; J. Immigrants organization (e.g. organization for the support or promotion of immigrants' interests, broadly defined); K. Ethnic organization (e.g., organization primarily for the advancement of the ethnic group); L. Antiracism organization; M. Educational organization, teachers', parents, and so on; N. Youth organization (e.g., scouts, youth clubs, etc.); O. Organization for the retired/elderly; P. Women's organization; Q. Residents, housing, or neighborhood organization; R. Other org.

Conclusion

Emerging Commonalities across New and Traditional Transatlantic Destinations

STEFANIE CHAMBERS

DIANA EVANS

ABIGAIL FISHER WILLIAMSON

I t is our hope that this book has initiated a process of bridging the gap between the existing scholarly literature on new immigrant destinations in Europe and the United States. In our view, gaining greater insight into the political and policy responses to increased diversity at the local, regional, and national levels as well as new immigration patterns at the transatlantic level promises to provide a fresh perspective on immigrant integration policies. On its own, comparative research on EU nations and their experiences with contemporary immigrant integration policy is tremendously valuable. Similarly, scholarship examining state and local variation in the United States can shed light on policies and patterns of immigrant integration. Although scholars have extensively researched issues pertaining to immigrant settlement on both sides of the Atlantic, this volume has attempted to generate thoughtful analysis about variation in immigrant integration outcomes in a variety of circumstances in Europe and the United States. Our objective in bringing together a carefully selected group of transatlantic case studies has been to initiate a dialogue on how parallel processes of immigrant dispersion across varied settings affect immigrant policies and integration outcomes.

Throughout the volume we have employed the concept of "new immigrant destinations" to identify those areas in which foreign-born persons have arrived in significant numbers relatively recently. Both European and U.S. scholars have started examining these areas only in the last decade (Marrow 2005; Morales 2014; Urso and Carammia 2014; Zúñiga and Hernández-León 2005b). In bringing these literatures together, we pursued two important goals. First, we hoped to generate theoretical and practical insights about what appear to be parallel transatlantic processes and experiences. As cited in the Introduction, the volume's central ambition was to identify the factors mediating the varied outcomes across new destinations and, in so doing, contribute to the formulation of middle-level theory (Messina 2013). Second, we aspired to shed new light on the important points of intersection and divergence among the various types of new immigrant destinations.

Our starting supposition in pursuing these objectives was that many if not most of the dilemmas, trade-offs, and general political costs and benefits related to contemporary immigration across locales, regions, and countries *are* likely similar. Nevertheless, the proliferation of new immigrant destinations now allows us to consider two key dimensions of variation across these destinations. Some new destinations are experiencing unprecedented diversity while others are experiencing new forms of diversity that overlay preexisting ethnic or cultural cleavages, which we refer to in the Introduction as superdiversity. Given this variation, we can investigate how these different compositions of diversity affect outcomes. Similarly, with some new destinations located within traditional destination countries and other new destination countries adjacent to traditional destination countries, examining transatlantic new destinations allows us to consider how interrelations with "old" destinations shape outcomes in the new. In examining these interrelations between new and traditional destinations, we expected to learn whether the politics of immigrant settlement in new destinations are following a trajectory similar to that of the traditional destinations (Messina 2009). Finally, we wanted to better understand the multifaceted and complex phenomenon of immigrant integration (Freeman 2004; van Tubergen 2006), and particularly the common political contexts in which the integration process typically unfolds across the new immigrant destinations (Crul and Schneider 2010: 1250; Palidda 2009: 357).

In drawing upon examples from ten EU countries and the United States and examining four regions and twelve cities, we found that the recency of immigrant settlement does not systematically determine immigrant policies or integration outcomes. In short, the relative novelty of immigrant settlement does not appear to set new destinations on a distinct political-policy pathway. Looking across the destinations with unprecedented diversity and nascent superdiversity, we observe that immigration can present unique challenges in those superdiverse new destinations where immigrants introduce perceived barriers to linguistic or cultural preservation. In contrast, our observations on the role of interrelations with traditional destinations are decidedly more complex. Traditional destinations can shape outcomes in new destinations to the extent that the former exercise influence over institutional responses in the latter, such as the EU influencing the early migration cycle member countries or the U.S. government shaping new destination cities' responses. Nonetheless, the examples across the chapters in this volume make abundantly clear that such influence flows not only down from higher levels of government long accustomed to immigration, but also up from new destination cities and regions. Thus, while we find some evidence of policy convergence, we also emphasize the importance of attending to gaps between popular attitudes and public policies, as well as gaps between national or supranational mandates and subnational implementation. We conclude by offering suggestions for research and policy, especially emphasizing three key sets of actors in integration processes: civil society organizations, bureaucrats, and elected/party officials.

In organizing the volume, we used Gary Freeman's (1995) typology as a starting point from which to categorize the various destinations. The book opened with an examination of Ireland and Italy, two intermediate European destinations that have attracted foreign laborers since the late 1980s or early 1990s. Both chapters investigated the responses to immigration at the subnational level, with a focus on those by city bureaucrats in Dublin and by regional authorities in Veneto and Emilio-Romagna. In the case of Ireland, Erica Dobbs's chapter shed light on the limitations of bureaucratic entities in facilitating immigrant electoral incorporation. Tiziana Caponio and Francesca Campomori's chapter illuminated how the differing ideological orientations of two regions in Italy resulted in variations in integration policy implementation, thus raising broader questions about influence of national-level immigrant integration policies and regimes.

The chapters in Part II addressed the question of variation in response to immigration amidst nascent superdiversity; that is, when a significant native-born or "historical" minority population is included in the integration equation (Barker 2015). Amado Alarcón considered linguistic and socioeconomic integration trends among recent immigrants in Catalonia. He found that immigrants largely remained socially isolated due to a mismatch between employment opportunities and social mobility among immigrants who were able to master Catalan. Helen Marrow's study of the American South shed light on the changing dynamics of ethno-racial hierarches in the United States. According to Marrow, the influx of Hispanics in the South has created a dynamic whereby black-white-Hispanic divisions vary based on elite versus nonelite status and depending on the institutional context. In some cases Hispanics share a lower status category with blacks, while in other areas they occupy a more privileged position relationally with whites.

Part III included chapters set in Europe and the United States that assessed subnational immigrant dispersion to new places within traditional destinations. Claudio Holzner and Melissa Goldsmith analyzed a large dataset that examined verified turnout among registered voters across the state of Utah. They found that local context matters. Smaller localities provide a setting in which immigrants are more readily politically incorporated than in larger cities, as immigrants who have dispersed to new, rural destinations are more likely to participate in the electoral process than those in larger cities. While Holzner and Goldsmith's data do not allow us to identify the mechanisms of political incorporation in smaller communities in Utah, Rhys Andrews's chapter on immigrant dispersion to rural destinations in England underscores the important work of nongovernmental actors, and especially the role of organized religion, in integrating new immigrants. He found that although immigration may negatively affect social cohesion, active, well-resourced NGOs, such as mainline churches, can mitigate its impact.

Part IV examined two early migration cycle destinations, Poland and Latvia, which have experienced substantial immigration only since the 2000s. Both countries' nascent immigration and integration policies have been significantly shaped by EU mandates. This said, the two cases vary in that Polish society was previously homogeneous, whereas Latvia's contemporary immigration picture is complicated by the long-standing presence of a non-citizen Russian minority, which has fed popular resistance to the presence of all non-Latvians. The examples of Poland and Latvia represent the frontier of new immigrant destinations, ground that is ripe for future exploration and theorizing.

The final section of this book included three chapters that addressed the extent to which new immigrant destinations differ from traditional destinations in terms of immigrant integration. In line with the analysis presented in the Introduction, all three chapters indicated that the relative recency of immigrants' arrival to a destination does not appear to be determinative of integration policies or outcomes. Monica Varsanyi and her coauthors examined policing practices and, in so doing, discovered that there are more similarities than differences between new and traditional destinations. Melissa Marschall's study of education policy similarly revealed that new destinations are addressing the needs of LEP students as well, if not better, than traditional destinations. Finally, Katia Pilati and Laura Morales found that across nine EU cities, immigrant civic and political engagement in new and older destinations is similar, with the exception of involvement in pan-immigrant organizations. In sum, both the analysis in the Introduction and the volume's three final chapters suggest that recency of immigrant settlement does not result in systematically different outcomes in new destinations.

Role of Novelty in Shaping New Destination Outcomes

The relative "novelty" of migration to a particular destination inevitably produces challenges and opportunities with regard to immigrant integration. On the one hand, the presence of foreign-born newcomers in a new setting is likely to precipitate expected threat responses (Walker and Leitner 2011). Similarly, new destinations are unlikely to have a preexisting infrastructure to facilitate immigrant integration efforts (Waters and Jiménez 2005). On the other hand, new destinations may be initially willing to respond to immigrant needs, while the public in traditional destinations may increasingly suffer from "immigration fatigue" ("Immigrants Have Worlds to Offer" 1992), thus leading to increasingly restrictive and exclusionary responses over time. As the summary above suggests, our findings do not support either hypothesis. Certainly, immigrant integration does not happen automatically or easily in new destinations. In this vein, Dobbs (Chapter 1, this volume) aptly describes a "chicken or egg" dilemma facing new destinations in that they lack organized immigrant constituencies and also the administrative experience or infrastructure to incorporate immigrant voices. Yet, despite these real challenges, our major finding is that new destinations are not distinctly less able or willing to integrate immigrants.

Collectively, the authors identified the ways in which new immigrant destinations are able to develop social and political structures, organizations, and practices to address the challenges of diversity and achieve positive immigrant integration outcomes. Marschall found that new destination schools are more involved in outreach to limited-English proficient parents, perhaps in an effort to compensate for the lack of preexisting civic infrastructure. Likewise, Varsanyi and her colleagues discovered that new destination police departments may be slightly lagging in developing formal policies toward immigrants, yet where they have done so, policies are not systematically more restrictive. Finally, while Dobbs's "chicken or egg" dilemma would otherwise lead us to expect especially low levels of immigrant political incorporation in new destinations, Morales and Pilati found few statistically significant differences between old and new destination cities in Europe. Indeed, the only systematically different factor between the two was that new destination immigrants are less involved in pan-immigrant organizations, perhaps because these umbrella groups have yet to emerge in the newest destination cities. Taken together, these findings suggest that new destinations do not differ systematically from traditional destinations in terms of their capacity to integrate newcomers.

Likewise, the political discourse surrounding immigrants across new destinations suggests that they do not diverge systematically in terms of ideology. In Poland, many elites appear quietly accepting of immigration flows, while in Latvia a notable contingent protests the presence of immigrants. In their discussion of Italy, Caponio and Campomori illustrate how two regions with similar patterns of immigrant settlement have responded very differently to their respective newcomers, with Veneto taking a more assimilationist tack as compared to Emilio-Romagna. In the United States, many states in the South have actively championed restrictive and exclusionary policies, while, at the local level, schools and police have actively incorporated immigrants, even in new destinations. Indeed, immigrants in Utah seem to have

incorporated more successfully in smaller localities, which are less traditional destinations for immigration than large cities. These and other examples suggest that early responses to immigrants in new destinations are not
uniformly restrictive, nor are they uniformly accommodating.

Variation in Responses amid Unprecedented Diversity and Superdiversity

While the recency of immigrant settlement is not independently determinative of integration outcomes, the collective essays in this volume do suggest
that one particular type of new destination *is* likely to be particularly resistant to the presence of newcomers. In particular, wherever the preservation
of a threatened ethnic identity is a central issue, as in Latvia and Catalonia,
new forms of diversity tend to raise unique challenges. In the Introduction,
we raised the possibility that nascent superdiversity in new destinations with
preexisting ethnic or cultural cleavages could actually facilitate the immigrant integration process. Destinations with previous experience navigating
native or historical forms of diversity could have existing institutions that
would also aid in integrating diversity precipitated by an influx of foreign-
born persons (Waters and Kasinitz 2013). Meanwhile, new destinations with
no previous experience of ethnic diversity might be uniquely threatened by
the unprecedented changes precipitated by immigration (Walker and Leitner
2011). While we found some evidence pointing in this direction, on the whole,
the examples of Latvia and Catalonia suggest that new immigrant destinations are less likely to be receptive to outsiders when ethnic or linguistic
preservation is of paramount political concern. The situations in Latvia and
Catalonia run contrary to Barker's (2015: 5) finding that in cases with a linguistic dimension, an inclusionary approach to membership is possible.

Turning to the possibility that native-born diversity supports the incorporation of foreign-born diversity, we did find evidence for this claim. In the U.S.
South, for instance, Marrow demonstrated that Latino newcomers can draw on
the legacy of the African American civil rights movement in making symbolic
claims and in accessing resources available through civil rights legislation. Yet,
institutions designed to address native-born diversity may not always provide
a good fit for addressing immigrants. In Catalonia, for instance, bilingual education historically facilitated the integration of internal Spanish migrants, but
it is not consistently achieving the same ends for the foreign born.

Similarly, we found some evidence for the claim that homogeneous destinations are especially threatened by new diversity. In Poland, elites are
especially concerned about the presence of Vietnamese immigrants, though
according to Aleksandra Kazłowska and Magdalena Lesińska, this concern
has not derailed the implementation of EU-mandated integration measures.
In his research on rural England, Andrews attributes declining social

cohesion amidst greater immigrant presence to the perceived threat to the identity of rural denizens. This said, rural England appears to be capable of addressing this challenge, in that well-resourced nongovernmental organizations (here, mainline churches) can successfully mitigate an erosion of overall social cohesion. And in Utah, a new destination state, local elections and affiliation with a political party enhance immigrant political incorporation. In sum, while unprecedented diversity may present some thorny challenges, it does not appear to systematically hamper political-policy responses.

In contrast, superdiversity may present greater challenges when the preservation of a threatened linguistic and/or ethnic identity is at risk. In Latvia, the presence of a sizeable Russian population presents a perceived threat to Latvian language and culture. Likewise, in Catalonia, the increasing presence of Spanish-speaking Latin Americans presents a threat to the primacy of the Catalan language. In analyzing these societies, both Dace Akule and Alarcón identify ways in which the struggle to maintain the privileged place of Latvians in Latvia and Catalan in Catalonia presents barriers to the integration of new immigrants. Latvia represents perhaps a unique case, in which the influence of Russian migrants in Latvian society during the Soviet period has led to especially negative popular attitudes toward immigration. The continued desire to exclude noncitizen Russians makes it difficult to contemplate integrating other new immigrant groups. The examples of Latvia and Catalonia suggest that there may be unique challenges to immigrant integration in what Alarcón refers to as "a receiving context already characterized by hybridity" (Chapter 3, this volume).

Yet not all superdiverse new destinations are confronted by these challenges to the same degree. In new superdiverse destinations in which the preservation of linguistic and cultural identity is not a central concern, intergroup dynamics appear to be more complex. In the U.S. South, Marrow reveals that, at times, elite African Americans have been wary of Latino newcomers because they perceive them as a threat to their status as the predominant minority group. In recent years, however, elite African Americans and Hispanics have collaborated to address common civil rights concerns. Marrow suggests that native and foreign subordinate groups in these new destinations are likely to have greater contact, thus opening avenues for both cooperation and conflict depending on the societal class of the actors and the domain in which they interact.

Variation in Interrelations between Traditional and New Destinations

Unlike superdiversity, which seems to present distinct challenges when it takes the form of ethnic preservation, we do not find that new destinations vary systematically in their immigrant integration outcomes due to their interrelations with traditional destinations. As anticipated, the experiences of older destinations appear to provide models that the new destinations can consider adopting as they attempt to integrate new groups at the local, regional, or national level. Several contributions to this volume provide examples of the power of national and supranational institutional arrangements in shaping new destinations' political and policy responses. However, the contributions also reveal that the influence does not always flow down from traditional national or supranational authorities. To the contrary, new destination cities, states, and regions can also influence traditional immigration-receiving nations from the bottom up.

Looking first at the influence of traditional destination authorities, our early migration cycle cases of Poland and Latvia provide key examples of the EU's supranational influence. While Poland and Latvia differ in terms of their political discourse concerning immigration, they do not differ markedly in their policies. Indeed, they have adapted to the changing demographics of their labor market and the subsequent migration of workers in ways that are not radically different from traditional European destination countries. Our contributors attribute these similarities to the influence of supranational mandates associated with EU accession. Indeed, Kazłowska and Lesińska describe Poland's integration policy as strictly "top-down" (Chapter 7, this volume). EU mandates include a requirement that EU citizens be allowed to participate in local elections and have access to basic social benefits outside of their native country. In addition, state incentives to support immigrant integration are linked to financial incentives offered by the EU. In this way, EU membership is a carrot for new EU countries, offering a network of "integration best practices" that can be adopted in countries like Poland and Latvia. These EU integration policies often evolved in Europe's traditional destinations over decades. The examples of Poland and Latvia raise the question of how immigrant integration will unfold when integration policies have been "transposed" on the ground, rather than emerging within the domestic context over time.

The contributions to this volume about the American case similarly illustrate the power of national mandates in traditional destinations in shaping political and policy responses in subnational new destinations. As Marschall indicates, federal education policies provide incentives for immigrant integration by insisting that schools demonstrate testing improvement among English-language learners. But, in some ways, federal policies have also influenced both new and traditional destinations to move away from accommodating immigrants. Marschall describes how local schools have moved away from providing bilingual education in response to federal moves toward intensive English acquisition. Likewise, as Varsanyi and Marrow describe in their respective chapters, federal policies that devolve immigration enforcement to the local level through programs such as 287g and Secure Communities have empowered states to restrict immigration locally.

With these examples in mind, one might assume that interrelations between established and new destinations will typically involve the former influencing the actions of the latter. However, several examples from this volume suggest that such influence does not necessarily or automatically flow from higher levels of government to new destination countries, regions, and cities. In observing Italy's regions, Caponio and Campomori describe how Veneto's assimilationist approach to immigrant integration has been "uploaded" to the national level. In the U.S. context, while federal devolution of enforcement opened avenues for local restriction, states in the U.S. South have also developed grassroots responses to immigration that influence national reform debates, such as efforts to deter unauthorized settlement through stricter hiring, housing, and benefits practices (Varsanyi 2010a). On the side of accommodation, grassroots efforts to welcome immigrants have influenced the national debate: President Obama's recent "Federal Strategic Action Plan on Immigrant and Refugee Integration" (White House Task Force on New Americans 2015) compiles local integration efforts. As these examples suggest, influence does not flow uniformly from traditional destinations to new destinations, nor does the influence of one type of destination on another necessarily result in a more accommodating or restrictive ideological approach.

Policy Convergence or Divergent Pathways?

Given these mixed outcomes, what do the contributions to this volume suggest about the likelihood of policy convergence? Comparisons between new and traditional destinations throughout the volume suggest that policies are not systematically different in new destinations, thus suggesting convergence. By the same token, however, they reveal that even as formal policies appear to converge at the national level, they can obscure differences in political dynamics and implementation across countries. Moreover, considerable variation at the subnational level suggests that a single political-policy pathway is not inevitable.

Contrasting Poland with Latvia suggests the limits of supranational EU influence in achieving policy convergence. Though the two countries acceded to the EU at the same time, Latvia has been more reluctant to implement the EU's immigrant integration directives due to concerns about its noncitizen Russian population. Even in Poland, which has more readily adopted EU mandates, elites do not necessarily embrace the policies imposed from above. Whereas EU influence led Poland to adopt more expansive integration measures than it otherwise would have, observing the experiences of Western European nations has led Polish elites to be concerned about the challenges associated with immigrant integration.

As these examples suggest, convergent policies do not necessarily result in convergent popular attitudes or policy outcomes. In Italy, for instance, even as we see moves toward civic integrationism paralleling other European nations, Caponio and Campomori demonstrate that the implementation of these policies differs across regions. Increasingly, a similar policy language is used in documents across regions such as Veneto and Emilio-Romagna, but local understandings and uses of this language nevertheless remain different. On the whole, our findings echo Cornelius and Tsuda's (2004) "gap hypothesis," which emphasizes the chasm between immigration policy intentions and outcomes. While we see convergence in policies, public attitudes often lag behind policies, meaning that similar policies do not necessarily result in similar outcomes on the ground. These findings suggest a need to continue to examine immigration policies and integration outcomes subnationally, rather than relying solely on national typologies. As Caponio and Campomori argue, examining the local and regional levels allows scholars to identify not only the policy rhetoric around immigrant integration, but also the actual practices implemented.

Lessons from Transatlantic New Destinations

Having reviewed our findings, we now consider what we have learned about the factors that influence immigrant integration in new and traditional destinations. As the preceding discussion indicates, we have discovered that societies that feel their linguistic or cultural preservation is threatened will tend to resist integrating foreign-born newcomers. Beyond this, we found that the decisive contributor to integration outcomes was the degree to which three sets of actors engaged in immigrant integration: civil society, bureaucrats, and elected/party officials. While various institutional characteristics shape the responses of these actors, as the aforementioned gap hypothesis suggests, no policy can determine the responses of actors, since political discourse and implementation differ even in the presence of similar policies. Thus, the process of immigrant integration appears more a matter of political will than discrete, facilitating conditions. This finding calls for a closer investigation of the factors shaping political will, including citizen attitudes and party competition.

Commitment of Civil Society Organizations

Both in Europe and the United States and across varying types of new destinations, the commitment of civil society organizations is a crucial factor in determining immigrant integration outcomes. For instance, Andrews's chapter sheds light on how the engagement of mainline religious institutions in rural England diminishes the extent to which growing diversity impacts overall social cohesion. These well-resourced institutions are able to play a bridging role between the native and foreign born, thus contributing to integration efforts. Morales and Pilati similarly draw our attention to the different types of local associations and their varying roles in immigrant integration. While they highlight the bridging function of native organizations that involve immigrants, they also underscore the importance of immigrant ethnic organizations in providing social support. Lastly, they introduce an intermediate type of organization that brings immigrants of different ethnicities together in pan-immigrant groups that can lobby for shared interests. Morales and Pilati suggest that this third type of organization may be less prevalent in new destinations cities in the EU.

While this represents a rare point of divergence between new and traditional destinations, other findings from the volume indicate that supranational or national influence can be particularly powerful in shaping a convergence of civil society integration efforts. In Latvia and Poland, as well as Italy, the European Integration Fund's support for NGOs incentivized organizations to undertake integration-related projects. Likewise, in rural England, Andrews reports that the National Labour agenda of partnering with faith-based groups to achieve social ends supported immigrant integration efforts. Thus, the accumulated evidence suggests that civil society actors play a crucial role in integration efforts and are especially sensitive to national and supranational efforts to incentivize immigrant integration activities.

Commitment of Bureaucrats

Consonant with the bureaucratic incorporation literature developed in the United States (Jones-Correa 2008; Lewis and Ramakrishnan 2007; Marrow 2009b), several contributions to this volume indicate that local bureaucrats in new destinations play a central role in immigrant integration processes. As Varsanyi notes, bureaucrats often develop an early awareness of immigrants' presence as they implement their conventional duties. While not all bureaucrats are eager to accommodate immigrants, many do so out of a professional service ethic (Jones-Correa 2008; Lewis and Ramakrishnan 2007; Marrow 2009b). In the absence of civic infrastructure, their efforts may be particularly crucial in early new destination settings. For instance, Marschall reveals that U.S. schools in new destinations are particularly likely to reach out to immigrant parents, perhaps because there are fewer bridging mechanisms available to them than in more established destinations. Indeed, bureaucrats may even be involved in efforts to generate civic infrastructure for political integration. In Dublin, Dobbs finds local government officials involved in attempts to convene civil society organizations to support immigrant integration efforts, successfully creating linkages among immigrant organizations.

Bureaucratic involvement in immigrant integration efforts may be particularly influential when bureaucrats include what Marschall refers to as "cultural brokers," that is, members of the immigrant ethnic group that serve a bridging function. In American schools, for example, hiring Hispanic and black teachers contributes to the ability of a school to teach English as a second language successfully and accommodate immigrant students in other ways. On the whole, the powerful role of bureaucrats in new destinations suggests that immigrant integration could be advanced by the appointment of bureaucrats (including but not necessarily restricted to coethnics) who are especially committed to that goal. Given bureaucratic discretion in many areas, these changes could result in the allocation of resources to such areas as employment training, English language acquisition (Marrow 2009b; Marschall), and other favorable policies (Varsanyi et al.). Yet, Dobbs's exploration of bureaucrats' efforts to spur immigrant electoral involvement in Dublin also reveals the limitations of the influence of bureaucratic agents. As she explains, the electoral incorporation of immigrants can only go so far without the active intervention of political parties that are, after all, responsible for identifying candidates and contesting elections.

Commitment of Party/Elected Officials

As Dobbs's chapter suggests, while we find many examples of civil society and bureaucratic involvement in integration efforts, political parties and elected officials may be inactive or restrictive. A political party's ideology influences its inclination to accommodate or restrict. Caponio and Campomori reveal that the political stance of the dominant political party in a given region influences both the development of regional policy and the implementation of national policy. Likewise, the presence of an anti-immigrant party can strongly shape integration outcomes, as in Latvia (Akule) and Veneto (Caponio and Campomori). In Italy, the center-right party that governs Veneto has stressed assimilation, including Italian language and culture courses and, simultaneously, preservation of the local culture. In contrast, the center-left governing party of Emilia Romagna has emphasized policies of integration and multiculturalism, including worker training, Italian-language skills, and protection against discrimination.

Political parties also influence integration outcomes through their influence over electoral structures that either support or hinder immigrant political participation. In the United States, there is unrealized potential for local political parties to include immigrants on election lists. In Utah, immigrants registered with a political party are more likely to vote (Holzner and Goldsmith). That said, political parties in the United States and elsewhere do not always respond to this potential. In Ireland, for instance, parties make relatively little effort to incorporate immigrants (Dobbs). Pointing to the absence of a critical mass of immigrant voters, several of the contributions to this volume suggest that there are barriers to convincing party officials of the need to attend to immigrants. This, of course, is at the heart of Dobbs's new destination "chicken or egg dilemma." We can expect that in societies that give immigrants and their children relatively easy access to citizenship the dilemma ultimately will be solved over time; elsewhere, barriers to citizenship may produce more lasting exclusion.

Final Reflections

In this Conclusion we have attempted to glean how the recency of immigrant settlement, as well as varying compositions of diversity and differing inter-relations with traditional destinations condition the successful integration of immigrants in new destinations. One of our key findings is that in their approaches to the integration of immigrants, new and traditional destinations do not differ in clearly patterned ways. Only superdiverse new destinations with an interest in ethnic or linguistic preservation demonstrate a consistent pattern of resisting or delaying the progress of immigrant integration. On the whole, we find evidence of considerable policy convergence across new and traditional destinations with respect to integration policy. Yet convergent national policies obscure subnational variation in policies and outcomes. We find that civil society, bureaucrats, and elected/party officials play key roles in shaping immigrant integration outcomes.

For policy makers, this volume suggests that supranational incentives can spur immigrant integration among civil society and bureaucrats. Non-governmental organizations seem particularly likely to engage in integration in response to financial incentives. Likewise, policies that direct bureaucrats to serve immigrants or provide discretion for them to do so can bolster integration efforts. Seeking out coethnic bureaucrats to serve as cultural brokers in new destinations may have particularly salutary effects. Encouraging support from political parties and elected officials presents greater challenges and may happen only over time. Thus, this volume indicates that one crucial area for further research is on citizen attitudes across destinations and their relationship to parties' ideological views on immigration.

Although we are limited by the countries examined and research questions raised by the assembled chapters, the volume nevertheless addresses, for the first time, questions with which scholars on both sides of the Atlantic have been grappling independently. In so doing, we hope that the volume initiates an ongoing transatlantic dialogue about the integration of immigrants, a dialogue in which examples of both policy innovations and failures help scholars and students better understand the circumstances in which immigrants can and do become full members of their host societies.

References

Achinstein, Betty, and Julia Aguirre. 2008. "Cultural Match or Culturally Suspect: How New Teachers of Color Negotiate Sociocultural Challenges in the Classroom." *Teachers College Record* 110 (8): 1505–1540.

Agadjanian, Victor. 2001. "Religion, Social Milieu, and the Contraceptive Revolution." *Population Studies* 55 (2): 135–148.

Akdenizli, Banu, E. J. Dionne Jr., and Roberto Suro. 2008. *Democracy in the Age of New Media: A Report on the Media and the Immigration Debate.* Washington, DC: Brookings Institution and University of Southern California. http://www.brookings .edu/research/reports/2008/09/25-immigration-dionne, accessed March 22, 2015.

Akule, Dace. 2010. *Imigrācija un emigrācija priekšvēlēšanu programmās pirms 2010.gada vēlēšanām.* Riga, Latvia: Centre for Public Policy PROVIDUS. http://providus.lv /article/imigracija-un-emigracija-prieksvelesanu-programmas-pirms-2010-gada -velesanam, accessed June 3, 2014.

———. 2011. *Political Participation of Third Country Nationals on National and Local Levels: Latvian Country Report.* Riga, Latvia: Centre for Public Policy PROVIDUS. http://pdc.ceu.hu/archive/00006544/, accessed May 30, 2014.

———. 2012. "Latvian Citizenship Changes: 'Exceptions Do Not Make the Rule.' " *Index MIPEZ Blog.* December 8. http://www.mipex.eu/blog/latvian-citizenship -amendments-bring-minor-improvements-to-integration, accessed June 7, 2014.

Alarcón, Amado, and Luis Garzón, eds. 2011. *Language, Migration and Social Mobility in Catalonia.* Leiden, Netherlands: Brill Academic Publishers.

———. 2013. "Children of Immigrants and Social Mobility in Officially Bilingual Societies: The Case of Catalonia." *Spanish in Context* 10 (1): 92–113.

Alarcón, Amado, and Sònia Parella Rubio. 2013. "Linguistic Integration of the Descendants of Foreign Immigrants in Catalonia." *Migraciones Internacionales* 7 (1): 101–130.

Alesina, Alberto, and Eliana La Ferrara. 2000. "Participation in Heterogeneous Communities." *Quarterly Journal of Economics* 115 (3): 847–904.

———. 2002. "Who Trusts Others?" *Journal of Public Economics* 85:207–234.

Alexander, Michael. 2004. "Local Policies towards Migrants as an Expression of Host-Stranger Relations: A Proposed Typology." *Journal of Ethnic and Migration Studies* 29 (3): 411–430.

Alford, Robert R., and Eugene C. Lee. 1968. "Voting Turnout in American Cities." *American Political Science Review* 62 (3): 796–813.

Allport, Gordon W. 1954. *The Nature of Prejudice.* Cambridge, MA: Addison-Wesley.

Almond, Gabriel A., and Sidney Verba. 1963. *The Civic Culture: Political Attitudes and Democracy in Five Nations.* Princeton, NJ: Princeton University Press.

Alvarado, Joel, and Charles Jaret. 2009. *Building Black-Brown Coalitions in the Southeast: Four African American–Latino Collaborations.* Atlanta, GA: Southern Regional Council.

Ambrosini, Maurizio. 2004. "Il futuro in mezzo a noi: Le seconde generazioni scaturite dall'immigrazione nella società italiana dei prossimi anni." In *Seconde generazioni: Un'introduzione al futuro dell'immigrazione in Italia,* edited by Maurizio Ambrosini and Stefano Molina, 1–53. Turin, Italy: Fondazione Giovanni Agnelli. http://www.academia .edu/2293863/Seconde_generazioni_unintroduzione_al_futuro_dellimmigrazione _In_Italia, accessed July 11, 2014.

———. 2013. "Immigration in Italy: Between Economic Acceptance and Political Rejection." *International Migration and Integration* 14 (1): 175–194.

American Civil Liberties Union (ACLU). 2013. "Opposition to HB 786: RECLAIM North Carolina Act." http://www.acluofnorthcarolina.org/files/Legislative_Fact_Sheet_HB _786_.pdf, accessed September 12, 2013.

American Community Surveys. 2008–2012. https://www.census.gov/programs-surveys/ acs/, accessed July 5, 2014.

Andersen, Kristi. 2008. "Parties, Organizations, and Political Incorporation: Immigrants in Six U.S. Cities." In *Civic Hopes and Political Realities: Immigrants, Community Organizations, and Political Engagement,* edited by S. Karthick Ramakrishnan and Irene Bloemraad, 77–106. New York: Russell Sage.

———. 2010. *New Immigrant Communities: Finding a Place in Local Politics.* Boulder, CO: Lynne Rienner.

André, Stéfanie, Jaap Dronkers, and Fenella Fleischmann. 2010. "Perceptions of In-group Discrimination by First and Second Generation Immigrants from Different Countries of Origin in EU Member-States." Unpublished paper. http://www.eui.eu/Personal /Dronkers/English/Andre.pdf, accessed April 5, 2014.

Appleseed. n.d. "Local Police and Federal Immigration Enforcement." Washington, DC: Appleseed. http://appleseednetwork.org/wp-content/uploads/2012/05/Forcing-Our -Blues-into-Gray-Areas.pdf, accessed June 15, 2014.

Aptekar, Sofya. 2009. "Organizational Life and Political Incorporation of Two Asian Immigrant Groups: A Case Study." *Ethnic and Racial Studies* 32 (9): 1511–1533.

Arango, Joaquín. 2012. "Early Starters and Latecomers: Comparing Countries of Immigration and Immigration Regimes in Europe." In *European Immigrations: Trends, Structures, and Policy Implications,* edited by Marek Okólski, 45–64. Amsterdam: Amsterdam University Press.

Argyris, Chris, and Donald A. Schön. 1978. *Organizational Learning: A Theory of Action Perspective.* Reading, MA: Addison-Wesley.

Arizona v. United States. 2012. 567 US, https://www.law.cornell.edu/supremecourt/ text/11-182, accessed April 21, 2015.

Armenta, Amada. 2012. "From Sheriff's Deputies to Immigration Officers: Screening Immigrant Status in a Tennessee Jail." *Law and Policy* 34 (2): 191–210.

Aud, Susan, William Hussar, Michael Planty, and Thomas Snyder. 2010. *The Condition of Education 2010*. NCES Report 2010-028. Washington, DC: National Center for Education Statistics, U.S. Department of Education. http://nces.ed.gov/pubsearch /pubsinfo.asp?pubid=2010028, accessed April 15, 2015.

Ayón, David R. 2006. "Spanish-Language Media and Mexican Civic Participation." In *Invisible No More*, edited by Xóchitl Bada, Jonathan Fox, and Andrew Selee, 27–30. Washington, DC: Mexico Institute, Woodrow Wilson International Center for Scholars. www.wilsoncenter.org/mexico, accessed September 5, 2011.

Bada, Xóchitl, Jonathan Fox, Robert Donnelly, and Andrew Selee. 2010. *Context Matters: Latino Immigrant Civic Engagement in Nine U.S. Cities*. Reports on Latino Immigrant Civic Engagement, National Report. Washington DC: Woodrow Wilson International Center for Scholars, April.

Bada, Xóchitl, Jonathan Fox, and Andrew Selee, eds. 2006. *Invisible No More: Mexican Migrant Civic Participation in the United States*. Washington, DC: Mexico Institute, Woodrow Wilson International Center for Scholars.

Badia i Margarit, Antoni Maria. 1964. *Llengua i Cultura als Països Catalans*. Barcelona: Edicions 62.

———. 1969. "La llengua dels Barcelonins; resultats d'una enquesta sociològico-lingüística." *Col·lecció Estudis i documents* 10. Barcelona: Edicions 62.

Bagnasco, Arnaldo. 1977. *Tre Italie: La Problematica Territoriale Dello Sviluppo Italiano: Studi E Ricerche 74*. Bologna: Il mulino.

Bankston, Carl L. 2007. "New People in the New South: An Overview of Southern Immigration." *Southern Cultures* 13 (4): 24–44.

Barber, Benjamin R. 1984. *Strong Democracy: Participatory Politics for a New Age*. Berkeley: University of California Press.

Barbulescu, Roxana. Forthcoming. *The Politics of Immigrant Integration in Post-Enlargement Europe: Migrants, Co-ethnics and European Citizens in Italy and Spain*. Notre Dame, IN: University of Notre Dame Press.

Barker, Fiona. 2015. *Nationalism, Identity and the Governance of Diversity: Old Politics, New Arrivals*. Houndsmill, UK: Palgrave Macmillan.

Barreto, Matt A. 2007. "Sí Se Puede! Latino Candidates and the Mobilization of Latino Voters." *American Political Science Review* 101 (3): 425–441.

Barreto, Matt A., Gary M. Segura, and Nathan D. Woods. 2004. "The Mobilizing Effect of Majority-Minority Districts on Latino Turnout." *American Political Science Review* 98 (1): 65–75.

Barreto, Matt A., Mario Villarreal, and Nathan D. Woods. 2005. "Metropolitan Latino Political Behavior: Voter Turnout and Candidate Preference in Los Angeles." *Journal of Urban Affairs* 27 (1): 71–91.

Barreto, Matt A., and Nathan Woods. 2005. "Latino Voting Behavior in an Anti-Latino Political Context: The Case of Los Angeles County." In *Diversity in Democracy: Minority Representation in the United States*, edited by Gary M. Segura and Shaun Bowler, 148–169. Charlottesville: University of Virginia Press.

Bass, Loretta E., and Lynne M. Casper. 1999. "Are there Differences in Registration and Voting Behavior between Naturalized and Native-born Americans?" Population Division Working Paper 28. Washington, DC: U.S. Census Bureau. https://www .census.gov/population/www/documentation/twps0028/twps0028.html, accessed March 17, 2016.

————. 2001. "Impacting the Political Landscape: Who Registers and Votes among Naturalized Americans?" *Political Behavior* 23 (2): 103–130.

Bebbington, David W. 2008. *Evangelicals in Modern Britain: A History from the 1730s to
the 1980s*. London: Allen & Unwin.

Bellair, Paul E. 1997. "Social Interaction and Community Crime: Examining the Importance of Neighbor Networks." *Criminology* 35 (4): 677–703.

Benito Pérez, Ricard, and Isaac González Balletbó. 2009. "The Intensity and Nature of
Linguistic Segregation in Catalan Schools." *Noves SL. Revista de Sociolingüística*
(Winter): 1–12. http://www.gencat.cat/llengua/noves/noves/hm09hivern/docs/a
_Benito_Isaac.pdf, accessed July 5, 2016.

Benjamin-Alvarado, Jonathan, Louis DeSipio, and Celeste Montoya. 2009. "Latino Mobilization in New Immigrant Destinations: The Anti-H.R. 4437 Protest in Nebraska's
Cities." *Urban Affairs Review* 44 (5): 718–735.

Bennett, Colin J. 1991. "What Is Policy Convergence and What Causes It?" *British Journal
of Political Science* 21 (2): 215–233.

Berger, Maria, Christian Galonska, and Ruud Koopmans. 2004. "Political Integration by
a Detour? Ethnic Communities and Social Capital of Migrants in Berlin." *Journal of
Ethnic and Migration Studies* 30 (3): 491–507.

Berkeley, Rob, and Savita Vij. 2008. *Right to Divide? Faith Schools and Community Cohesion*. London: Runnymede Trust.

Bertossi, Christophe, and Jam Willem Duyvendak. 2009. "Modèles d'intégration et intégration des modèles? Une étude comparative entre la France et les Pays-Bas." *Migrations Sociétés* 21 (122): 27–37.

Beyerlein, Kraig, and John R. Hipp. 2005. "Social Capital, Too Much of a Good
Thing? American Religious Traditions and Community Crime." *Social Forces* 84
(2): 995–1013.

Bijl, Rob, and Arjen Verweij. 2012. "Measuring and Monitoring Immigrant Integration
in Europe: Facts and Views." In *Measuring and Monitoring Immigrant Integration
in Europe*, edited by Rob Bijl and Arjen Verweij, 11–42. The Hague: The Netherlands
Institute for Social Research.

Blakely, Tony A., and Alistair J. Woodward. 2000. "Ecological Effects in Multi-level Studies." *Journal of Epidemiology and Community Health* 54 (5): 367–374.

Blalock, Hubert M. 1967. *Toward a Theory of Minority-Group Relations*. London:
Wiley.

Blau, Peter M. 1977. *Inequality and Heterogeneity: A Primitive Theory of Social Structure*.
New York: Free Press.

Bleich, Erik. 2003. *Race Politics in Britain and France: Ideas and Policymaking since the
1960s*. New York: Cambridge University Press.

Bloemraad, Irene. 2005. "The Limits of de Tocqueville: How Government Facilitates
Organisational Capacity in Newcomer Communities." *Journal of Ethnic and Migration Studies* 31 (5): 865–887.

————. 2006a. *Becoming a Citizen: Incorporating Immigrants and Refugees in the United
States and Canada*. Oakland: University of California Press.

————. 2006b. "Becoming a Citizen in the United States and Canada: Structured Mobilization and Immigrant Political Incorporation." *Social Forces* 85 (2): 667–695.

Blommaert, Jan, and Jef Verschueren. 1998. *Debating Diversity: Analysing the Discourse of
Tolerance*. London: Routledge.

Blot, Richard K. 2003. *Language and Social Identity*. Westport, CT: Greenwood Publishing
Group.

Bobo, Lawrence, and Vincent L. Hutchings. 1996. "Perceptions of Racial Group Competition: Extending Blumer's Theory of Group Position to a Multiracial Social Context." *American Sociological Review* 61 (6): 951–972.

Böcker, Anita, Ines Michalowski, and Dietrich Thränhardt. 2004. "Succès et échecs des politiques d'intégration: Réévaluer les modèles allemand et néerlandais." In *Les modèles d'intégration en questions: Enjeux et perspectives*, edited by Michel Pélissier, Arthur Paecht, and Alexandre Adler, 25–46. Paris: Iris.

Bonifazi, Corrado, Salvatore Strozza, and Mattia Vitiello. 2012. "Measuring Integration in a Reluctant Immigration Country: The Case of Italy." In *Measuring and Monitoring Immigrant Integration in Europe*, edited by Rob Bijl and Arjen Verweij, 183–199. The Hague: The Netherlands Institute for Social Research.

Bonilla-Silva, Eduardo. 2004. "From Bi-Racial to Tri-Racial: Towards a New System of Racial Stratification in the USA." *Ethnic and Racial Studies* 27 (6): 931–950.

Boswell, Christina. 2009. *The Political Uses of Expert Knowledge: Immigration Policy and Social Research*. New York: Cambridge University Press.

Boswell, Christina, Andrew Geddes, and Peter Scholten. 2011. "The Role of Narratives in Migration Policy-Making: A Research Framework." *British Journal of Politics and International Relations* 13 (1): 1–11.

Boucher, Gerry. 2008. "Ireland's Lack of a Coherent Integration Policy." *Translocations* 3 (1). http://www.ucd.ie/mcri/resources/Roundtable%20Reading%201.pdf, accessed April 10, 2014.

Bousetta, Hassan. 2009. "Multinational Federalism and Immigrant Multiculturalism in Brussels." In *Immigration and Self-Government of Minority Nations*, edited by Ricard Zapata-Barrero, 87–102. Brussels: P.I.E. Peter Lang.

Bowerman, Bruce L., and Richard T. O'Connell. 1990. *Linear Statistical Models: An Applied Approach*. 2nd ed. Belmont, CA: Duxbury.

"Boycott Tropiano Hearing." 1991. *The Morning Call*, July 7. http://articles.mcall.com/1991 -07-07/news/2818931_1_hispanic-immigrants-darker-side, accessed September 5, 2013.

Boyer, Spencer P. 2009. *Learning from Each Other: The Integration of Immigrant and Minority Groups in the United States and Europe*. Washington, DC: Center for American Progress, April. http://www.americanprogress.org/issues/2009/04/pdf /immigrant_integration.pdf, accessed May 8, 2014.

Brady, Henry E., Sidney Verba, and Kay Lehman Schlozman. 1995. "Beyond SES: A Resource Model of Political Participation." *American Political Science Review* 89 (2): 271–294.

Brambor, Thomas, William R. Clark, and Matt Golder. 2006. "Understanding Interaction Models: Improving Empirical Analyses." *Political Analysis* 14 (1): 63–82.

Brands-Kehris, Ilze. 2010. "Citizenship, Participation and Representation." In *How Integrated Is Latvian Society? An Audit of Achievements, Failures and Challenges*, edited by Nils Muižnieks, 93–124. Riga: University of Latvia Advanced Social and Political Research Institute.

Brehm, Joan M., Bruce W. Eisenhauer, and Richard S. Krannich. 2004. "Dimensions of Community Attachment and Their Relationship to Well-Being in the Amenity-Rich Rural West." *Rural Sociology* 69 (3): 405–429.

Brettell, Caroline B. 2008. "'Big D': Incorporating New Immigrants in a Sunbelt Suburban Metropolis." In *Twenty-First-Century Gateways: Immigrant Incorporation in Suburban America*, edited by Audrey Singer, Susan Wiley Hardwick, and Caroline Brettell, 53–86. Washington, DC: Brookings Institution.

British Council and Migration Policy Group. 2011. *Migrant Integration Policy Index*. British Council and Migration Policy Group.

Brown, Anna, and Eileen Patten. 2014. "Statistical Portrait of the Foreign-Born Population in the United States, 2012." Pew Research Center, April 29. http://www.pewhispanic .org/2014/04/29/statistical-portrait-of-hispanics-in-the-united-states-2012/, accessed August 25, 2014.

Brown, Ralph B., Shawn F. Dorius, and Richard S. Krannich. 2005. "The Boom-Bust Recovery Cycle: Dynamics of Change in Community Satisfaction and Social Integration in Delta, Utah." *Rural Sociology* 70 (1): 28–49.

Browne, Irene, and Mary Odem. 2012. "'Juan Crow' in the Nuevo South?" *Du Bois Review: Social Science Research on Race* 9 (2): 321–337.

Browne, Irene, Beth Reingold, Mary Odem, and Anne Kronberg. 2013. "Race, Politics, and Anti-Immigration Legislation in the Nuevo South: Do African American Lawmakers Support or Oppose 'Juan Crow'?" Paper presented at the Annual Meeting of the Social Science History Association, Chicago, IL, November 21–24.

Brubaker, Rogers. 1992. *Citizenship and Nationhood in France and Germany*. Cambridge, MA: Harvard University Press.

———. 2001. "The Return of Assimilation? Changing Perspectives on Immigration and Its Sequels in France, Germany, and the United States." *Ethnic and Racial Studies* 24 (4): 531–548.

Bruce, Steve. 1995. *Religion in Modern Britain*. Oxford: Oxford University Press.

Buckley, David T. 2013. "Citizenship, Multiculturalism and Cross-National Muslim Minority Public Opinion." *West European Politics* 36 (1): 150–175.

Bueker, Catherine Simpson. 2005. "Political Incorporation among Immigrants from Ten Areas of Origin: The Persistence of Source Country Effects." *International Migration Review* 39 (1): 103–140.

Bullock, Charles S., III. 1990. "Turnout in Municipal Elections." *Policy Studies Review* 9 (3): 539–549.

Burgess, Richard. 2009. "African Pentecostal Spirituality and Civic Engagement: The Case of the Redeemed Church of God in Britain." *Journal of Beliefs and Values* 30 (3): 255–273.

Bursick, Robert J. 1988. "Social Disorganization and Theories of Crime and Delinquency: Problems and Prospects." *Criminology* 26 (4): 519–551.

Caponio, Tiziana. 2005. "Policy Networks and Immigrants' Associations in Italy: The Cases of Milan, Bologna and Naples." *Journal of Ethnic and Migration Studies* 31 (5): 931–950.

———. 2010. "Grassroots Multiculturalism in Italy: Milan, Bologna and Naples Compared." In *The Local Dimension of Migration Policymaking*, edited by Tiziana Caponio and Maren Borkert, 57–84. Amsterdam: Amsterdam University Press.

———. 2012. "Theories of Multiculturalism Italian Style: Soft or Weak Recognition?" In *Challenging Multiculturalism: European Models of Diversity*, edited by Ray Taras, 216–235. Edinburgh: Edinburgh University Press.

Caponio, Tiziana, and Maren Borkert. 2010. *The Local Dimension of Migration Policymaking*. IMISCOE Report. Amsterdam: Amsterdam University Press.

Caponio, Tiziana, and Paolo R. Graziano. 2011. "Towards a Security-Oriented Migration Policy Model? Evidence from the Italian Case." In *Migration and Welfare in the New Europe: Social Protection and the Challenges of Integration*, edited by Emma Carmel, Alfio Cerami, and Theodoros Papadopoulos, 105–120. Bristol, UK: Policy Press.

Caponio, Tiziana, Alistair Hunter, and Stijn Verbeek. 2015. "(De)constructing Expertise: Comparing Knowledge Utilization in the Migrant Integration 'Crisis.'" *Journal of Comparative Policy Analysis: Research and Practice* 17 (1): 26–40.

Caren, Neal. 2007. "Big City, Big Turnout? Electoral Participation in American Cities." *Journal of Urban Affairs* 29 (1): 31–46.

Caritas Italiana. 2011. *Dossier Statistico Immigrazione Caritas-Migrantes 2011.* Rome: Caritas Italiana.

Castles, Stephen, Maja Korac, Ellie Vasta, and Steven Vertovec. 2002. *Integration: Mapping the Field.* London: Home Office Immigration Research and Statistics Service. http://forcedmigrationguide.pbworks.com/w/page/7447907/Integration%3A%20Mapping%20the%20Field, accessed April 11, 2014.

Castles, Stephen, and Mark J. Miller. 2003. *The Age of Migration: International Population Movements in the Modern World.* 3rd ed. New York: Guilford Press.

CCES (Cooperative Congressional Election Study). 2012. http://projects.iq.harvard.edu/cces/home, accessed July 15, 2014.

Central Bureau of Statistics, Latvia. n.d. http://www.csb.gov.lv/, accessed June 3, 2013.

———. 2016. "CNA31: Population by Country of Birth, County and Year 1981–2006." Online StatBank, Census Time Series, Usual Residence and Place of Birth. http://www.cso.ie/en/databases/, accessed July 22, 2016.

Centro de Investigaciones Sociológicas. 2012. *Barómetro autonómico (III).* Madrid: http://www.cis.es/cis/export/sites/default/-Archivos/Marginales/2940_2959/2956/Es2956_mapa_pdf.html, accessed January 28, 2014.

Chakraborti, Neil, and Jon Garland, eds. 2004. *Rural Racism.* Cullompton, UK: Willan.

Chapa, Jorge, and Belinda De La Rosa. 2004. "Latino Population Growth, Socioeconomic and Demographic Characteristics, and Implications for Educational Attainment." *Education and Urban Society* 36 (2): 130–149.

Chaves, Mark. 2004. *Congregations in America.* Cambridge, MA: Harvard University Press.

Chavez, Jorge M., and Doris Marie Provine. 2009. "Race and the Response of State Legislatures to Unauthorized Immigrants." *Annals of the American Academy of Political and Social Science* 623 (1): 78–92.

Chavez, Sergio. 2005. "Community, Ethnicity, and Class in a Changing Rural California Town." *Rural Sociology* 70 (3): 314–335.

Chen, Chen-Su. 2011. *Public Elementary and Secondary School Student Enrollment and Staff Counts from the Common Core of Data: School Year 2009–2010. First Look.* NCES Report 2011-347. Washington, DC: National Center for Education Statistics, U.S. Department of Education.

Chen, Ming Hsu. 2012. *Where You Stand Depends on Where You Sit: Bureaucratic Incorporation of Immigrants in Federal Workplace Agencies.* SSRN Scholarly Paper 33. Rochester, NY: Berkeley Journal of Employment and Labor Law. http://papers.ssrn.com/abstract=2019181, accessed April 1, 2015.

Chiba, Yuko. 2010. "Educational Integration in a Divided Society: Lived Experiences of Settled Immigrants in Northern Ireland." *Translocations: Migration and Social Change* 6 (2). http://www.translocations.ie/docs/v06i02/Vol%206%20Issue%202%20-%20Peer%20review%20-%20Chiba.pdf, accessed May 4, 2014.

Church Urban Fund. 2008. *Believing in Local Action.* London: Church Urban Fund.

Cinalli, Manlio, and Marco Giugni. 2011. "Institutional Opportunities, Discursive Opportunities and the Political Participation of Migrants in European Cities." In *Social Capital, Political Participation and Migration in Europe,* edited by Laura Morales and Marco Giugni, 43–62. New York: Palgrave.

Cloke, Paul, Mark Goodwin, Paul Milbourne, and Chris Thomas. 1995. "Deprivation, Poverty and Marginalisation in Rural Lifestyles in England and Wales." *Journal of Rural Studies* 11 (4): 351–365.

Coenders, Marcel, and Peer Scheepers. 1998. "Support for Ethnic Discrimination in the Netherlands 1979–1993: Effects of Period, Cohort, and Individual Characteristics." *European Sociological Review* 14 (4): 405–422.

Coleman, James S. 1994. *Foundations of Social Theory*. Cambridge, MA: Harvard University Press.

Coleman, Mathew. 2012. "The 'Local' Migration State: The Site-Specific Devolution of Immigration Enforcement in the US South." *Law and Policy* 34 (2): 159–190.

Colombo, Asher, and Giuseppe Sciortino. 2004. "Italian Immigration: The Origins, Nature and Evolution of Italy's Migratory Systems." *Journal of Modern Italian Studies* 9 (1): 49–70.

Contreras, A. Reynaldo. 2002. "The Impact of Immigration Policy on Education Reform Implications for the New Millennium." *Education and Urban Society* 34 (2): 134–155.

Cook, Nancy. 2014. "Was Utah's Much-Heralded Immigration Law All It Promised?" *Atlantic Monthly*, April 16.

Cornelius, Wayne A., and Takeyuki Tsuda. 2004. "Controlling Immigration: The Limits of Government Intervention." In *Controlling Immigration: A Global Perspective*, 2nd ed., edited by Wayne A. Cornelius, Takeyuki Tsuda, Phillip L. Martin, and James F. Hollifield, 3–48. Palo Alto, CA: Stanford University Press.

Cotter, David A. 2004. "Communities of Work: Rural Restructuring in Local and Global Contexts." *Rural Sociology* 69 (4): 581–584.

Council of the European Union. 2004a. "Common Basic Principles for Immigrant Integration Policy in the European Union." Press release, 2618th Council Meeting. Brussels: Justice and Home Affairs. http://www.consilium.europa.eu/uedocs/cms_data/docs/pressdata/en/jha/82745.pdf, accessed April 12, 2014.

———. 2004b. *The Hague Programme: Strengthening Freedom, Security and Justice in the European Union*. Council Document 16054/04 JAI559. Brussels.

Countryside Agency. 2000. *The State of the Countryside, 2000*. London: Countryside Agency.

Crowley, Martha, and Daniel T. Lichter. 2009. "Social Disorganization in New Latino Destinations?" *Rural Sociology* 74 (4): 573–604.

Crul, Maurice, and Jens Schneider. 2010. "Comparative Context Integration Theory: Participation and Belonging in Europe's Large Cities." *Journal of Ethnic and Racial Studies* 34 (4): 1249–1268.

CSO (Central Statistics Office). 2008. *Census 2006. Non-Irish Nationals Living In Ireland*. Dublin: CSO. http://www.cso.ie/en/census/census2006reports/non-irishnationalslivinginireland/, accessed September 5, 2013.

———. 2016. "CNA31: Population by Country of Birth, County and Year 1981–2006." Online StatBank, Census Time Series, Usual Residence and Place of Birth. http://www.cso.ie/en/databases/, accessed July 22, 2016.

Dahl, Robert A. (1961) 2005. *Who Governs? Democracy and Power in an American City*. 2nd ed. New Haven, CT: Yale University Press.

Daniel-White, Kimberly. 2002. "Reassessing Parent Involvement: Involving Language Minority Parents in School Work at Home." *Working Papers in Educational Linguistics* 18 (1): 29–49.

Davis, Andrew. 2009. "Multi-nation Building? Immigrant Integration Policies in the Autonomous Communities of Catalonia and Madrid." In *Citizenship Policies in the Age of Diversity: Europe at the Crossroads*, edited by Ricard Zapata-Barrero, 137–155. Barcelona: Fundació CIDOB.

Dawney, Leila. 2008. "Racialisation of Central and East European Migrants in Hereford-shire." Working Paper 53. Brighton, UK: Sussex Centre for Migration Research.

DCC (Dublin City Council). 2008. "Migrant Voters Campaign." Press release. Dublin City Council, Office of the Mayor.

DECLG (Department of the Environment, Community, and Local Government). 2013. *Referendum Results, 1937–2014.* Dublin: DECLG. http://www.environ.ie/en /LocalGovernment/Voting/Referenda/PublicationsDocuments/FileDown Load,1894,en.pdf, accessed July 15, 2016.

Deeb-Sossa, Natalia. 2013. *Doing Good: Racial Tensions and Workplace Inequalities at a Community Clinic in El Nuevo South.* Tucson: University of Arizona Press.

de Graauw, Els. 2008. "Nonprofit Organizations and the Contemporary Politics of Immi-grant Incorporation in San Francisco." Ph.D. diss., University of California, Berkeley.

De la Garza, Rodolfo O., Martha Menchaca, and Louis DeSipio, eds. 1994. *Barrio Ballots: Latino Politics in the 1990 Elections.* Boulder, CO: Westview.

Department for Communities and Local Government. 2007. *Best Value User Satisfaction Surveys 2006–07.* London: Department for Communities and Local Government.

———. 2008a. *Face to Face and Side by Side: A Framework for Partnership in Our Multi-Faith Society.* London: HMSO.

———. 2008b. *National Indicators for Local Authorities and Local Authority Partnerships: Handbook of Definitions.* London: Department for Communities and Local Govern-ment.

———. 2011. *International Migration and Rural Economies.* London: Department for Com-munities and Local Government.

Department of Homeland Security. 2013. *DHS Budget-in-Brief FY 2013.* Department of Homeland Security. http://www.dhs.gov/dhs-budget, accessed March 30, 2015.

DeSipio, Louis. 2001. "Building America, One Person at a Time: Naturalization and Politi-cal Behavior of the Naturalized in Contemporary American Politics." In *E Pluribus Unum: Contemporary and Historical Perspectives on Immigrant Political Incorpora-tion,* edited by Gary Gerstle and John Mollenkopf, 67–106. New York: Russell Sage.

Diani, Mario, and Doug McAdam, eds. 2003. *Social Movements and Networks: Relational Approaches to Collective Action.* Oxford: Oxford University Press.

Díaz McConnell, Eileen. 2008. "The US Destinations of Contemporary Mexican Immi-grants." *International Migration Review* 42 (4): 767–802.

Diena. 2012. "Pētnieki uzsver saziņas nozīmi ar Latvijas iedzīvotājiem ārvalstīs." Novem-ber 7. http://dzirkstele.diena.lv/lietotaju-raksti/petnieki-uzsver-sazinas-nozimi-ar -latvijas-iedzivotajiem-arvalstis-3792, accessed January 20, 2015.

Di Paolo, Antonio, and Josep Lluís Raymond. 2010. "Language Knowledge and Earnings in Catalonia." Working Paper XREAP20107. Xarxa de Referència en Economia Apli-cada (XREAP), revised July.

Donato, Katharine M., Melissa Stainback, and Carl L. Bankston, III. 2006. "The Economic Incorporation of Mexican Immigrants in Southern Louisiana: A Tale of Two Cities." In *New Destinations: Mexican Immigration to the United States,* edited by Victor Zúñiga and Rubén Hernández-León, 76–100. New York: Russell Sage.

Donato, Katherine M., Charles M. Tolbert, Alfred Nucci, and Yukio Kawano. 2007. "Recent Immigrant Settlement in the Nonmetropolitan United States: Evidence from Internal Census Data." *Rural Sociology* 72 (4): 537–559.

———. 2008. "Changing Faces, Changing Places: The Emergence of New Nonmetropolitan Immigrant Gateways." In *New Faces in New Places: The Changing Geography of Amer-ican Immigration,* edited by Douglas S. Massey, 75–98. New York: Russell Sage.

Douglas, Karen Manges, and Rogelio Sáenz. 2013. "The Criminalization of Immigrants and the Immigration-Industrial Complex." *Daedalus* 142 (3): 199–227.

Drbohlav, Dušan. 2009. "Determinants of Migration." In *Experiencing Immigration: Comparative Analysis of the Czech Republic, Hungary and Poland*, edited by Dušan Drbohlav, Ágnes Hárs, and Izabela Grabowska-Lusińska. IDEA Working Paper 14, July. http://www.6fp.uw.edu.pl/pliki/WP14_Experiencing_immigration.pdf, accessed May 12, 2013.

———. 2012. "Patterns of Immigration in the Czech Republic, Hungary, and Poland." In *European Immigrations: Trends, Structures, and Policy Implications*, edited by Marek Okólski, 180–209. Amsterdam: Amsterdam University Press.

Drinkwater, Stephen, John Eade, and Michal Garapich. 2009. "'Poles Apart'? EU Enlargement and the Labour Market Outcomes of Immigrants in the UK." *International Migration* 47 (1): 161–190.

Duchón, Deborah A., and Arthur D. Murphy. 2001. "Introduction: From Patrones and Caciques to Good Ole Boys." In *Latino Workers in the Contemporary South*, edited by Arthur D. Murphy, Colleen Blanchard, and Jennifer A. Hill, 1–9. Athens: University of Georgia Press.

Dustmann, Christian, Maria Casanova, Michael Fertig, Ian Preston, and Christoph Schmidt. 2003. *The Impact of EU Enlargement on Migration Flows*. Home Office Online Report 25/03. London: Home Office Research, Development and Statistics Directorate.

Duszczyk, Maciej, and Magdalena Lesińska. 2010. "Migration Policy in Poland: Towards a Migration Doctrine." In *Immigration to Poland: Policy, Employment, Integration*, edited by Izabela Grabowska-Lusinska, Marek Okólski, Magdalena Lesinska, and Agata Górny, 57–61. Warsaw: Scholar Publishing House.

Eade, John, Stephen Drinkwater, and Michal P. Garapich. 2006. *Class and Ethnicity: Polish Migrant Workers in London*. Guildford: CRonEM, University of Surrey. http://www.surrey.ac.uk/cronem/files/POLISH_FINAL_RESEARCH_REPORT_WEB.pdf, accessed August 14, 2013.

Eagly, Ingrid V. 2013. "Criminal Justice for Noncitizens: An Analysis of Variation in Local Enforcement." *New York University Law Review* 88 (4): 1126–1223.

Earnest, David C. 2006. "Neither Citizen nor Stranger: Why States Enfranchise Resident Aliens." *World Politics* 58 (2): 242–275.

Elder, Glen H., Jr., and Rand D. Conger. 2000. *Children of the Land: Adversity and Success in Rural America*. Chicago, IL: University of Chicago Press.

Ēlerte, Sarmīte. 2013. "Nepilsoņu kongresa marginālās spēles. *Delfi*, March 24. http://www.delfi.lv/news/comment/comment/sarmite-elerte-nepilsonu-kongresa-marginalas-speles.d?id=43171826, accessed May 5, 2013.

Elmore, Richard F. 1979. "Backward Mapping: Implementation Research and Policy Decisions." *Political Science Quarterly* 94 (4): 601–616.

Engbersen, Godfried, Arjen Leerkes, Izabela Grabowska-Lusinska, Erik Snel, and Jack Burgers. 2013. "On the Differential Attachments of Migrants from Central and Eastern Europe: A Typology of Labour Migration." *Journal of Ethnic and Migration Studies* 39 (6): 959–981.

Engbersen, Godfried, and Erik Snel. 2013. "Liquid Migration: Dynamic and Fluid Patterns of Post-Accession Migration Flows." In *Mobility in Transition: Migration Patterns after EU Enlargement*, edited by Birgit Glorius, Izabela Grabowska-Lusinska, and Aimee Kuvik, 21–40. Amsterdam: Amsterdam University.

Engbersen, Godfried, Erik Snel, and Jan de Boom. 2010. "'A Van Full of Poles': Liquid Migration from Central and Eastern Europe." In *A Continent Moving West?*, edited by Richard Black, Godfried Engbersen, Marek Okólski, and M. C. Pantiru, 115–140. Amsterdam: Amsterdam University Press.

Epp, Charles R. 2010. *Making Rights Real*. Chicago, IL: University of Chicago Press.

Erie, Steven P. 1988. *Rainbow's End: Irish-Americans and the Dilemmas of Urban Machine Politics, 1840–1985*. Oakland: University of California Press.

Eriksen, Thomas Hylland. 2006. "Diversity versus Difference: Neo-liberalism in the Minority Debate." In *The Making and Unmaking of Difference*, edited by Richard Rottenburg, Burkhard Schnepel, Shingo Shimada, 13–36. Bielefeld, Germany: Transaction.

Escandell, Xavier, and Alin M. Ceobanu. 2010. "Nationalisms and Anti-Immigrant Sentiment in Spain." *South European Society and Politics* 15 (2): 157–179.

European Commission. 2005. *Special Eurobarometer: Social Values, Science and Technology*. European Commission. http://ec.europa.eu/public_opinion/archives/ebs/ebs_225_report_en.pdf, accessed September 14, 2011.

———. 2007. *Eurobarometer 217: Intercultural Dialogue in Europe: Analytical Report*. Brussels: European Commission, November.

———. 2012. *Eurobarometer 393: Discrimination in the EU in 2012*. Brussels: European Commission, November.

———. 2013. *Eurobarometer 80: Public Opinion in the European Union*. Brussels: European Commission, December.

European Ministerial Conference on Integration. 2010. Zaragoza, Spain. http://ec.europa.eu/ewsi/UDRW/images/items/docl_13055_519941744.pdf, accessed April 20, 2014.

European Union Agency for Fundamental Rights. 2005. *Majorities' Attitudes towards Migrants and Minorities: Key Findings from the Eurobarometer and the European Social Survey*. Report Summary. European Union Agency for Fundamental Rights. http://fra.europa.eu/en/publication/2005/majorities-attitudes-towards-migrants-and-minorities-key-findings-eurobarometer-a-0, accessed July 7, 2015.

European Website on Integration. 2013. http://ec.europa.eu/ewsi/en/news/newsdetail.cfm?ID_ITEMS=37631, accessed May 28, 2013.

Faist, Thomas. 2009. "Diversity: A New Mode of Incorporation?" *Ethnic and Racial Studies* 32 (1): 171–190.

Fanning, Bryan, ed. 2007. *Immigration and Social Change in the Republic of Ireland*. Manchester, UK: Manchester University Press.

———. 2009. *New Guests of the Irish Nation*. Dublin: Irish Academic Press.

Fanning, Bryan, and Fidéle Mutwarasibo. 2007. "Nationals/Non-Nationals: Immigration, Citizenship and Politics in the Republic of Ireland." *Ethnic and Racial Studies* 30 (3): 439–460.

Fanning, Bryan, Fidéle Mutwarasibo, and Neitah Chadamoyo. 2003. *Positive Politics: Participation of Immigrants and Ethnic Minorities in the Electoral Process*. Dublin: Africa Solidarity Centre. http://www.ucd.ie/mcri/resources/PositivePolitics-03pdf.pdf, accessed June 10, 2014.

Fanning, Bryan, Jo Shaw, Jane-Ann O'Connell, and Marie Williams. 2007. *Irish Political Parties, Immigration and Integration in 2007*. Dublin: University College Dublin. http://www.ucd.ie/mcri/Political%20Parties,%20Immigration%20and%20Integration.pdf, accessed April 22, 2015.

Farnell, Richard, Jill Hopkinson, David Jarvis, Jeremy Martineau, and Jane Ricketts Hein. 2006. *Faith in Rural Communities: Contributions of Social Capital to Community Vibrancy*. Stoneleigh Park, UK: Acora.

Faßmann, Heinz, and Ursula Reeger. 2012. "Old Immigration Countries: The Concept and Empirical Examples." In *European Immigrations: Trends, Structures, and Policy Implications*, edited by Marek Okólski, 65–90. Amsterdam: Amsterdam University Press.

Favell, Adrian. 2001. *Philosophies of Integration: Immigration and the Idea of Citizenship in France and Britain*. New York: Palgrave Macmillan.

Fennelly, Katherine. 2008. "Prejudice toward Immigrants in the Midwest." In *New Faces in New Places: The Changing Geography of American Immigration*, edited by Douglas Massey, 151–178. New York: Russell Sage.

Fennema, Meindert. 2004. "The Concept and Measurement of Ethnic Community." *Journal of Ethnic and Migration Studies* 30 (3): 429–447.

Fennema, Meindert, and Jean Tillie. 1999. "Political Participation and Political Trust in Amsterdam: Civic Communities and Ethnic Networks." *Journal of Ethnic and Migration Studies* 25 (4): 703–726.

———. 2001. "Civic Community, Political Participation and Political Trust of Ethnic Groups." *Connections* 24:26–41.

Fernández-Huertas Moraga, Jésus, and Ada Ferrer-i-Carbonell. 2007. "Immigration in Catalonia." Unpublished paper. http://www.iae.csic.es/specialMaterial/a8263153727sp5537.pdf, accessed April 20, 2014.

Ferris, Emily. 2012. "Local Latino Elected Officials' Leadership Behavior: Policy Positions and Concerns." Paper presented at Southern Political Science Association Conference, New Orleans, LA, January 12–14.

Fihel, Agnieszka, Agata Górny, Aleksandra Grzymała-Kazłowska, Ewa Kępińska, and Piekut Aneta. 2007. "Od zbiorowości do społeczności: rola migrantów osiedleńczych w tworzeniu się społeczności imigranckich w Polsce." CMR Working Paper 27/(85). Warsaw: CMR.

Finifter, Ada, and Paul R. Abramson. 1975. "City Size and Feelings of Political Competence." *Political Opinion Quarterly* 39 (2): 842–868.

Fishman, Joshua A. 1991. *Reversing Language Shift: Theoretical and Empirical Foundations of Assistance to Threatened Languages*. Bristol, UK: Multilingual Matters.

Fix, Michael, Jeffrey S. Passel, and Jorge Ruiz de Velasco. n.d. "School Reform: The Demographic Imperative and Challenge." Unpublished manuscript. http://www.iza.org/conference_files/iza_ui_2004/fix.pdf, accessed April 20, 2015.

Fleury-Steiner, Ben, and Jamie Longazel. 2010. "Neoliberalism, Community Development, and Anti-Immigrant Backlash in Hazleton, Pennsylvania." In *Taking Local Control: Immigration Policy Activism in US Cities and States*, edited by Monica Varsanyi, 157–172. Stanford, CA: Stanford University Press.

Ford, Robert, and Matthew J. Goodwin. 2014. *Revolt on the Right: Explaining Support for the Radical Right in Britain*. New York: Routledge.

Fortuny, Karina, Ajay Chaudry, and Paul Jargowsky. 2010. "Immigration Trends in Metropolitan America, 1980–2007." Brief No. 1. Washington, DC: Urban Policy Institute. http://www.urban.org/uploadedpdf/412273-immigration-trends-in-metro-america.pdf, accessed October 20, 2012.

Fox, Cybelle, and Thomas A. Guglielmo. 2012. "Defining America's Racial Boundaries: Blacks, Mexicans, and European Immigrants." *American Journal of Sociology* 118 (6): 1753–1763.

Francis, Leslie J. 2008. "Family, Denomination, and the Adolescent World View: An Empirical Enquiry among 13- to 15- Year-old Girls in England and Wales." *Marriage and Family Review* 43 (3–4): 185–204.

Francis, Leslie J., and David W. Lanksheart. 1992. "The Rural Rectory: The Impact of Resident Priest on Local Church Life." *Journal of Rural Studies* 8 (1): 97–103.

Fraser, Cait, Henry Jackson, Fiona Judd, Angela Komiti, Garry Robins, Greg Murray, John Humphrys, Pip Pattison, and Gene Hodgins. 2005. "Changing Places: The Impact of Rural Restructuring on Mental Health in Australia." *Health and Place* 11 (2): 157–171.

Freeman, Gary P. 1995. "Modes of Immigration Politics in Liberal Democratic States." *International Migration Review* 24 (4): 881–902.

———. 2004. "Immigrant Incorporation in Western Democracies." *International Migration Review* 28 (3): 945–969.

Friedkin, Noah E. 2004. "Social Cohesion." *Annual Review of Sociology* 30:409–425.

Funacja Energia dla Europy. 2013. *Imigranci Pilnie Potrzebni*. Warsaw: Fundacja Energia dla Europy. http://fede.org.pl/wp-content/uploads/2013/03/raport-08-26.021.pdf, accessed January 26, 2014.

Furbey, Robert, Adam Dinham, Richard Farnell, Doreen Finneron, and Guy Wilkinson. 2006. *Faith as Social Capital: Connecting or Dividing*. York, UK: Joseph Rowntree Foundation.

Fussell, Elizabeth. 2010. "Sources of Pro-Immigrant Sentiment: The Reception of Latino Immigrants in New Orleans after Hurricane Katrina." Paper presented at the Annual Meeting of the American Sociological Association, Atlanta, GA, August 14.

Gal, Susan, and Kathryn A. Woolard. 1995. "Constructing Languages and Publics: Authority and Representation." *Pragmatics* 5 (2): 129–138.

Gans, Herbert J. 1992. "Second-generation Decline: Scenarios for the Economic and Ethnic Futures of the Post-1965 American Immigrants." *Ethnic and Racial Studies* 15 (2): 173–192.

———. 2012. "'Whitening' and the Changing American Racial Hierarchy." *Du Bois Review: Social Science Research on Race* 9 (2): 267–279.

Ganz, Marshall. 2011. "Public Narrative, Collective Action, and Power." In *Accountability through Public Opinion*, edited by Sina Odugbemi and Taeku Lee, 273–289. Washington, DC: The World Bank.

Garzón, Luis, and Amado Alarcón. 2008. "Second Generation Argentinean Migrants in Catalonia: Ethnic Mobility and Mobilization." *Comparative Sociology* 7 (4): 434–456.

Gay, Claudine. 2001. "The Effect of Black Congressional Representation on Political Participation." *American Political Science Review* 95 (3): 589–602.

General Assembly of North Carolina. 2013. House Bill 786: RECLAIM NC Act. April 11. http://www.ncleg.net/Sessions/2013/Bills/House/PDF/H786v1.pdf, accessed December 4, 2014.

Gerber, Alan S., Donald P. Green, and Ron Shachar. 2003. "Voting May Be Habit-Forming: Evidence from a Randomized Field Experiment." *American Journal of Political Science* 47 (3): 540–550.

Gibson, Campbell, and Kay Jung. 2006. "Historical Census Statistics on the Foreign-born Population of the United States: 1850 to 2000." Working Paper 81. Washington, DC: U.S. Census Bureau, Population Division.

Gill, Hannah. 2010. *The Latino Migration Experience in North Carolina: New Roots in the Old North State*. Chapel Hill: University of North Carolina Press.

Gilligan, Chris, Paul Hainsworth, and Aidan McGarry. 2014. "Fractures, Foreigners and Fitting in: Exploring Attitudes towards Immigration and Integration in Northern Ireland." In *Migration and Divided Societies*, edited by Chris Gilligan and Susan Ball, 101–117. London: Routledge.

Givens, Terri E. 2014. "Nationalism versus Multiculturalism: European Identity and the Impact of the Radical Right on Antidiscrimination Policy in Europe." In *Europe's Contending Identities: Supranationalism, Ethnoregionalism, Religion, and New Nationalism*, edited by Andrew C. Gould and Anthony M. Messina, 203–218. New York: Cambridge University Press.

Glanton, Dahleen. 2001. "Changing Demographics Force South to Confront Prejudices." *Chicago Tribune*, March 18. http://www.highbeam.com/doc/1G1-121185071.html, accessed January 20, 2015.

Gleeson, Shannon, and Roberto G. Gonzales. 2012. "When Do Papers Matter? An Institutional Analysis of Undocumented Life in the United States." *International Migration* 50 (4): 1–19.

Goerres, Achim. 2007. "Why Are Older People More Likely to Vote? The Impact of Ageing on Electoral Turnout in Europe." *British Journal of Politics and International Relations* 9 (1): 90–121.

Goldsmith, Melissa, and Claudio A. Holzner. 2014. "Foreign-Born Voting Behavior in Local Elections: Evidence from New Immigrant Destinations." *American Politics Research* 58 (April): 1–32.

Golubeva, Marija, Iveta Kažoka, and Anda Rozukalne. 2007. *Shrinking Citizenship: Analytical Report on the Monitoring of Printed Media, Parliamentary Debates and Legislative Initiative Concerning Civic Participation in Latvia*. Riga, Latvia: Centre for Public Policy PROVIDUS, http://providus.foo.lv/public/27124.html, accessed January 10, 2015.

González, M. Jesús, and M. Luisa de Lázaro y Torres. 2005. "La Localización de la Inmigrante en España a través del Censo de la Población del 2001: Principales Características." *Cuadernos Geográficos* 36 (1): 35–49.

González-Ferrer, Amparo, and Laura Morales. 2013. "Do Citizenship Regimes Shape Political Incorporation? Evidence from Four European Cities." *European Political Science* 12:455–466.

Gordon, Daniel N. 1970. "Immigrants and Municipal Voting Turnout: Implications for the Changing Ethnic Impact on Urban Politics." *American Sociological Review* 38 (4): 665–681.

Gore, Sarah. 2002. "The Catalan Language and Immigrants from Outside the European Union." *International Journal of Iberian Studies* 15 (2): 91–102.

Górny, Agata, Izabela Grabowski-Lusińska, Magdalena Lesińska, and Marek Okólski, eds. 2009. *Poland: Becoming a Country of Sustained Immigration*. IDEA Working Paper 10, May. http://www.idea6fp.uw.edu.pl/pliki/WP10_Poland.pdf, accessed May 18, 2013.

Goździak, Elzbieta M., and Micah N. Bump, eds. 2008. *New Immigrants, Changing Communities: Best Practices for a Better America*. Lanham, MD: Lexington Books.

Goździak, Elzbieta M., and Susan F. Martin. 2005. *Beyond the Gateway: Immigrants in a Changing America*. Lanham, MD: Lexington Books.

Grabowska-Lusińska, Izabela, and Marek Okólski. 2009. *Emigracja ostatnia?* Warsaw: Wydawnictwo Naukowe Scholar.

Granovetter, Michael S. 1973. "The Strength of Weak Ties." *American Journal of Sociology* 78 (6): 1360–1380.

Gray, Ian. 1994. "The Changing Structure of Rural Communities." *Rural Society* 4 (3–4): 17–21.

Green, Donald P., Alan S. Gerber, and David W. Nickerson. 2003. "Getting Out the Vote in Local Elections: Results from Six Door-to-Door Canvassing Experiments." *Journal of Politics* 65 (4): 1083–1096.

Green, John C. 2005. *The American Religious Landscape and Political Attitudes: A Baseline for 2004*. Report for the Pew Forum on Religion and Public Life. Washington, DC: Pew Research Center.

Green, Simon. 2007. "The Challenge of Immigrant Integration in Europe." *European View* 5 (1): 47–52.

Griffith, David. 2008. "New Midwesterners, New Southerners: Immigration Experiences in Four Rural American Settings." In *New Faces in New Places: The Changing Geography of American Immigration*, edited by Douglas S. Massey, 179–210. New York: Russell Sage.

Grzymała-Kazłowska, Aleksandra, ed. 2008. *Między jednością a wielością: Integracja odmiennych grup i kategorii imigrantów w Polsce*. Warsaw: CMR.

———. 2012. "Paradoksy polskiej tolerancji. Postawy wobec mniejszości I imigrantów w Polsce na tle Europy." In *Wartości i zmiany: Przemiany postaw Polaków w jednoczącej się Europie*, edited by Aleksandra Jasińska-Kania, 131–164. Warsaw: Scholar.

———. 2015. "The Role of Different Forms of Bridging Capital for Immigrant Adaptation and Upward Mobility: The Case of Ukrainian and Vietnamese Immigrants Settled in Poland." *Ethnicities* 15 (3): 460–490.

Grzymała-Kazłowska, Aleksandra, and Marek Okólski. 2010. "Amorphous Population Movements into Poland and Ensuing Policy Challenges." In *Immigration Worldwide: Policies, Practices and Trends*, edited by Uma A. Segal, Doreen Elliott, and Nazeen S. Mayadas, 224–256. New York: Oxford University Press.

Grzymała-Kazłowska, Aleksandra, and Agnieszka Weinar. 2006. "The Polish Approach to Integration." *Canadian Diversity* 5 (1): 72–75.

Hagan, Jacqueline. 2006. "Making Theological Sense of the Migration Journey from Latin America: Catholic, Protestant, and Interfaith Perspectives." *American Behavioral Scientist* 49 (11): 1554–1573.

Hainsworth, Paul, ed. 1998. *Divided Society: Ethnic Minorities and Racism in Northern Ireland*. London: Pluto Press.

Hajnal, Zoltan L., and Paul G. Lewis. 2003. "Municipal Institutions and Voter Turnout in Local Elections." *Urban Affairs Review* 38 (5): 645–668.

Hall, Matthew. 2013. "Residential Integration on the New Frontier: Immigrant Segregation in Established and New Destinations." *Demography* 50 (5): 1873–1896.

Hall, Peter A., and Rosemary C. R. Taylor. 1996. "Political Science and the Three New Institutionalisms." *Political Studies* 44 (5): 936–957.

Halseth, Greg. 1999. "We Came for the Work: Situating Employment Migration in BC's Small, Resource-Based Communities." *Canadian Geographer* 43 (4): 363–381.

Hamilton, Howard D. 1971. "The Municipal Voter: Voting and Nonvoting in City Elections." *American Political Science Review* 65 (4): 1135–1140.

Hammar, Tomas, ed. 1985. *European Immigration Policy: A Comparative Study*. Cambridge: Cambridge University Press.

Handy, Femida, and Itay Greenspan. 2009. "Immigrant Volunteering: A Stepping Stone to Integration?" *Nonprofit and Voluntary Sector Quarterly* 38 (6): 956–982.

Hardwick, Susan W. 2008. "Toward a Suburban Immigrant Nation." In *Twenty-First Century Gateways: Immigrant Incorporation in Suburban America*, edited by Audrey Singer, Susan W. Hardwick, and Caroline B. Brettell, 31–50. Washington, DC: Brookings Institution.

Hazans, Mihails. 2011. "The Changing Face of Latvian Emigration . . . and the Changing Face of Latvia." Unpublished paper. Riga, Latvia: University of Latvia.

Heath, Anthony F., Stephen D. Fisher, Gemma Rosenblatt, David Sanders, and Maria Sobolewska. 2013. *The Political Integration of Ethnic Minorities in Britain.* Oxford: Oxford University Press.

Heckman, James J. 1979. "Sample Selection Bias as a Specification Error." *Econmetrica* 47 (1): 153–161.

Heleniak, Timothy. 2006. "Latvia Looks West, But Legacy of Soviets Remains." *Migration Policy Institute,* February. http://www.migrationpolicy.org/article/latvia-looks-west-legacy-soviets-remains, accessed July 5, 2014.

Helmke, Gretchen, and Steven Levitsky. 2004. "Informal Institutions and Comparative Politics: A Research Agenda." *Perspectives on Politics* 2 (4): 725–740.

Hethmon, Michael M. 2004. "The Chimera and the Cop: Local Enforcement of Federal Immigration Law." *University of the District of Columbia David A. Clarke School of Law Law Review* 8:83–140.

Hochschild, Jennifer. 2010. "Immigrant Political Incorporation: Comparing Success in the United States and Western Europe." *Ethnic and Racial Studies* 33 (1): 19–38.

Hochschild, Jennifer, Jacqueline Chattopadhyay, Claudine Gay, and Michael Jones-Correa, eds. 2013. *Outsiders No More? Models of Immigrant Political Incorporation.* New York: Oxford University Press.

Hochschild, Jennifer L., and John H. Mollenkopf. 2009a. *Bringing Outsiders In: Transatlantic Perspectives on Immigrant Political Incorporation.* Ithaca, NY: Cornell University Press.

———. 2009b. "Modeling Immigrant Political Incorporation." In *Bringing Outsiders In: Transatlantic Perspectives on Immigrant Political Incorporation,* edited by Jennifer L. Hochschild and John H. Mollenkopf, 15–30. Ithaca, NY: Cornell University Press.

———. 2009c. "Setting the Context." In *Bringing Outsiders In: Transatlantic Perspectives on Immigrant Political Incorporation,* edited by Jennifer L. Hochschild and John H. Mollenkopf, 3–14. Ithaca, NY: Cornell University Press.

Hoge, Dean R., Charles Zech, Patrick McNamara, and Michael J. Donahue. 1998. "The Value of Volunteers as Resources for Congregations." *Journal for the Scientific Study of Religion* 37 (3): 470–480.

Hollinger, David A. 1995. *Postethnic America: Beyond Multiculturalism.* New York: Basic Books.

Honohan, Iseult. 2010. "Citizenship Attribution in a New Country of Immigration: Ireland." *Journal of Ethnic and Migration Studies* 36 (5): 811–827.

Hopkins, Daniel. 2010. "Politicized Places: Explaining Where and When Immigrants Provoke Local Opposition." *American Political Science Review* 104 (1): 4–60.

Huguet Canalís, Ángel, and José Luis Navarro Sierra. 2005. "Inmigrantes en la escuela: Una revisión de es tu dios sobre las relaciones entre rendimiento escolar e inmigración." In *Multilingüismo, competencia lingüística y nuevas tecnologías,* edited by David Lasagabaster and Juan Manuel Sierra, 53–74. Barcelona: Horsori.

Huntington, Samuel P. 2004a. "The Hispanic Challenge." *Foreign Affairs* 141 (March/April): 30–45.

———. 2004b. *Who Are We? The Challenges to American National Identity.* New York: Simon & Schuster.

Iannacone, Laurence R. 1994. "Why Strict Churches Are Strong." *American Journal of Sociology* 99 (5): 1180–11211.

IDESCAT. 2009. *Enquesta d'usos lingüistics de la població 2008.* Barcelona: IDESCAT. http://www.idescat.cat/cat/idescat/publicacions/cataleg/pdfdocs/eulp2008.pdf, accessed July 5, 2014.

Iglicka, Kristyna, Katarzyna Gmaj, and Wojciech Borodzicz-Smoliński. 2011. *Circular Migration Patterns: Migration between Ukraine and Poland*. Florence, Italy: European University Institute. http://www.eui.eu/Projects/METOIKOS/Documents/CaseStudies/METOIKOScasestudyPolandUkraine.pdf, accessed May 1, 2015.

"Immigrants Have Worlds to Offer." 1992. *Businessweek*, July 12. http://www.businessweek.com/stories/1992-07-12/immigrants-have-worlds-to-offer, accessed January 7, 2015.

Indāns, Ivars. 2004. *Imigrācijas ietekme uz etniskajām attiecībām Latvijā ES paplašināšanās kontekstā*. Riga, Latvia: Latvian Institute for International Relations, Friedrich-Ebert Foundation.

Instituto Nacional Estadística. 2013. "El número de extranjeros inscritos baja en 216.125 hasta 5,5 millones, de los cuales 2,4 millones son ciudadanos de la UE." http://www.ine.es/prensa/np776.pdf, accessed March 29, 2014.

International Association of Chiefs of Police. 2007. *Police Chief's Guide to Immigration Issues*. Washington, DC: International Association of Chiefs of Police.

Ireland, Patrick. 1994. *The Policy Challenge of Ethnic Diversity: Immigrant Politics in France and Switzerland*. Cambridge, MA: Harvard University Press.

———. 2004. *Becoming Europe: Immigration, Integration, and the Welfare State*. Pittsburgh, PA: University of Pittsburgh Press.

ISTAT. n.d. http://demo.istat.it/.

———. 2012. *Italian Statistical Abstract 2011*. Rome: Instituto Nazionale di Statistica. http://www3.istat.it/dati/catalogo/20120531_00/compendio_statistico_italiano%20 2011.pdf, accessed April 2, 2014.

Itzigsohn, José, and Silvia Giorguli-Saucedo. 2005. "Incorporation, Transnationalism, and Gender: Immigrant Incorporation and Transnational Participation as Gendered Processes." *International Migration Review* 39 (4): 895–920.

Jaccard, James, and Robert Turrisi. 2003. *Interaction Effects in Multiple Regressions*. London: Sage.

Jacobs, Dirk, Karen Phalet, and Marc Swyngedouw. 2004. "Associational Membership and Political Involvement among Ethnic Minority Groups in Brussels." *Journal of Ethnic and Migration Studies* 30 (3): 543–559.

Jeram, Sanjay. 2013. "Immigrants and the Basque Nation: Diversity as a New Marker of Identity." *Ethnic and Racial Studies* 36 (11): 1770–1788.

Johnson, James H., Jr., Karen D. Johnson-Webb, and Walter C. Farrell Jr. 1999. "Newly Emerging Hispanic Communities in the United States: A Spatial Analysis of Settlement Patterns, In-migration Fields, and Social Receptivity." In *Immigration and Opportunity: Race, Ethnicity, and Employment in the United States*, edited by Frank D. Bean and Stephanie Bell-Rose, 263–310. New York: Russell Sage.

Johnson, Kenneth M., and Daniel T. Lichter. 2008. "Natural Increase: A New Source of Population Growth in Emerging Hispanic Destinations in the United States." *Population and Development Review* 34 (2): 327–346.

Jones, Jennifer A. 2012. "Blacks May Be Second Class, but They Can't Make Them Leave: Mexican Racial Formation and Immigrant Status in Winston-Salem." *Latino Studies* 10 (1): 60–80.

Jones-Correa, Michael. 1998a. *Between Two Nations: The Political Predicament of Latinos in New York City*. Ithaca, NY: Cornell University Press.

———. 1998b. "Different Paths: Gender, Immigration and Political Participation." *International Migration Review* 32 (2): 326–349.

———. ed. 2001a. *Governing American Cities: Inter-ethnic Coalitions, Competition, and Conflict*. New York: Russell Sage.

———. 2001b. "Institutional and Contextual Factors in Immigrant Naturalization and Voting." *Citizenship Studies* 5 (1): 41–56.

———. 2005a. "Bringing Outsiders In: Questions of Immigration Incorporation." In *The Politics of Democratic Inclusion*, edited by Christina Wolbrecht and Rodney E. Hero with Peri E. Arnold and Alvin B. Tillery, 75–101. Philadelphia, PA: Temple University Press.

———. 2005b. "The Bureaucratic Incorporation of Immigrants in Suburbia." Unpublished paper. https://www.princeton.edu/csdp/events/JonesCorrea051007/Jones-Correa051007.pdf, accessed July 5, 2016.

———. 2008. "Immigrant Incorporation in Suburbia: The Role of Bureaucratic Norms in Education." In *New Faces in New Places*, edited by Douglas S. Massey, 308–340. New York: Russell Sage.

———. 2011. *All Migration Is Local: Receiving Communities and Their Role in Successful Immigrant Integration*. Washington, DC: Center for American Progress. http://www.scribd.com/doc/65648743/All-Immigration-Is-Local, accessed April 15, 2014.

———. 2013. "Thru-Ways, By-Ways, and Cul-de-Sacs of Immigrant Political Immigration." In *Outsiders No More? Models of Immigrant Political Incorporation*, edited by Jennifer L. Hochschild, Jacqueline Chattopadhyay, Claudine Gay, and Michael Jones-Correa, 176–191. New York: Oxford University Press.

Jones-Correa, Michael, and Katherine Fennelly. 2009. "Immigration Enforcement and Its Effects on Latino Lives in Two Rural North Carolina Communities." Paper presented at the "Undocumented Hispanic Migration: On the Margins of a Dream" Conference, Connecticut College, October 16.

Jones-Correa, Michael, Helen B. Marrow, Dina G. Okamoto, and Linda R. Tropp. 2013. "Immigrant-Native Relations in 21st-Century America: Intergroup Contact, Trust, and Civic Engagement." Project Award, Russell Sage.

Joppke, Christian. 2007. "Beyond National Models: Civic Integration Policies for Immigrants in Western Europe." *West European Politics* 30 (1): 1–22.

Joppke, Christian, and F. Leslie Seidle, eds. 2012. *Immigrant Integration in Federal Countries*. Montreal and Kingston, Canada: McGill-Queens University Press.

Jost, Kenneth. 2009. "Bilingual Education vs. English Immersion." *CQ Researcher* 19 (43): 1029–1052.

Juhasz, Attila. 2010. "Anti-Immigrant Prejudice in Central and Eastern Europe." Political Capital Policy Research and Consulting Institute. http://www.riskandforecast.com/post/bulgaria/anti-immigrant-prejudice-in-central-and-eastern-europe_581.html, accessed February 19, 2014.

Kaczmarczyk, Paweł, ed. 2014. "Recent Trends in International Migration in Poland: The 2012 SOPEMI Report." Warsaw: Center for Migration Research, University of Warsaw.

———. 2015. "Recent Trends in International Migration in Poland: The 2014 SOPEMI Report." Warsaw: Center for Migration Research, University of Warsaw.

Kandel, William, and John Cromartie. 2004. *New Patterns of Hispanic Settlement in Rural America*. Rural Development Research Report 99. Washington, DC: U.S. Department of Agriculture Economic Research Service. http://www.ers.usda.gov/publications/rdrr-rural-development-research-report/rdrr99.aspx#.U8WHYI1dV8M, accessed September 4, 2014.

Karnig, Albert K., and B. Oliver Walter. 1983. "Decline in Municipal Voter Turnout: A Function of Changing Structure." *American Politics Research* 11 (4): 491–505.

Karnite, Raita, and Krišs Karnītis. 2009. *Iedzīvotāju starpvalstu ilgtermiņa migrācijas ietekme uz Latvijas tautsaimniecību*. Riga, Latvia: Centre for Public Policy PROVI-

DUS. http://providus.lv/article/iedzivotaju-starpvalstu-ilgtermina-migracijas-ietekme-uz-latvijas-tautsaimniecibu, accessed October 14, 2014.

Kasarda, John, and Morris Janowitz. 1974. "Community Attachment in Mass Society." *American Sociological Review* 39 (3): 328–339.

Kasileva, Katya. 2011. "6.5% of the EU Population Are Foreigners and 9.4% are Born Abroad." Brussels: Eurostat.

Kasinitz, Philip, John H. Mollenkopf, Mary C. Waters, and Jennifer Holdaway. 2008. *Inheriting the City: The Children of Immigrants Come of Age.* New York: Russell Sage.

Katz, Susan Roberta. 2004. "Does NCLB Leave the US behind in Bilingual Teacher Education?" *English Education* 36 (2): 141–152.

Kaufmann, Karen. 2004. *The Urban Voter: Group Conflict and Mayoral Voting Behavior in American Cities.* Ann Arbor: University of Michigan Press.

Kaufmann, Karen M., and Antonio Rodriguez. 2010. "Local Context and Latino Political Socialization: Why Immigrant Destinations Matter." Unpublished paper. http://www.bsos.umd.edu/gvpt/apworkshop/kaufmann2010.pdf, accessed October 16, 2011.

Kearns, Ade, and Ray Forrest. 2000. "Social Cohesion and Multilevel Urban Governance." *Urban Studies* 37 (5–6): 995–1017.

Kelleher, Christine A., and David Lowery. 2009. "Central City Size, Metropolitan Institutions and Political Participation." *British Journal of Political Science* 39 (1): 59–92.

Kępińska, Ewa, and Dariusz Stola. 2004. "Migration Policies and Politics in Poland." In *The New Europe: East-West Revisited*, edited by Agata Górny and P. Ruspini, 156–179. New York: Palgrave Macmillan.

Ķešāne, I., and R. Kaša. 2008. "Learning to Welcome: Integration of Immigrants in Latvia." In *The Integration of Immigrants in Latvia and Poland*, 37–79. Riga, Latvia: Centre for Public Policy PROVIDUS. http://www.migpolgroup.com/public/docs/148.part_2_LearningtoWelcome_20.08.08.pdf, accessed July 10, 2014.

Key, V. O. 1949. *Southern Politics in State and Nation.* New York: Alfred A. Knopf.

Khashu, Anita. 2009. *The Role of Local Police: Striking a Balance between Immigration Enforcement and Civil Liberties.* Washington, DC: Police Foundation. http://www.policefoundation.org/content/role-of-local-police, accessed August 5, 2013.

Kicinger, Anna. 2005. *Between Polish Interests and the EU Influence: Polish Migration Policy Development 1989–2004.* Warsaw: Central European Forum for Migration Research. http://www.cefmr.pan.pl/docs/cefmr_wp_2005-09.pdf, accessed December 5, 2014.

Kicinger, Anna, and Izabela Koryś. 2011. "The Case of Poland." In *Migration Policymaking in Europe: The Dynamics of Actors and Contexts in Past and Present*, edited by Giovanna Zincone, Rinus Penninx, and Maren Borkert, 347–376. Amsterdam: Amsterdam University Press.

Ķīlis, R. 2009. "Why Is Migration Inevitable?" Paper presented at the conference "Inclusion Unaffordable? The Uncertain Fate of Integration Policies in Europe." Riga, Latvia, November 16. http://pdc.ceu.hu/archive/00006542/, accessed July 10, 2014.

King, Carole. 2009. "The Rise and Decline of Village Reading Rooms." *Rural History* 20 (2): 163–186.

King, Russell, and Nicola Mai. 2008. *Out of Albania: From Crisis Migration to Social Inclusion in Italy.* New York: Berghahn Books.

Kinney, Jenn, and Elizabeth F. Cohen. 2013. "Multilevel Citizenship in a Federal State: The Case of Noncitizens' Rights in the United States." In *Multilevel Citizenship*, edited by Willem Maas, 70–86. Philadelphia: University of Pennsylvania Press.

Klementjeviene, Ana. 2010. "Lithuania as a New Country of Immigration." Migration online.cz. http://www.migrationonline.cz/en/lithuania-as-a-new-country-of-immigration, accessed August 16, 2013.

Kochhar, Rakesh, Roberto Suro, and Sonya Tafoya. 2005. *The New Latino South: The Context and Consequences of Rapid Population Growth.* Washington, DC: Pew Hispanic Center. http://www.pewhispanic.org/2005/07/26/the-new-latino-south/, accessed October 14, 2014.

Koff, Harlan. 2006. "Does Hospitality Translate into Integration? Subnational Variations of Italian Responses to Immigration." In *Local Citizenship in Recent Countries of Immigration: Japan in Comparative Perspective*, edited by Takeyuki Tsuda, 173–203. Lanham, MD: Lexington Books.

———. 2008. *Fortress Europe or a Europe of Fortresses? The Integration of Migrants in Western Europe.* Brussels: P.I.E. Peter Lang.

Koopmans, Ruud. 2003. "Good Intentions Sometimes Make Bad Policy: A Comparison of Dutch and German Integration Policies." In *The Challenge of Diversity: European Social Democracy Facing Migration, Integration, and Multiculturalism*, edited by R. Cuperus, 47–58. Innsbruck, Austria: Studienverlag.

Koopmans, Ruud, and Merlin Schaeffer. 2013. "De-Composing Diversity: In-Group Size and Out-Group Entropy and Their Relationship to Neighbourhood Cohesion." WZB Discussion Paper SP VI 2013-104. Berlin: WZB.

Koopmans, Ruud, Paul Statham, Marco Giugni, and Florence Passy. 2005. *Contested Citizenship: Immigration and Cultural Diversity in Europe.* Minneapolis: University of Minnesota Press.

Kovalenco, Julia, Peter Mensah, Tadas Leončikas, and Karolis Žibas. 2010. *New Immigrants in Estonia, Latvia and Lithuania.* Talinn: Legal Information Centre for Human Rights.

Kraft, Randy. 2014. "Allentown City Council Takes a Stand for US Immigration Reform." *WFMZ-TV*, March 20. http://www.wfmz.com/news/news-regional-lehighvalley/Local/allentown-city-council-takes-a-stand-for-us-immigration-reform/25069284, accessed May 4, 2014.

Krissman, Fred. 2000. "Immigrant Labor Recruitment: US Agribusiness and Undocumented Immigrants from Mexico." In *Immigration Research for a New Century: Multidisciplinary Perspectives*, edited by Nancy Foner, Rubén G. Rumbaut, and Steven J. Gold, 277–300. New York: Russell Sage.

Krūma, Kristīne. 2010. "Integration and Naturalisation Tests: The New Way to European Citizenship: Country Report Latvia." Centre for Migration Law, Radboud University Nijmegen, November.

Kymlicka, Will. 2001. "Immigrant Integration and Minority Nationalism." In *Minority Nationalism and the Changing International Order*, edited by Michael Keating and John McGarry, 61–83. Oxford: Oxford University Press.

Lane, Robert E. 1965. *Political Life: Why and How People Get Involved in Politics.* New York: The Free Press.

Latvian Centre for Human Rights. 2013. "Second Alternative Report on the Implementation of the Council of Europe Framework Convention for the Protection of National Minorities in Latvia." http://cilvektiesibas.org.lv/site/attachments/27/09/2013/LCHR_Minority_Shadow_Report_2309_1.pdf, accessed March 1, 2013.

Lee, Jennifer, and Frank D. Bean 2010. *The Diversity Paradox: Immigration and the Color Line in 21st Century America.* New York: Russell Sage.

Lee, Matthew R. 2008. "Civic Community in the Hinterland: Toward a Theory of Rural Social Structure and Violence." *Criminology* 46 (2): 447–478.

Lee, Matthew R., and John P. Bartowski. 2004. "Love Thy Neighbour? Moral Communities, Civic Engagement, and Juvenile Homicide in Rural Areas." *Social Forces* 82: 1001–1035.

Lee, Taeku, S. Karthick Ramakrishnan, and Ricardo Ramírez, eds. 2007. *Transforming Politics, Transforming America: The Political and Civic Incorporation of Immigrants in the United States.* Charlottesville: University of Virginia Press.

Leerkes, Arjen, Monica Varsanyi, and Godfried Engbersen. 2012. "Local Limits to Migration Control Practices of Selective Migration Policing in a Restrictive National Policy Context." *Police Quarterly* 15 (4): 446–475.

Lekwa, Verl L., Tom W. Rice, and Matthew V. Hibbing. 2007. "The Correlates of Community Attractiveness." *Environment and Behavior* 39 (2): 198–216.

Lentin, Ronit. 2007. "Ireland: Racial State and Crisis Racism." *Ethnic and Racial Studies* 30 (4): 610–627.

Lesińska, Magdalena. 2014. "The European Backlash against Immigration and Multiculturalism." *Journal of Sociology* 50 (1): 37–50.

Lewis, Paul G., Doris Marie Provine, Monica W. Varsanyi, and Scott H. Decker. 2012. "Why Do (Some) City Police Departments Enforce Federal Immigration Law? Political, Demographic, and Organizational Influences on Local Choices." *Journal of Public Administration Research and Theory* 23 (1): 1–25.

Lewis, Paul G., and S. Karthick Ramakrishnan. 2007. "Police Practices in Immigrant-Destination Cities: Political Control or Bureaucratic Professionalism?" *Urban Affairs Review* 42 (6): 874–900.

Lewis, Paul G., Monica W. Varsanyi, Marie Provine, and Scott Decker. 2011. "New Destinations or Old Politics? Explaining Local Immigration Policing Practices in the United States." Paper presented at the American Political Science Association annual meeting, Seattle, WA, September.

———. 2013. "New Destinations or Old Politics? Explaining Local Immigration Policing Practices in the United States." Unpublished paper.

Lichter, Daniel T., and Kenneth M. Johnson. 2006. "Emerging Rural Settlement Patterns and the Geographic Redistribution of America's New Immigrants." *Rural Sociology* 71 (1): 109–131.

———. 2009. "Immigrant Gateways and Hispanic Migration to New Destinations." *International Migration Review* 43 (3): 496–518.

Lichter, Daniel T., Domenico Parisi, Michael C. Taquino, and Steven Michael Grice. 2010. "Residential Segregation in New Hispanic Destinations: Cities, Suburbs, and Rural Communities Compared." *Social Science Research* 39 (2): 215–230.

Licona, Adela C., and Marta Maria Maldonado. 2014. "The Social Production of Latino/a Visibilities and Invisibilities: Geographies of Power in Small Town America." *Antipode* 46 (2): 517–536.

Lien, Pei-te, Christian Collet, Janelle Wong, and S. Karthick Ramakrishnan. 2001. "Asian Pacific-American Public Opinion and Political Participation." *PS: Political Science and Politics* 34 (3): 625–630.

Lien, Pei-te, M. Margaret Conway, and Janelle Wong. 2004. *The Politics of Asian America.* New York: Routledge.

Linton, April. 2004. "A Critical Mass Model of Bilingualism among US-Born Hispanics." *Social Forces* 83 (1): 279–314.

Lippard, Cameron D., and Charles A. Gallagher, eds. 2011. *Being Brown in Dixie: Race, Ethnicity, and Latino Immigration in the New South.* Boulder, CO: First Forum Press.

Lipsky, Michael. 1980. *Street-Level Bureaucracy: Dilemmas of the Individual in Public Services.* New York: Russell Sage.

Lovato, Roberto. 2008. "Juan Crow in Georgia." *The Nation*, May 8. http://www.thenation. com/article/juan-crow-georgia#, accessed March 30, 2015.

Loyal, Steven. 2011. *Understanding Immigration in Ireland: State Labour and Capital in a Global Age*. Manchester, UK: Manchester University Press.

Luebke, Paul. 2011. "Anti-Immigrant Mobilization in a Southern State." In *Being Brown in Dixie: Race, Ethnicity, and Latino Immigration in the New South*, edited by Cameron D. Lippard and Charles A. Gallagher, 261–278. Boulder, CO: Lynne Rienner.

Mac Thomais St.-Hilaire, Aonghas. 2001. "Segmented Assimilation." In *Encyclopedia of American Immigration*, edited by James Ciment, 460–467. Armonk, NY: M.E. Sharpe.

Mahnig, Hans. 2004. "The Politics of Minority-Majority Relations: How Immigrant Policies Developed in Paris, Berlin and Zurich." In *Citizenship in European Cities: Immigrants, Local Politics and Integration Policies*, edited by Rinus Penninx, Karen Kraal, Marco Martiniello, and Steven Vertovec, 17–38. Aldershot: Ashgate.

Makarovs, Viktor, and Aleksejs Dimitrovs. 2009. *Latvijas nepilsoņi un balsstiesības: kompromisi un risinājumi*. Riga, Latvia: Centre for Public Policy PROVIDUS. http:// providus.lv/article/latvijas-nepilsoni-un-balstiesibas-kompromisi-un-risinajumi, accessed May 10, 2013.

Marrow, Helen B. 2005. "New Destinations and Immigrant Incorporation." *Perspectives on Politics* 3 (4): 781–799.

———. 2009a. "Immigrant Bureaucratic Incorporation: The Dual Roles of Professional Missions and Government Policies." *American Sociological Review* 74 (5): 756–776.

———. 2009b. "New Immigrant Destinations and the American Colour Line." *Ethnic and Racial Studies* 32 (6): 1037–1057.

———. 2011. *New Destination Dreaming: Immigration, Race, and Legal Status in the Rural American South*. Palo Alto, CA: Stanford University Press.

Marschall, Melissa. 2006. "Parent Involvement and Educational Outcomes for Latino Students." *Review of Policy Research* 23 (5): 1053–1076.

Marschall, Melissa J., Elizabeth Rigby, and Jasmine Jenkins. 2011. "Do State Policies Constrain Local Actors? The Impact of English Only Laws on Language Instruction in Public Schools." *Publius: The Journal of Federalism* 41 (3): 586–609.

Marschall, Melissa J., Paru R. Shah, and Katharine Donato. 2012. "Parent Involvement Policy in Established and New Immigrant Destinations." *Social Science Quarterly* 93 (1): 130–151.

Marshall, T. H. 1964. *Class, Citizenship, and Social Development*. Garden City, NY: Doubleday.

Massey, Douglas S. 2008a. "Assimilation in a New Geography." In *New Faces in New Places: The Changing Geography of American Immigration*, edited by Douglas S. Massey, 343–353. New York: Russell Sage.

———. 2008b. *Categorically Unequal: The American Stratification System*. New York: Russell Sage.

———, ed. 2008c. *New Faces in New Places: The Changing Geography of American Immigration*. New York: Russell Sage.

Massey, Douglas S., and Chiara Capoferro. 2008. "The Geographic Diversification of American Immigration." In *New Faces in New Places: The Changing Geography of American Immigration*, edited by Douglas S. Massey, 25–50. New York: Russell Sage.

Massey, Douglas S., Jorge Durand, and Noland J. Malone. 2002. *Beyond Smoke and Mirrors: Mexican Immigration in an Era of Economic Integration*. New York: Russell Sage.

Matysiak, Anna, and Beata Nowok. 2007. "Stochastic Forecast of the Population of Poland, 2005–2050." Working Paper WP 2006-026. Rostock, Germany: Max Planck

Institute for Demographic Research, MPIDR. http://www.demographic-research
.org/Volumes/Vol17/11/17-11.pdf, accessed April 15, 2014.

McClain, Paula D. 2006. "North Carolina's Response to Latino Immigrants and Immigration." In *Immigration's New Frontiers: Experiences from the Emerging Gateway States*,
edited by Greg Anrig and Tova Andrea Wang, 7–32. New York: Century Foundation
Press.

McClain, Paula D., Niambi M. Carter, Victoria M. DeFrancesco, J. Alan Kendrick,
Monique L. Lyle, Shayla C. Nunnally, Thomas J. Scotto, Jeffrey D. Grynaviski, and
Jason A. Johnson. 2003. "St. Benedict the Black Meets the Virgin of Guadalupe: Inter-
group Relations in a Southern City." Paper presented at the Color Lines Conference,
Harvard Law School, Cambridge, MA, August 29–September 1.

McClain, Paula D., Niambi M. Carter, Victoria M. DeFrancesco Soto, Monique L. Lyle,
Jeffrey D. Grynaviski, Shayla C. Nunnally, Thomas J. Scotto, J. Alan Kendrick,
Gerald F. Lackey, and Kendra Davenport Cotton. 2006. "Racial Distancing in a
Southern City: Latino Immigrants' Views of Black Americans." *Journal of Politics*
68 (3): 571–584.

McClain, Paula D., Gerald F. Lackey, Efrén O. Pérez, Niambi M. Carter, Jessica Johnson
Carew, Eugene Walton Jr., and Candace Watts Smith. 2011. "Intergroup Relations in
Three Southern Cities: Black and White Americans and Latino Immigrants' Atti-
tudes." In *Just Neighbors? Research on African American and Latino Relations in the
United States*, edited by Edward Telles, Mark Sawyer, and Gaspar Rivera-Salgado,
201–241. New York: Russell Sage.

McClain, Paula D., Monique L. Lyle, Niambi M. Carter, Victoria M. DeFrancesco Soto,
Gerald F. Lackey, Kendra Davenport Cotton, Shayla C. Nunnally, Thomas J. Scotto,
Jeffrey D. Grynaviski, and J. Alan Kendrick. 2007. "Black Americans and Latino
Immigrants in a Southern City: Friendly Neighbors or Economic Competitors?" *Du
Bois Review: Social Science Research on Race* 4 (1): 97–117.

McClurg, Scott D. 2003. "Social Networks and Political Participation: The Role of Social
Interaction in Explaining Political Participation." *Political Research Quarterly* 56 (4):
449–464.

McDermott, Monica. n.d. *Mixed Communities, Mixed Emotions: Life in a Changing Southern City*. Unpublished book manuscript.

———. 2011. "Black Attitudes and Hispanic Immigrants in South Carolina." In *Just Neighbors?: Research on African American and Latino Relations in the United States*, edited
by Edward Telles, Mark Sawyer, and Gaspar Rivera-Salgado, 242–263. New York:
Russell Sage.

McDonnell, Lorraine, and Paul Thomas Hill. 1993. *Newcomers in American Schools: Meeting the Educational Needs of Immigrant Youth*. Santa Monica, CA: Rand.

Mellin, Ted. 1986. "Tropiano Plans to Ask Reversal on Sanctuary: City Should Encourage
Respect, Obedience of Law, She Says." *The Morning Call*, December 16. http://articles
.mcall.com/1986-12-16/news/2546553_1_sanctuary-resolution-refugees-from
-central-america-sanctuary-movement, accessed April 10, 2014.

Menjívar, Cecilia. 2003. "Religion and Immigration in Comparative Perspective: Catholic
and Evangelical Salvadorans in San Francisco, Washington, D.C., and Phoenix." *Sociology of Religion* 64 (1): 21–45.

Messina, Anthony M. 1989. *Race and Party Competition in Britain*. Oxford: Oxford University Press.

———. 1992. "The Two Tiers of Ethnic Conflict in Western Europe." *The Fletcher Forum
of World Affairs* 16 (2): 51–66.

———. 2001. "The Impacts of Post–WWII Migration to Britain: Policy Constraints, Political Opportunism and the Alteration of Representational Politics." *Review of Politics* 63 (2): 259–285.

———. 2007. *The Logics and Politics of Post–WWII Migration to Western Europe.* New York: Cambridge University Press.

———. 2009. "The Politics of Migration to Western Europe: Ireland in Comparative Perspective." *West European Politics* 32 (1): 1–26.

———. 2013. "The Limits of Grand Migration Theory: Embedding Experiences of Immigration and Immigrant Incorporation within Their Appropriate National, Regional, and Local Settings." In *The Multicultural Dilemma: Migration, Ethnic Politics, and State Intermediation*, edited by Michelle Hale Williams, 15–29. New York: Routledge.

Messina, Anthony M., Luis R. Fraga, Laurie A. Rhodebeck, and Frederick D. Wright, eds. 1992. *Ethnic and Racial Minorities in Advanced Industrial Democracies.* New York: Greenwood Press.

Michelson, Melissa R. 2003. "Getting Out the Latino Vote: How Door-to-Door Canvassing Influences Voter Turnout in Rural Central California." *Political Behavior* 25 (3): 247–263.

Miera, Frauke. 2012. "Not a One-Way Road? Integration as a Concept and a Policy." In *European Multiculturalisms: Cultural, Religious and Ethnic Challenges*, edited by Anna Triandafyllidou, Tariq Modood, and Nasar Meer, 192–212. Edinburgh: Edinburgh University Press.

Migration Observatory. 2013. *COMMENTARY: Bordering on Confusion: International Migration and Implications for Scottish Independence.* Oxford: Migration Observatory, University of Oxford. http://www.migrationobservatory.ox.ac.uk/sites/files/migobs/commentary%20-%20bordering%20on%20confusion.pdf, accessed May 29, 2014.

Migration Policy Institute. 2008. *Foreign-Born Population and Foreign Born as Percentage of the Total US Population, 1850 to 2008.* Migration Policy Institute Data Hub. http://www.migrationpolicy.org/sites/default/files/source_charts/final.fb.shtml, accessed March 24, 2015.

Milly, Deborah J. 2014. *New Policies for New Residents: Immigrants, Advocacy, and Governance in Japan and Beyond.* Ithaca, NY: Cornell University Press.

Ministry of Social Policy, Poland. 2005. "Proposals of Actions Aimed at Establishing a Comprehensive Immigrant Integration Policy in Poland." Warsaw. https://ec.europa.eu/migrant-integration/index.cfm?action=furl.go&go=/librarydoc/proposals-of-actions-aimed-at-establishing-a-comprehensive-immigrant-integration-policy-in-poland, accessed December 12, 2016.

Ministry of the Interior of the Republic of Latvia. 2007. "Izsludina Koncepciju Par Migrācijas Politiku Nodarbinātības Kontekstā." http://www.iem.gov.lv/eng/aktualitates/jaunumi/?doc=14046, accessed June 17, 2014.

Mitnik, Pablo A., and Jessica Halpern-Finnerty. 2010. "Immigration and Local Governments: Inclusionary Local Policies in the Era of State Rescaling." In *Taking Local Control: Immigration Policy Activism in US Cities and States*, edited by Monica W. Varsanyi, 51–72. Palo Alto, CA: Stanford University Press.

Mittelberg, David, and Mary C. Waters. 1992. "The Process of Ethnogenesis among Haitian and Israeli Immigrants in the United States." *Ethnic and Racial Studies* 15 (3): 412–436.

Mollenkopf, John H., and Jennifer L. Hochschild. 2009. "Setting the Context." In *Bringing Outsiders In: Transatlantic Perspectives on Immigrant Political Incorporation*, edited by Jennifer L. Hochschild and John H. Mollenkopf, 3–14. Ithaca, NY: Cornell University Press.

———. 2010. "Immigrant Political Incorporation: Comparing Success in the United States and Europe." *Ethnic and Racial Studies* 33 (1): 19–38.

Mollenkopf, John H., David Olson, and Tim Ross. 2001. "Immigrant Political Participation in New York and Los Angeles." In *Governing Cities*, edited by Michael Jones-Correa, 17–70. New York: Russell Sage.

Mollenkopf, John H., and Manuel Pastor. 2013. "Struggling over Strangers or Receiving with Resilience? The Metropolitics of Immigrant Integration." Paper presented at the "Building Resilient Regions Closing Symposium at the Urban Institute," Washington, DC, May 31. http://brr.berkeley.edu/wp-content/uploads/2013/05/Mollenkopf-Pastor -struggling-strangers.pdf, accessed May 3, 2014.

Mollenkopf, John H., and Raphael Sonenshein. 2009. "The New Urban Politics of Integration: A View from the Gateway Cities." In *Bringing Outsiders In*, edited by Jennifer L. Hochschild and John H. Mollenkopf, 74–92. Ithaca, NY: Cornell University Press.

Moody, James, and Douglas R. White. 2003. "Social Cohesion and Embeddedness: A Hierarchical Conception of Social Groups." *American Sociological Review* 68 (1): 103–127.

Morales, Laura. 2014. "Party Reactions to Immigration in New Destination Countries." Paper presented to the ECPR General Conference, Glasgow, Scotland, September 6.

Morales, Laura, Eva Anduiza, Bo Bengtsson, Cinalli Manlio, Mario Diani, Marco Giugni, Antal Orkeny, Jon Rogstad, and Paul Statham. 2013. "LOCALMULTIDEM and MDE Individual Survey (WP4) Dataset, 2004–2008." Harvard Dataverse Network. http://dx .doi.org/10.7910/DVN/24987, accessed November 14, 2014.

Morales, Laura, and Alfonso Echazarra. 2013. "Will We All Hunker Down? The Impact of Immigration and Diversity on Local Communities in Spain." *Journal of Elections, Public Opinion & Parties* 23 (3): 343–366.

Morales, Laura, and Marco Giugni, eds. 2011. *Social Capital, Political Participation and Migration in Europe: Making Multicultural Democracy Work?* New York: Palgrave Macmillan.

Morales, Laura, and Katia Pilati. 2011. "The Role of Social Capital in Migrants' Engagement in Local Politics in European Cities." In *Social Capital, Political Participation and Migration in Europe: Making Multicultural Democracy Work?*, edited by Laura Morales and Marco Giugni, 87–114. New York: Palgrave Macmillan.

Morales, Laura, and Luis Ramiro. 2011. "Gaining Political Capital through Social Capital: Policy-Making Inclusion and Network Embeddedness of Migrants' Associations in Spain." *Mobilization* 16 (1): 147–164.

Moorhead, James H. 1999. *World without End: Mainstream American Protestant Visions of the Last Things, 1880–1925.* Bloomington: Indiana University Press.

NALEO (National Association of Latino Elected and Appointed Officials). 2012. "National Directory of Latino Elected Officials." http://www.naleo.org/downloads/2012_Directory.pdf, accessed June 7, 2014.

Naples, Nancy. 1994. "Contradictions in Agrarian Ideology: Restructuring Gender, Race-Ethnicity, and Class." *Rural Sociology* 59 (1): 110–135.

NCELA (National Clearinghouse for English Language Acquisition). 2011. "What Language Instruction Educational Programs Do States Use to Serve English Learners?" NCELA Fact Sheet. http://www.ncela.us/files/uploads/5/LIEPs0406BR.pdf, accessed April 11, 2015.

NCES (National Center for Educational Statistics). 2014. "Schools and Staffing Survey (SASS)." Various years. http://nces.ed.gov/surveys/sass/, accessed June 30, 2014.

NCP (New Communities Partnership). 2010. *Our Vote Can Make a Difference: Voter Registration & Education Campaign, November 2008–June 2009.* http://www.newcommunities.

ie/download/pdf/ncp_ac_vep__report_full_colour_final_version.pdf, accessed May 5, 2014.

Neal, Sarah. 2002. "Rural Landscapes, Representations and Racism: Examining Multicultural Citizenship and Policy-Making in the English Countryside." *Ethnic and Racial Studies* 25 (3): 442–461.

Nelson, Margaret K. 1999. "Economic Restructuring, Gender, and Informal Work: A Case Study of a Rural County." *Rural Sociology* 64 (1): 18–46.

Newman, Michael. 2011. "Different Ways to Hate a Language in Catalonia: Interpreting Low Solidarity Scores in Language Attitude Studies." In *Selected Proceedings of the 5th Workshop on Spanish Sociolinguistics*, edited by Jim Michnowicz and Robin Dodsworth, 40–49. Somerville, MA: Cascadilla Proceedings Project.

Newman, Michael, Mireia Trenchs-Parera, and Shukhan Ng. 2008. "Normalizing Bilingualism: The Effects of the Catalonian Linguistic Normalization Policy One Generation After." *Journal of Sociolinguistics* 12 (3): 306–333.

Newton, Anne L. 2005. "It Is Not a Question of Being Anti-Immigration: Categories of Deservedness in Immigration Policy Making." In *Deserving and Entitled: Social Constructions and Public Policy*, edited by Anne L. Schneider and Helen M. Ingram, 139–172. Albany, NY: SUNY Press.

Nie, Norman H., G. Bingham Powell Jr., and Kenneth Prewitt. 1969a. "Social Structure and Political Participation: Developmental Relationships, Part I." *American Political Science Review* 63 (2): 361–378.

———. 1969b. "Social Structure and Political Participation: Developmental Relationships, II." *American Political Science Review* 63 (3): 808–832.

Niessen, Jan. 2000. *Diversity and Cohesion: New Challenges for the Integration of Immigrants and Minorities*. Strasbourg, France: Council of Europe.

Niven, David. 2004. "The Mobilization Solution? Face-to-Face Contact and Voter Turnout in Municipal Elections." *Journal of Politics* 66 (3): 868–885.

Núñez, Xosé-Manoel. 2002. "History and Collective Memories of Migration in a Land of Migrants: The Case of Iberian Galicia." *History and Memory* 14 (1–2): 229–258.

OCMA (Office of Citizenship and Migration Affairs). 2013. *Par Trešo Valstu Valstspiederīgo Un Latvijas Nepilsoņu Viedokli Par Latvijas Pilsonību Un Iemesliem, Kas Veicina Vai Kavē Pilsonības Iegūšanu*. Riga: Office of Citizenship and Migration Affairs. http://www.pmlp.gov.lv/lv/sakums/jaunumi/publikacijas/petijumi/2013.gada-p%C4%93t%C4%ABjums-latvijas.pdf, accessed January 10, 2015.

OECD. 2013. *International Migration Outlook 2013*. Paris: OECD.

———. 2015. *International Migration Outlook 2015*. Paris: OECD.

OECD SOPEMI. 1995. *Trends in International Migration*. Paris: OECD.

———. 2007. *International Migration Outlook*. Paris: OECD.

Office of Citizenship and Migration Affairs, Latvia. n.d. http://www.pmlp.gov.lv/en/statistics/residence.html, accessed December 15, 2016.

Office of the Deputy Prime Minister. 2002. *Urban and Rural Area Definitions: A User Guide*. London: Office of the Deputy Prime Minister.

Okamoto, Dina G. 2003. "Toward a Theory of Panethnicity: Explaining Asian American Collective Action." *American Sociological Review* 68 (6): 811–842.

Okamoto, Dina, and Kim Ebert. 2010. "Beyond the Ballot: Immigrant Collective Action in Gateways and New Destinations in the United States." *Social Problems* 57 (4): 529–558.

Okólski, Marek. 2009. "General Introduction." In *Poland: Becoming a Country of Sustained Immigration*, edited by Agata Górny, Izabela Grabowski-Lusińska, Magdalena

Lesińka, and Marek Okólski. IDEA Working Paper 10, May. http://www.idea6fp. uw.edu.pl/pliki/WP10_Poland.pdf, accessed May 18, 2013.

———. 2010. "General Introduction." In *Immigration to Poland: Policy, Employment, Integration*, edited by Agata Górny, Izabela Grabowski-Lusińska, Magdalena Lesińka, and Marek Okólski, 17–53. Warsaw: Wydawnictwo Naukowe Scholar.

———, ed. 2012. *European Immigrations: Trends, Structures and Policy Implications.* Amsterdam: Amsterdam University Press.

Oliver, J. Eric. 2000. "City Size and Civic Involvement in Metropolitan America." *American Political Science Review* 94 (2): 361–373.

Oller, Judith. 2008. *El coneixement de la llengua catalana i la llengua castellana per part de l'alumnat estranger escolaritzat a l'educació primària de Catalunya: factors explicatius i relacions d'interdependència lingüística.* Ph.D. diss., Department of Psychology, University of Girona, Spain.

O'Neil, Kevin. 2010. "Hazleton and Beyond: Why Communities Try to Restrict Immigration." *Migration Information Source.* http://www.migrationpolicy.org/article/hazleton-and-beyond-why-communities-try-restrict-immigration, accessed May 1, 2015.

O'Neil, Kevin, and Marta Tienda. 2010. "A Tale of Two Counties: Natives' Opinions toward Immigration in North Carolina." *International Migration Review* 44 (3): 728–761.

ORAC (Office of the Refugee Applications Commissioner). 2001. *Annual Report 2001.* Dublin, Ireland.

———. 2004. *Annual Report 2003.* Dublin, Ireland.

Ó'Riain, Sean. 2014. *The Rise and Fall of Ireland's Celtic Tiger: Liberalism, Boom and Bust.* New York: Cambridge University Press.

Oropesa, R. S. 2012. "Neighbourhood Disorder and Social Cohesiveness among Immigrants in a New Destination: Dominicans in Reading, PA." *Urban Studies* 49 (1): 115–132.

Oropesa, R. S., and Leif Jensen. 2010. "Dominican Immigrants and Discrimination in a New Destination: The Case of Reading, Pennsylvania." *City and Community* 9 (3): 274–298.

Osgood, D. Wayne, and Jeff M. Chambers. 2000. "Social Disorganization outside the Metropolis: An Analysis of Rural Youth Violence." *Criminology* 38 (1): 81–116.

Palacios, Irene, and Laura Morales. 2013. *LOCALMULTIDEM and MDE Individual Surveys (WP4) Technical Report.* Version 1. Leicester, UK: University of Leicester.

Palidda, Salvatore. 2009. "Insertion, Integration and Rejection of Immigration in Italy." In *Illiberal Liberal States: Immigration, Citizenship and Integration in the EU*, edited by Elspeth Guild, Kees Groenendijk, and Sergio Carrera, 357–372. Surrey, UK: Ashgate.

Pandya, Chhandasi, Margie McHugh, and Jeanne Batalova. 2011. "Limited English Proficient Individuals in the United States: Number, Share, Growth, and Linguistic Diversity." Migration Policy Institute Fact Sheet, December. http://migrationpolicy.org /research/limited-english-proficient-individuals-united-states-number-share-growth -and-linguistic, accessed November 10, 2014.

Pantoja, Adrian D., Cecilia Menjívar, and Lisa Magana. 2008. "The Spring Marches of 2006: Latinos, Immigration, and Political Mobilization in the 21st Century." *American Behavioral Scientist* 52 (4): 499–506.

Pantoja, Adrian D., Ricardo Ramirez, and Gary M. Segura. 2001. "Citizens by Choice, Voters by Necessity: Patterns in Political Mobilization by Naturalized Latinos." *Political Research Quarterly* 54 (4): 729–750.

Pantoja, Adrian D., and Gary M. Segura. 2003. "Fear and Loathing in California: Contextual Threat and Political Sophistication among Latino Voters." *Political Behavior* 25 (3): 265–286.

Papademetriou, Demetrios G. 2006. "Managing International Migration Better: Principles and Perspectives for Gaining More from Migration." In *Europe and Its Immigrants in the 21st Century: A New Deal or a Continuing Dialogue of the Deaf?*, edited by Demetrios G. Papademetriou, xiv–lxiii. Washington, DC: Migration Policy Institute.

Parella, Sonia and Amado Alarcón. 2015. "Preferencias Lingüísticas de los descendientes de inmigrantes en Barcelona." In *Lengua Española, Contacto Lingüístico y Globalización*, edited by Roland Terborg, Amado Alarcón, and Lourdes Neri, 319–340. Mexico City: CELE-UNAM.

Parisi, Domenico, Daniel T. Lichter, and Michael C. Taquino. 2011. "Multi-Scale Residential Segregation: Black Exceptionalism and America's Changing Color Line." *Social Forces* 89 (3): 829–852.

Pateman, Carole. 1970. *Participation and Democratic Theory*. Cambridge: Cambridge University Press.

Peixoto, João, Joaquín Arango, Corrado Bonifazi, Claudia Finotelli, Catarina Sabino, Salvatore Strozza, and Anna Triandafyllidou. 2012. "Immigrants, Markets, and Policies in Southern Europe: The Making of an Immigration Model?" In *European Immigrations: Trends, Structures, and Policy Implications*, edited by Marek Okólski, 107–148. Amsterdam: Amsterdam University Press.

Penninx, Rinus. 2003. "Integration: The Role of Communities, Institutions, and the State." *Migration Information Source*, October 1. Washington, DC: Migration Policy Institute. http://www.migrationpolicy.org/article/integration-role-communities-institutions-and-state, accessed April 1, 2014.

Penninx, Rinus, and Marco Martiniello. 2004. "Integration Processes and Policies: State of the Art and Lessons." In *Citizenship in European Cities: Immigrants, Local Politics and Integration Policies,* edited by Rinus Penninx, Karen Kraal, Marco Martiniello, and Steven Vertovec, 139–163. Aldershot, UK: Ashgate.

Pettigrew, Thomas F., and Linda R. Tropp. 2006. "A Meta-Analytic Test of Intergroup Contact Theory." *Journal of Personality and Social Psychology* 90 (5): 751–783.

Pham, Huyen. 2004. "The Inherent Flaws in the Inherent Authority Position: Why Inviting Local Enforcement of Immigration Laws Violates the Constitution." *Florida State University Law Review* 31:965–1003.

Pieterse, Jan Nederveen. 2001. "The Case of Multiculturalism: Kaleidoscopic and Long-Term Views." *Social Identities* 7 (3): 393–407.

Pilati, Katia. 2010. *La partecipazione politica degli immigrati: Il caso di Milano.* Rome: Armando Editore.

———. 2012. "Network Resources and the Political Engagement of Migrant Organisations in Milan." *Journal of Ethnic and Migration Studies* 38 (4): 671–688.

Pilati, Katia, and Laura Morales. 2016. "Ethnic and Immigrant Politics vs. Mainstream Politics: The Role of Ethnic Organizations in Shaping the Political Participation of Immigrant-Origin Individuals in Europe." *Ethnic and Racial Studies* 39 (15): 2796–2817.

Police Executive Research Forum. 2008. "Critical Issues in Policing Series: Police Chiefs and Sheriffs Speak Out on Local Immigration Enforcement." Washington, DC: Police Executive Research Forum. http://www.policeforum.org/assets/docs/Free_Online_Documents/Immigration/police%20chiefs%20and%20sheriffs%20speak%20out%20on%20local%20immigration%20enforcement%202008.pdf, accessed July 5, 2016.

Political Capital. 2010. "Back by Popular Demand: Demand for Right-Wing Extremism (DEREX) Index." Budapest: Political Capital Policy Research and Consulting Institute. http://www.riskandforecast.com/useruploads/files/derex_study.pdf, accessed January 24, 2014.

Ponzo, Irene, Ben Gidley, Emanuela Roman, Francesco Tarantino, Ferruccio Pastore, and Ole Jensen. 2013. "Researching Functioning Policy Practices in Local Integration in Europe: A Conceptual and Methodological Discussion Paper." Oxford: ICT-ILO, FIERI and COMPAS. http://www.eu-mia.eu/Eumia%20meth%20paper3.pdf, accessed August 22, 2016.

Portes, Alejandro. 1998. "Social Capital: Its Origins and Applications in Modern Sociology." *Annual Review of Sociology* 24:1–24.

Portes, Alejandro, Cristina Escobar, and Renelinda Arana. 2008. "Bridging the Gap: Transnational and Ethnic Organizations in the Political Incorporation of Immigrants in the United States." *Ethnic and Racial Studies* 31 (6): 1056–1090.

———. 2013. "Transnational and Ethnic Organizations in the Political Incorporation of Immigrants in the United States." In *Migration in the 21st Century: Rights, Outcomes, and Policy*, edited by Thomas N. Maloney and Kim Korinek, 126–157. New York: Routledge.

Portes, Alejandro, and Lingxin Hao. 1998. "E Pluribus Unum: Bilingualism and Language Loss in the Second Generation." *Sociology of Education* 71 (4): 269–294.

Portes, Alejandro, and Ruben G. Rumbaut. 1996. *Immigrant America: A Portrait.* 2nd ed. Berkeley: University of California Press.

———. 2001. *Legacies: The Story of the Immigrant Second Generation.* Oakland: University of California Press.

Portes, Alejandro, and Min Zhou. 1993. "The New Second Generation: Segmented Assimilation and Its Variants." *Annals of the American Academy of Political and Social Science* 530 (November): 74–96.

Post, Harry. 1989. *Pillarization: An Analysis of Dutch and Belgian Society.* Brookfield, VT: Gower.

Primo, David M., Matthew L. Jacobsmeier, and Jeffrey Milyo. 2007. "Estimating the Impact of State Policies and Institutions with Mixed-Level Models." *State Politics & Policy Quarterly* 7 (4): 446–459.

Public Religion Research Institute. 2013. "Religion, Values and Immigration Reform Survey 2013." Public Religion Research Institute. http://publicreligion.org/site/wp-content/uploads/2013/03/2013-Religion-Values-and-Immigration-Reform-Survey-Topline1.pdf, accessed March 20, 2014.

Pujolar, Joan. 2010. "Immigration and Language Education in Catalonia: Between National and Social Agendas." *Linguistics and Education: An International Research Journal* 21 (3): 229–243.

Putnam, Robert D. 2000. *Bowling Alone: The Collapse and Revival of American Community.* New York: Simon & Schuster.

———. 2007. "*E Pluribus Unum*: Diversity and Community in the Twenty-first Century: The 2006 Johan Skytte Prize Lecture." *Scandinavian Political Studies* 30 (2): 137–174.

Putnam, Robert D., Robert Leonardi, and Raffaella Y. Nanetti. 1993. *Making Democracy Work: Civic Traditions in Modern Italy.* Princeton, NJ: Princeton University Press.

Quillian, Lincoln. 1995. "Prejudice as a Response to Perceived Group Threat: Population Composition and Anti-immigrant and Racial Prejudice in Europe." *American Sociological Review* 60 (4): 586–611.

Rakove, Milton L. 1976. *Don't Make No Waves . . . Don't Back No Losers: An Insiders' Analysis of the Daley Machine.* Bloomington: Indiana University Press.

Ramakrishnan, S. Karthick. 2006. *Democracy in Immigrant America: Changing Demographics and Political Participation.* Palo Alto, CA: Stanford University Press.

Ramakrishnan, S. Karthick, and Irene Bloemraad, eds. 2008a. *Civic Hopes and Political Realities: Immigrants, Community Organizations, and Political Engagement.* New York: Russell Sage.

———. 2008b. "Making Organizations Count: Immigrant Civic Engagement in California Cities." In *Civic Hopes and Political Realities: Immigrants, Community Organizations, and Political Engagement,* edited by Karthick S. Ramakrishnan and Irene Bloemraad, 45–76. New York: Russell Sage.

Ramakrishnan, S. Karthick, and Thomas J. Espenshade. 2001. "Immigrant Incorporation and Political Participation in the United States." *International Migration Review* 35 (3): 870–909.

Ramakrishnan, S. Karthick, and Tom Wong. 2010. "Partisanship, Not Spanish: Explaining Municipal Ordinances Affecting Undocumented Immigrants." In *Taking Local Control: Immigration Policy Activism in US Cities and States,* edited by Monica W. Varsanyi, 73–93. Palo Alto, CA: Stanford University Press.

Randall, Nancy Horak, and Spencer Delbridge. 2005. "Perceptions of Social Distance in an Ethnically Fluid Community." *Sociological Spectrum* 25 (1): 103–122.

Rendón, Silvio. 2007. "The Catalan Premium: Language and Employment in Catalonia." *Journal of Population Economics* 20 (3): 669–686.

Ribas, Vanessa. 2016. *On the Line: Slaughterhouse Lives and the Making of the New South.* Oakland: University of California Press.

Rice, Tom W., and Brent Steele. 2001. "White Ethnic Diversity and Community Attachment in Small Iowa Towns." *Social Science Quarterly* 82 (2): 397–407.

Rich, Brian, and Marta Miranda. 2005. "The Sociopolitical Dynamics of Mexican Immigration in Lexington, Kentucky, 1997–2002." In *New Destinations,* edited by Victor Zúñiga and Rubén Hernández-León, 187–219. New York: Russell Sage.

Rios, Victor. 2011. *Punished: Policing the Lives of Black and Latino Boys.* New York: New York University Press.

Rodríguez, Cristina M. 2008. "The Significance of the Local in Immigration Regulation." *Michigan Law Review* 106:567–642.

Rodríguez, Cristina, Muzaffar Chishti, Randy Capps, and Laura St. John. 2010. *A Program in Flux: New Priorities and Implementation Challenges for 287(g).* Washington, DC: Migration Policy Institute. http://www.migrationpolicy.org/research/program-flux-new-priorities-and-implementation-challenges-287g, accessed May 22, 2014.

Rodríguez, Néstor. 2012. "New Southern Neighbors: Latino Immigration and Prospects for Intergroup Relations between African-Americans and Latinos in the South." *Latino Studies* 10 (1): 18–40.

Rodríguez-García, Dan, John Biles, Lara Winnemore, and Ines Michalowski. 2007. *Policies and Models of Incorporation: A Transatlantic Perspective: Canada, Germany, France and the Netherlands.* Barcelona, Spain: Fundació CIDOB.

Romaniszyn, Krystyna. 1996. "The Invisible Community: Undocumented Polish Workers in Athens." *New Community* 22 (2): 321–333.

Rosenstone, Steven J., and John Mark Hansen. 2002. *Mobilization, Participation, and Democracy in America.* New York: Pearson.

Rosenstone, Steven J., and Raymond Wolfinger. 1978. "The Effect of Registration Laws on Voter Turnout." *American Political Science Review* 72 (1): 22–45.

Ruhs, Martin. 2003. "Emerging Trends and Patterns in the Immigration and Employment of Non-EU Nationals in Ireland: What the Data Reveal." Working Paper 6. The Policy Institute, Trinity College Dublin.

Russell, Anthony. 1986. *The Country Parish.* London: SPCK.

———. 2005. "A Time of Transition." *Journal of the Royal Agricultural Society of England* 166: 1–3.

Saint-Fort, Pradine, Noëlle Yasso, and Susan Shah. 2012. *Engaging Police in Immigrant Communities: Promising Practices from the Field.* New York: Vera Institute for Justice. http://www.vera.org/pubs/engaging-police-immigrant-communities-promising-practices-field, accessed September 22, 2014.

Sampson, Robert J., Doug McAdam, Heather MacIndoe, and Simon Weffer-Elizondo. 2005. "Civil Society Reconsidered: The Durable Nature and Community Structure of Collective Civic Action." *American Journal of Sociology* 111 (3): 673–714.

Sampson, Robert J., Jeffrey D. Morenoff, and Felton Earls. 1999. "Beyond Social Capital: Spatial Dynamics of Collective Efficacy for Children." *American Sociological Review* 64 (5): 633–660.

Sanchez, Gabriel R. 2008. "Latino Group Consciousness and Perceptions of Commonality with African Americans." *Social Science Quarterly* 89 (2): 428–444.

Sanchez, Gabriel R., and Natalie Masuoka. 2010. "Brown-Utility Heuristic? The Presence and Contributing Factors of Latino Linked Fate." *Hispanic Journal of Behavioral Sciences* 32 (4): 519–531.

Schaeffer, Merlin. 2014. *Ethnic Diversity and Social Cohesion: Immigration, Ethnic Fractionalization and Potentials for Civic Action.* Farnham Surrey, UK: Ashgate.

Schier, Steven E. 2002. "From Melting Pot to Centrifuge: Immigrants and American Politics." *The Brookings Review* 20 (1): 16–19.

Schmid, Carol. 2003. "Immigration and Asian and Hispanic Minorities in the New South: An Exploration of History, Attitudes, and Demographic Trends." *Sociological Spectrum* 23 (2): 129–157.

Schneider, Anne L., and Helen M. Ingram. 2014. *Policy Design for Democracy.* Lawrence: University Press of Kansas.

Schneider, Cathy Lisa. 2008. "Police Power and Race Riots in Paris." *Politics and Society* 36 (1): 133–159.

Schneider, Jo Anne. 2007. "Connections and Disconnections between Civic Engagement and Social Capital in Community-based Nonprofits." *Nonprofit and Voluntary Sector Quarterly* 36:572–597.

Schnell, Philipp and Davide Azzolini. 2015. "The Academic Achievements of Immigrant Youths in New Destination Countries: Evidence from Southern Europe." *Migration Studies* 3 (2): 217–240.

Scholten, Peter. 2011. *Framing Immigrant Integration: Dutch Research-Policy Dialogues in Comparative Perspective.* Amsterdam: Amsterdam University Press.

Schön, Donald A., and Martin Rein. 1994. *Frame Reflection: Toward the Resolution of Intractable Policy Controversies.* New York: Basic Books.

Sennett, Richard. 1970. *The Uses of Disorder: Personal Identity and City Life.* New York: W. W. Norton.

Shah, Paru. 2009. "Motivating Participation: The Symbolic Effects of Latino Representation on Parent School Involvement." *Social Science Quarterly* 90 (1): 212–230.

Shaw, Clifford R., and Henry D. McKay. 1969. *Juvenile Delinquency and Urban Areas.* Rev. ed. Chicago: University of Chicago Press.

Shields, Gerard. 1991. "Three Allentown Residents Argue for Keeping Sanctuary Status." *The Morning Call,* May 9. http://articles.mcall.com/1991-05-09/news/2800268_1_sanctuary-city-city-seal-status, accessed June 30, 2014.

Shumaker, Sally A., and Daniel Stokols. 1982. "Residential Mobility as a Social Issue and Research Topic." *Journal of Social Issues* 38 (3): 1–19.

Sigel, Roberta S., and Marilyn B. Hoskin. 1981. *The Political Involvement of Adolescents.* New Brunswick, NJ: Rutgers University Press.

Singer, Audrey. 2004. *The Rise of New Immigrant Gateways.* Washington, DC: Brookings Institution. http://www.brookings.edu/research/reports/2004/02/demographics-singer, accessed July 5, 2014.

———. 2008. "Twenty-First-Century Gateways: An Introduction." In *Twenty-First-Century Gateways: Immigrant Incorporation in Suburban America,* edited by Audrey Singer, Susan B. Hardwick, and Caroline B. Brettell, 3–30. Washington, DC: Brookings Institution.

SKDS Public Poll Institute. 2011. *DNB Latvijas barometrs: Emigrācija.* https://www.dnb.lv /sites/default/files/dnb_latvian_barometer/documents/2011/290.dnb-nord-latvijas -barometrs-nr35.pdf, accessed February 10, 2015.

———. 2012. *Nacionālo ideju popularitāte sabiedrībā, Latvijas iedzīvotāju aptauja.* Alliance of European Conservatives and Reformists, SKDS Public Poll Institute, July. http://www.skds .lv/doc/Nacionalo_ideju_popularitate_sabiedriba_072012_LV.pdf, accessed June 4, 2014.

Smith, Barbara Ellen. 2009. "Market Rivals or Class Allies? Relations between African American and Latino Immigrant Workers in Memphis." In *Global Connections and Local Receptions: New Latino Immigration to the Southeastern United States,* edited by Fran Ansley and Jon Shefner, 299–317. Knoxville: University of Tennessee Press.

Smith, Buster G., and Byron Johnson. 2010. "The Liberalization of Young Evangelicals: A Research Note." *Journal for the Scientific Study of Religion* 49 (2): 351–360.

Smith, Greg. 2002. "Religion, and the Rise of Social Capitalism: The Faith Communities in Community Development and Urban Regeneration in England." *Community Development Journal* 37 (2): 167–177.

Sniderman, Paul M., and Louk Hagendoorn. 2007. *When Ways of Life Collide: Multicultural-ism and Its Discontents in the Netherlands.* Princeton, NJ: Princeton University Press.

Sociālās Alternatīvas Institūts. 2008. *Migration, Employment and Labour Market Integra-tion Policies in the European Union (2000–2009): Latvian Country Report.* Brussels: Sociālās Alternatīvas Institūts.

Solé, Carlota. 1981. *La integración sociocultural de los inmigrantes en Cataluña.* Madrid: Centro de Investigaciones Sociológicas.

———. 1988. *Catalunya, societat receptora d'immigrants: anàlisi comparativa de dues enquestes 1978 i 1983.* Barcelona: Institute of Catalan Studies.

SOPEMI Report. 2012. "Poland: Système d'Observation Permanente sur les Migrations." Unpublished manuscript.

Sorokin, Pitrim. 1928. *Contemporary Sociological Theories.* London: Harper.

Soss, Joe. 2000. *Unwanted Claims: The Politics of Participation in the US Welfare System.* Ann Arbor: University of Michigan Press.

Soysal, Yasemin Nuhoğlu. 1994. *Limits of Citizenship: Migrants and Postnational Member-ship in Europe.* Chicago, IL: University of Chicago Press.

Spanje, Joost van. 2010. "Contagious Parties: Anti-Immigration Parties and Their Impact on Other Parties' Immigration Stances in Contemporary Western Europe." *Party Politics* 16 (5): 563–586.

Stark, Rodney, Daniel P. Doyle, and Lori Kent. 1980. "Rediscovering Moral Communities: Church Membership and Crime." In *Understanding Crime,* edited by Travis Hirschi and Michael Gottfredson, 43–50. Beverly Hills, CA: Sage.

Stola, Dariusz. 2001. "Międzynarodowa mobilność zarobkowa w PRL." In *Ludzie na huśtawce: migracje między peryferiami Polski i Zachodu,* edited by E. Jaźwinska and Marek Okólski, 62–100. Warsaw: Wydawn Nauk Scholar.

Strömblad, Per, and Per Adman. 2010. "Political Integration through Ethnic or Nonethnic Voluntary Associations?" *Political Research Quarterly* 63 (4): 721–730.

Strömblad, Per, Gunnar Myrberg, and Bo Bengtsson. 2011. "Optimal Opportunities for Ethnic Organization and Political Integration? Comparing Stockholm with Other European Cities." In *Social Capital, Political Participation and Migration in Europe: Making Multicultural Democracy Work?*, edited by Laura Morales and Marco G. Giugni, 115–139. New York: Palgrave Macmillan.

Stuesse, Angela C. 2016. *Scratching out a Living: Latinos, Race, and Work in the Deep South*. Oakland: University of California Press.

Stuesse, Angela, and Mathew Coleman. 2014. "Automobility, Immobility, Altermobility: Surviving and Resisting the Intensification of Immigrant Policing." *City and Society* 26 (1): 51–72.

Stuesse, Angela C., Mary E. Odem, and Elaine Lacy. 2009. "Race, Migration, and Labor Control: Neoliberal Challenges to Organizing Mississippi." In *Latino Immigrants and the Transformation of the US South*, edited by Mary E. Odem and Elaine Lacy, 91–111. Athens: University of Georgia Press.

Stuesse, Angela C., Cheryl Staats, and Andrew Grant-Thomas. Forthcoming. "As Others Pluck Fruit Off the Tree of Opportunity: Immigration, Racial Hierarchies, and Intergroup Relations Efforts in the United States." *Du Bois Review*.

Stunell, Andrew. 2010. "Keeping Faith in the Big Society." Presented by parliamentary undersecretary in the Department of Communities and Local Government at the Inter-Faith Network for the UK meeting, July 12, London.

Stuppini, Andrea. 2012. "Le Politiche Regionali per L'integrazione. Quattro Regioni a Confronto: Lombardia, Veneto, Emilia-Romagna E Toscana."*Rapporto Annuale sull'Economia dell'Immigrazione*. Venice: Fondazione Leone Moressa.

Šūpule, Inese, Līga Krastiņa, Inguna Peņķe, and Jolanta Krišāne. 2004. *Etniskā tolerance un Latvijas sabiedrības integrācija*. Riga, Latvia: Baltijas Sociālo Zinātņu institūts. http://providus.lv/article/etniska-tolerance-un-latvijas-sabiedribas-integracija, accessed August 11, 2013.

Suro, Roberto, and Jeffrey S. Passel. 2003. *The Rise of the Second Generation: Changing Patterns in Hispanic Population Growth*. Washington, DC: Pew Hispanic Center.

Suro, Roberto, and Sonya Tafoya. 2004. *Dispersal and Concentration: Patterns of Latino Residential Settlement*. Washington, DC: Pew Hispanic Center.

Tajfel, Henri, and John C. Turner. 1979. "An Integrative Theory of Intergroup Conflict." In *The Social Psychology of Intergroup Relations*, edited by William G. Austin and Stephen Worchel, 33–47. Monterey, CA: Brooks-Cole.

———. 1986. "The Social Identity Theory of Inter-group Behavior." In *Psychology of Intergroup Relations*, edited by William G. Austin and Stephen Worchel, 7–24. Chicago, IL: Nelson-Hall.

Takle, Marianne. 2013. "Democratic Mobilization in Immigrant Organizations." *Nordic Journal of Migration Research* 3 (3): 126–134.

Tam Cho, Wendy K. 1999. "Naturalization, Socialization, Participation: Immigrants and (Non-) Voting." *Journal of Politics* 61 (4): 1140–1155.

Tarchi, Marco. 2007. "Recalcitrant Allies: The Conflicting Foreign Policy Agenda of the Alleanza Nazionale and the Lega Nord." In *Europe for Europeans: The Foreign and Security Policy of the Populist Radical Right*, edited by Christina Schori Liang, 187–208. Hampshire, UK: Ashgate.

Tatalovich, Raymond. 1995. *Nativism Reborn?: The Official English Language Movement and the American States*. Lexington: University Press of Kentucky.

Teorell, Jan, Mariano Torcal, and José Ramón Montero. 2007. "Political Participation: Mapping the Terrain." In *Citizenship and Involvement in European Democracies: A Comparative Analysis*, edited by Jan W. Van Deth, José Ramón Montero, and Anders Westholm, 66–87. Abingdon, UK: Taylor and Francis.

Terrazas, Aaron. 2011. "Immigrants in New-Destination States." *Migration Information Source*, February 8. Washington, DC: Migration Policy Institute. http://www.migrationpolicy.org/article/immigrants-new-destination-states, accessed April 16, 2014.

Terrazas, Aaron, and Michael Fix. 2009. *The Binational Option: Meeting the Instructional Needs of Limited English Proficient Students*. Washington, DC: Migration Policy Institute. http://www.migrationpolicy.org/research/binational-option-meeting-instructional-needs-limited-english-proficient-students, accessed July 14, 2014.

Theodore, Nik, and Nina Martin. 2007. "Migrant Civil Society: New Voices in the Struggle over Community Development." *Journal of Urban Affairs* 29 (3): 269–397.

Thompson, Robert J., and Joseph R. Rudolph Jr. 1989. "The Ebb and Flow of Ethnoterritorial Politics in the Western World." In *Ethnoterritorial Politics, Policy, and the Western World*, edited by Joseph R. Rudolph Jr. and Robert J. Thompson, 1–14. Boulder, CO: Lynne Rienner.

Tillie, Jean. 2004. "Social Capital of Organisations and Their Members: Explaining the Political Integration of Immigrants in Amsterdam." *Journal of Ethnic and Migration Studies* 30 (3): 529–541.

Tipton, Steven M. 2008. *Public Pulpits: Methodists and Mainline Churches in the Moral Argument of Public Life*. Chicago, IL: University of Chicago Press.

Togeby, Lise. 2004. "It Depends . . . How Organisational Participation Affects Political Participation and Social Trust among Second-generation Immigrants in Denmark." *Journal of Ethnic and Migration Studies* 30 (3): 509–528.

Trawick, Michelle W., and Roy M. Howsen. 2006. "Crime and Community Heterogeneity: Race, Ethnicity, and Religion." *Applied Economics Letters* 13 (6): 341–345.

Triandafyllidou, Anna. 2009. "Integration and Citizenship Policies." In *The Making of an Immigration Model: Inflows, Impacts and Policies in Southern Europe*, edited by Joaquin Arango, Corrado Bonifazi, Claudia Finotelli, Joao Peixoto, Catarina Sabino, Salvatore Strozza, and Anna Triandafyllidou. IDEA Working Paper 9, May. www.idea6fp.uw.edu.pl/pliki/WP_9_Southern_countries_synthesis.pdf, accessed August 4, 2014.

———. 2010. "Greece: The Challenge of Native and Immigrant Muslim Populations." In *Muslims in 21st Century Europe: Structural and Cultural Perspectives*, edited by Anna Triandafyllidou, 199–217. New York: Routledge.

———. 2012. "Addressing Cultural, Ethnic, and Religious Diversity Challenges in Europe: A Comparative Overview of 15 European Countries." In *Accept Pluralism*. San Domenico di Fiesole, Italy: European University Institute. http://ec.europa.eu/ewsi/UDRW/images/items/docl_21233_187704397.pdf, accessed April 14, 2014.

Trounstine, Jessica. 2009. "All Politics Is Local: The Reemergence of the Study of City Politics." *Perspectives on Politics* 7 (3): 611–618.

———. 2010. "Representation and Accountability in Cities." *Annual Review of Political Science* 13:407–423.

Uhlaner, Carole. 1991. "Perceived Discrimination and Prejudice and the Coalition Prospects of Blacks, Latinos, and Asian Americans." In *Racial and Ethnic Politics in California*, edited by Byran O. Jackson and Michael B. Preston, 339–371. Berkeley, CA: Institute of Governmental Studies Press.

University of Latvia, Faculty of Social Sciences. 2010. "NI. Dimensijas. Vēsturiskā atmiņa." Public opinion survey, http://dspace.lu.lv/dspace/handle/7/50/browse?value

=Aptaujas+%22NI%3A+Dimensijas.+V%C4%93sturisk%C4%81+atmi%C5%86a.+LU +SZF%2C+2010%22+tehnisk%C4%81+inform%C4%81cija&type=subject, accessed December 14, 2016.

Urso, Ornella, and Marcello Carammia. 2014. "Political Parties and the Politicisation of Migration in Italy, 1994–2008." Paper delivered to the ECPR General Conference, Glasgow, Scotland, September 6.

U.S. Census Bureau. 1990. http://www.census.gov/main/www/cen1990.html, accessed January 22, 2011.

———. 2010. *American Community Survey 5-Year Estimates, 2006–2008.* http://www.census. gov/acs/www/data_documentation/2009_release/, accessed December 22, 2010.

———. 2008–2012. American Community Surveys. https://www.census.gov/programs -surveys/acs/, accessed July 5, 2014.

———, Population Division. 2011. Table 4. "Annual Estimates of the Resident Population for Incorporated Places in Utah: April 1, 2000 to July 1, 2009" (SUB-EST2009-04-49). http:// www.census.gov, accessed March 13, 2011.

Utah League of Cities and Towns. 2010. *2010 City Directory.* Salt Lake City: Utah League of Cities and Towns.

Vallas, Steven P., and Emily Zimmerman. 2007. *Sources of Variation in Attitudes toward Illegal Immigration.* Mason Immigration Survey of Virginia Residents. Fairfax, VA: Center for Social Science Research, George Mason University. http://www.cj-network.org/cj/wp-content/uploads/2011/01/2007sharplydivided.pdf, accessed March 6, 2014.

Vallas, Steven P., Emily Zimmerman, and Shannon N. Davis. 2009. "Enemies of the State? Testing Three Models of Anti-Immigrant Sentiment." *Research in Social Stratification and Mobility* 27 (4): 201–217.

Van Tubergen, Frank. 2006. "Religious Affiliation and Attendance among Immigrants in Eight Western Countries: Individual and Contextual Effects." *Journal for the Scientific Study of Religion* 45 (1): 1–22.

Varsanyi, Monica W. 2010a. "Immigration Policy Activism in U.S. States and Cities: Inter-disciplinary Perspectives." In *Taking Local Control: Immigration Policy Activism in U.S. Cities and States,* edited by Monica W. Varsanyi, 1–27. Palo Alto, CA: Stanford University Press.

———, ed. 2010b. *Taking Local Control: Immigration Policy Activism in US Cities and States.* Palo Alto, CA: Stanford University Press.

———. 2011. "Neoliberalism and Nativism: Local Anti-Immigrant Policy Activism and an Emerging Politics of Scale." *International Journal of Urban and Regional Research* 35 (2): 295–311.

Varsanyi, Monica, Paul G. Lewis, Doris Provine, and Scott Decker. 2012. "A Multilayered Jurisdictional Patchwork: Immigration Federalism in the United States." *Law and Policy* 34 (2): 138–158.

Vasta, Ellie. 2007. "From Ethnic Minorities to Ethnic Majority Policy: Multiculturalism and the Shift to Assimilationism in the Netherlands." *Ethnic and Racial Studies* 30 (5): 713–740.

Vēbers, E. 1994. *Etnosituācija Latvijā: Fakti un komentāri.* Riga, Latvia: Latvijas Zinātņu akadēmijas Filozofijas un socioloģijas institūts.

Venturini, Alessandra. 2004. *Postwar Migration in Southern Europe: An Economic Analysis.* Cambridge: Cambridge University Press.

Verba, Sidney. 1965. "Organizational Membership and Democratic Consensus." *Journal of Politics* 27 (3): 467–497.

Verba, Sidney, and Norman H. Nie. 1972. *Participation in America: Political Democracy and Social Equality.* New York: Harper and Row.

Verba, Sidney, Kay Lehman Schlozman, and Henry Brady. 1995. *Voice and Equality: Civic Voluntarism in American Politics.* Cambridge, MA: Harvard University Press.

Vermeulen, Floris. 2006. *The Immigrant Organising Process: Turkish Organisations in Amsterdam and Berlin and Surinamese Organisations in Amsterdam, 1960–2000.* Amsterdam: Amsterdam University Press.

Vertovec, Steven. 2007. "Super-Diversity and Its Implications." *Ethnic and Racial Studies* 30 (6): 1024–1054.

Voas, David, and Alasdair Crockett. 2005. "Religion in Britain: Neither Believing nor Belonging." *Sociology* 39 (1): 11–28.

Voyer, Andrea M. 2013. *Strangers and Neighbors: Multiculturalism, Conflict, and Community in America.* New York: Cambridge University Press.

Walker, Kyle E., and Helga Leitner. 2011. "The Variegated Landscape of Local Immigration Policies in the United States." *Urban Geography* 32 (2): 156–178.

Wals, Sergio C. 2011. "Does What Happens in Los Mochis Stay in Los Mochis? Explaining Post Migration Political Behavior." *Political Research Quarterly* 64 (3): 600–611.

Walsh, Katherine C. 2006. "Communities, Race and Talk: An Analysis of the Occurrence of Civic Intergroup Dialogue Programs." *Journal of Politics* 68 (1): 22–33.

Warren, Roland L. 1978. *The Community in America.* Chicago, IL: Rand McNally.

Waslin, Michele. 2010. "Immigration Enforcement by State and Local Police: The Impact on the Enforcers and Their Communities." In *Taking Local Control: Immigration Policy Activism in US Cities and States,* edited by Monica W. Varsanyi, 97–114. Palo Alto, CA: Stanford University Press.

Waters, Mary C., and Tomás Jiménez. 2005. "Assessing Immigrant Assimilation: New Empirical and Theoretical Challenges." *Annual Review of Sociology* 31:105–125.

Waters, Mary C., and Philip Kasinitz. 2013. "Immigrants in New York: Reaping the Benefits of Continuous Migration." *Daedalus* 142 (3): 92–116.

Waters, Mary C., Philip Kasinitz, and Asad L. Asad. 2014. "Immigrants and African Americans." *Annual Review of Sociology* 40 (July): 369–390.

WBRC (Fox 6 News). 2011. "NAACP Ups the Focus on the Immigration Law." October 14. http://www.myfoxal.com/story/15693527/naacp-ups-the-focus-on-the-immigration-law, accessed February 4, 2015.

Weeks, Liam, and Aodh Quinlivan. 2009. *All Politics Is Local: A Guide to Local Elections in Ireland.* Cork, Ireland: Collins Press.

Weinar, Agnieszka. 2006. *Europeizacja polskiej polityki migracyjnej, 1900–2003.* Warsaw: Scholar.

Weise, Julie M. 2012. "Dispatches from the 'Viejo' New South: Historicizing Recent Latino Migrations." *Latino Studies* 10 (1–2): 41–59.

Welch, Michael R., Charles R. Tittle, and Thomas Petee. 1991. "Religion and Deviance among Adult Catholics: A Test of the 'Moral Communities' Hypothesis." *Journal for the Scientific Study of Religion* 30 (2): 159–172.

Weldon, Steven A. 2006. "The Institutional Context of Tolerance for Ethnic Minorities: A Comparative, Multilevel Analysis of Western Europe." *American Journal of Political Science* 50 (2): 331–349.

Wessendorf, Susanne. 2014. *Commonplace Diversity: Social Relations in a Super-Diverse Context.* New York: Palgrave.

Whitby, Kenny J. 2007. "The Effect of Black Descriptive Representation on Black Electoral Turnout in the 2004 Elections." *Social Science Quarterly* 88 (4): 1010–1023.

White, Stephen, Neil Nevitte, André Blais, Elisabeth Gidengil, and Patrick Fournier. 2008. "The Political Resocialization of Immigrants: Resistance or Lifelong Learning?" *Political Research Quarterly* 61 (2): 268–281.

White House Task Force on New Americans. 2015. "Strengthening Communities by Welcoming All Residents: Federal Strategic Action Plan on Immigrant and Refugee Integration." https://www.whitehouse.gov/blog/2015/04/15/strengthening-communities-welcoming-and-integrating-immigrants-and-refugees, accessed May 5, 2015.

Wilkinson, Betina, and Natasha Bingham. n.d. "The Aftermath of a Hurricane: African Americans' Attitudes toward Latino Immigration in New Orleans." Unpublished journal article.

Wilkinson, Betina Cutaia, and Natasha Bingham. 2016. "Getting Pushed Back Further in Line? Racial Alienation and Black Attitudes toward Immigration and Immigrants." *PS: Political Science and Politics* 49 (2): 221–227.

Wilkinson, Kenneth P. 1984. "Rurality and Patterns of Social Disruption." *Rural Sociology* 49 (1): 25–36.

———. 1991. *The Community in Rural America.* Westport, CT: Greenwood.

Williams, Kim M. 2016. "Black Elite Opinion on American Immigration Policy: Evidence from Black Newspapers, 2000–2013." *Journal of African American Studies* 20: 248–271.

Williams, Kim M., and Lonnie Hannon. 2016. "Immigrant Rights in a Deep South City: The Effects of Anti-Immigrant Legislation on Black Elite Opinion in Birmingham, Alabama." *Du Bois Review* 13(1): 139–157.

Wilson, John, and Thomas Janoski. 1995. "The Contribution of Religion to Volunteer Work." *Sociology of Religion* 56 (2): 137–152.

Winders, Jamie. 2008. "Nashville's New 'Sonido': Latino Migration and the Changing Politics of Race." In *New Faces in New Places: The Changing Geography of American Immigration*, edited by Douglass S. Massey, 249–273. New York: Russell Sage.

———. 2013. *Nashville in the New Millennium: Immigrant Settlement, Urban Transformation, and Social Belonging.* New York: Russell Sage.

———. 2014. "New Immigrant Destinations in Global Context." *International Migration Review* 48 (1): 149–179.

Wishnie, Michael J. 2004. "Civil Liberties in a New America: State and Local Police Enforcement of Immigration Laws." *University of Pennsylvania Journal of Constitutional Law* 6:1084–1115.

Włoch, Renata. 2013. "Poland: Multiculturalism in the Making." In *Challenging Multiculturalism: European Models of Diversity*, edited by Raymond Taras, 257–278. Edinburgh: Edinburgh University Press.

Wong, Janelle S. 2005. "Mobilizing Asian American Voters: A Field Experiment." *Annals of the American Academy of Political and Social Science* 601 (September): 102–114.

———. 2006. *Democracy's Promise: Immigrants and American Civic Institutions.* Ann Arbor: University of Michigan Press.

Wood, Curtis. 2002. "Voter Turnout in City Elections." *Urban Affairs Review* 38 (2): 209–231.

Woolard, Kathryn A. 1985. "Language Variation and Cultural Hegemony: Toward an Integration of Sociolinguistic and Social Theory." *American Ethnologist* 12 (4): 738–748.

———. 1989. *Double Talk: Bilingualism and the Politics of Ethnicity in Catalonia.* Palo Alto, CA: Stanford University Press.

———. 2003. "We Don't Speak Catalan Because We Are Marginalized: Ethnic and Class Connotations of Language in Barcelona." In *Language and Social Identity*, edited by Richard Blot, 85–103. Westport, CT: Praeger.

———. 2013. "Is the Personal Political? Chronotopes and Changing Stances toward Catalan Language and Identity." *International Journal of Bilingual Education and Bilingualism* 16 (2): 210–224.

Woolard, Kathryn A., and Tae-Joong Gahng. 1990. "Changing Language Policies and Attitudes in Autonomous Catalonia." *Language in Society* 19 (3): 311–330.

Wuthnow, Robert. 2004. *Saving America?* Princeton, NJ: Princeton University Press.

Žagar, Mitja. 2008. "Diversity Management and Integration: From Ideas to Concepts." *European Yearbook of Minority Issues* 6 (2006/2007): 307–327.

Zald, Meyer N. 1996. "Culture, Ideology, and Strategic Framing." In *Comparative Perspectives on Social Movements: Political Opportunities, Mobilizing Structures, and Cultural Framings*, edited by Doug McAdam, John D. McCarthy, and Mayer N. Zald, 261–274. New York: Cambridge University Press.

Zamora, Sylvia. 2016. "Racial Remittances: The Effect of Migration on Racial Ideologies in Mexico." *Sociology of Race and Ethnicity* 2 (4): 466–481.

Zamora-Kapoor, Anna. 2013. "A Structural Explanation for Anti-Immigrant Sentiment." Ph.D. diss., Columbia University. http://academiccommons.columbia.edu/catalog/ac%3A163309, accessed February 14, 2014.

Zanfrini, Laura. 2011. "Labour." In *The Sixteenth Italian Report on Migrations 2010*, edited by Vincenzo Cesareo, 51–69. Milan: McGraw-Hill.

Zankovska-Odiņa, Sigita. 2005. "Imigranti-etniskās spriedzes avots vai integrācijas veicinātāji?" Centre for Public Policy PROVIDUS, January 10. http://providus.lv/article/imigranti-etniskas-spriedzes-avots-vai-integracijas-veicinataji, accessed July 3, 2014.

———. 2009. "Situation of Roma in Latvia." www.gesis.org/fileadmin/upload/dienstleistung/fachinformationen/series_ssee_01/Roma_in_Central_and_Eastern_Europe.pdf, accessed July 30, 2014.

Zapata-Barrero, Ricard. 2009. "Policies and Public Opinion towards Immigrants: The Spanish Case." *Ethnic and Racial Studies* 32 (7): 1101–1120.

———. 2010. "Managing Diversity in Spanish Society: A Practical Approach." *Journal of Intercultural Studies* 31 (4): 383–402.

———. 2013. *Diversity Management in Spain: New Dimensions, New Challenges.* Manchester, UK: Manchester University Press.

Zapata-Barrero, Ricard, Rocío Faúndez García, and Elena Sánchez Montijano. 2009. "Temporary and Circular Labour Migration: Reassessing Established Public Policies." Working Paper 1 (Autumn). http://www.upf.edu/gritim/_pdf/GRITIM_UPF_WP_Series_1_Zapata_Faundez_Sanchez.pdf, accessed April 15, 2014.

Zelče, Vita. 2011. "Major Flows of Migration Early 19th Century to 1991." In *Latvia Human Development Report 2010/2011: National Identity, Mobility and Capability*, edited by Brigita Zepa and Evija Kļave, 53–69. Riga, Latvia: Advanced Social and Political Research Institute of the University of Latvia. http://www.biss.soc.lv/downloads/resources/TAP/TAP2010_2011_ENG.pdf, accessed August 1, 2014.

Zepa, Brigita, Inese Šūpule, Iveta Ķešāne, Aija Lulle, Mihails Hazans, Oksana Žabko, Iveta Bebriša, and Līga Krastiņa. 2009. *Imigranti Latvijā: Iekļaušanās iespējas un nosacījumi.* Riga, Latvia: Baltic Institute of Social Sciences. http://providus.lv/article/imigranti-latvija-ieklausanas-iespejas-un-nosacijumi, accessed September 5, 2014.

Zhou, Min. 1999. "Coming of Age: The Current Situation of Asian American Children." *Amerasia Journal* 25 (1): 1–27.

Zhou, Stephen J., and John R. Logan. 2003. "Increasing Diversity and Persistent Segregation: Challenges of Educating Minority and Immigrant Children in Urban America."

References

251

References

351

In *The End of Desegregation?*, edited by Stephen J. Caldas and Carl L. Bankston, 177–194. Hauppauge, NY: Nova Science Publishers.

Zincone, Giovanna. 2011. "The Case of Italy." In *Migration Policymaking in Europe*, edited by Giovanna Zincone, Rinus Penninx, and Maren Borkert, 247–290. Amsterdam: Amsterdam University Press.

Zúñiga, Victor, and Rubén Hernández-León, eds. 2005a. *New Destinations: Mexican Immigration to the United States*. New York: Russell Sage.

———. 2005b. "The Sociopolitical Dynamics of Mexican Immigration in Lexington, Kentucky, 1977 to 2002: An Ambivalent Community Responds." In *New Destinations: Mexican Immigration in the United States*, edited by Victor Zúñiga and Rubén Hernández-León, 187–219. New York: Russell Sage.

Contributors

Dace Akule was the director of the PROVIDUS Centre for Public Policy in Riga, Latvia, from 2013 to 2016. In 2009 she published a country report within the framework of the Open Society's Institute-Sofia research project and coauthored a handbook on select aspects of the Lisbon Treaty published by the European Commission Representation in Latvia. She has conducted field research on legal-institutional and socioeconomic aspects of the employment of Belarusians, Moldovans, and Ukrainians in Latvia for the International Organization for Migration.

Amado Alarcón is professor of sociology at Universitat Rovira I Virgili in Catalonia, Spain, and Fulbright scholar at the Center for InterAmerican and Border Studies at University of Texas at El Paso, Texas. His research deals with language, migrations, education, and occupations in bilingual societies. He is the president of the Research Committee on Language and Society of the International Sociological Association. His most recent edited book is *Lengua Española, Contacto Lingüístico y Globalización* (2016).

Rhys Andrews is professor of public management at Cardiff Business School at Cardiff University in Wales. His research interests focus on strategic management, social capital, and public service performance. He has published widely in refereed journals and is the coauthor of *Strategic Management and Public Service Performance* (2011) and *Public Service Efficiency: Reframing the Debate* (2013).

Francesca Campomori is senior researcher at the University of Venice (Ca' Foscari), where she teaches social policy and political science. Her research interests focus on immigrant integration policies and refugee policies. She has published widely in refereed journals and is the author of *Immigrazione e cittadinanza locale* (2008).

Tiziana Caponio is associate professor of political science and of dynamics and policies of migration in the Department of Cultures, Politics, and Society at the University of Turin, and a research fellow at Collegio Carlo Alberto. She is coleader of the standing committee The Multilevel Governance of Immigrant and Immigration Policy of the IMIS-COE Research Network. She is author of *Città italiane e immigrazione* (2006) and coeditor of *The Local Dimension of Migration Policymaking* (2010). She is currently working on a special journal issue on the multilevel governance of migration.

Stefanie Chambers is Charles A. Dana Research Professor of Political Science at Trinity College in Hartford, Connecticut. Her research and teaching focus on mayoral leadership, urban education, and environmental justice. In addition to her journal articles and book chapters, she is the author of two Temple University Press books: *Mayors and Schools: Minority Voices and Democratic Tensions in Urban Education* (2006); and *Somalis in the Twin Cities and Columbus: Immigrant Incorporation in New Destinations* (2017).

Scott Decker is Foundation Professor in the School of Criminology and Criminal Justice at Arizona State University. He is the author of 17 books and over 120 scientific articles. The former include *Life in the Gang: Family, Friends and Violence* (1996), *Confronting Gangs: Crime and Community* (2015), and *Policing Immigrants: Local Law Enforcement on the Front Lines* (2016). He is an active and contributing member of the Eurogang Research Group. He has testified before the President's Task Force on Twentieth-Century Policing.

Erica Dobbs is a postdoctoral fellow and visiting assistant professor in the Department of Political Science at Swarthmore College. Her research focuses on how migration reshapes the dynamics of political and social citizenship in both sending and receiving countries.

Diana Evans is professor of political science at Trinity College in Hartford, Connecticut. Her research interests include the American Congress, pork barrel politics, and Latino politics. In addition to numerous journal articles and book chapters, she is the author of *Greasing the Wheels: The Use of Pork Barrel Projects to Build Majority Coalitions in Congress*, which received the Richard F. Fenno Jr. Prize for the best book on legislative studies published in 2004.

Melissa M. Goldsmith is research analyst at the Urban Institute for Teacher Education at the University of Utah. Her research interests include political participation at the local and national levels and, more recently, issues in higher education. She has published on the subjects of local political involvement, immigration, and educator preparation.

Claudio A. Holzner is associate professor of political science and director of the Center for Latin American Studies at the University of Utah. His research focuses on the political participation of poor and marginal political actors in Latin America and immigrants in the United States. He is the author of *Poverty of Democracy: The Institutional Roots of Political Participation in Mexico* (2011).

Aleksandra Kazłowska is visiting lecturer at the University of Birmingham and assistant professor at the University of Warsaw. She specializes in research into immigrants' adaptation and integration policy and has authored or coauthored over sixty academic articles, monographs, and special issues. She currently serves as vice editor in chief for *Central and Eastern European Migration Review*.

Magdalena Lesińska is assistant professor at the Centre of Migration Research at the University of Warsaw. Her current research includes migration policy at the state and EU levels, the political and public participation of immigrants, and diaspora politics. She is coeditor of several books and the author of dozens of articles and working papers, among them analyses of the migration policy of Poland and other central and East European countries.

Paul G. Lewis is associate professor in the School of Politics and Global Studies at Arizona State University. Much of his research has examined the determinants and effects of local public policies, with a particular focus on urban development, community change, and local policies toward immigrants. He is coauthor of *Policing Immigrants* (2016) and *Custodians of Place: Governing the Growth and Development of Cities* (2009) and the author of *Shaping Suburbia: How Political Institutions Organize Urban Development* (1996).

Helen B. Marrow is associate professor of sociology and interim director of the Program in Latino Studies at Tufts University. Her research interests focus on immigration, race and ethnicity, inequality and social policy, research methods, and health. In addition to her journal articles, she is the author of *New Destination Dreaming: Immigration, Race, and Legal Status in the Rural American South* (2011) and coauthor of *The New Americans: A Guide to Immigration since 1965* (2007).

Melissa Marschall is professor of political science and director of the Center for Local Elections in American Politics at Rice University. Her research focuses on representation, local politics, education policy, and political behavior. Her work appears in a wide range of political science, education, and urban studies journals. She is the coauthor (with Mark Schneider and Paul Teske) of *Choosing Schools: Consumer Choice and the Quality of American Schools*, which received the Policy Studies Association's Aaron Wildavsky Award for the best policy book published during 2000–2001.

Anthony M. Messina is John R. Reitemeyer Professor of Political Science at Trinity College in Hartford, Connecticut. His research focuses on the politics of migration to Europe. He is the author of *Race and Party Competition in Britain* (1989) and *The Logics and Politics of Post–World War II Migration to Western Europe* (2007) and the editor or coeditor of *Ethnic and Racial Minorities in the Advanced Industrial Democracies* (1992), *West European Immigration and Immigrant Policy in the New Century* (2002), *The Migration Reader* (2006), *The Year of the Euro* (2006), and *Europe's Contending Identities: Supranationalism, Ethnoregionalism, Religion, and New Nationalism* (2014).

Laura Morales is professor of comparative politics at the University of Leicester in the United Kingdom. Her research focuses on political behavior, the political consequences of immigration, and comparative politics. She is the author of *Joining Political Organisations* (2009) and coeditor of *Political Discussion in Modern Democracies in a Comparative Perspective* (2010) and *Social Capital, Political Participation and Migration in Europe* (2011). She has published in numerous journals and is currently conducting research on the political representation of citizens of immigrant origin in Europe in the context of the Pathways Project (http://www.pathways.eu/).

Katia Pilati is assistant professor in the Department of Sociology and Social Research (DSRS) at the University of Trento, Italy. Before joining DSRS, she was a Marie Curie fellow at the Department of Political Science at the University of Geneva and a research fellow at the Université Libre de Bruxelles. Her research interests include political participation, immigration, social movements, and social networks. She has published in refereed journals and is the author of *Migrants' Political Participation in Exclusionary Contexts: From Subcultures to Radicalization* (2016).

Doris Marie Provine is Professor *Emerita* of the Justice Studies faculty in the School of Social Transformation at Arizona State University. She previously taught in the Maxwell School at Syracuse University. She has been a Judicial Fellow, the director of the Law and Social Sciences Program at the National Science Foundation, and a Fulbright Fellow. Her recent books include *Unequal under Law: Race in the War on Drugs* (2007) and *Policing Immigrants: Local Law Enforcement on the Front Lines* (2016).

Monica W. Varsanyi is associate professor of political science at the John Jay College of Criminal Justice, CUNY, and a member of the Doctoral Faculties in Geography and Criminal Justice at the CUNY Graduate Center. Her research addresses the politics of unauthorized immigration in the United States, specifically the growing tensions among local, state, and federal governments vis-à-vis immigration policy and enforcement. She is the editor of *Taking Local Control: Immigration Policy Activism in U.S. Cities and States* (2010) and coauthor of *Policing Immigrants: Local Law Enforcement on the Front Lines* (2016).

Abigail Fisher Williamson is assistant professor of political science and public policy & law at Trinity College in Hartford, Connecticut. Her research focuses on municipal government responses to immigrants and their role in shaping political incorporation. She recently completed a book manuscript entitled *Welcoming New Americans? Local Governments and Immigrant Incorporation*.

Index